P9-DND-409

Prentice Hall

GRAMMAR AND COMPOSITION

SERIES CONSULTANTS

Grade 6

Joleen Johnson
Curriculum Writer, Office of Secondary Instruction
San Bernardino City Unified Schools
San Bernardino, California

Grade 7

Ellen G. Manhire
English Consultant Coordinator
Fresno, California

Grade 8

Elizabeth A. Nace
Supervisor, Language Arts
Akron, Ohio

Grade 9

Jerry Reynolds
Supervisor, Language Arts
Rochester, Minnesota

Grade 10

Marlene Corbett
Chairperson, Department of English
Charlotte, North Carolina

Grade 11

Gilbert Hunt
Chairperson, Department of English
Manchester, Connecticut

Grade 12

Margherite LaPota
Curriculum Specialist
Tulsa, Oklahoma

CRITIC READERS

Sheila Bridges
J.L. Wilkinson Middle School
Middleburg, FL

John Elias
Wilkes-Barre Area School District
Wilkes-Barre, PA

Linda Fiddler
Pulaski County Schools
Little Rock, AR

Beverly J. Follendorf
Sweetwater Union High School
San Diego, CA

Jeri B. Jackson
Mt. Gap Middle School
Huntsville, AL

Druscilla L. Jones
Fayette County Public Schools
Lexington, KY

Wilbert J. Lindwall
San Diego City Schools
San Diego, CA

George Comer
Gary Public Schools
Gary, IN

Gloria A. Peirsol-Marino
Lockhart Junior High School
Orlando, FL

Starlyn M. Norman
Howard Junior High School
Orlando, FL

Dora H. Patterson
Meadowbrook Junior High School
Orlando, FL

Margaret A. Reed
Minneapolis Public Schools
Minneapolis, MN

Kathleen A. Sherman
Carroll High School
Fort Wayne, IN

Annette R. Van Dusen
Oklahoma City Public Schools
Oklahoma City, OK

Mary Ann Weathers
Shelby City Schools
Shelby, NC

Prentice Hall

GRAMMAR AND COMPOSITION

SERIES AUTHORS

Gary Forlini — **Senior Author**
Pelham High School, Pelham, New York

Mary Beth Bauer — Harris County Department of Education,
Houston, Texas

Lawrence Biener — Locust Valley Junior-Senior High School,
Locust Valley, New York

Linda Capo — Pelham Junior High School,
Pelham, New York

Karen Moore Kenyon — Saratoga High School,
Saratoga, California

Darla H. Shaw — Ridgefield School System,
Ridgefield, Connecticut

Zenobia Verner — University of Houston,
Houston, Texas

PRENTICE HALL
Englewood Cliffs, New Jersey
Needham, Massachusetts

SUPPLEMENTARY MATERIALS

Annotated Teacher's Edition
Teacher's Resource Book
Computer Exercise Bank
Writing Model Transparencies

Acknowledgments: page 590

PRENTICE HALL Grammar and Composition
Fourth Edition

Printed in the United States of America.

ISBN 0-13-711805-8

10

PRENTICE HALL

Englewood Cliffs, New Jersey 07632

Contents

Grammar Usage Mechanics

II Usage 145

Composition and Allied Skills

UNIT I

Grammar

Chapter 1

Nouns

Auto mechanics know the parts of a car. They know how each part works together with others to make the car go. In a similar way, grammarians—people who study grammar—know the parts of our language. They have names for the eight parts of speech used in English sentences. These names—*noun, pronoun, verb, adjective, adverb, preposition, conjunction,* and *interjection*—tell the different kinds of work that words do. Naming these parts of speech helps people talk about language. As you learn about the parts of speech, you will learn how the words you use everyday express what you want to say.

This chapter is about nouns. First, you will learn what makes nouns a special category of words and how you can identify them. Then, you will learn about a special type of noun, the compound noun. Finally, you will learn about the two basic classes of nouns, common and proper nouns. Above all, you will see that nouns are the words you use whenever you name something.

1.1 The Noun

A *noun* is one of the eight parts of speech. It is a word that names something. Some nouns name people, some name places, and some name things. *Dr. Fitzgerald, Washington, D. C.,* and *automobile,* for example, are all nouns.

A noun is the name of a person, place, or thing.

Nouns name both living and nonliving things. Some nouns name what can be seen, such as *elephant.* Others name ideas, such as *strength*.

The nouns in the following chart are grouped under the headings People, Places, and Things. Notice that the nouns in the third column include both those that name things you can see and those that name ideas.

NOUNS		
People	**Places**	**Things**
writer	Ohio	movie
Mrs. Fisher	theater	hunger
Ann	ocean	guitar
sailor	Rocky Mountains	love

In order to find out if a word is a noun, look at how it is used in a sentence. If the word names a person, place, or thing, it is a noun. The nouns in the following sentences are underlined.

EXAMPLES: Keith lives nearby.
We vacationed in Canada.
Her laughter was loud.

Almost every time you speak, you talk about people, places, or things. When you talk about them, you are using nouns.

EXERCISE A: Identifying Nouns. List the nouns in each sentence.

EXAMPLE: My favorite author is James Ullman.
author James Ullman

1. James Ullman wrote many books and stories.
2. Ullman was born in America but also lived in the mountains of Tibet.
3. This experienced adventurer loved to climb mountains.
4. Ullman joined an expedition to climb Mount Everest.
5. The climb is described in a novel.
6. Another story by Ullman unfolds in the Amazon.
7. People enjoy the adventures described in his books.
8. Readers admire his knowledge and his daring.
9. Ullman traveled throughout the world as a reporter.
10. This famous man was a traveler, a writer, and a fascinating person.

EXERCISE B: More Work with Nouns. Follow the directions for Exercise A.

1. The proper ingredients for making bread are flour, water, milk, butter, and yeast.
2. First, dissolve the yeast in warm water.
3. Add sugar and flour and let the mixture rise in a bowl.
4. Add warm milk and more flour and knead the dough on a wooden board.
5. Again, let the dough rise, punch it down, shape it, and bake each loaf for thirty minutes.

DEVELOPING WRITING SKILLS: Using Nouns to Describe a Room. List ten nouns that name things you can see in your classroom or in a room in your home. Then, use the nouns to write a paragraph describing the room. Underline each of the ten nouns.

1.2 Compound Nouns

Some nouns are made up of two or more words. *Classroom* is made up of *class* and *room.* The noun *classroom* is a *compound noun*. Another compound noun is *homework*. It is made up of the words *home* and *work*.

A compound noun is one noun made by joining two or more words.

Sometimes the meaning of a compound noun is more than just the meaning of two or more words put together. Words such as *drumstick, bookworm, bootcamp,* and *housecoat* have meanings that are different from the meanings of the words that make them up. Do you know the meanings of the underlined words below?

EXAMPLES: The king, who was too ill to rule, was really just a figurehead (a person who has a title but no real power).

The soldier kept his clothing in a footlocker (a small trunk).

Check a dictionary when you are not sure of the meaning of a compound noun.

Compound nouns are written in three different ways. Some are written as single words, others are hyphenated words, and still others as two or more separate words.

The chart below shows several examples of compound nouns.

COMPOUND NOUNS		
Single Words	**Hyphenated Words**	**Separate Words**
heartbeat	father-in-law	dinner jacket
firefighter	right-hander	test tube
thunderstorm	tie-up	pen pal

EXERCISE: Finding Compound Nouns. Copy each sentence, underlining the compound nouns.

EXAMPLE: The <u>Golden Gate Bridge</u> shone in the <u>sunlight</u>.

1. The salesclerk sold me a goldfish
2. My sister-in-law has a basketful of potatoes.
3. Like clockwork, each day she turns on the soap opera.
4. The left-hander threw a fastball.
5. Take your backpack and your snowshoes on the expedition.
6. Is any member of your family a sleepwalker?
7. The short story was about a cowboy and a farmhand.
8. Will you watch basketball or football this weekend?
9. My girlfriend owns a sheep dog and a Siamese cat.
10. I know a folktale about people in the Russian countryside.
11. After playing handball, Eddie had a milkshake.
12. The lawyer played the tape recording in the courtroom.
13. Put a book mark in the book and return it to the bookcase.
14. I brought my armchair closer to the fireplace.
15. An eyewitness told the policeman what she had seen.
16. The mail carrier left greeting cards in my mailbox.
17. An attorney-at-law is the chairperson of our committee.
18. I need eyeglasses to see the handwriting on the blackboard.
19. The housekeeper answered the doorbell and smiled.
20. Do you prefer applesauce or rice pudding for dessert?

DEVELOPING WRITING SKILLS: Writing Sentences with Compound Nouns. Write five sentences describing a vacation. Include one of the following compound nouns in each sentence: *classmates, wristwatch, record player, amusement park,* and *football.*

1.3 Common and Proper Nouns

Nouns can be grouped in several different ways. For example, all nouns are either *common nouns,* or *proper nouns.* To decide if a noun is common or proper, you must know whether it names something in a specific way or a general way.

A common noun names any one of a group of people, places, or things.

A proper noun names a specific person, place, or thing.

It is easy to recognize common nouns. Common nouns are not capitalized (except at the beginning of a sentence or in a title). Words such as *author, city,* and *month* are common nouns because they can apply to many different people, places, or things. In addition, a common noun can be a single word such as *carpenter* or *state* or a compound word such as *travel agent* or *post office.*

Proper nouns, on the other hand, are always capitalized. *Mary Stewart, Chicago,* and *April* are proper nouns because they name specific people, places, and things. Proper nouns are often made up of more than one word. When a proper noun such as *Avenue of the America's* contains words such as *a, an, the,* and *of,* these words are not capitalized.

Common Nouns	Proper Nouns
scientist	Madam Curie
relative	Aunt Carol
city	Atlanta
state	Kentucky
book	*Julie of the Wolves*
bridge	Golden Gate Bridge
holiday	Columbus Day

EXERCISE A: Identifying Common and Proper Nouns. Make a chart with two columns labeled Common Nouns and Proper Nouns. Put each noun listed below in the correct column. Then, for each common noun, write a related proper noun. For each proper noun, write a related common noun.

EXAMPLES:	*Common Nouns*	*Proper Nouns*
car	car	Oldsmobile
White House	building	White House

1. singer
2. Lake Superior
3. computer
4. neighbor
5. Poland
6. football team
7. university
8. girl
9. Einstein
10. Franklin D. Roosevelt
11. World War II
12. Joan of Arc
13. Snoopy
14. Macy's
15. comedian
16. Iowa
17. club
18. doctor
19. airline
20. London

EXERCISE B: More Work with Common and Proper Nouns. Follow the directions for Exercise A.

1. China
2. Yankee Stadium
3. school
4. Civil War
5. Spanish
6. George Washington
7. gulf
8. friend
9. San Diego
10. canal
11. hero
12. baseball team
13. Amazon River
14. town
15. Andes Mountains
16. monument
17. ocean
18. building
19. Betsy Ross
20. Saturn

DEVELOPING WRITING SKILLS: Using Common and Proper Nouns in Sentences. Write ten sentences. In each sentence include both a common noun and a proper noun. Underline each common noun and circle each proper noun.

Skills Review and Writing Workshop

Nouns

CHECKING YOUR SKILLS

Write the nouns in each sentence. Compound nouns, common nouns, and proper nouns have been included.

EXAMPLE: The hawk left the giant oak.
hawk oak

1. Some animals that live in cities are not pets.
2. Falcons have been seen on several bridges in New York City.
3. Coyotes roam the suburbs of California.
4. People in the city sometimes see skunks and opossums.
5. There are kinds of birds and insects that have remained in neighborhoods for centuries.
6. Why have these creatures moved to crowded areas?
7. Scientists say there are several reasons.
8. Citizens have become more interested in wildlife.
9. New guides and booklets are becoming available to readers.
10. Investigators can search attics, cellars, backyards, and parks.

USING GRAMMAR SKILLS IN WRITING

Writing a News Story

Think of something that happened to you or something you saw recently that you think a friend would enjoy hearing about. You are going to write a news story about that event. Remember to be specific. Be sure each word you use says exactly what you mean.

A reporter includes all the information he or she has so the reader can understand the story fully. Organize your facts so the main ones are in the first paragraph and the less important ones are in the following paragraphs.

Chapter 2

Pronouns

Pronouns are useful words. They make speaking and writing easy to follow. Without them, a person talking about the President of the United States might sound like this: "The President is a powerful person. The President sees that laws are carried out. Agencies help the President with the President's work. The President and the President's advisors prepare the budget. The President and the President's advisors present the budget to Congress. The President does important work."

Thanks to pronouns, people can talk like this: "The President is a powerful person. *He* sees that laws are carried out. Agencies help *him* with *his* work. The President and *his* advisors prepare the budget. *They* present *it* to Congress. The President does important work."

The words in italics are pronouns. These pronouns act as substitutes for the words *President, advisors,* and *budget* so that they do not have to be repeated again and again.

In this chapter you will learn to recognize pronouns. You will also practice using them in sentences of your own.

2.1 The Pronoun

Pronouns are useful words because they can "stand-in" for nouns. They prevent people from having to use the same nouns over and over again.

A pronoun takes the place of a noun.

EXAMPLES: Jerry noticed the dog before Maria noticed it.
(*It* takes the place of *dog*.)
Emily decided that she would take gymnastics.
(*She* takes the place of *Emily*.)

The noun that is replaced by a pronoun is called the *antecedent*. Usually, the antecedent comes before the pronoun. The antecedent is the name of a person, place, or thing. The chart below shows how pronouns are used to replace antecedents.

PRONOUNS AND ANTECEDENTS	
Person	Marie (ANTECEDENT) said she (PRONOUN) would visit on Tuesday.
Place	Florida (ANTECEDENT) is popular because it (PRONOUN) has a warm climate.
Thing	Our rusty old bicycles (ANTECEDENT) cannot be used until they (PRONOUN) are repaired.

A pronoun and its antecedent will often be in the same sentence, as they are in the examples above. Sometimes, however, a pronoun and its antecedent will be in different sentences.

EXAMPLES: Jane sings well. Many people have enjoyed listening to her.
Michael collects rocks. His collection is valuable.

EXERCISE A: Recognizing Pronouns and Antecedents. Each of the sentences below contains one pronoun. Copy each sentence, underlining the pronoun and its antecedent. Then, draw an arrow connecting the pronoun and antecedent.

EXAMPLE: The settlers grew corn and ate it often.

The settlers grew corn and ate it often.

1. The colonists worked hard when they first came to America.
2. Farmers spent their time working the land.
3. A woman invented a machine she could use to grind corn.
4. Sybilla Masters sold her cornmeal in Philadelphia.
5. The people enjoyed their evenings.
6. The colonists enjoyed tall tales and told them often.
7. A child would listen to a bird and imitate its call.
8. A girl who owned a doll could dress it in fancy clothes.
9. A settler wrote that he was glad to live in America.
10. If a boy had free time, he might play ball.

EXERCISE B: More Work with Pronouns and Antecedents. Follow the directions for Exercise A.

1. Every seashell has its own look.
2. There are 70,000 varieties, and they are all different.
3. An interesting fact about shells is that they have no backbones.
4. Shells with skeletons have them on the outside.
5. The animals that live in shells are affected by their surroundings.

DEVELOPING WRITING SKILLS: Using Pronouns and Antecedents in Sentences. Write five sentences about people you know. Include antecedents and pronouns in all of the sentences.

2.2 Personal Pronouns

Personal pronouns refer to people and what they speak or write about.

Personal pronouns refer to (1) the person speaking or writing, (2) the person listening or reading, or (3) the topic (person, place, or thing) being discussed or written about.

The first-person pronouns *I, me, my, mine, we, us, our* and *ours* refer to the person speaking.

EXAMPLE: I favor the new plan.

The second-person pronouns you, your, and yours refer to the person spoken to.

EXAMPLE: You will see the picture.

The third-person pronouns he, him, his, she, her, hers, it, its, they, them, them, their, and theirs refer to the person, place, or thing spoken about.

EXAMPLE: He wants to listen to music.

The chart below presents the personal pronouns. Included are personal pronouns that indicate ownership *(my, mine, your, yours, his, her, hers, its, their,* and *theirs).* Notice also that the second-person personal pronouns are the same in both the singular and the plural.

PERSONAL PRONOUNS		
	Singular	**Plural**
First Person	I, me, my, mine	we, us, our, ours
Second Person	you, your, yours	you, your, yours
Third Person	he, him, his she, her, hers it, its	they, them, their, theirs

EXERCISE A: Recognizing Personal Pronouns. List the personal pronoun in each sentence. Then label it as *first-person, second-person,* or *third-person.*

EXAMPLE: Marlene and I examined the building.
I (first-person)

1. Have you ever heard of a rockscraper?
2. It could be called an underground skyscraper.
3. The designer says he believes in space above ground.
4. His prediction is for more underground buildings.
5. We may have buildings more than 110 feet underground.
6. People may not realize how far down they are.
7. My concern is whether there will be enough light.
8. I read that lenses could beam light downwards.
9. A worker said that the amount of light inside surprised him.
10. A woman said she liked the constant temperature underground.

EXERCISE B: More Work with Personal Pronouns. Follow the directions for Exercise A.

1. Was your summer vacation pleasant?
2. I spent the summer traveling in Mexico.
3. The entire family went with me.
4. There are five of us in all.
5. Henry brought along his camera and took pictures.
6. Andrea brought her sketch pad and charcoals.
7. Of course, our journals were packed.
8. Sometimes Andrea spent her time in the park.
9. Other times, they went to the museum.
10. In the evening we all got together for dinner.

DEVELOPING WRITING SKILLS: Using Personal Pronouns. Write a brief paragraph in which you discuss a movie. Use personal pronouns, and underline them.

2.3 Demonstrative Pronouns

Demonstrative pronouns point to people, places, and things much as you point to them with your finger.

A demonstrative pronoun points out a person, place, or thing.

There are four demonstrative pronouns. They are *this, that, these,* and *those.*

This and *that* are singular demonstrative pronouns.

EXAMPLES: This is a new invention.

That is silk.

These and *those* are plural demonstrative pronouns.

EXAMPLES: I bought some sweaters. These are for you.

Those appear to be lilacs.

Demonstrative pronouns tell whether something is near or far from the speaker. *This* and *these* point to what is nearby. *That* and *those* point to what is more distant.

NEAR: This is the desk where I sit.

Of all the books I own, these are my favorites.

FAR: Is that the road to take?

Those are frisky puppies.

A demonstrative pronoun can point to a noun in the same sentence or in a different one.

SAME SENTENCE: These are the cards I received.

DIFFERENT SENTENCE: You have a red pencil. That is what I'm looking for.

EXERCISE A: Recognizing Demonstrative Pronouns. Find the demonstrative pronoun in each sentence. Write both the demonstrative pronoun and the noun it refers to.

EXAMPLE: This is a new magazine.
This magazine

1. These are paintings by Charles Willson Peale.
2. This is a portrait of George Washington.
3. Do you know if those are also paintings by Peale?
4. Peale set up a gallery of paintings for the public. This was the first in America.
5. He created a portable bathtub. That was quite useful.
6. He kept live birds. These were admired by friends.
7. This was a household full of artists.
8. That was the studio Thomas Jefferson praised.
9. Yes, these are pictures by Peale's brother.
10. I think those are letters Peale wrote.

EXERCISE B: More Work with Demonstrative Pronouns. Follow the directions for Exercise A.

1. This is the street I live on.
2. That is our house.
3. Those are the bushes I planted.
4. Of all my coins, that is the one I value most.
5. This is a coin from Africa.
6. My pennies come from different places. These were minted in San Francisco.
7. Those are French francs.
8. This is a buffalo-head nickel.
9. Yes, that is money from Italy.
10. These are some coins for you.

DEVELOPING WRITING SKILLS: Using Demonstrative Pronouns. Write a paragraph in which you point out interesting things in your school to a visitor. Use all four demonstrative pronouns.

Skills Review and Writing Workshop

Pronouns

CHECKING YOUR SKILLS

List the pronoun in each sentence. Then, label each pronoun as a *personal pronoun* or a *demonstrative pronoun.*

EXAMPLE: Joanne said her goal is to become an editor.
her (personal pronoun)

1. You may know Earth is part of the Milky Way galaxy.
2. This is a galaxy made up of billions of stars.
3. We are learning more and more about stars.
4. The center of the galaxy is called its core.
5. The core is hidden from us by dust clouds.
6. Scientists spend their time studying radio waves.
7. These are radio waves from giant antennas.
8. They study the waves to learn about the galaxy.
9. I have been reading a scientific report.
10. Three scientists released their latest findings.

USING GRAMMAR SKILLS IN WRITING

Writing a Journal

Writers often keep journals. They make notes of their experiences, observations, and ideas. They often use that material in stories and novels.

Write a page for a journal. It could be about a real day, or it could be about an imaginary day. You could, for example, see yourself in another city or another country. You could be with people you know or people you invent.

Remember you are writing this page because you might include the events, sounds, or sights in a story. So be sure to include your thoughts and feelings.

When you finish writing, read your page carefully. Have you written enough? Could you use the material? Be sure the antecedents of your pronouns are clear.

3

Verbs

When you studied nouns and pronouns, you learned about words that name or represent the people, places, and things you speak or write about. But since the world is made up not only of people, places, and things but also of actions and happenings, another kind of word is needed. The words that let you say what people are doing or what is happening are verbs. Nouns and verbs, pronouns and verbs—these are the words that do the important work when you speak or write.

In this chapter, you will learn several things about verbs. First, you will learn how to recognize a verb. Then you will read about three different groups of verbs—verbs that express action, verbs that link the parts of a sentence, and verbs that help other verbs. You will also practice using verbs in sentences of your own.

3.1 The Verb

A verb is an important part of every sentence. No sentence is complete without one. A verb tells what someone or something does or is. In other words, a verb shows action or condition.

A verb expresses the action or condition of a person, place, or thing.

Many verbs express actions or activities that can be completed. They show what someone or something *does* or *did*. In the example below the verbs showing action are underlined.

EXAMPLES: Claude painted the scenery.

Sandra designed the costumes.

Other verbs express condition. Such verbs link a noun or pronoun with words that describe the condition of the noun or pronoun. In the examples below, verbs that express condition are underlined. Notice that they link the nouns that come before them with the descriptive words that follow.

EXAMPLES: The book is wonderful.

This wood feels smooth.

The chart lists examples of verbs that express action and verbs that express condition.

VERBS	
Action	**Condition**
build	is
examine	seem
reply	appear
jog	taste
solve	sound

EXERCISE A: Recognizing Verbs. List the verb in each of the sentences below.

EXAMPLE: Mrs. Bethune received donations from the school.
received

1. Mary McLeod Bethune dreamed of a school for black children.
2. She explored different locations.
3. Daytona, Florida, was her choice.
4. She felt sure of herself and her idea.
5. Five students paid fifty cents a week as tuition.
6. Mrs. Bethune taught her pupils useful skills.
7. The school grew larger each year.
8. In the evening, adults studied there.
9. The students worked very hard.
10. Mrs. Bethune became a famous educator.

EXERCISE B: More Work with Verbs. List the verb in each of the following sentences.

1. My friend Mark enjoys skiing.
2. Last year his family spent two weeks in Vail, Colorado.
3. He and his brother Paul tried the beginner slopes.
4. Soon they felt confident.
5. Mark and Paul attended some classes in skiing.
6. They seemed excited about the sport.
7. Several days later, the boys attempted a steeper slope.
8. This attempt was successful.
9. Mark skillfully raced past a group of people.
10. Now he is an experienced skier.

DEVELOPING WRITING SKILLS: Using Verbs in Sentences. Write a paragraph of five or more sentences explaining how to do or make something. Underline the verbs in your sentences.

3.2 Action Verbs

There are several different kinds of verbs. One kind, *action verbs,* show someone doing something or something being done. *Dance, swim, fall,* and *explode* are all action verbs.

An action verb indicates the action of a person or thing. The action can be visible or mental.

Some action verbs show visible action.

EXAMPLES: Ellen plays soccer.
Jeffrey lifted weights.
Nancy shouted to her friends.

The verbs *play* and *lift* indicate visible actions. These actions can be seen.

Other verbs indicate mental actions. These actions cannot be seen or heard directly. They are thinking activities, but they are still actions.

EXAMPLES: The students understand the assignment.
Everyone believes you.

The verbs *understand* and *believe* express mental actions.

The chart below shows the two types of action verbs.

ACTION VERBS	
Visible Actions	**Mental Actions**
entertain	feel
jump	imagine
announce	love
throw	dislike

Strong, specific action verbs make your speech and writing interesting. They help you communicate clearly.

EXERCISE A: Identifying Action Verbs. Copy the sentences below. Underline the action verb in each sentence.

EXAMPLE: The audience applauded the performers.

1. A glassblower built an unusual glass instrument.
2. The glass armonica produces a loud, unforgettable sound.
3. People remember its unusual tones.
4. A player gently rubs the glass rims with his hands.
5. An electric motor twirls the glasses of this instrument.
6. Modern composers appreciate the sound of the armonica.
7. They wonder about its future as a concert instrument.
8. Eighteenth-century composers wrote music for armonica.
9. Some people feared the strange music.
10. In fact, a few towns in Europe banned the instrument.

EXERCISE B: More Work with Action Verbs. Follow the directions for Exercise A.

1. I selected three mystery books for you.
2. The campers gathered together for a meeting.
3. Larry signaled to his friend across the room.
4. I understand the unusual nature of this case.
5. The judge awarded the prize to Alice's dog.
6. Suddenly, I realized my mistake.
7. Pedro recognized the bearded man immediately.
8. She heard incomprehensible sounds over the radio.
9. He adjusted the sound of the television.
10. After a few moments, the student chose a topic for her composition.

DEVELOPING WRITING SKILLS: Using Action Verbs to Tell What Is Happening. Observe someone working or playing. Then write ten sentences describing what the person did. Try to use exact, specific verbs. Underline the verbs you use.

3.3 Linking Verbs

Linking verbs join nouns or pronouns with words that identify or describe them.

A linking verb joins a noun or pronoun at or near the beginning of a sentence with a word at or near the end. The word at the end identifies or describes the noun or pronoun.

The most common linking verbs are all forms of the verb *be: am, are, is, was,* and *were.* In each example below, the linking verb joins a noun or pronoun with a word that identifies or describes it.

EXAMPLES: Laura is the editor. (*Editor* identifies *Laura.*)

Elliot was ready. (*Ready* describes *Elliot.*)

The jars are full. (*Full* describes *jars.*)

Several other verbs also work as linking verbs. They work the same way as the forms of *be* do to connect the parts of a sentence.

EXAMPLES: The pilot remained calm. (*Calm* describes *pilot.*)

Jean and Katy became lawyers. (*Lawyers* identifies *Jean* and *Katy.*)

The following chart presents some of these other linking verbs.

OTHER LINKING VERBS		
appear	look	sound
become	remain	stay
feel	seem	taste
grow	smell	turn

EXERCISE A: Recognizing Linking Verbs. Copy the sentences below. Underline each linking verb. Then, draw a double-headed arrow to connect the words that are linked by the verb.

EXAMPLE: Wolves are shy.

1. Rita is an artist.
2. The candidates seem confident.
3. Some trees grow tall.
4. The fresh bread smelled delicious.
5. My neighbor sounded frightened on the phone.
6. This new magazine looks interesting.
7. Mr. Davis was a farmer in the Midwest.
8. The old couple's store stayed open all week.
9. We remained partners for five years.
10. The inexperienced traveler felt tired.

EXERCISE B: More Work with Linking Verbs. Copy each of the following sentences. Underline the linking verb. Then, draw a double-headed arrow to show which words are linked by the verb.

1. The speaker appeared relaxed.
2. This new report sounds accurate.
3. I am a relative of the senator.
4. My sister remained calm during the emergency.
5. John became impatient after ten minutes.
6. Michelle turned red with embarrassment.
7. The small horses were Shetlands.
8. Every item looked new.
9. Ted seemed fit for the job.
10. This holiday dinner smells delicious.

DEVELOPING WRITING SKILLS: Using Linking Verbs in Sentences. Write a paragraph about a stranger who has knocked at your door. Use one of the following linking verbs in each sentence: *sound, seem, remain, appear, become, is, am, are, were,* and *look.*

3.4 Helping Verbs

Verbs such as *jump, talk,* and *wait* are called *main verbs.* Sometimes, however, verbs are made up of several words such as *had jumped, might have talked, would have understood,* and *could have been waiting.* In this case, the verbs that come before the main verb are called *helping verbs.* They help express the meaning of the main verb.

A helping verb is a verb that comes before the main verb and adds to its meaning.

A main verb and one or more helping verbs form a *verb phrase.* In the sentences below, the helping verbs are underlined and the main verbs are boxed. Together, the two kinds of verbs make up verb phrases.

EXAMPLES: Sheila was [sleeping.]
Sheila had been [sleeping.]
Sheila should have been [sleeping.]

The various forms of *be* and *have* are the most common helping verbs. The following chart of helping verbs includes some of the forms of *be* and *have,* as well as other helping verbs.

COMMON HELPING VERBS		
am	have	may
are	has	might
is	had	must
was	can	shall
were	could	should
be	do	will
being	does	would
been	did	

EXERCISE A: Identifying Helping Verbs. Copy the verb phrase (main verb plus helping verb) in each sentence. Then, underline the helping verbs and circle the main verbs.

EXAMPLE: A snowflake is created from a fleck of dust.

is (created)

1. No one can explain the exact formation of snowflakes.
2. A snowflake might begin as an uncomplicated shape.
3. Eventually it will look like crystal.
4. Its growth could be caused by a slight push.
5. It will grow even more with a second push.
6. One scientist has been working on a theory.
7. This scientist might be solving the snowflake mystery.
8. A computer is being used in the scientist's work.
9. He has written many mathematical formulas.
10. The formulas have been fed into the computer.

EXERCISE B: More Work with Helping Verbs. Follow the directions in Exercise A.

1. Historians have written about Nathan Hale's bravery.
2. He was serving in the army during the American Revolution.
3. Later, he would become a spy.
4. He was captured by British soldiers and was sentenced to die.
5. We should remember him as a hero.

DEVELOPING WRITING SKILLS: Writing Sentences with Helping Verbs. Write five sentences explaining something you like to do at home or at school. Use helping verbs in each sentence.

Skills Review and Writing Workshop

Verbs

CHECKING YOUR SKILLS

Write the verb or verb phrase in each sentence below. There are action verbs, linking verbs, and helping verbs in this exercise.

EXAMPLE: Early Native Americans hunted wild bison.
hunted

1. The first Americans arrived in North America 20,000 years ago.
2. That was during the Ice Age.
3. A land bridge had formed between Asia and America.
4. The Asians were searching for food.
5. They crossed the land bridge into North America.
6. This explanation seems believable to scientists.
7. The travelers must have moved south slowly.
8. They followed a path near the Rocky Mountains.
9. Some Asians may have used boats.
10. Eventually they settled the continent.

USING GRAMMAR SKILLS IN WRITING

Writing About a Sports Event

Imagine that you have been chosen to explain a sports event to someone who has been away. You need to explain clearly what the event is all about.

What sports event are you going to explain? Be sure your verbs are lively. Of course you need to explain the rules of the sport you have selected. But you want to make that explanation as interesting as possible. Look your work over carefully.

Chapter 4

Adjectives

Some words make language come alive for a reader or listener. They turn an otherwise gray, dull description into one that is stimulating and detailed. Readers who are reading about a particular house, for example, need information that can help them picture it and tell it apart from other houses. The house could be *old* and *shabby*, or *new* and *luxurious*.

Adjectives such as *shabby* and *luxurious* are words that help make meaning clear. Without adjectives, people would communicate in only a vague, general way. With adjectives, people can show how things are unique and special. Adjectives can make your writing and speaking more interesting. Those that create clear pictures in a reader's or listener's mind are particularly effective.

In this chapter, you will read more about adjectives. You will learn to identify them. You will also learn about several types of adjectives—articles, proper adjectives, and possessive adjectives. Each type of adjective helps a reader or listener understand a message by making it more specific.

4.1 The Adjective

Adjectives are words that make language more specific. For example, *car* is a general word, but a *red, two-door '67 Chevrolet* is far more specific. Adjectives such as *red* and *two-door* make nouns and pronouns more clear and vivid.

An adjective is a word that describes something.

Adjectives are often called *modifiers,* because they modify, or change, the meaning of a noun or pronoun. Notice how *sweater* is modified by each set of adjectives.

EXAMPLES: lightweight sweater
thick wool sweater
red turtleneck sweater

Adjectives answer several questions about nouns and pronouns. They tell *What kind? Which one? How many?* or *How much?*

QUESTIONS ANSWERED BY ADJECTIVES		
What Kind?	*expensive* toys	*colorful* caps
Which One?	*this* man	*these* boots
How Many? How Much?	*few* cars	*many* people

Adjectives usually come before the nouns they modify. They can come after nouns, but this is less common.

BEFORE: Kevin has three apples.

Large, colorful flowers bloomed everywhere.

AFTER: Kevin's apples are ripe.

Flowers, large and colorful, bloomed everywhere.

In a similar way, one or more adjectives can come before or after a pronoun.

BEFORE: Intelligent and active, he commands attention.

AFTER: She is talented.

EXERCISE: Recognizing Adjectives. List each adjective in the sentences below.

EXAMPLE: Dream houses often have large rooms.

Dream large

1. I like to fish in clear, cold, deep lakes.
2. Old clothes are often comfortable.
3. Vera enjoys frisky, playful kittens.
4. Dad's new car uses less gas than his old one.
5. Red and white roses were everywhere.
6. Hot cocoa is my favorite beverage.
7. I like to watch old silent films.
8. Sunsets can be magnificent around here.
9. Blue, green, brown, and orange sweaters were on display.
10. Chocolate, vanilla, and strawberry ice cream was served in gleaming cups.
11. I know of two good and cheap restaurants nearby.
12. The long race left the runner exhausted.
13. Frightened and confused, small children hugged their mothers.
14. My ideal home would have large rooms.
15. My older sister is both artistic and athletic.
16. Used cars can sometimes be good bargains.
17. Three small sunfish were all my brother caught.
18. Look at Don's fancy new sneakers!
19. Large wet flakes were falling in swirls of bitter wind.
20. Andy writes funny and interesting letters.

DEVELOPING WRITING SKILLS: Using Adjectives to Describe a Movie. Write a paragraph of ten sentences in which you describe the characters, setting, and plot of a movie. Use one or more adjectives in each sentence.

4.2 Articles

Three frequently used adjectives are the words *a, an,* and *the.* They are called *articles.* Articles can be *definite* or *indefinite.* Both types of articles indicate that a noun will soon follow.

***The* is the definite article. It points to a specific person, place, or thing.**

***A* and *an* are the indefinite articles. They point to any member of a group of similar people, places, or things.**

DEFINITE: Mr. Ryan is the man to see. (a specific person)

Go into the garden. (a specific place)

I want the notebook. (a specific thing)

INDEFINITE: I need to see a doctor (any doctor).

Let's go to a park. (any park)

A is used before consonant sounds and *an* is used before vowel sounds. The chart below gives several examples of the indefinite articles used correctly before consonant sounds and before vowel sounds.

HOW TO USE *A* AND *AN*	
***A* Before Consonant Sounds**	***An* Before Vowel Sounds**
a pineapple	an ivory tusk
a *u*seful item (*y* sound)	an eraser
a *o*ne-way street (*w* sound)	an angry look
a taxi	an opportunity
a lamp	an umbrella

EXERCISE: Using Indefinite Articles. Copy each phrase. Replace the blank with the correct indefinite article.

EXAMPLE: ______ delicate instrument
a delicate instrument

1. ______ new film
2. ______ successful deal
3. ______ uninterrupted game
4. ______ foreign language
5. ______ idea
6. ______ one-time senator
7. ______ innocent mistake
8. ______ endless task
9. ______ brilliant idea
10. ______ uniform to wear
11. ______ gold ring
12. ______ agreeable partner
13. ______ early appointment
14. ______ impatient customer
15. ______ graceful leap
16. ______ original painting
17. ______ telegram message
18. ______ unpleasant time
19. ______ unwilling person
20. ______ special report
21. ______ telephone directory
22. ______ evergreen tree
23. ______ additional feature
24. ______ radio program
25. ______ unusual time

DEVELOPING WRITING SKILLS: Using Articles in Sentences. Write a paragraph describing some of the presents you have received during your life. When you are finished writing, underline each definite and indefinite article.

4.3 Proper Adjectives

The words *African sunset, Siberian climate,* and *American art* all have something in common. An adjective based on a proper noun begins each pair of words. Such adjectives are called *proper adjectives.*

A proper adjective is (1) a proper noun used as an adjective or (2) an adjective formed from a proper noun.

When a proper noun is used as an adjective, it answers the question *What kind?* or *Which one?* about the noun it modifies. The chart below lists proper nouns and then shows how they can be used as proper adjectives.

Proper Nouns	Proper Nouns Used as Adjectives
Baltimore	Baltimore newspaper
April	April showers
Kennedy	Kennedy family

Endings called *suffixes* are added to many proper nouns to make them into proper adjectives. A few proper nouns and their adjective forms are shown below.

Proper Nouns	Proper Adjective Forms
America	American jazz
Inca	Incan empire
Queen Victoria	Victorian novel

Notice that an ending such as *-n* or *-ian* has been added to each of the proper nouns.

The following sentences give additional examples of proper adjectives.

EXAMPLES: Colombian coffee was served.

I won a European vacation.

EXERCISE A: Identifying Proper Adjectives. List the proper adjectives in each sentence. Then list the noun it modifies.

EXAMPLE: My family dined at an Italian restaurant.
Italian restaurant

1. Georgia peaches are famous for their sweet taste.
2. Patricia prefers French dressing on her salad.
3. We have tickets to hear a Beethoven symphony.
4. Put the Swiss watch on the counter.
5. The actor wore a Panama hat and carried a cane.
6. A Parisian designer made this dress.
7. We read several examples of Spanish literature.
8. The Canadian team is well prepared.
9. March winds howled around us as we landed in Chicago.
10. Michelle wrote to the Venezuelan embassy for information.

EXERCISE B: More Work with Proper Adjectives. Follow the directions for Exercise A.

1. Last year we vacationed on a Hawaiian island.
2. A Chaplin movie is playing nearby.
3. Have you seen the Portuguese coins?
4. Susan wants to read the Carter memoirs.
5. My mother chose Mediterranean furniture.
6. Our club met during the Christmas vacation.
7. An Irish leprechaun is the team mascot.
8. The Swedish film has a good plot.
9. We decided to go to a Mexican restaurant.
10. I can play a Chopin waltz on the piano.

DEVELOPING WRITING SKILLS: Writing Sentences with Proper Adjectives. Imagine that you took a trip around the world. Write five sentences about things you saw and did. Use a proper adjective, such as *French, Spanish, Mexican, Peruvian,* or *Greek,* in each sentence.

4.4 Possessive Adjectives

Not only can nouns be used as adjectives, but pronouns can, also. In the word pairs *my computer, our class,* and *its cover,* the personal pronouns are working as adjectives.

A personal pronoun can be used as an adjective if it modifies a noun.

The following examples show personal pronouns used as adjectives. Because they show possession, they are called *possessive adjectives.*

EXAMPLES: Eddie recopied his notes.

Jane said, "My coat is warm."

The students hoped their team would win.

Notice that each underlined pronoun modifies, or describes, the noun that follows it.

PERSONAL PRONOUNS USED AS POSSESSIVE ADJECTIVES		
Singular		**Plural**
my	her	our
your	its	your
his		their

Each pronoun in the examples above refers back to a noun, its antecedent. The examples below show that personal pronouns (1) work as adjectives and (2) take the place of nouns. The arrows point back to antecedents and forward to the nouns modified.

EXAMPLES: All students can leave their books here.

Ben predicted his score in the game.

The club wants to increase its membership.

EXERCISE A: Recognizing Possessive Adjectives. Copy each sentence. Underline the possessive adjective. Then, draw one arrow connecting the possessive adjective to its antecedent and another arrow connecting it to the noun it modifies.

EXAMPLE: Eric wrote his story on a microcomputer.

1. Andrea said that computers make her life easier.
2. Computers don't lose their patience.
3. Eric added, "My homework was done on a computer."
4. Juan spends his time designing programs.
5. A student who uses a computer will learn its uses.
6. Michael, has your school developed any software for science classes?
7. Mary will show her program to you.
8. "Donna, your program is saved on a diskette."
9. The boys have made revisions in their compositions.
10. Chris says his skills in word processing have improved.

EXERCISE B: More Work with Recognizing Possessive Adjectives. Follow the directions for Exercise A.

1. Dr. Alice Hamilton is known for her work in medicine.
2. She helped people in Chicago care for their children.
3. Dr. Hamilton received her degree in 1893.
4. The governor appointed the doctor to head one of his committees.
5. She studied workers' diseases and their causes.

DEVELOPING WRITING SKILLS: Using Possessive Adjectives in Sentences. Write ten sentences giving your opinion and the opinion of your classmates about popular music or a popular-music group. Use a possessive adjective in each sentence.

Skills Review and Writing Workshop

Adjectives

CHECKING YOUR SKILLS

Copy the sentences below. Underline each adjective. Look for ordinary adjectives as well as articles, proper adjectives, and possessive adjectives. The number in parentheses tells how many adjectives to look for.

EXAMPLE: The history class had an exciting debate. (4)

1. Our school has an outstanding program. (3)
2. The useful courses are taught by a talented faculty. (4)
3. Ten exciting programs are offered in the science department. (4)
4. The students, talented and determined, learn their lessons. (4)
5. French teachers and Spanish teachers are experienced and able instructors. (4)
6. Folk dancing and jazz dancing are taught in the gym. (3)
7. My favorite classes are computer science and creative writing. (4)
8. This school has a capable principal. (3)
9. Your first visit will show you small classes and solid learning in action. (4)
10. Visit our African art gallery on the third floor. (5)

USING GRAMMAR SKILLS IN WRITING

Writing Description

Write about a beautiful person or an ugly one. Pick a real person or an imaginary one. As you write, try not to use the first word you think of. Take a minute to think of a second and perhaps better word. It is, for example, easy to say someone's hair is not straight. It is much more interesting to say that someone's head was covered with brown snake-like curls. Check your work to be sure your adjectives are vivid.

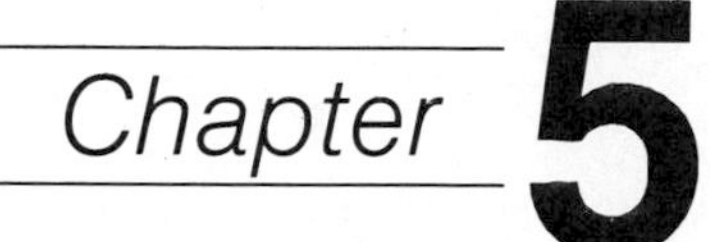

Chapter 5

Adverbs

Like adjectives, adverbs are modifiers. They modify verbs, adjectives, and other adverbs, making them clear and exact. Adverbs often describe actions. If a woman is working, for example, she could be working *quickly, efficiently, slowly, hurriedly, nearby,* or *late.* An adverb can tell you *how* she is working. Choosing adverbs that describe vividly helps readers or listeners better understand your meaning.

This chapter is about adverbs. You will learn how to recognize them. You will also learn about the differences between adjectives and adverbs.

5.1 The Adverb

Adverbs are words that modify other words, just as adjectives do. Adverbs most often modify verbs. The first word in each of the following phrases is an adverb: *slowly twisted, skillfully reads, quickly hides.*

Adverbs also modify adjectives and adverbs. In the sentence *The game was very exciting,* the adverb *very* modifies the adjective *exciting.* In *They played extremely well,* the adverb *extremely* modifies the adverb *well.*

An adverb is a word that modifies a verb, an adjective, or another adverb.

Adverbs answer several questions when they modify verbs.

WHAT ADVERBS TELL ABOUT VERBS	
Where?	He lives nearby. I looked inside.
When?	Janice played yesterday. The message arrived early.
In What Way?	The musician performed perfectly. The dancers moved gracefully.
To What Extent?	Amy fully agrees with me. I am totally opposed to it.

When adverbs modify adjectives or adverbs, they answer the question *To what extent?*

ADVERB MODIFYING A VERB: Grace tenderly spoke to Sam.

ADVERB MODIFYING AN ADJECTIVE: A very kind woman helped me.

ADVERB MODIFYING ANOTHER ADVERB: Tim draws extremely well.

EXERCISE A: Finding Adverbs. Find the adverb that modifies each underlined word.

EXAMPLE: We playfully created a new symbol.
playfully

1. I often think about numbers.
2. Yesterday I read about large numbers.
3. A boy once created a new number word.
4. He jokingly named it a googol.
5. Carefully write *1* with one hundred *0*'s.
6. Mathematicians accepted the idea most enthusiastically.
7. Eventually he created another large number expression.
8. He very quickly named this one the googolplex.
9. I rarely hear about the Mega, another amazingly large number.
10. A scientist carefully gave it a serious name.

EXERCISE B: More Work with Adverbs. For each sentence, list the adverb that modifies the underlined word.

1. All our relatives gather yearly.
2. Joyously, we celebrate our good fortunes.
3. We hold a barbecue outside.
4. I received my engraved invitation early.
5. This year we celebrated uptown.
6. A restaurant carefully catered the affair.
7. This change utterly surprised us.
8. Eagerly, the restaurant promised an unusually favorable rate.
9. They guaranteed everything fully.
10. I dine at that restaurant quite often.

DEVELOPING WRITING SKILLS: Using Adverbs in Sentences. Write ten sentences using an adverb in each sentence.

5.2 Adverb or Adjective?

You may sometimes have to think carefully before identifying a word as an adverb or an adjective. This is because some words may be used as an adverb in one sentence and an adjective in the next.

If a noun or pronoun is modified by a word, that word is an adjective. If a verb, adjective, or adverb is modified by a word, that word is an adverb.

The example below shows how the word *right* is used as an adverb in the first sentence and as an adjective in the second.

ADVERB: When you reach Spring Street, turn right. (Right modifies the verb *turn.*)

ADJECTIVE: A ninety-degree angle is called a right angle. (*Right* modifies the noun *angle.*)

Adjectives and adverbs also answer different questions. Adjectives answer the questions *What kind? Which one? How many?* and *How much?* Adverbs answer the questions *Where? When? In what way?* and *To what extent?*

To decide whether a word is an adjective or adverb, look at the part of speech of the word it modifies. If it is a noun or pronoun, the word is an adjective. If it is a verb, adjective, or adverb, the word is an adverb. If the word answers the question *What kind? Which one? How many?* or *How much?* it is an adjective. If it answers the question *Where? When? In what way?* or *To what extent?* it is an adverb.

ADVERB: The bus stopped short. (*Short* modifies the verb *stopped* and tells *in what way* the bus stopped.)

ADJECTIVE: The bus made a short stop. (*Short* modifies the noun *stop* and tells *what kind* of stop.)

EXERCISE A: Recognizing Adverbs and Adjectives. Tell whether each underlined word in the sentences below is an adverb or an adjective.

EXAMPLE: I bought an electric clock.
adjective

1. She gazed at the far horizon.
2. He traveled far.
3. I know that you write well.
4. Sarah is well and so am I.
5. A daily flight leaves from here.
6. The flight leaves daily at 10 a.m.
7. The crowd pushed forward.
8. The forward movement pulled me along.
9. In order to see better, George moved near.
10. It was a near miss.

EXERCISE B: More Work with Adverbs and Adjectives. Tell whether each underlined word in the sentences below is an adverb or an adjective.

1. I heard a humorous story.
2. He spoke endlessly.
3. She gave a farewell speech.
4. My recent offer is a generous one.
5. The builder successfully completed the house.
6. They actively swap ideas.
7. He carefully recorded the music.
8. Have you seen the valuable jewel?
9. The giant tree amazed the hikers.
10. The group meets weekly.

DEVELOPING WRITING SKILLS: Using Adverbs and Adjectives in Sentences. Watch a person doing something. Write ten sentences describing what the person is doing. Use an adverb or an adjective in each sentence, and underline it.

Skills Review and Writing Workshop

Adverbs

CHECKING YOUR SKILLS

Copy each sentence below. Underline the adverb. Then draw an arrow connecting the adverb to the word it modifies.

EXAMPLE: George Washington skillfully commanded the troops.

1. Washington tried hard to improve the army.
2. He eagerly trained them in military matters.
3. Washington wisely sent Henry Knox to Ticonderoga.
4. Knox went north for cannons.
5. He worked continually to deliver the weapons.
6. Washington carefully planned his next move.
7. General Howe sadly withdrew the British from Boston.
8. Washington fully believed in his plan.
9. Cautiously, he moved his army to New York.
10. The British soon followed them.

USING GRAMMAR SKILLS IN WRITING

Writing About Your Earliest Memory

What is the earliest thing you remember? Some people can remember all the way back to when they were babies. Others remember their first day at school or the first time they went on a trip.

Instead of telling someone about the earliest thing you remember, you are going to write about it. What facts will you write about? Will you tell how something looked or felt?

You can write as if everything you describe were happening now. Or you can put that memory in the past. Perhaps you will want to compare the way things seemed to you then with what you know to be true now. When you are finished, read your work carefully. Be sure you have chosen words that say what you want them to say. Use adjectives and adverbs to make your memory come alive.

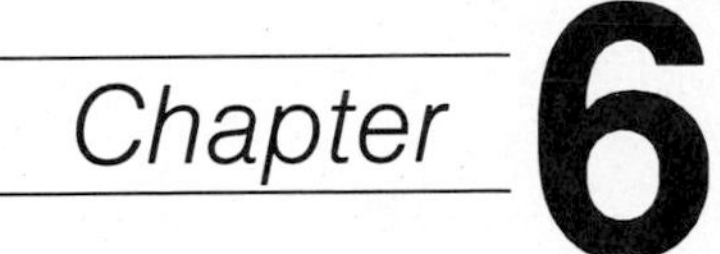

Prepositions

Some words are important simply because they show how other, more important words are related to each other. They may not provide as much meaning as these other words, but they make it possible for them to do their work.

Prepositions are one of the kind of words that serve this necessary function. Although many prepositions are short words—*by, up, in*—they have a big effect on meaning. For example, would you rather be *by* a creek, *up* a creek, or *in* a creek?

This chapter tells about prepositions. You will learn how to recognize them. Then you will learn how to tell if a word is being used as a preposition or an adverb. Finally, you will practice using prepositions.

6.1 The Preposition

Prepositions help a reader or listener understand the relationship of one word to another.

A preposition relates a noun or pronoun to another word in the sentence.

In the examples below, notice how changing prepositions changes meaning.

EXAMPLES: My report is inside my notebook.

My report is beside my notebook.

My report is underneath my notebook.

Some frequently used prepositions are listed in the following chart.

FIFTY PREPOSITIONS				
about	behind	during	off	to
above	below	except	on	toward
across	beneath	for	onto	under
after	beside	from	opposite	underneath
against	besides	in	out	until
along	between	inside	outside	up
among	beyond	into	over	upon
around	but	like	past	with
at	by	near	since	within
before	down	of	through	without

A few prepositions are made up of more than one word.

EXAMPLES: That is the answer according to Mary.

We need stamps in addition to the paper.

The football is next to the soccer ball.

I took the bus instead of the train.

The picnic was postponed on account of rain.

EXERCISE A: Supplying Prepositions. Copy each sentence, replacing the blank with a preposition. Use the chart on the opposite page to help you.

EXAMPLE: I will meet you ______ the store.
I will meet you outside the store.

1. Put your briefcase ______ the table.
2. Tie the string ______ the package.
3. We have been waiting for a reply ______ yesterday.
4. The game will not be held ______ noon.
5. The restaurant is ______ a lake.
6. Draw a line ______ the paper.
7. I will search for the letter ______ my desk.
8. The covering was placed ______ the furniture.
9. Look ______ the telescope to see Saturn.
10. Call me any day ______ Tuesday.

EXERCISE B: More Work with Prepositions. Copy each sentence, replacing the blank with a preposition. Use the chart on the opposite page to help you.

1. Pull the chair out from ______ the table.
2. The liquid smells ______ perfume.
3. The plants reach ______ the light.
4. There is a garage ______ the grocery store.
5. I traveled ______ the town on a bicycle.
6. I voted ______ the changes suggested by the mayor.
7. The meat and vegetables were already ______ the table.
8. Wait ______ tomorrow for the results of the survey.
9. We looked for the pad ______ the pile of papers.
10. Please leave the newspaper ______ the front door.

DEVELOPING WRITING SKILLS: Using Prepositions in Sentences. Write ten sentences telling where a number of things in your home are located. Use a preposition in each sentence. Use as many different ones as you can.

6.2 Preposition or Adverb?

Many words can be used both as prepositions and as adverbs. In order to tell the part of speech, you must see how a word is being used in a sentence.

A preposition will always be part of a prepositional phrase.

An adverb can stand alone.

PREPOSITION: The ball rolled outside the playground. (PREPOSITIONAL PHRASE: outside the playground)

ADVERB: Pat is waiting outside.

Prepositional phrases always include a preposition and a noun or pronoun. They may also include words that modify the noun.

EXAMPLES: The blizzard started in Canada. (PREP: in; NOUN: Canada)

Rest stops are located along the interstate highway. (PREP: along; MODIFIERS: the interstate)

The phrases "in Canada," and "along the interstate highway" are prepositional phrases. Adverbs, on the other hand, are used alone. They can end a sentence. Also, they answer questions that prepositions do not: *Where? When? In what way?* and *To what extent?*

The following chart shows more examples of words used as both prepositions and adverbs.

Prepositions	Adverbs
We performed before a crowd.	I've seen him before.
They raced down the path.	The man sat down.
The cat leaped off the sofa.	Harry walked off.
The room is behind the den.	Barbara stayed behind.

EXERCISE A: Recognizing Prepositions and Adverbs. Tell whether the underlined word is a *preposition* or an *adverb.*

EXAMPLE: Mr. Elliot stopped by.
adverb

1. Marilyn sat down.
2. The plumber went down the stairs.
3. The runners stood behind the white line.
4. The runner fell behind.
5. I saw you leap across and run away.
6. Ben ran across the street.
7. I asked Jane to come inside for a chat.
8. Mary placed the casserole inside the oven.
9. I read past the second chapter.
10. The train roared past.

EXERCISE B: More Work with Recognizing Prepositions and Adverbs. Follow the directions in Exercise A.

1. The child came out.
2. Helen raced out the door.
3. Miriam has been waiting since last Tuesday.
4. No one has visited since.
5. We took the notice off the bulletin board.
6. After dinner, they took off for the movies.
7. Mark painted on the smooth surface.
8. After you brush your teeth, put your shoes on.
9. This chair spins around.
10. A new store opened around the corner.

DEVELOPING WRITING SKILLS: Using Prepositions and Adverbs in Sentences. Use each of the words below in *two* sentences. In the first sentence, use the word as a preposition. In the second sentence, use the word as an adverb. The words to use are *after, before, over, off,* and *around.*

Skills Review and Writing Workshop

Prepositions

CHECKING YOUR SKILLS

List the preposition in each sentence. Then, give a different preposition that could also fit in the sentence.

EXAMPLE: Your copy is beside the telephone.
beside behind

1. The music begins before the dancing.
2. Arthur sent an invitation to my mother.
3. The debate was held in the conference room.
4. The witness fainted during the trial.
5. The families will camp along the river.
6. The teacher strolled around the room.
7. My house is located between the school and the pond.
8. Our congresswoman is respected by the community.
9. We placed the cover over the machine.
10. The large dog moved near the group of children.

USING GRAMMAR SKILLS IN WRITING

Writing Travel Directions

You are going to write a description of how you get to school for someone who just moved into your neighborhood. That person is going to do exactly what you do. So you need to be as clear as possible. Decide exactly what information you are going to put into this piece. Start with the first thing you do, then the second, third, and so on. End up at the school entrance.

Be sure to describe what you see on the way to school as well as the way you travel. You might indicate certain landmarks. For example, you turn left at the red house or you pass the gas station on the left before turning into the driveway. Think about all the things you see on the way to school so you will be able to describe them. Proofread your work carefully. Check that your prepositions help make your description clear.

Conjunctions

Conjunctions and prepositions have been called the "glue" of language. Both parts of speech help hold sentences together. The words *and, but,* and *or* are three conjunctions you probably use almost every time you speak. In fact, these conjunctions, as well as *so,* tend to be used so often that writers and speakers must try not to overuse them. In this chapter, you will learn more about conjunctions. You will read about what they do within sentences. You will also learn to identify common conjunctions and practice using them in sentences of your own. When used correctly, conjunctions help make sentences smooth and clear.

7.1 The Conjunction

Conjunctions connect. They often join words in pairs, such as *Romeo and Juliet, light but sturdy,* and *swimming or running.* Conjunctions also connect larger word groups, such as phrases and sentences.

Conjunctions connect words, groups of words, and whole sentences.

Coordinating conjunctions connect words or groups of words that are similar in form: noun with noun, phrase with phrase, sentence with sentence, and so on.

The following chart presents the seven coordinating conjunctions.

COORDINATING CONJUNCTIONS						
and	but	for	nor	or	so	yet

In the chart below, each coordinating conjunction is boxed and each set of connected words is underlined.

USING COORDINATING CONJUNCTIONS	
Words Connected	**Examples**
Nouns	The pens and pencils are here.
Pronouns	He or I will lead the discussion.
Verbs	The players planned and practiced.
Adjectives	That coat is attractive but expensive.
Adverbs	He works quickly yet carefully.
Prepositional Phrases	The campers followed the trail up the hill and around the lake.
Sentences	You should come soon, for next week we will be leaving.

EXERCISE A: Recognizing Coordinating Conjunctions. For each sentence, list the coordinating conjunction and the words or word groups it connects. Circle the conjunction.

EXAMPLE: The first humans did not use tools or fire.
tools (or) fire

1. Today I have tests in mathematics and social studies.
2. I went to the game, but I left early.
3. Cars were parked in the street and in the driveways.
4. Bob reads slowly and carefully.
5. Mary wanted to buy those jeans, so she saved her allowance money.
6. The book was long but enjoyable.
7. The runner stumbled and fell.
8. I did not like the movie, nor did she.
9. Are you going with us or with them?
10. Bill phoned all day, yet nobody answered.

EXERCISE B: More Work with Coordinating Conjunctions. Follow the directions for Exercise A.

1. Jill could not get tickets, nor could Ed.
2. Do you want lemonade or soda?
3. The weather was sunny but cool.
4. I'm excited, for today is my birthday.
5. Put your bicycle in the garage or in the basement.
6. Did they fly or drive to Kansas City?
7. The song was simple but beautiful.
8. The boat glided silently yet rapidly.
9. Please put in my sandwich lettuce and mayonnaise.
10. Either you or she will be asked to speak.

DEVELOPING WRITING SKILLS: Using Coordinating Conjunctions in Sentences. Write ten sentences telling about two people you know. Use a coordinating conjunction in each sentence.

7.2 Correlative Conjunctions

Correlative conjunctions are conjunctions that are used in pairs. Like coordinating conjunctions, they connect similar types of words or word groups.

Correlative conjunctions are pairs of conjunctions that connect words or word groups.

There are five pairs of correlative conjunctions: both . . . and, either . . . or, neither . . . nor, not only . . . but also, and whether . . . or. They can connect nouns, pronouns, verbs, adjectives, adverbs, prepositional phrases, and sentences.

USING DOUBLE CONJUNCTIONS	
Words Connected	**Examples**
Nouns	Both oranges and grapefruits are on sale.
Pronouns	Neither you nor I could have known.
Verbs	I'll either walk or jog to your house.
Adjectives	Her car is not only new but also custom-built.
Adverbs	He draws both skillfully and creatively.
Prepositional Phrases	Our team is not only in the playoffs but also in the division lead.
Sentences	Either we hold the race here, or we will hold it in Canada.
Sentences	Not only did we get to meet the comedian, but we also got to take his picture.

EXERCISE: Finding Correlative Conjunctions. Copy each sentence. Circle both parts of the correlative conjunction and underline the words or word groups it connects.

EXAMPLE: Basketball players need both ability and spirit.

1. Neither the bat nor the ball belongs to me.
2. My sister reads both novels and plays.
3. Ralph could not decide whether to go or to stay at the party.
4. She neither agreed nor disagreed.
5. Your brother is both funny and intelligent.
6. The ball landed either in the lake or in that bush.
7. The food here is both inexpensive and tasty.
8. Not only did we go to the fair but we also won a prize.
9. The coach would not say whether Phil or Don would pitch.
10. On ice you must drive both slowly and carefully.
11. Both Eric and Aaron play tennis.
12. They not only compete but also practice.
13. They feel neither nervous nor upset in a game.
14. Eric studies his opponent both before a game and during a game.
15. They both play either singles or doubles.
16. It is hard to say whether Eric or Aaron is the better player.
17. They select not only their equipment but also the courts where they will play.
18. Aaron plays either during the day or during the evening.
19. To play well, they should be neither tired nor angry.
20. Instead, they should feel both focused and calm.

DEVELOPING WRITING SKILLS: Using Correlative Conjunctions to Write About a Sport. Write five sentences using a correlative conjunction in each one. Tell about games and sports you have played.

Skills Review and Writing Workshop

Conjunctions

CHECKING YOUR SKILLS

Copy the sentences below. Circle the conjunctions. Underline the words or word groups connected by each conjunction. Both coordinating conjunctions and correlative conjunctions have been included.

EXAMPLE: We can listen to tapes (or) records of music.

1. People play and listen to music.
2. They listen to music both at home and at concerts.
3. No one knows whether singing or dancing came first.
4. The first instruments were natural, so they didn't have to be invented.
5. The ancient Greeks played music, but few songs have survived.
6. Folk songs were not written down, yet many remain.
7. Music can make you not only silly but also serious.
8. Janet likes to attend operas and concerts.
9. Music is very old, so it has a long history.
10. I want to study either piano or violin.

USING GRAMMAR SKILLS IN WRITING

Writing About a Family Dinner

Imagine you have fifteen brothers and sisters. You all just finished eating dinner. Write a letter to a good friend telling what went on at the dinner table.

You might want to start out by telling your friend where everyone sat. Then you can tell what food you ate and how the food was passed around. Tell about the conversation at the dinner table and how everyone behaved.

Since so many people are involved, you need to organize them into groups. Otherwise your friend might not understand what happened. Proofread your piece. Be sure you have established the seating pattern at the table so what you say is clear. Check that you have used conjunctions properly.

Chapter 8

Interjections

Words such as *darn! ah! oh! what!* and *oops!* express feelings and emotions. These words are called interjections.

Interjections are usually reserved for dialogue in stories or for adventure comic books. In other kinds of writing, an occasional interjection may add liveliness, but as a rule interjections should seldom be used in essays and reports.

In this chapter you will examine several examples of interjections and practice fitting them into sentences. You will also use interjections in sentences of your own.

8.1 The Interjection

When you want to show strong feeling or excitement, you can use words that exclaim. In the sentence *Terrific! I will begin right now,* the word *terrific* shows strong feeling. *Terrific* is being used as an *interjection.*

Interjections are words that express sudden excitement or strong feeling.

Sometimes an interjection is followed by an exclamation mark and is separated from the sentence that follows it.

EXAMPLE: Wow! That was a powerful serve.

Ouch! That pan is still hot.

Other times an interjection is followed by a comma and connected to a sentence. This happens when the interjection expresses a mild feeling instead of a strong one.

EXAMPLE: My, that was an exciting story.

Oh, I wish I could find it.

Interjections are used more in speech than in writing. They are informal, rather than formal expressions. When you do see them in writing, they are often included in dialogue. The chart below lists words often used as interjections.

INTERJECTIONS				
ah	fine	huh	oops	ugh
aha	golly	hurray	ouch	well
alas	gosh	my	psst	what
boy	great	never	sh	whew
darn	heavens	nonsense	terrible	wonderful
eureka	hey	oh	terrific	wow

EXERCISE A: Supplying Interjections. Substitute an interjection for each of the blanks below. Use the interjections listed in the chart on page 70 or think of others.

EXAMPLE: ______ ! I'm so happy you were selected.

Wow! I'm so happy you were selected.

1. ______ ! It's 10:30 a.m. and he is not here yet.
2. ______ ! I just shut the door on my finger.
3. ______ ! Elizabeth and I can hardly believe the news.
4. ______ , I can't hear the music.
5. ______ ! My briefcase is missing.
6. ______ ! This new recipe I tried tastes awful.
7. ______ ! She could not have been in Baltimore.
8. ______ ! It's a dramatic discovery.
9. ______ ! We just made it in time for the next train.
10. ______ , don't forget the records.

EXERCISE B: More Work with Supplying Interjections. Follow the directions in Exercise A.

1. ______ , I didn't realize it was so late.
2. ______ ! We won the city championships.
3. ______ ! I almost missed my appointment.
4. ______ , you have an impressive coin collection.
5. ______ ! This idea is really great.
6. ______ , what an original painting.
7. ______ , it's impossible to meet this deadline.
8. ______ ! I scraped my knee on the sidewalk.
9. ______ ! You dropped the stack of books.
10. ______ ! Have you heard about Melissa's new plan?

DEVELOPING WRITING SKILLS: Using Interjections in Sentences. Write ten sentences about exciting events you have experienced. Use an interjection in each sentence. Place a comma or an exclamation point after each interjection.

Skills Review and Writing Workshop

Interjections

CHECKING YOUR SKILLS

List the interjections in each of the sentences below. Interjections that express strong feelings are followed by exclamation marks. Interjections that express mild feelings are followed by commas.

EXAMPLE: Randy yelled, "Ouch! I just twisted my ankle."
Ouch

1. Oh, I just heard my named called.
2. The student said, "Darn! I can't find my homework."
3. Terrific! I'm so glad your story was printed.
4. Ugh! What miserable weather.
5. "Boy, I never saw such a smart dog," said Arnel.
6. The traveler exclaimed, "Golly! What a night."
7. Whew! That test was a rough one.
8. Hey! Haven't you learned how to ride a bike yet?
9. Wow! This exhibit is the best one I've ever seen.
10. Hal replied, "Nonsense! Thirteen is not an unlucky number."

USING GRAMMAR SKILLS IN WRITING
Writing Thoughts

It's your birthday. A lot of people have come to your party and you are opening your presents. Since you are polite, you say you like everything. But now's your chance to say what you really think!

Write your thoughts as you open each box. Remember, some of your gifts are just what you want, so your enthusiasm is real. But those others . . . !

As you write, be sure to say what the gift is and describe it. Then express exactly what your real thoughts are about it. Put in as many interjections and exclamation points as you want to. You can get as excited as you want since no one can read your mind!

Chapter 9

Reviewing Parts of Speech

Until now you have been reading about the specific jobs of each of the eight parts of speech. In this chapter you will see how these parts all work together to form clear sentences. Becoming aware of how the separate parts of language work together is a step toward learning to use your own language more effectively.

When you see an interesting piece of writing or you hear an original sentence, ask yourself why it seems so interesting or original. Is it because the nouns and verbs are strong and specific? Is it because the adjectives and adverbs add precise details? Is it because the conjunctions and prepositions clearly explain the relationships between words? If so, then the parts of speech are working together effectively.

In this chapter you will review the role of each of the parts of speech. As you study the definitions and examples, notice the different roles the parts of speech have. How are the roles similar? How are they different? You will also practice identifying and using each of the parts of speech.

9.1 Identifying Parts of Speech

Chapters 1 to 8 explained and discussed the eight parts of speech—nouns, pronouns, verbs, adjectives, adverbs, prepositions, conjunctions, and interjections. Each of these words does a different job within a sentence.

The eight parts of speech all do different kinds of work within sentences.

The chart below summarizes the information you have already learned about the parts of speech.

THE EIGHT PARTS OF SPEECH		
Parts of Speech	**What They Do in a Sentence**	**Examples**
Noun	Names a person, place, or thing	Emily is a doctor.
Pronoun	Takes the place of a noun	He sent it to me.
Verb	Expresses an action or condition	Ted hit the ball. Mark seems tired.
Adjective	Modifies a noun or pronoun	He is smart.
Adverb	Modifies a verb, an adjective, or another adverb	Eugene responded quickly.
Preposition	Relates a noun or pronoun to another word	Alan dived into the pool.
Conjunction	Connects words, groups of words, or sentences	Miriam and Bob want to go, but I want to stay.
Interjection	Shows sudden excitement or strong feeling	Ouch! That hurts. Oh, what a fascinating tale.

9.1 Identifying Parts of Speech

Before labeling a word as a particular part of speech, see how it is used in a sentence. Remember that many words can be used as different parts of speech. The only way to tell the part of speech is to see what the word does in a sentence. In the following examples, the words *spring* and *inside* are each used as three different parts of speech.

EXAMPLES: Taste the spring water.

(*Spring* is an adjective. It describes the noun *water*.)

Some people spring out of bed in the morning.

(*Spring* is a verb. It expresses an action.)

The spring in my sister's toy broke and needs to be replaced.

(Spring is a noun. It names a thing.)

The inside of the kitchen cabinet is painted beige.

(*Inside* is a noun. It names a place.)

The monthly meeting was held inside the clubhouse.

(*Inside* is a preposition. It relates the noun *clubhouse* to the word *held*.)

Bob stayed inside.

(*Inside* is an adverb. It modifies the verb *stayed*.)

The chart at the bottom of page 74 should help you determine the part of speech of any word in a sentence. The following examples show how the different parts of speech work together in a sentence.

	ADJ	ADJ	NOUN	VERB	PREP	ADJ	NOUN
EXAMPLES:	The	carefree	tourists	sat	beside	the	pool.

INTERJ	NOUN	CONJ	PRON	VERB		ADV
Alas,	Rebecca	and	he	have	parted	forever.

EXERCISE A: Identifying Parts of Speech. Identify the part of speech of each underlined word below. All eight parts of speech—nouns, pronouns, verbs, adjectives, adverbs, prepositions, conjunctions, and interjections—are included in this exercise.

EXAMPLE: Harry Houdini liked magic.
noun

1. As a child, Harry Houdini learned all he could about locks.
2. He thought long and seriously about becoming a magician.
3. Harry and his brother Theo were known as the Houdini Brothers.
4. They rehearsed a trick escape from a locked box.
5. Once, the trick did not work.
6. Theo was stuck inside the box.
7. Reporters took pictures of Houdini's successful escapes.
8. Houdini's wonderful act became famous.
9. Wow! He escaped from a locked prison cell.
10. He was a success in America and in Europe.

EXERCISE B: More Work with Parts of Speech. Follow the directions for Exercise A.

1. My room is arranged for comfort and efficiency.
2. As you enter, you will find a wooden work table on the left.
3. I write and type there.
4. There is a bookshelf near the table.
5. On this bookshelf, I keep both my pencils and paper supplies.
6. I spend many hours in this room.
7. I often read or write there during the evening.
8. My, what a relief to have this quiet place.
9. Sometimes I rearrange the furniture.
10. Then things look strange for a while.

EXERCISE C: Using the Parts of Speech. Supply a specific word according to the direction in parentheses. The word should fit the meaning of the sentence.

EXAMPLE: Sam is an (adjective) swimmer.
expert

1. The (noun) Sam received was handwritten.
2. It was on (adjective) paper.
3. He (adverb) placed it in his pocket.
4. He was asked to swim (conjunction) to dive in the show.
5. (Interjection)! What a talented person.
6. (Pronoun) is an accomplished athlete.
7. Cindy also (verb) well.
8. She dives (adverb) into the water.
9. Stephanie and (pronoun) usually practice music lessons daily.
10. They have been serious swimmers (preposition) last year.
11. My favorite food is (noun).
12. I like it because it tastes (adjective).
13. (Interjection)! It is tasty.
14. You should try some, (conjunction) it will soon be gone.
15. My mother often makes turkey (preposition) the holidays.
16. Another food I like is (noun).
17. (Pronoun) has a wonderful flavor and aroma.
18. (Interjection), haven't I offered you any?
19. It has been (adverb) prepared.
20. It's made from one of my grandmother's (adjective) recipes.

DEVELOPING WRITING SKILLS: Using the Parts of Speech in Sentences. Write eight sentences about a day that was special for you. Underline a different part of speech in each sentence.

Skills Review and Writing Workshop

Reviewing the Parts of Speech

CHECKING YOUR SKILLS

Identify the part of speech of each underlined word in the paragraph below. Each of the eight parts of speech has been included: nouns, pronouns, verbs, adjectives, adverbs, prepositions, conjunctions, and interjections.

EXAMPLE: Laura Ingalls Wilder had an interesting life.
adjective

(1) Laura Ingalls Wilder wrote books about her experiences. (2) The earliest book tells about part of her childhood. (3) Other books tell about the family's journeys and Laura's memories of people and places. (4) Laura traveled out West with her parents and her sister. (5) They met with many difficulties, but they never lost heart. (6) Laura always managed to cope with daily problems. (7) Later, her husband, Almanzo, who suffered from health problems, successfully managed a farm. (8) Laura wrote about her home, her family, and her friends. (9) Indeed, readers can learn much about her life from her books. (10) Two generations of readers have enjoyed her "Little House" books.

USING GRAMMAR SKILLS IN WRITING

Writing a Thank-You Letter

Remember all those gifts you received at the birthday party? Now you need to write thank-you letters.

Pick a gift you didn't like. Then try to think of some good things about that gift. For example, someone might have made you a green sweater with orange bees on it. You might not like it because you were once stung by a bee. But you can say something nice about the color or the style. Be sure to proofread. The person who gave you the sweater went to a lot of trouble, so you want to take the trouble to be sure your letter is grammatically correct.

Chapter 10

Subjects and Predicates

Sentences help people make sense when they speak or write. They make it possible for people to express complete ideas. Consider the following two messages: *A test in science* and *We are having a test in science tomorrow.* The first is just a group of words. The second is a complete sentence. If you were getting ready to study, which message would you find more useful?

To write clear and useful sentences, it helps to know the main parts of a sentence. Every sentence must have two basic parts: a *subject* and a *predicate.* In this chapter you will learn about these two basic parts and practice using them.

10.1 The Two Basic Parts of a Sentence

The sentence is a basic unit of speech and writing. It is by using sentences that people make themselves understood, particularly in writing. If you study the way sentences are put together, you will learn to recognize correct, well-formed sentences. You will learn which parts are necessary and which parts are not.

Every complete sentence contains a subject and a predicate. The subject tells who or what the sentence is about. The predicate tells something about the subject.

The Subject. Sentences can be about anything. Any person, place, or thing can be a subject. The *simple subject* of a sentence is the noun or pronoun that answers the question *Who?* or *What?* about the sentence.

EXAMPLES: He asked me to help.

Atlanta is the site of the new factory.

Democracy is a form of government.

Usually the simple subject is a noun or pronoun found at the beginning of a sentence. However, there are some exceptions. First, there are simple subjects that consist of more than one word. These include titles, names, and compound nouns.

EXAMPLES: *The Wizard of Oz* was on television last night.

Pen pals sometimes get the chance to meet.

Second, subjects sometimes appear at the middle or the end of a sentence. Notice their positions in the following examples.

EXAMPLES: After the debate, Marion went for a walk.

On the table sat the precious jewel.

Third, a sentence that requests or commands can have an unstated but understood subject. The subject *you* is not stated.

EXAMPLE: Answer the phone. (The sentence is understood to mean "*You* answer the phone.")

The Predicate. Every sentence also has a predicate. The *simple predicate* is the verb that tells what action the subject performs, what action is performed on the subject, or what the condition of the subject is.

EXAMPLES: Connie drew the picture for the cover.

The plans were changed.

Marvin is ready.

Every sentence has a simple subject and a simple predicate. In addition, modifiers (descriptive words) can be added to the simple subject and the simple predicate. In the sentences shown in the chart, the simple subjects are underlined once and the simple predicates are underlined twice.

SIMPLE SUBJECTS AND PREDICATES

Donna paints.

The plant in the corner blooms every summer.

My blue raincoat is hanging in the hallway,

It is easy to find the simple subject and simple predicate if you ask yourself the following questions.

SIMPLE SUBJECT: What noun or pronoun answers the question *Who?* or *What?* before the verb?

SIMPLE PREDICATE: What verb expresses the action done by or to the subject or tells the condition of the subject?

EXERCISE A: Finding Simple Subjects and Simple Predicates. Copy the sentences below. Underline the simple subject once and the simple predicate twice. Remember that the simple subject will be a noun or a pronoun that answers the question *Who?* or *What?* before the verb. The simple predicate will be a verb.

EXAMPLE: Colonial women cooked in a fireplace.

1. English settlers arrived in Plymouth Colony in 1620 after a long voyage.
2. The governor called these settlers "pilgrims."
3. Some people came to Plymouth Colony for religious reasons.
4. Their ship was called the *Mayflower.*
5. The settlers wanted a better life.
6. The men worked in the fields.
7. Women, too, helped on the farm.
8. Even children were expected to work.
9. Most houses were small.
10. These homes pleased the settlers.

EXERCISE B: More Work with Simple Subjects and Simple Predicates. Copy the sentences below. Underline the simple subject once and the simple predicate twice.

1. Yesterday we moved the old furniture out of our house.
2. My Uncle Jonathan will sell it at his garage sale this weekend.
3. I remember how every scratch in that old table was made.
4. The wooden chair wobbles a bit.
5. Many letters were written at that table.
6. Robert often studied there.
7. We felt a little sentimental about losing it.
8. The new furniture looks modern.
9. The table holds more books and papers.
10. The padded seat swivels.

EXERCISE C: Writing Subjects and Predicates. For each sentence, supply a word according to the direction in parentheses. Underline each simple subject or simple predicate you supply.

EXAMPLE: (Subject) enjoys fishing.

Albert enjoys fishing.

1. She (predicate) that the event was extraordinary.
2. (Subject) became interested in photography.
3. Muriel (predicate) the conversation.
4. You (predicate) the cabin near the lake.
5. The (subject) is located beside the basketball court.
6. Across the room (predicate) our cat.
7. My (subject) encouraged me to travel.
8. Nora (predicate) her science project.
9. Keith (predicate) to find a quiet spot.
10. Each (subject) returned to the cruise ship.

EXERCISE D: More Practice Writing Subjects and Predicates. Supply a word according to the direction in parentheses. Underline each simple subject or simple predicate you supply.

1. (Subject) believe in what we are doing.
2. Our family (predicate) what to do over vacation.
3. Recently, (subject) solved the problem.
4. Our teacher (predicate) us to keep diaries.
5. (Subject) began the experiment.
6. The child (predicate) his eyes.
7. (Subject) admitted the chief was right.
8. The youngsters reluctantly (predicate).
9. (Subject) noticed the crowd in the distance.
10. (Subject) seems like the material we need.

DEVELOPING WRITING SKILLS: Using Subjects and Predicates in Sentences. Write ten sentences about one or more events you remember. Underline each simple subject once and each simple predicate twice.

10.2 Complete Subjects and Predicates

Sentences can be expanded. A writer can add to both the subject and the predicate of a sentence.

The complete subject of a sentence is the simple subject and the words related to it. The complete predicate is the verb and the words related to it.

A sentence can have just a simple subject and a simple predicate. Such a sentence will usually be quite brief. In the following sentence, the vertical line separates the simple subject *fish* from the simple predicate *swim.*

EXAMPLE: Fish | swim.

This sentence could be expanded by adding words to the subject and the predicate. These words would be part of the *complete subject* and the *complete predicate.*

EXAMPLE: Exotic fish of different colors and shapes | swim in my new heated fish tank.

The chart below shows the complete subject and the complete predicate of several sentences. Each simple subject is underlined once and each simple predicate is underlined twice.

COMPLETE SUBJECTS AND PREDICATES	
Complete Subjects	**Complete Predicates**
My old friend	returned for a visit.
A new pair of skates	sits in the store window.
That horror movie	frightened my brother.
The talented actor	received the starring role.

EXERCISE A: Complete Subjects and Predicates. Copy each sentence. Put *a vertical line* between the complete subject and the complete predicate. Underline the simple subject once and the simple predicate twice.

EXAMPLE: The guests in the drawing room |looked suspicious.

1. The elegant lady glanced nervously at the clock.
2. Old Dr. Wentworth walked up and down the room.
3. A man in a blue suit looked out the window.
4. The famous artist mumbled some words to herself.
5. The pianist, pleasant and handsome, spoke constantly.
6. The alert hostess tried to relieve the tension.
7. A young woman offered the guests cold drinks.
8. This thoughtful offer helped a bit.
9. All the guests welcomed the distraction.
10. The conversation returned to normal.

EXERCISE B: More Work with Complete Subjects and Predicates. Follow the directions for Exercise A.

1. My older cousin works on his car every weekend.
2. He checks the pressure in the tires.
3. Paul opens the hood to check the oil.
4. The oil must be at the proper level.
5. The old radiator needs more water.
6. Several quarts of water must be added.
7. A friend from school sometimes helps Paul with these chores.
8. The two boys clean the inside of the car.
9. Other boys from town wash the outside.
10. Waxing is the last chore.

DEVELOPING WRITING SKILLS: Using Complete Subjects and Predicates. Write ten sentences about a mysterious, funny, or unusual event. Separate each complete subject and complete predicate with a vertical line.

10.3 Compound Subjects and Predicates

A sentence can have more than one simple subject and more than one verb.

A compound subject is two or more simple subjects that are related to the same verb.

Compound subjects are connected by conjunctions such as *and* or *or.*

EXAMPLES: Bob or Sue will go.

Hockey and football are my favorite sports.

Steve or Jane will bring the refreshments.

A sentence can also have a *compound predicate.*

EXAMPLE: At camp I sang songs, made friends, and went hiking.

A compound predicate is two or more verbs that are related to the same subject.

The following chart shows several examples of compound predicates. The verbs that make up each compound predicate are underlined twice.

COMPOUND PREDICATES
At camp we sang songs, met new friends, and went hiking.
My dog fetches a ball, plays with me, and does tricks.
During the winter, I ski, skate, and play hockey.

Occasionally, a sentence may have both a compound subject and a compound predicate.

EXAMPLE: Sandy and Marie called and asked for help.

EXERCISE: Recognizing Compound Subjects and Predicates. Copy the sentences below. Underline the parts of each compound subject once and the parts of each compound predicate twice. Circle the conjunction.

EXAMPLE: English (and) math are my favorite subjects.

1. In English class, we read and discuss literature.
2. Mark Twain and Edgar Allan Poe are authors we discuss.
3. Marilyn or Evan will lead a debate this week.
4. We reread and corrected our papers.
5. My dog eats, sleeps, and plays all day.
6. Decimals and percents are taught in math class.
7. Ellen or Hal will lead the discussion today.
8. Jim and Jane saw that movie.
9. Pairs of students check and correct each other's work.
10. Julia added and divided to solve that problem.
11. In the nineteenth century, few boys and girls stayed in school for as many years as students do today.
12. Instead, they worked on farms or labored in factories.
13. A boy or girl from a rich family might have a tutor.
14. Sometimes parents hired a teacher and started a school.
15. Books and supplies were sometimes scarce.
16. Horace Mann visited schools and taught about learning improvements.
17. He and Mary Mann were interested in education.
18. Horace Mann wrote and spoke about schooling.
19. Schools and books were regularly inspected.
20. Horace Mann taught, practiced law, and ran a college.

DEVELOPING WRITING SKILLS: Writing Sentences with Compound Subjects and Predicates. Write ten sentences describing a classroom activity. Use a compound subject or a compound predicate in each one.

10.4 Hard-to-Find Subjects

This section shows how to identify simple subjects in three different kinds of sentences.

The Subject of a Command or Request. If a sentence commands or requests someone to do something, the subject is often unstated.

The subject of a command or request is understood to be the word *you*.

Sentences	How the Sentences Are Understood
Stop!	You stop!
Begin at once.	You begin at once.
Audrey, make a list	Audrey, you make a list.
Bob, get the tickets.	Bob, you get the tickets.

Even though a command or request may begin with the name of the person spoken to, the subject is still understood to be *you.*

The Subject of a Question. If a sentence asks a question, the subject usually follows the verb. This is called *inverted order.*

In questions, the subject often follows the verb or is located between a helping verb and the main verb.

EXAMPLES: How can Claude remember all the lines in the play?

Is a movie playing this evening?

If you are not sure of the subject of a question, turn the question into a statement. It will be easier to find the subject when the words are in normal order.

Questions	Questions Changed to Statements
Has Ruth been practicing?	Ruth has been practicing.
Will David start tomorrow?	David will start tomorrow.
Can this container hold a quart?	This container can hold a quart.

The Subject of a Sentence Beginning with *There* or *Here*. *There* and *here* often begin sentences.

The words *there* and *here* are never subjects.

Sometimes *there* and *here* are used as adverbs that answer the question *Where? There* can also be used as a sentence starter.

ADVERBS: There is my coat.

Here are the albums.

SENTENCE STARTERS: There are fifty states in the United States.

There was a young boy here.

You can see that the order of subject and verb in each sentence above is inverted—that is, the subject follows the verb. If you have trouble finding the subject of sentences like these, rewrite the sentence so that it does not begin with *there* or *here.*

Sentences	Rewritten Sentences
Here is your package.	Your package is here.
There in the window was a tiny monkey.	A tiny monkey was there in the window.
There are two senators elected from every state.	Two senators are elected from every state.

EXERCISE A: Recognizing Commands or Requests. List the simple subject of each sentence. Five of the sentences are commands or requests.

EXAMPLE: Jennifer, look for Australia on the map.
you

1. Remind me to take a picture of a koala bear.
2. Australia is a large country.
3. The British settled in Australia almost 200 years ago.
4. Look at the Australian flag.
5. Arlene, find the location of the capital, Canberra, on this map.
6. Most people in Australia speak English.
7. Listen to them speak.
8. Some Australian words are different from American English words.
9. Sydney is the largest city in Australia.
10. Maria, take a picture of that kangaroo.

EXERCISE B: Finding the Subject of Sentences That Ask Questions. Write the simple subject of each question. Remember to change the question into a statement if you are not sure of the subject.

EXAMPLE: Why did Laura send us a letter?
Laura

1. What is the capital of Greece?
2. Has Richie decided on a career?
3. How did you spend the afternoon?
4. Did June remember to bring her racket?
5. When will the show begin?
6. Where is the museum?
7. Are swimming lessons given today?
8. Is the Arctic Ocean the smallest ocean?
9. Have scientists studied this animal?
10. Were advertisements printed in the magazine and in the newspaper?

EXERCISE C: Recognizing Hard-to-Find Subjects. Write the simple subject of each sentence. Commands and requests, questions, and sentences beginning with *there* and *here* are all included.

EXAMPLE: Is a cat a mammal?

cat

1. Is the whale the largest mammal?
2. There are some very large whales.
3. Would the class like to visit the zoo?
4. Rita, find out the zoo's opening and closing times.
5. Look at the seal asleep on the rock.
6. Can a giraffe lie down?
7. Here is a good place for watching the otters.
8. Can a porcupine "shoot" its quills?
9. Don't feed the elephants in the zoo.
10. There is a hamster in our science class.

EXERCISE D: More Work with Hard-to-Find Subjects. Write the simple subject of each sentence.

1. Where is the map of Massachusetts?
2. Show me Boston on the map.
3. There is a scale of miles for measuring distance.
4. Here is an atlas with many maps in it.
5. Why is this globe more accurate than that map?
6. Is this symbol for mountains?
7. Evelyn, color each river on this map.
8. There is a list of cities in the back of the atlas.
9. Don, take the map with you.
10. Can the passengers read a road map?

DEVELOPING WRITING SKILLS: Writing Sentences with Subjects in Different Positions. Write ten sentences explaining a simple task, such as sharpening a pencil. Write some (1) commands, (2) questions, and (3) sentences that begin with *there* and *here.*

Skills Review and Writing Workshop

Subjects and Predicates

CHECKING YOUR SKILLS

Copy each sentence. Underline each simple subject once and each simple predicate twice. If the subject is understood, write it in.

EXAMPLE: Abraham Lincoln's family lived on a farm.

1. Abraham Lincoln was the sixteenth President of our country.
2. Did he really live in a log cabin?
3. Jordan, ask the librarian for a book about Lincoln.
4. There is a famous one by Carl Sandburg.
5. Listen to a recording of the Gettysburg Address.
6. That speech was written in 1863.
7. He was President during the Civil War.
8. Here is a list of his accomplishments.
9. Where is his monument?
10. Find a city named for our sixteenth President.

USING GRAMMAR SKILLS IN WRITING

Writing an Argument for Yourself

Imagine someone said to you, "You can do anything you want to do for the next two hours. But you have to convince me that you should do it." Decide what you would like to do. Then think of all the reasons why you should be given the chance to do that thing or those things.

As you write, remember it is not enough to say, "I want to go to the moon" or "I want to eat a gallon of chocolate ice cream." In order to get that trip or that ice cream you have to explain why you, and not someone else, should be chosen. Can you think of some very good reasons why eating a gallon of ice cream would make you a better person? Or what you could do on the moon that no one else could do?

When you reread your work, be sure you have used subjects and predicates correctly. What you have to say is important, but so is how you say it. Proofread carefully.

Direct Objects and Indirect Objects

Every sentence needs a simple subject and a simple predicate. Often, however, these two parts alone are not enough. Most sentences need additional words in order to give a full idea of what the speaker or writer means to say. The words *David fought* make up a sentence, but if the speaker's meaning is that David fought Goliath, then the word *Goliath* is needed—*David fought Goliath.* In this case, *Goliath* is what grammarians call a *complement*—a word that is needed to complete the meaning of a sentence.

In this chapter, you will read about two types of complements: *direct objects* and *indirect objects.* You will learn what they are, and you will practice using them.

11.1 Direct Objects

You already know that a sentence must have two parts—a simple subject and a simple predicate.

Other sentences need additional words to complete their meaning. These words are called *complements.* In the sentence *Janet gave a speech, speech* is a complement. It completes the meaning of *Janet gave*.

A *direct object* is one type of complement. It is used to complete many sentences with action verbs.

A direct object is a noun or pronoun that appears with an action verb and receives the action of the verb.

A direct object answers the question *Whom?* or *What?*

EXAMPLES: Mrs. Gomez picked us. (DO: us)

(Picked *whom? Answer:* us)

Fred asked a question. (DO: question)

(asked *what? Answer:* question)

The detective followed Abe into the garden. (DO: Abe)

(Followed *whom? Answer:* Abe)

The chart below shows how simple subjects, simple predicates, and direct objects form complete sentences. As you can see, a direct object may be *compound.* That means that one verb can have two or more direct objects.

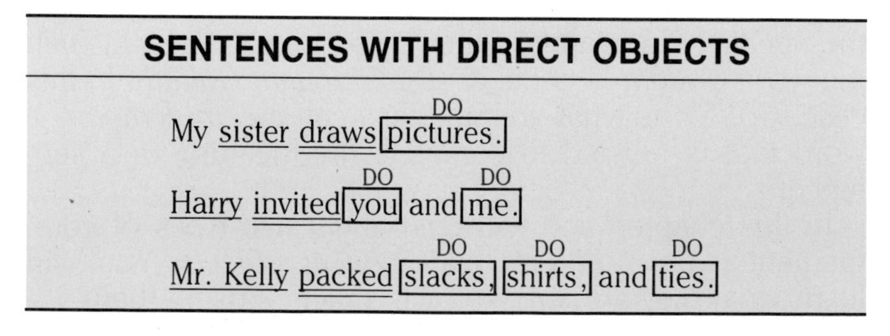

SENTENCES WITH DIRECT OBJECTS

My sister draws pictures. (DO: pictures)

Harry invited you and me. (DO: you; DO: me)

Mr. Kelly packed slacks, shirts, and ties. (DO: slacks; DO: shirts; DO: ties)

EXERCISE A: Finding Direct Objects. Copy each sentence. Then, underline each direct object.

EXAMPLE: Ivan often plays football.

1. The jeweler displayed the bracelet in his window.
2. Kathy sings the opening song at the concert tonight.
3. One lucky person won the lottery.
4. The boss told the truth.
5. Patty noticed the daisies and lilies that I planted in my yard.
6. In the gym, Randy performed acrobatics on the mat.
7. Justine practices piano each Tuesday afternoon.
8. Mr. Murray locks the door at 6:00 p.m.
9. The plumber fixed the faucet and the drain.
10. Dr. Travis examined my teeth yesterday and said I have no cavities.

EXERCISE B: More Work with Direct Objects. Follow directions for Exercise A.

1. I put film in the camera.
2. Mr. Brown grows flowers and vegetables every summer.
3. His family built a house in the country.
4. My mother listed the ingredients to buy.
5. The gift delighted them.
6. The student toured England and France.
7. Our committee appointed Mrs. Percy.
8. The child placed the dishes on the table.
9. The speaker showed charts, pictures, and graphs.
10. An announcer reported the news of the day.

DEVELOPING WRITING SKILLS: Using Direct Objects in Sentences. Write ten sentences about something that happened in school last year. Use a direct object in each sentence.

11.2 Indirect Objects

A sentence that has a direct object can also have an *indirect object.* An indirect object is another type of complement. It also helps complete the meaning of sentences.

An indirect object is a noun or pronoun usually located between an action verb and a direct object. It tells the person or thing something is given to or done for.

An indirect object answers the question *To or for whom?* or *To or for what?* after an action verb.

EXAMPLES: Yolanda sent Marge [IO] a letter [DO].

(Sent *to whom? Answer:* Marge)

We gave the magazine [IO] a title [DO].

(Gave *to what? Answer:* magazine)

An indirect object cannot be part of a prepositional phrase. In the sentence *Yolanda sent a letter to Martha. Martha* belongs to a prepositional phrase. It is not an indirect object.

Indirect objects can be compound. That is, a verb can be followed by two or more indirect objects.

EXAMPLE: Rose sold John [IO] and Eric [IO] the tickets [DO].

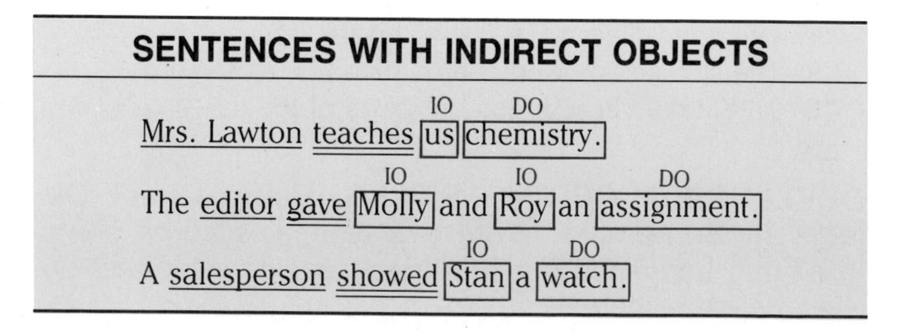

SENTENCES WITH INDIRECT OBJECTS

Mrs. Lawton teaches us [IO] chemistry [DO].

The editor gave Molly [IO] and Roy [IO] an assignment [DO].

A salesperson showed Stan [IO] a watch [DO].

EXERCISE A: Recognizing Indirect Objects. Copy each sentence and underline each indirect object.

EXAMPLE: I owe Martin a letter.

1. Several students brought the teacher an apple.
2. Sandra, please give him this message.
3. The family lent the museum their paintings.
4. Our agency finds people beautiful apartments.
5. My aunt wrote me the news of the new baby.
6. The architect showed her the plans for the house.
7. The company offered writers and lawyers good jobs.
8. Senator Alexander Blackwell sent the committee his report.
9. Please teach Kenny and me a tongue twister.
10. My watch tells me the time and the date.

EXERCISE B: More Work with Indirect Objects. Copy each sentence and underline each indirect object.

1. Brenda told her mother, father, and brother the story.
2. Will you show my cousin and me your stamp collection?
3. The celebrity granted our magazine an interview.
4. A clever rcmark landed him the job.
5. The man in the tan sweater told me a tall tale.
6. Ron baked the children some bread.
7. The shiny penny could bring me some luck.
8. The teacher promised the class a party.
9. Before leaving, give us your new address.
10. The owner of the horse offered Chris a ride.

DEVELOPING WRITING SKILLS: Using Indirect Objects in Sentences. Write ten sentences about your activities last week. Include an indirect object in each sentence. Remember that the sentence pattern should be Subject + Action Verb + Indirect Object + Direct Object. Modifiers can be added.

Skills Review and Writing Workshop

Direct Objects and Indirect Objects

CHECKING YOUR SKILLS

Make two columns on your paper. Label one column Indirect Objects and the other column Direct Objects. Then, list the indirect objects and the direct objects in the sentences below.

EXAMPLE: Arnold read Jean a scene from a play.

Indirect Objects	Direct Objects
Jean	scene

1. Our science teacher showed us several fossils.
2. We will send Marilyn an invitation.
3. The librarian read us "Rip Van Winkle."
4. Frances bought her friend a present.
5. The principal taught the class a history lesson.
6. After today, you will owe me a favor.
7. The coach taught the team a new play.
8. Grandma sent Nick, Amanda, and Peter a postcard from Europe.
9. The owner might sell you that jacket at a discount.
10. The speaker told the audience an interesting story.

USING GRAMMAR SKILLS IN WRITING

Writing a Book Review

You have probably written or given a book report. And when you did that, you might have told what was in the book and perhaps how that information helped you learn something. A book review in a newspaper or magazine is similar to a book report. That is, the writer gives his or her opinion about the book.

Choose a book you liked or didn't like. Then tell something about the book—the story or the kind of information it has. Finally, say why you liked or didn't like the book. Remember to give reasons for your opinion. Check that direct and indirect objects have been used correctly and that you have organized your review clearly.

Chapter 12

Predicate Nouns and Adjectives

In this chapter you will be reading about two special kinds of words that are found in the complete predicate. *Predicate nouns* and *predicate adjectives* are called *subject complements.* A predicate noun renames the subject. A predicate adjective describes the subject. Both types of subject complements help complete the meaning of sentences by telling more about the subject.

This chapter describes these two types of subject complements and shows how they are used in sentences. You will practice identifying predicate nouns and predicate adjectives. Then, you will practice using them in sentences and in a composition.

12.1 Predicate Nouns

A subject and a linking verb will generally be followed by one or more words that are needed to form a complete sentence. Predicate nouns are often used to complete this kind of sentence.

A predicate noun is a noun that appears with a subject and a linking verb. It renames or identifies the subject.

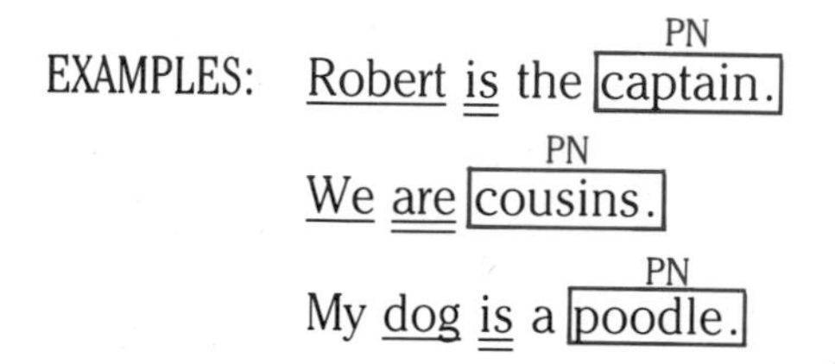

All the verbs in the sentences above are linking verbs. These verbs are forms of the verb *be,* the most common linking verb.

A linking verb links almost like an equal sign. In the first sentence above, *Robert is the captain* means *Robert = the captain.* The word *is* links *Robert* and *the captain* by saying that the one equals the other.

A sentence can have a compound predicate noun. That means that two or more nouns can follow a linking verb and identify or rename a subject.

EXAMPLE: The speakers today are [Jim] (PN) and [Rebecca.] (PN)

Predicate nouns, like other complements, can never be part of prepositional phrases.

EXAMPLE: Chemistry is an interesting [branch] (PN) of science.

Branch is a predicate noun, but *science* is not. It is part of the prepositional phrase *of science.*

The chart at the top of the next page shows sentences with predicate nouns boxed.

SENTENCES WITH PREDICATE NOUNS

George Washington was our first President.

Miss Alexander should be the director.

EXERCISE: Recognizing Predicate Nouns. List the predicate nouns in each sentence below.

EXAMPLE: Janet became a reporter.
reporter

1. These books are novels.
2. Sarah was the illustrator of that story.
3. The young man is a beginner.
4. Our neighbor Georgia became an astronomer.
5. The group remained friends for many years.
6. This computer should be the machine for you.
7. I am an amateur tennis player.
8. The animals here are dogs, cats, and birds.
9. Dr. Parker has been my dentist for five years.
10. Mrs. Gomez is the school nurse.
11. A raccoon is a mammal.
12. That tree might be a maple.
13. Eddie will remain class treasurer for another year.
14. The brave fireman is my uncle.
15. This green stone must be an emerald.
16. Phil could become a professional golfer.
17. This flower with three petals must be an orchid.
18. I was a volunteer in the city hospital.
19. Broccoli and spinach are green vegetables.
20. Balboa and Magellan were Spanish explorers.

DEVELOPING WRITING SKILLS: Using Predicate Nouns in Sentences. Write ten sentences about characters from books, movies, or TV. Use a linking verb and a predicate noun in each sentence.

12.2 Predicate Adjectives

An adjective may also follow a linking verb. If it completes the sentence, it is called a predicate adjective.

A predicate adjective is an adjective that appears with a subject and a linking verb. It describes or modifies the subject of the sentence.

Predicate adjectives always modify the subject of a sentence. The arrows in the examples below connect the boxed predicate adjectives with the subjects they modify.

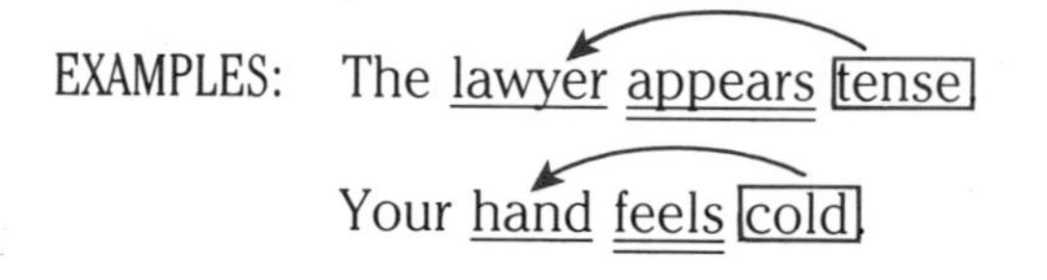

Predicate adjectives follow linking verbs, such as the ones in the examples above. Other linking verbs include *be, become, grow, look, smell, sound, stay,* and *turn.*

A sentence may also have a compound predicate adjective—two or more adjectives following a linking verb.

EXAMPLES: I felt tired and hungry after the long climb.

The room grew crowded and stuffy.

The chart below gives more examples of sentences with one or more predicate adjectives. An arrow connects each predicate adjective with the subject it modifies.

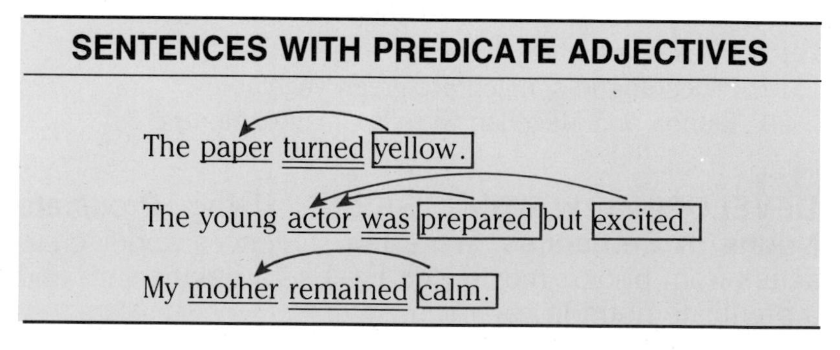

EXERCISE A: Recognizing Predicate Adjectives. Copy each of the sentences below. Underline each predicate adjective. Then draw an arrow connecting it to the subject it modifies. Compound predicate adjectives are included.

EXAMPLE: The audience grew silent.

1. This winter has been cold and damp.
2. The plans sound perfect to me.
3. We were ready before noon.
4. That marching music is lively.
5. My pet cat is intelligent but mischievous.
6. Your home cooking always tastes wonderful.
7. The room looks strange without furniture.
8. The house will be empty all summer.
9. I became impatient with the slow service.
10. The listeners remained quiet and attentive.

EXERCISE B: More Work with Predicate Adjectives. Follow the directions in Exercise A.

1. Mike is interested in computers.
2. You must be mistaken about the time and place.
3. I remained awake and restless all night.
4. The path became narrow and steep.
5. My parents will be happy with this news.
6. This large sculpture is attractive but unsteady.
7. You seem healthy and rested after your vacation.
8. This new fabric feels smooth.
9. My aunt appeared tired after her trip.
10. We were nervous about the noise.

DEVELOPING WRITING SKILLS: Using Predicate Adjectives in Sentences. Write ten sentences advertising one or more "new" products. Use a predicate adjective in each sentence. Remember to use only linking verbs.

Skills Review and Writing Workshop

Predicate Nouns and Adjectives

CHECKING YOUR SKILLS

Copy each sentence below. Underline each predicate noun or predicate adjective. Label each underlined word PN (predicate noun) or PA (predicate adjective).

EXAMPLE: The blue whale is large. (PA)

1. This graceful animal is a jaguar.
2. The dog appears tame to me.
3. The elephant could become extinct in the future.
4. The fawn was fearful but curious.
5. The fastest flying animals are birds.
6. Chimpanzees are the most intelligent apes.
7. Some birds seem friendly with larger animals.
8. A lion's den can be a cave near a mountain.
9. Monkeys are careful with their babies.
10. That large alligator looks ferocious to me.

USING GRAMMAR SKILLS IN WRITING

Writing a New Ending

You just wrote a book review in which you considered elements such as plot. Now think of that story or another story you read. Think how that story or perhaps a novel would be with a different ending. You are going to write that ending.

Before you write, think about the characters in the story. Would they be likely to do something different? Would they be likely to say something different? You can change what they do or say, but they still must remain true to themselves. For example, if a character cannot read or write, you cannot have him or her writing a letter at the end of the book unless you send that character to school! Be sure you don't have people doing things they really can't do.

After you have decided what your new ending will be, write a description of it. Check that you have used predicate nouns and adjectives correctly.

Chapter 13

Recognizing and Diagraming Sentences

You are already quite experienced at sentence building. Think of all the notes you have written and all the phone conversations you have had. You were giving and receiving information. Other times you are likely to have used sentences to get information. You may have asked a friend, "Where should we meet?" Or you may have startled someone by yelling, "Look out!"

This chapter will help you examine the sentences you are already using. It will answer the following questions: What kinds of sentences are there? What are the most common sentence patterns? Can sentence patterns be changed? What is a sentence diagram?

As you learn more about the way sentences are put together, you should experiment with sentence patterns. There are a number of ways you can say the same thing. Decide which way seems best for your purpose.

13.1 Four Kinds of Sentences

Every sentence can be grouped according to its purpose. To determine the purpose of a sentence, ask yourself, "What is this sentence trying to do?"

There are four kinds of sentences: declarative, interrogative, imperative, and exclamatory.

Declarative sentences make statements. They declare facts or ideas. They always end with a period.

EXAMPLE: American schools began in the 1600's.

Interrogative sentences ask questions. They always end with a question mark.

EXAMPLE: What is the name of that river?

Imperative sentences make commands or requests. A mild command or request ends with a period. A strong command or request ends with an exclamation mark.

EXAMPLES: Place your books under your seat.
Tell me now!

Exclamatory sentences express strong feelings or emotion. They end with an exclamation mark.

EXAMPLE: What an exciting race that was!

The chart below gives more examples of the four kinds of sentences.

FOUR KINDS OF SENTENCES	
Kinds of Sentences	**Examples**
Declarative	Columbus was a great navigator.
Interrogative	Who was a great navigator?
Imperative	Tell me about a great navigator.
Exclamatory	What a great navigator he was!

EXERCISE A: Recognizing the Four Kinds of Sentences. Label each sentence *declarative, interrogative, imperative,* or *exclamatory.* Then, show what punctuation is needed at the end.

EXAMPLE: Have you ever been to New England
interrogative ?

1. Maine is a New England state
2. What is the population
3. Visit Acadia National Park
4. Why is Maine called the Pine Tree State
5. What a rocky coast this is
6. How thrilling it is to ski down these mountains
7. Maine has many small, white churches
8. Try a Maine lobster
9. Have you ever been to the Tate House in Portland
10. The winters in this Northeastern state are very cold and long

EXERCISE B: More Work with the Four Kinds of Sentences. Follow the directions for Exercise A.

1. Our neighbor bought a new computer
2. Look at the color monitor
3. The computer has a large memory
4. Try this new piece of software
5. Can you save this report on a disk
6. How fast it prints
7. Can you make color graphics
8. What a fabulous device this is
9. You can write your own programs
10. A computer may change the way you write

DEVELOPING WRITING SKILLS: Writing Four Kinds of Sentences. Write ten sentences about early morning sights, sounds, and thoughts. Use all four kinds of sentences.

13.2 Basic Sentence Patterns

The several ways that words are arranged to form sentences are known as sentence patterns.

Basic sentence patterns describe how subjects, verbs, and complements are arranged in a sentence.

The S-V Pattern. This is the simplest pattern. It consists of a simple subject and a verb. Words that modify the subject and verb can also be included.

EXAMPLE: Three birds (S) nested (V) in the tree.

The S-V-DO Pattern. This pattern includes a subject, an action verb, and a direct object.

EXAMPLE: My dad (S) sells (V) cars (DO).

The S-V-IO-DO Pattern. This includes a subject, an action verb, indirect object, and direct object.

EXAMPLE: Aunt Ruth (S) offered (V) Mary (IO) a snack (DO).

The S-LV-PN Pattern. This pattern includes a subject, a linking verb, and a predicate noun.

EXAMPLE: Steven (S) is (LV) an automobile mechanic (PN).

The S-LV-PA Pattern. This pattern includes a subject, a linking verb, and a predicate adjective.

EXAMPLE: Madeline (S) looks (LV) bored (PA).

The chart on the following page shows each of the sentence patterns that have been introduced.

BASIC SENTENCE PATTERNS	
Patterns	**Examples**
S-V	S V The telephone rang.
S-V-DO	S V DO We arranged the desks.
S-V-IO-DO	S V IO DO William gave me a smile.
S-LV-PN	S LV PN The boys were teammates.
S-LV-PA	S LV PA This message sounds important.

Within these basic patterns, any of the parts can be compound. There can be two simple subjects, two verbs, and so on. In the following examples, a number of different possibilities are shown.

EXAMPLES:

S S V
Angela and Theresa traveled to New York.

S V V
Danny sings well but dances poorly.

S V DO DO
Cindy repairs bicycles and skateboards.

S V IO IO DO
Keith sent Toby and Eric their invitations.

S V PN PN
Emily is a writer and a teacher.

S V PA PA
The corn is fresh and sweet.

In addition, more than one part of a basic sentence pattern can be compound. For example, the sentence below has a compound subject and a compound direct object.

EXAMPLE:

S S V DO DO
Ted and Jane washed the car and the van.

EXERCISE A: Identifying Basic Sentence Patterns. Copy each sentence. Underline the subject once and the verb twice. Put boxes around the main words of the complement: direct objects, indirect objects, predicate nouns, and predicate adjectives. Add labels as shown in the example below.

EXAMPLE: The detective gave [me] a [clue.]

1. My brother collects insects.
2. Marsha practices ballet.
3. Mr. Fisher gave us his opinion.
4. Wendy chose that scarf.
5. That shape is a pentagon.
6. Your behavior is satisfactory.
7. The weather changed suddenly.
8. Sal threw me the ball.
9. Laughter is a pleasant sound.
10. These old shoes feel comfortable.

EXERCISE B: More Work with Identifying Basic Sentence Patterns. Copy each sentence below. Underline the subject once and the verb twice. Put boxes around the main words of the complement: direct objects, indirect objects, predicate nouns, and predicate adjectives. Add labels as shown in the example given for Exercise A.

1. The night was gloomy.
2. The old house was huge.
3. It aroused my curiosity.
4. I entered.
5. Inside, a sudden movement startled me.
6. Wings flapped noisily.
7. I saw a bat.
8. It gave me a scare.
9. I opened the door.
10. I left fast.

EXERCISE C: Completing Sentence Patterns. Copy the sentences below, replacing the blanks with your own words.

EXAMPLE:	S	V	IO	DO
	Mike	gave	me	______.
	Mike	gave	me	courage.

	S	V	IO	DO
1.	The letter	______	me	news.
2.	______	lent	Bob	money.
3.	______	brought	us	cake.
4.	We	______	Sheila	nothing.
5.	They	bought	us	______.
6.	Mr. Horst	sent	______	mail.
7.	He	served	me	______.
8.	Aunt Linda	______	her	stories.
9.	______	taught	Lucy	Spanish.
10.	She	assigned	______	homework.

EXERCISE D: More Practice Completing Sentence Patterns. Copy the sentences below, replacing the blanks with your own words.

	S	LV	PA
1.	Craig	looks	______.
2.	______	tastes	sweet.
3.	Marsha	became	______.
4.	I	______	different.
5.	Rover	______	hungry.

DEVELOPING WRITING SKILLS: Using Basic Sentence Patterns. Write ten sentences about good news you would like to hear. Use each basic sentence pattern at least once.

13.3 Diagraming Sentences

When you study sentences, it is often helpful to draw a diagram of them.

A diagram shows how the parts of a sentence are related.

Sentence diagrams begin with two lines—one horizontal and one vertical. The horizontal line is called a *base line* and the vertical line is called a *bar.*

FORM OF A DIAGRAM: ______|______

The simple subject of a sentence is written to the left of the bar. The verb is written to the right. No punctuation is used in diagrams.

DECLARATIVE SENTENCE: Dogs bark.

Dogs	bark

Put the subject on the left—even when the sentence begins with a verb.

INTERROGATIVE SENTENCE: Did he remember?

he	Did remember

To diagram an imperative sentence, you must remember that the subject *you* is understood. Put it on the base line within parentheses.

IMPERATIVE SENTENCE: Wait!

(you)	Wait

DIAGRAMING A SENTENCE

1. Draw two lines, the base line and the bar.
2. Write the simple subject on the left and the verb on the right.
3. Capitalize the first word of the sentence.
4. If the sentence is imperative, write the subject as *(you)*.

EXERCISE A: Making Sentence Diagrams. Diagram each of the sentences below, following the explanation on the preceding page.

EXAMPLE: Aunt Deborah called.

Aunt Deborah	called

1. Iron rusts.
2. Jeffrey will be coming.
3. Is it moving?
4. Cyclones move.
5. Begin.
6. Will language change?
7. Must we leave?
8. Congress has been meeting.
9. Decide!
10. Crickets jump.

EXERCISE B: More Practice Diagraming Sentences. Diagram each of the following sentences.

1. Karen has been waiting.
2. Did he understand?
3. Opportunities come.
4. Try!
5. Robert was pretending.
6. Concentrate.
7. Shall we try?
8. Mrs. Young hesitated.
9. Has Shelley decided?
10. Finish.

DEVELOPING WRITING SKILLS: Explaining Sentence Diagrams. Write a brief paragraph explaining how to diagram a sentence. You can include a sample diagram of your own along with your explanation. Use the following words: *subject, verb, base line, bar, punctuation, capital letter.*

Skills Review and Writing Workshop

Recognizing and Diagraming Sentences

CHECKING YOUR SKILLS

Tell whether each sentence is *declarative, interrogative, imperative,* or *exclamatory*. Show the punctuation mark that should be used at the end of each sentence.

EXAMPLE: What are bones made of
interrogative ?

1. Not all animals have bones
2. Watch this movie about bones
3. Animals with backbones are called vertebrates
4. Are birds vertebrates
5. Examine this bone
6. How soft it feels
7. Bones harden slowly
8. What foods help bones to grow
9. What are bones made of
10. What an unusual topic this is

USING GRAMMAR SKILLS IN WRITING

Writing a Blurb

In the last lesson you wrote a new ending for a story or novel. Now you are going to tell the whole world about that new ending. How? By writing a blurb. That is the material on the book jacket that tells readers what the book is about and tries to excite their interest in it. It is somewhat like an advertisement.

Remember the main purpose of a blurb is to excite the reader. Use plenty of adjectives and make the language as exciting as possible. There are a lot of stories out there and you want the reader to choose yours. Be careful about your sentence structure. Grammatical mistakes will not make readers open your book. Proofread carefully, too.

Chapter 14

Phrases

One way to expand your sentences is to use *phrases.* One kind of phrase, the verb phrase, has already been discussed. (See Section 3.4.) Verb phrases are made up of a main verb and one or more helping verbs. For example, *should have called* is a verb phrase. The entire phrase does the work of a single verb, as in the sentence *I should have called the repairman.*

There are other kinds of phrases besides verb phrases. All phrases, however, are alike in two ways. First, every phrase is made up of a group of words that do the work of a single part of speech. For example, a phrase can do the work of a single adverb or a single adjective. Second, a phrase never has a subject *and* a verb.

This chapter tells more about phrases. You will read about prepositional phrases that act as adjectives and prepositional phrases that act as adverbs. You will also read about *appositive phrases.* Several exercises are included that will give you practice in identifying phrases and diagraming them.

14.1 Phrases That Act as Adjectives

You may already know that a prepositional phrase is generally made up of a preposition and a noun. Sometimes, however, a modifier is also part of a prepositional phrase.

EXAMPLES: before (PREP) dawn (NOUN)   with (PREP) great (ADJ) strength (NOUN)

When a prepositional phrase acts as an adjective, it is called an *adjective phrase.*

An adjective phrase is a prepositional phrase that modifies a noun or a pronoun.

Like a single adjective, an adjective phrase answers the question *What kind? Which one? How many?* or *How much?* While single adjectives usually come before nouns, adjective phrases usually come after them.

SINGLE ADJECTIVE: The fur-trimmed coat is mine.

ADJECTIVE PHRASE: The coat with the fur trim is mine.

Adjective phrases can modify nouns used as subjects, direct objects, or predicate nouns.

SENTENCES WITH ADJECTIVE PHRASES

A woman from Canada made this film. (Modifies a subject)

Ted told me the story about the cat. (Modifies a direct object)

This is a book of short stories. (Modifies a predicate noun)

A sentence can have more than one adjective phrase.

EXAMPLE: The laboratory on the first floor of this building is new.

EXERCISE A: Finding Adjective Phrases. Copy the sentences below. Underline each prepositional phrase used as an adjective. There can be more than one in a sentence. Then draw an arrow connecting the phrase to the word it modifies.

EXAMPLE: The surface <u>of the earth</u> holds water.

1. The water near the bottom of this lake is cold.
2. The water in the ocean is not drinking water.
3. Many people from the city enjoy water sports.
4. Faucets in houses bring us a good supply of water.
5. Water from the ocean evaporates.
6. Later, the moisture in the atmosphere returns as rain.
7. Industries along rivers often use the available water.
8. A house beside a lake is well located.
9. The tap water in this village tastes wonderful.
10. The water behind the dam is being saved.

EXERCISE B: More Work with Adjective Phrases. Follow the directions for Exercise A.

1. The sound of the machinery made us shout.
2. I will share my ideas on the subject.
3. The field across the road is where we play softball.
4. The sign near the road was an advertisement.
5. Today is a good day for a picnic.
6. The seat with the cushion is comfortable.
7. The car behind us was a convertible.
8. Irene heard the noise of the carpenter repairing the house next door.
9. The ground outside the building is muddy.
10. You should follow the advice of this expert.

DEVELOPING WRITING SKILLS: Using Adjective Phrases in Sentences. Write a brief paragraph about some goals you have set for yourself. Use an adjective phrase in each sentence.

14.2 Phrases That Act as Adverbs

A prepositional phrase can also do the work of an adverb. When it does, it is called an *adverb phrase.*

An adverb phrase is a prepositional phrase that modifies a verb, an adjective, or an adverb.

ADVERBS: The group met here. (Where?)

Yesterday, I played basketball. (When?)

Ellen wrote carefully. (In what way?)

ADVERB PHRASES: The group met at my house. (Where?)

At noon I played basketball. (When?)

Ellen wrote with care. (In what way?)

Because adverb phrases consist of more words than individual adverbs, they can be more exact than adverbs.

EXAMPLES: Park your car there. (adverb)

Park your car beside the van. (adverb phrase)

The chart below shows how adverb phrases modify verbs, adjectives, and adverbs.

SENTENCES WITH ADVERB PHRASES
He ran to the corner. (Modifies a verb)
The grass is wet with dew. (Modifies an adjective)
He works late at night. (Modifies an adverb)

A sentence may contain more than one adverb phrase.

EXAMPLE: In June divers searched within the old wreck.

EXERCISE A: Recognizing Adverb Phrases. Copy the sentences below. Underline each adverb phrase. Then, draw an arrow connecting the phrase with the word it modifies.

EXAMPLE: The boy took his toy boat to the pond.

1. She placed my umbrella beside my coat.
2. Jim plays softball after school.
3. The books fell with a loud bang.
4. On Sunday afternoon I read the sports section.
5. During the meeting Jean explained her ideas.
6. The housekeeper led the visitor to the study.
7. The entire class agrees with our plan.
8. He seems afraid of the dark.
9. We studied that question in the fall.
10. The old newspapers and magazines were piled evenly in stacks.

EXERCISE B: More Work with Adverb Phrases. Follow the directions for Exercise A.

1. E. B. White first lived in Mount Vernon, New York.
2. He studied at Cornell University.
3. He later wrote for *The New Yorker* magazine.
4. His writing is famous for its clarity and simplicity.
5. His essays are graceful in style.
6. His children's books appeal to many adults.
7. In *Charlotte's Web*, he wrote about a spider.
8. In his books, readers find fascinating details.
9. His stories are often full of his own experiences.
10. His book *Stuart Little* describes in detail a mouse's adventures.

DEVELOPING WRITING SKILLS: Writing Sentences with Adverb Phrases. Write ten sentences about a day you will never forget. Use an adverb phrase in each sentence.

14.3 Phrases That Rename, Identify, or Explain

"Babe Ruth, *the famous home-run king,* played mostly for the Yankees." In this sentence, the phrase in italics gives more information about *Babe Ruth,* the preceding noun.

Phrases that rename, identify, or explain the nouns they follow are called *appositive phrases.*

An appositive phrase renames, identifies, or explains the noun with which it appears.

Appositive phrases are generally set off by commas. This is because most appositive phrases are not necessary to the meaning of the sentences in which they appear.

Notice how each underlined phrase in the chart below identifies and explains the noun before it.

APPOSITIVE PHRASES

The harp, the oldest stringed instrument, is played with the fingers.

Austin, the capital of Texas, was named after Stephen Austin.

The Clydesdale, a handsome breed of horse, is often chosen to be in parades.

Appositive phrases can also be compound. Two or more complete phrases can be used to rename, identify, or explain the same noun. In the following example, the underlined appositive phrases identify the noun *prizes*.

EXAMPLE: The two prizes, a trip to Europe and a new car, were awarded.

EXERCISE A: Finding Appositive Phrases. Copy the sentences below. Underline each appositive phrase. Then draw an arrow from the phrase to the noun it identifies or explains.

EXAMPLE: This book, <u>a suspense novel</u>, is very popular.

1. Jim Kelly, the star of our show, was on TV.
2. Gym, my favorite class, is scheduled for today.
3. This car, an inexpensive model, uses gas efficiently.
4. We considered two choices, a Mexican restaurant and a French restaurant.
5. This letter, a message from my mother, arrived today.
6. Aunt Clara, my mother's sister, lives in Tennessee.
7. This cabinet was made by Bill Webster, my great-uncle.
8. The music, jazz of the 1930's, was great.
9. My friend, a computer whiz, leads a busy life.
10. The home, an elegant mansion, is owned by a millionaire.

EXERCISE B: More Work with Appositive Phrases. Copy the sentences below. Underline each appositive phrase. Then draw an arrow from the phrase to the noun it identifies or explains.

1. Atlanta, the capital of Georgia, is a busy city.
2. Main Street, a busy thoroughfare, was closed to traffic.
3. Lisa, my cousin from Maine, will visit us.
4. The movie, an unusually long show, was a documentary.
5. We joined the club, a group of serious chess players.

DEVELOPING WRITING SKILLS: Using Appositive Phrases. Write ten sentences about people, places, and events you know well. Use an appositive phrase in each sentence.

14.4 Diagraming Phrases

To diagram a prepositional phrase, draw a slanted line for the preposition and a horizontal line for the noun. Put modifiers on slanted lines beneath the noun.

PREPOSITIONAL PHRASE: near (PREP) the red barn (NOUN)

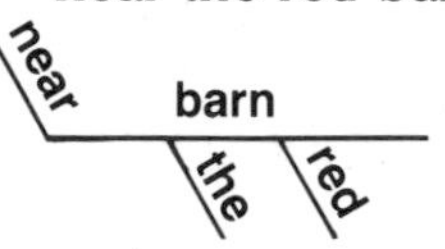

Adjective Phrases. A prepositional phrase that acts as an adjective is written beneath the noun or pronoun it modifies.

EXAMPLE: Our neighbor *down the road* jogs often.

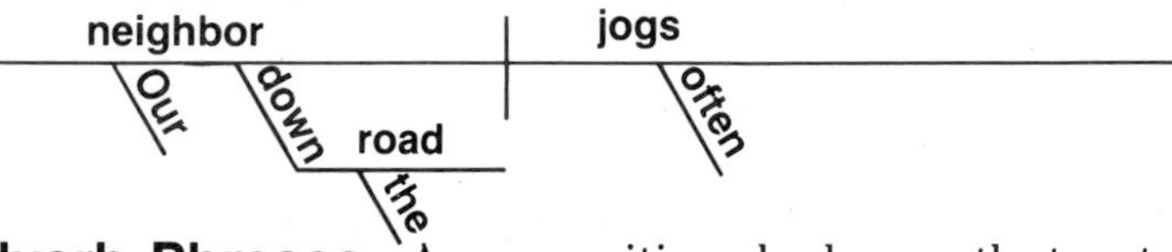

Adverb Phrases. A prepositional phrase that acts as an adverb is placed beneath the verb, adjective, or adverb it modifies.

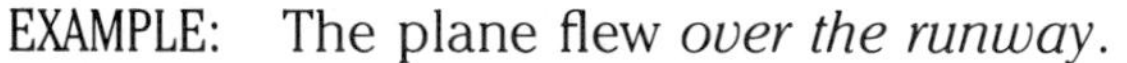

EXAMPLE: The plane flew *over the runway*.

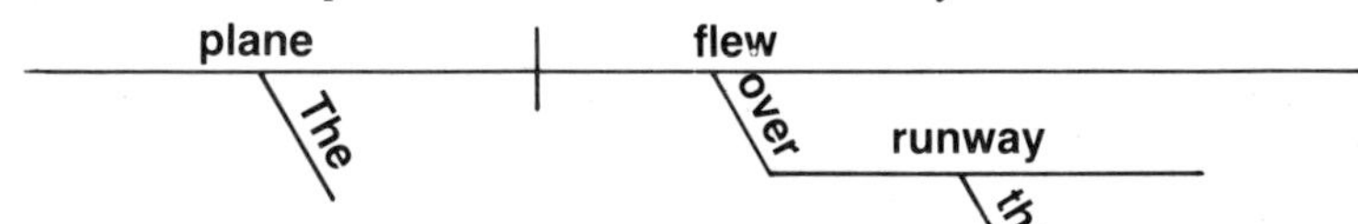

Appositive Phrases. To diagram an appositive phrase, put the most important noun in the phrase in parentheses and place it next to the noun it renames, identifies, or explains. Place the modifiers beneath the noun.

EXAMPLE: Sam, *the manager of a store*, works hard.

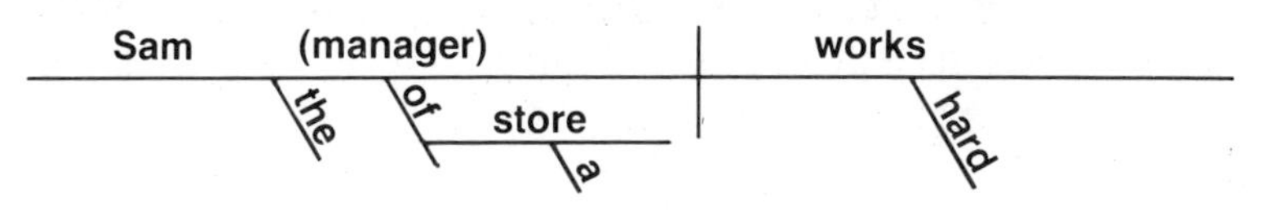

EXERCISE A: Diagraming Phrases. Diagram the sentences below. Each contains at least one prepositional or appositive phrase.

EXAMPLE: Poe, the author of the story, was born in Boston.

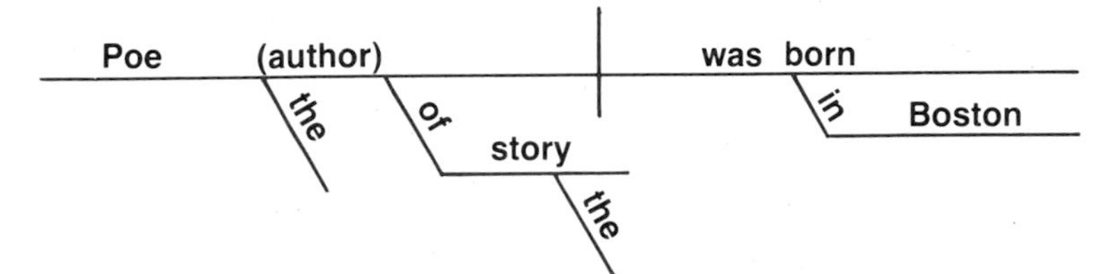

1. The flowers outside my window are blooming.
2. Mrs. Winters, the new principal, speaks clearly.
3. The restaurant around the corner is expanding.
4. The conversation during dinner was interrupted.
5. Our dog ran past the house.
6. The runner beside me had stopped.
7. A child strolled beyond the gate.
8. Directions with many examples explain clearly.
9. Our vacation, a week in Hawaii, begins tomorrow.
10. The president spoke before a large audience.

EXERCISE B: More Practice Diagraming Phrases. Diagram the following sentences. Each contains a prepositional or appositive phrase.

1. These one-act plays, two amusing comedies, are staged frequently.
2. Your bicycle belongs inside the garage.
3. Wendy scurried up the stairs.
4. The woman, an experienced nurse, worked rapidly.
5. The camera on the table loads easily.

DEVELOPING WRITING SKILLS: Explaining How to Diagram a Phrase. Write a paragraph telling a student your age how to diagram a phrase. You may use a sample diagram to help you.

Skills Review and Writing Workshop

Phrases

CHECKING YOUR SKILLS

Each sentence contains an adjective phrase, adverb phrase, or appositive phrase. Copy each sentence and underline each phrase. Draw an arrow from the phrase to the word it modifies.

EXAMPLE: The horses in this country work on farms.

1. The shire, a draft horse, is the largest horse.
2. Quarter horses often work on ranches.
3. I need a horse with strength and speed.
4. Ponies usually measure under four feet.
5. Thoroughbred horses are the descendants of Arabian horses.
6. Here is a Shetland pony, a favorite children's horse.
7. The horse with the white mane has blue eyes.
8. Mustangs, beautiful wild horses, roam about the countryside.
9. A Tennessee walking horse is a good choice for new riders.
10. Appaloosas have pale bodies with dark spots.

USING GRAMMAR SKILLS IN WRITING

Writing an Argument

Did you ever argue in favor of something and later argue against it? Suppose your class wants class officers. They could be elected or they could be appointed by the teacher. If you think you would be elected, you might want elections. If you think you would lose an election, you might want the teacher to choose.

Think of a situation or an idea that you could be for and be against, too. Then write one paragraph in favor of the idea and one paragraph against it. Be as persuasive as you can. Check that your phrases are clear and expressive.

Chapter 15

Clauses

Chapter 14 dealt with groups of related words called phrases. Phrases can expand your sentences and make them more interesting. Another type of word group—*the clause*—can also add variety and detail to your writing.

Clauses are different from phrases. They are sometimes but not always complete sentences. *She went to the movies* is a clause that is a complete sentence. However, *when she went to the movies* is also a clause, but it is not a complete sentence. What these two clauses have in common is that they both have a subject and a verb.

In this chapter you will learn more about clauses. First, you will learn to recognize them. Then you will learn how to build sentences using clauses. You will also practice writing sentences of your own that contain one or more clauses. In addition, you will learn to diagram sentences with more than one clause.

15.1 Recognizing Independent Clauses

Unlike phrases, clauses are often complete sentences. Every clause has a subject and a verb.

A clause is a group of words that contains both a subject and a verb.

There are two types of clauses: *independent clauses* and *subordinate clauses.*

An independent clause has a subject and a verb and can stand on its own as a complete sentence.

EXAMPLES: I am going to the movies.

Last Tuesday, Jim began judo lessons.

Mrs. Anderson will be showing a film now.

Subordinate clauses cannot function as complete sentences.

A subordinate clause has a subject and verb but cannot stand on its own as a complete sentence.

EXAMPLES: after Marie left school

unless we hurry

In each example above, some information is missing. *After Marie left school*, what happened? *Unless we hurry,* what will happen? A subordinate clause depends on other words to complete its meaning. It must be attached to an independent clause.

EXAMPLES: (SUBORDINATE CLAUSE) After Marie left school, (INDEPENDENT CLAUSE) she went shopping with Barbara and Ellen.

(SUBORDINATE CLAUSE) Unless we hurry, (INDEPENDENT CLAUSE) we will miss the bus.

EXERCISE A: Recognizing Independent Clauses. Label each group of words as an *independent clause* or a *subordinate clause.*

EXAMPLE: Harriet was almost trapped by a posse
independent clause

1. Harriet Tubman was born a slave
2. when she was six years old
3. she heard about slave uprisings
4. although Harriet was still a child
5. while she worked in the fields
6. Harriet Tubman escaped from slavery
7. she decided to help other slaves escape
8. after one group escaped
9. the Underground Railroad became famous
10. this woman of courage led many people to freedom

EXERCISE B: More Practice Recognizing Independent Clauses. Label each group of words as an *independent clause* or a *subordinate clause.*

1. Jan got his chance
2. until the senator began to speak
3. during the time that she worked in the factory
4. he stood there and fumbled for words
5. although the enemy destroyed the city
6. the guest told jokes during dinner
7. since everyone agrees with the plan
8. when they had all gathered in the hall
9. our teacher showed us some slides
10. while we were waiting for the trolley

DEVELOPING WRITING SKILLS: Writing Independent Clauses. Write ten independent clauses, adding a capital at the beginning and a period at the end. Each should describe someone you know. Make sure each has a subject and verb and is a complete sentence.

15.2 Forming Compound Sentences

A sentence that is made up of a single independent clause is called a *simple sentence.* But two or more independent clauses can be joined to form a *compound sentence.*

A compound sentence is made up of two or more independent clauses.

Independent clauses are generally joined by a comma and a coordinating conjunction *(and, but, for, nor, or, so,* or *yet).*

EXAMPLES: I wanted to relax after supper, so I did my homework early.

My brother was watching the game on television, but he soon fell asleep.

Another way to join the clauses is with a semicolon(;).

EXAMPLES: I am reading about Plymouth colony; I am also writing a report about it.

Phil enjoys science; I prefer math.

The chart below shows several compound sentences. The simple subject in each independent clause is underlined once. The verb in each independent clause is underlined twice. The coordinating conjuctions are circled.

COMPOUND SENTENCES
Eddie went to Dallas, and Mindy went to Houston.
Ellen likes basketball, but Jean prefers softball.
I should call home, for my parents will be expecting me.
Grandmother did not expect the rubber frog, nor was she ready for the invisible ink.

EXERCISE: Writing Compound Sentences. Combine each pair of independent clauses into one compound sentence. Use a comma and the coordinating conjunction shown in brackets.

EXAMPLE: The forecast is for rain.
The sun is still shining. [but]
The forecast is for rain, but the sun is still shining.

1. Ted brought the rolls.
   Robin brought the orange juice. [and]
2. The fans cheered the players on.
   The team couldn't even the score. [but]
3. I want to sell my old bicycle.
   I have outgrown it. [for]
4. We can take a bus to the theater.
   We can leave early and walk there. [or]
5. Susan helped me with my math.
   I helped her with her English. [and]
6. I have long, straight hair.
   My sister has short, curly hair. [but]
7. Bowling is a very old game.
   Balls and pins have been found in Egyptian tombs. [for]
8. Dinosaurs were very large.
   Their brains were very small. [yet]
9. In 1910 there were no electric washing machines.
   There were no electric toasters. [and]
10. Frisbees today are made of plastic.
    Earlier models were made of metal. [but]

DEVELOPING WRITING SKILLS: Creating Compound Sentences. Write ten compound sentences. In five of them, use a comma and a coordinating conjunction. In the other five, use a semicolon to join the independent clauses. Underline each simple subject once and each verb twice.

15.3 Diagraming Compound Sentences

The clauses of a compound sentence are diagramed separately, one under the other. They are connected by a dotted line that looks like a step. The coordinating conjunction or semicolon is written on the step.

EXAMPLES: Bob (S) plays (V) the piano (DO), and Sarah (S) plays (V) the violin (DO).

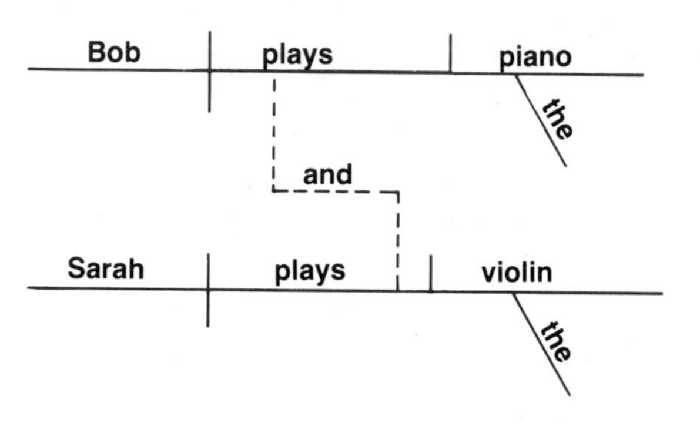

Simon (S) wrote (V) the story (DO), but Ted (S) read (V) it (DO) aloud.

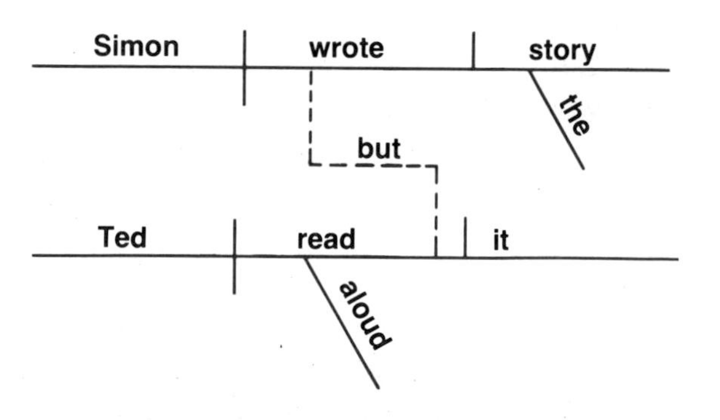

Notice that a direct object is placed on the same line as the subject and verb. A short line separates the direct object from the verb.

EXERCISE: Diagraming Compound Sentences. Diagram each of the following compound sentences.

EXAMPLE: I read mysteries, but my friend chooses fantasies.

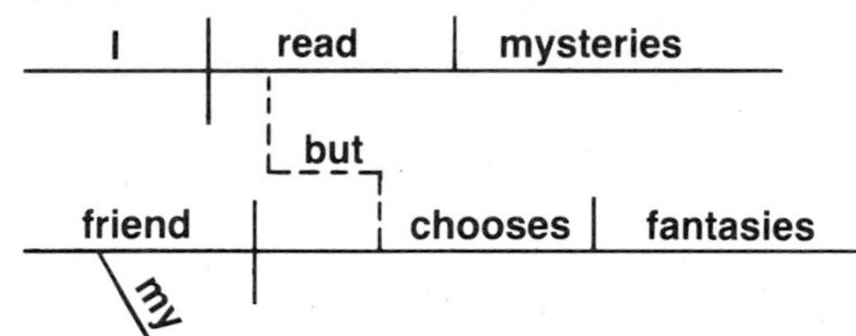

1. The buildings trembled, and the land shook.
2. We picked fresh strawberries, and they gathered beans.
3. Texas has mountains, and it has sandy beaches.
4. This model changes often, but that model stays the same.
5. We measured the pool in feet; they measured it in meters.
6. We can spend our money, or we can save it.
7. The player leaped up; he made the shot.
8. Some members came by plane, but others arrived by bus.
9. The blizzard could hit the city, or it could move east.
10. She told a story, and I listened attentively.
11. Michael received the message, but his older brother wrote a reply.
12. Amy can plant her seeds now, or she can wait until June.
13. The children arrived early, and they stayed late.
14. Mark hit a homerun, but the visiting team still lost the game.
15. I tried hard, but some questions stumped me.

DEVELOPING WRITING SKILLS: Explaining Sentence Diagrams. Write a paragraph explaining how to diagram a compound sentence. Explain the procedure in the correct order.

Skills Review and Writing Workshop

Clauses

CHECKING YOUR SKILLS

Tell whether each underlined clause is an *independent clause* or a *subordinate clause*. Remember that only an independent clause can stand on its own as a sentence.

EXAMPLE: Because Pocahontas saved his life, John Smith was grateful.
subordinate clause

1. When the settlers arrived, the Indians helped them.
2. John Smith visited the Indians after the fort was built.
3. The Indians didn't know if they should trust him.
4. While he was traveling, Smith was captured by Indians.
5. Although he was close to death, Pocahontas helped him.
6. He taught her to speak English while he was a prisoner.
7. Before he was released, the Indians asked him for guns.
8. If he gave the guns, he would be released and given land.
9. The settlers held Pocahontas hostage until her father agreed to their terms.
10. After she was married, Pocahontas went to England.

USING GRAMMAR SKILLS IN WRITING

Writing a Nature Report

You are the nature reporter on a newspaper. But where you live there is not much striking scenery or wild plants and animals. Then you realize people, dogs and cats, and blades of grass poking through sidewalks are parts of nature.

Write what you see of nature around your town. When you review your work, check that your clauses are grammatically correct.

Chapter 16

Fragments

Most people know that a sentence begins with a capital letter and ends with a period, a question mark, or an exclamation mark. But confusion sometimes sets in when writers have to decide where one sentence ends and another sentence begins. When a group of words is written as a sentence but does not have all the necessary sentence parts, the result is called a *fragment.*

Fragments are normally not acceptable in writing. Try to turn any fragments you find in your compositions into complete sentences. One way to do this is to read a sentence aloud. If something seems to be missing, it probably is. You can then supply the words needed to turn a phrase or subordinate clause into a complete sentence.

This chapter will explain more about fragments. You will learn to recognize when a group of words is a sentence and when it is a fragment. Then you will learn how to change fragments into complete sentences. This is important information to remember when you go over and revise your writing.

16.1 Recognizing Fragments

Fragments are parts of sentences. They are not complete sentences because they are missing something necessary for a complete thought.

A fragment is a group of words that does not express a complete thought.

The cat lives is a sentence. The words include a subject and a verb and express a complete thought. The words *The cat with the black and white paws* do not express a complete thought. A main verb (predicate) is missing, so the words do not express a complete thought. The following chart presents some of the many different kinds of fragments.

Fragments	What Is Missing
This opportunity.	A verb
Demanded immediate action.	A subject
The band playing a march.	A complete verb
Beside the sofa.	A subject and a verb
After Matthew left home.	An independent clause

Phrases and subordinate clauses are fragments if they are written as if they were sentences. Even though the subordinate clause *after Matthew left home* has a subject and a verb, it is not a complete sentence. It must be combined with an independent clause in order not to be a fragment—for example, *After Matthew left home, he stopped at the post office.*

You should keep in mind that length is no indication whether a group of words is a sentence or a fragment. *The cat lives* is a shorter group of words than *the cat with the black and white paws,* but it is a complete sentence. *The cat with the black and white paws* is longer, but it is still just a fragment.

EXERCISE A: Recognizing Fragments. Tell whether each group of words is a *sentence* or a *fragment.*

EXAMPLE: The package on the steps.
fragment

1. The day was dark and gray.
2. After we ate dinner.
3. On our street.
4. A bunch of flowers in her hand.
5. My brother and I explored the rooms in the vast, ancient castle.
6. Yelled back at us in a loud voice.
7. I didn't realize how cold it was.
8. In the middle of a big commotion.
9. My cousin chased me up the stairs.
10. A sharp turn into the driveway.

EXERCISE B: More Work with Fragments. Tell whether each group of words is a sentence or a fragment.

1. My neighbors went on an African safari.
2. We saw some bighorn sheep.
3. Jumped out from behind the door.
4. Watching for the arrival of the plane.
5. When I was living in Columbus, Ohio, with my grandparents.
6. A few of us waited outside.
7. Every Saturday before practice.
8. Should have guessed immediately.
9. After the first week at camp.
10. The conductor checked the tickets.

DEVELOPING WRITING SKILLS: Writing About Fragments and Sentences. Make up an example of a complete sentence and an example of a sentence fragment. Then write a paragraph explaining the difference between the two groups of words.

16.2 Correcting Fragments

Fragments leave a reader with the feeling that something has been left out. They prevent clear communication of meaning. If you notice a fragment in your writing, you can easily correct it by making up for the missing part or parts.

To correct a fragment, use one of these methods:

(1) Connect the fragment to a nearby sentence.
(2) Add the necessary words to change the fragment into a sentence.

Connecting Fragments to Nearby Sentences. A phrase can often be connected to the sentence that comes before or after it.

PHRASE: In a moment. She had vanished from sight.

SENTENCE: In a moment she had vanished from sight.

In a similar way, a subordinate clause can often be connected to the sentence before or after it.

CLAUSE: We can land safely. If we find a big field.

SENTENCE: We can land safely if we find a big field.

Adding Necessary Words to Fragments. To change a phrase into a sentence, you can add the missing subject, verb, or both.

PHRASE: Into the water.

SENTENCE: I jumped into the water.

You can also add words to a subordinate clause in order to make it a sentence. To each subordinate clause, you must add an independent clause.

CLAUSE: When the thundershower began.

SENTENCE: We ran inside when the thundershower began.

EXERCISE A: Changing Fragments into Sentences. Change the following fragments into complete sentences by adding the necessary words.

EXAMPLE: At the station.

I can meet you at the station tomorrow morning.

1. Before the dance.
2. While we worked on the experiment.
3. Once the baseball season begins.
4. Ahead of me.
5. After the summer vacation.
6. Without a pen or pencil.
7. Opposite the park.
8. When she began to speak.
9. Even though the temperature is warm.
10. From my seat.

EXERCISE B: More Work with Fragments and Sentences. Change the following fragments into complete sentences.

1. Next to the library.
2. How the rumor spread.
3. On top of my dresser.
4. Past the principal's office.
5. When they are found.
6. Unless the pitch is low.
7. Since he was on TV.
8. During the previous week.
9. As long as we have the right.
10. Beneath this stack of papers.

DEVELOPING WRITING SKILLS: Writing Complete Sentences. Write five titles for stories. Use the following words to begin the titles: *where, while, before, since,* and *if.* Then change each title into a complete sentence.

Skills Review and Writing Workshop

Fragments

CHECKING YOUR SKILLS

Tell whether each group of words is a *sentence* or a *fragment*. Then, rewrite each fragment as a complete sentence. There are five fragments in all.

EXAMPLE: Toward the city.
fragment At dusk he rode off toward the city.

1. Beside the fresh tracks.
2. We stepped into the tent.
3. The special-delivery message on your desk.
4. Shouting and dancing with joy.
5. April and May are my favorite months.
6. From the beginning of the trip.
7. The musician smiled and bowed to the audience.
8. When I realized the time, I began to hurry.
9. Promised to return in an hour.
10. You can borrow my brown jacket.

USING GRAMMAR SKILLS IN WRITING

Writing an Idea for a TV Show

Imagine that the president of the World Broadcasting Company has hired you to create a new TV show. Think about the kind of show you would like to see on TV. Is it a serious show or a comic one? Does it have many people on it or just a few? Maybe you would like to start a new game show. Perhaps you want to write a show about your school and some of the things that happen there.

Once you have imagined your show, think about how you are going to explain it. You want to tell where it takes place. You want to write about the people who will be on it. You want to give some idea of what is going to happen. If it is a game show, explain what people have to do and what prizes are offered. Read your work carefully. Be sure you have written no sentence fragments. Proofread carefully.

Chapter 17

Run-Ons

The last chapter was about fragments—parts or pieces of sentences. A fragment confuses a reader because not enough information is given to express a complete thought. The reader needs to know more.

A different kind of sentence error is writing a sentence with too much information. This type of sentence is called a *run-on.* Run-ons not only have too much information, but the information is not connected or punctuated properly. A reader doesn't know when one sentence stops and another sentence begins.

This chapter deals with run-ons. First, you will learn to recognize them. Then you will read about how to correct run-ons when you find them. In addition, you will practice writing complete sentences and proofreading them to see that none of your sentences are run-ons.

As you become more aware of the way sentences are put together, you should learn to avoid writing either fragments or run-ons. If you want to be understood, it is important to write complete sentences.

17.1 Recognizing Run-ons

A writer's ideas may come very quickly. When they do, the writer often tries to get these ideas down in a hurry. The result can be a run-on sentence.

A run-on sentence is two or more sentences written as if they were one sentence.

If you know what run-ons are, you can correct them in your writing. Some run-ons are made up of two sentences that are not separated by any punctuation; one sentence simply runs into another. Other run-ons are made up of two sentences separated by a comma but no conjunction. Remember, however, a sentence is not necessarily a run-on just because it is long.

The chart below gives examples of the two types of run-on sentences. In parentheses are explanations of what is wrong.

RUN-ONS
New York is called the Empire State the nickname was given by George Washington. (No punctuation at all after "State")
Birds can live in all kinds of climates some birds even live near the North Pole. (No punctuation at all after "climates")
Water becomes ice when frozen, it becomes steam when heated. (Just a comma after "frozen")
First we took a guided tour, later we wandered around the city by ourselves. (Just a comma after "tour")

Since most run-ons are the result of thinking quickly and writing hastily, the way to correct them is to go over your writing carefully. If you see your sentences need punctuation, put it in. Run-ons can be very confusing to the reader. That is why they are considered serious sentence errors.

EXERCISE: Recognizing Run-ons. Tell whether each of the following groups of words is a *run-on* or a *sentence.*

EXAMPLE: The human brain is very complicated, it receives information from other parts of the body.

run-on

1. The size of your brain does not determine how smart you are, a genius may have an average-sized brain, a large brain, or a small brain.
2. Until you are about 15 years old, your brain will continue to grow.
3. Scientists study the brain they have many unanswered questions.
4. The brain of a human adult weighs about three pounds the brain of an elephant weighs about eleven pounds.
5. Different parts of your brain control different activities.
6. I want to go to Spain, I have been studying Spanish for two years and want to test my knowledge of it in real life.
7. The capital of Colombia is Bogotá it is located in the Andes Mountains.
8. Brazil is the largest country in South America most of the people live along the Atlantic coast.
9. The bark of some birch trees peels off in layers like sheets of paper.
10. Because they are thin, many birch trees are bent over but not destroyed during storms that do great damage to other kinds of trees.

DEVELOPING WRITING SKILLS: Avoiding Run-ons. Write a paragraph about the advantages or disadvantages of watching television. Check to see that none of your sentences are run-ons.

17.2 Correcting Run-ons

There are three ways to correct run-ons: with end marks, commas and coordinating conjunctions, and semicolons.

Using End Marks. An *end mark*—a period, a question mark, or an exclamation mark—is the most obvious way to correct a run-on.

An end mark can divide a run-on into two separate sentences.

RUN-ON: When are you leaving, I am leaving now.

SEPARATED SENTENCES: When are you leaving? I am leaving now.

Using Commas and Coordinating Conjunctions. If the two sentences in a run-on are related in meaning, they can be joined into one compound sentence with a coordinating conjunction.

A comma and a coordinating conjunction (*and, but, for, or, nor, so,* or *yet*) can combine the two parts of a run-on.

RUN-ON: Deserts are not completely dry they receive a small amount of rain.

COMPOUND SENTENCE: Deserts are not completely dry, for they receive a small amount of rain.

Using Semicolons. Another way to connect closely related sentences is to use a semicolon.

A semicolon can connect the two parts of a run-on.

RUN-ON: A diamond is the hardest natural material, it is mostly made of carbon.

SENTENCE WITH A SEMICOLON: A diamond is the hardest natural material; it is mostly made of carbon.

EXERCISE A: Correcting Run-ons. Correct the following run-ons by one of the three methods given in this section.

EXAMPLE: My dog can do tricks, he can shake hands.
My dog can do tricks. He can shake hands.

1. The smallest dog is the chihuahua, the tallest dog is the Irish wolfhound.
2. A husky can pull a sled through snow, a collie can herd sheep.
3. A St. Bernard is the heaviest dog some St. Bernards weigh over 200 pounds.
4. A person can see better than a dog, a dog can hear better than a person.
5. Do wild dogs still exist I heard that there were some living in India.

EXERCISE B: More Work with Run-ons. Correct each of the following run-ons. Use the methods given in this section.

1. What sites did you see in Boston, we saw Faneuil Hall.
2. Last night we had a snowstorm the accumulation was over a foot.
3. George visited the historic city of Williamsburg, a blacksmith there explained his work.
4. The farm produces several kinds of fresh vegetables, most of them are sold locally.
5. Timothy's desk is made of oak Martha's desk is made of mahogany.

DEVELOPING WRITING SKILLS: Proofreading for Run-ons. Write a paragraph about a pet you have or one that you would like to have. Then, proofread your paragraph carefully to see that none of your sentences are run-ons.

Skills Review and Writing Workshop

Run-ons

CHECKING YOUR SKILLS

Tell whether each item below is a *sentence* or a *run-on*.

EXAMPLE: The radio is too loud, I can hardly hear you.
run-on

1. Tell me the problem, I'll see if I can help you.
2. I sent Jenny a birthday card, and she still has it.
3. A detective searched the room he was looking for clues.
4. We read about Beowulf, a poem tells how he killed the monster Grendel.
5. Rose buys the newspaper every day, for she likes to read the editorials.
6. There are many rooms in this mansion the largest is the living room.
7. Some people wore costumes; others were dressed casually.
8. We couldn't decide who should be leader, we finally decided to take turns.
9. Daniel is our representative he goes to meetings.
10. E. B. White has written children's books, but he has also written essays.

USING GRAMMAR SKILLS IN WRITING

Writing a Newspaper Article

You are furious. You have just learned that next summer's vacation has been canceled. Everyone will have to come to school all summer long. Luckily you own a newspaper, so you can write an article against this idea.

However, you just can't write "terrible idea" and let it go at that. People need to be convinced. Before you write, think carefully of how you will argue your point. Write about 100 words, and don't forget to proofread for run-on sentences.

UNIT **II**

Usage

Chapter 18

Levels of Language

What is the difference between the sentence *We're trying to come up with an answer* and the sentence *Our group is attempting to develop a solution?* The difference is in the wording, for the meaning is essentially the same. Because of the way each is worded, the second sentence is more formal (serious sounding) than the first.

The sentences above are examples of two different levels of English—formal and informal. In order to know which level to use, you should first think about your *audience.* For example, you would probably write and speak more formally to a government official than to a friend.

Another thing to consider is *what* you are writing. An article for the school newspaper would be written differently from a scribbled note left on the refrigerator. So you see, *whom* you write to and *what* you are trying to accomplish will decide the level of English that is right for the situation.

This chapter will give you more information about the levels of English. First you will read about formal English—the more serious kind of language. Then you will read about informal English—the more relaxed kind.

18.1 Formal English

Sometimes you must speak or write to someone you do not know very well. If the things you discuss are important and serious, you should use formal English.

Formal English is the language of serious subjects discussed in a serious, careful way.

Formal English is the language used in laws and legal writing, in important speeches by the President, in business letters, in wedding invitations, in other important announcements, and in school reports.

Many of the words used in formal English are more likely to be words found in written English than in spoken English. The chart below lists some suggestions for writing formal English.

WRITING FORMAL ENGLISH
1. Do not use contractions. (For example, use *are not* instead of *aren't* and *it is* instead of *it's*.)
2. Do not use slang. (Words such as *goof* are not acceptable.)
3. Do not use the pronoun *you* in a general way to mean "a person." (Use a noun or the pronoun *one* instead.)
4. Use serious, straightforward sentences. (A sentence that sounds like relaxed conversation is usually not formal English.)

The sentences below are examples of formal English.

EXAMPLES: He will disclose the results of his experiment.

One cannot be too careful when choosing a pet.

In the first sentence, *he will* is used instead of *he'll*. In the second sentence, the pronoun *one* is used instead of the more conversational word *you*.

EXERCISE A: Recognizing Formal English. Rewrite each sentence below. Choose the more formal word or phrase shown in parentheses.

EXAMPLE: They (shouldn't, should not) replace the program.
They should not replace the program.

1. (It's, It is) clearly a routine matter.
2. Mr. Brown seems more (energetic, peppy) now.
3. (You, One) should avoid, if possible, an unsafe situation.
4. The (kids, students) answered the questionnaires.
5. The (intellectual, high-brow) discussion raised new ideas.
6. The game left us (wrecked, exhausted).
7. Settlers were assured (they'd, they would) receive land.
8. The unfortunate news made them feel (sorrowful, blue).
9. The recently discovered document is (phony, counterfeit).
10. (They're, They are) likely to face some opposition.

EXERCISE B: More Work with Formal English. Rewrite each sentence, using the more formal word or phrase.

1. Women (could not, couldn't) vote in the 1800's.
2. Lucretia Mott and Elizabeth Cady Stanton (pushed, supported) women's rights.
3. (One, You) must admire their determination.
4. (It's, It is) fortunate that these two women met.
5. They met to (discuss, chat about) their ideas.

DEVELOPING WRITING SKILLS: Using Formal English. Write a letter to your principal suggesting ways to promote safety in school. Use formal English.

18.2 Informal English

When educated people talk to each other, write notes, or compose friendly letters, they generally use informal English.

Informal English is the language used by educated people in their everyday lives. It is more relaxed than formal English.

Informal English is just as correct as formal English, but it is most often used when people know each other well. You can find informal language in casual conversations, in friendly letters, in diaries, in newspaper sports stories, and in speeches of characters in many stories and plays. In informal English, words and sentences seem more like speech than writing. Many words and phrases that are acceptable for informal English are not acceptable in situations that call for formal English.

The chart below lists some suggestions for writing and recognizing informal English.

WRITING INFORMAL ENGLISH
1. Contractions are acceptable. (For example, *Who's going to make the announcement?*)
2. Popular expressions, specialized vocabulary (such as sports terms), and words and expressions used in friendly conversations are acceptable if they are not overdone. (For example, *The game was a total washout.*)
3. The pronoun *you* is often used in a general way to mean *a person* or *one*. (For example, *You should try to save energy.*)
4. Sentences are often looser and more conversational, more humorous, or more personal. (For example, *We'll meet in the morning—at no special time—and tinker with our bikes.*)

EXERCISE: Recognizing Informal English. One sentence in each pair uses formal English; the other uses informal English. Label each sentence in the pair *formal* or *informal.*

EXAMPLE: A. He'd stay around after school.
B. He would remain after school.
A. informal B. formal

1. A. Because of our nutty behavior, everyone looked at us.
   B. Our peculiar activities were clearly noticeable by everyone present.
2. A. You'd need three hands to run that machine.
   B. One needs considerable skill to operate that machine.
3. A. My schoolmates enjoy different forms of recreation.
   B. My pals like different kinds of fun.
4. A. His performance was remarkable.
   B. His performance was really wild.
5. A. She'd get the idea right away.
   B. She would understand the idea at once.
6. A. We'd usually chip in for his present.
   B. We would usually contribute money for his present.
7. A. Your mother excels as a cook.
   B. Your mom's cooking is out of this world.
8. A. Your parents seem to enjoy lavish vacations.
   B. Your folks always splurge on their vacations.
9. A. It's snowing—if you can believe it—even in April.
   B. Although it is April, it is snowing.
10. A. A lot of people think she's brainy.
    B. Many people consider her intelligent.

DEVELOPING WRITING SKILLS: Writing Informal English. Write a paragraph about your favorite subject in school. Use informal but correct English.

Skills Review and Writing Workshop

Levels of Language

CHECKING YOUR SKILLS

Tell whether the following sentences are written in *formal* or *informal* English.

EXAMPLE: It's interesting to learn about a place like Antarctica.
informal

1. Scientists have declared Antarctica to be the coldest location on earth.
2. As you know, it's completely covered with ice.
3. Temperatures of −126°F. are too nippy for me.
4. Although Captain Cook explored the area around Antarctica, he never saw land.
5. I'm pretty sure that other explorers stumbled on fossils and live bugs in Antarctica.
6. We've got some proof that Antarctica hasn't always been so cold.
7. Explorers have found fossils of warm-weather plants.
8. Some guys who were exploring got frozen in for a year.
9. Penguins, seals, and birds inhabit the Antarctic region.
10. Scientists predict that in the future Antarctica will be extremely useful to the people of the world.

USING USAGE SKILLS IN WRITING

Writing an Invitation

You are going to have a party and you plan to invite all your friends. You dash off an informal invitation. Your aunt, who is visiting the family, sees the invitation and insists you write it in a more formal way.

Write two versions, one in informal English, the other in formal English. Proofread both versions carefully.

Chapter 19

Using the Right Verb

Whether you are writing formally or informally, it is important to be able to use verbs correctly, according to the rules of standard English. Verbs in English have different forms. Changing from one form to another is generally a simple operation. This is because most verbs are *regular.* They change in regular ways according to a simple pattern. Other verbs, however, are *irregular.* They do not follow this simple pattern. It is up to you to learn how these irregular verbs change form.

This chapter deals with both regular and irregular verbs. First you will read about the way most verbs change. Then you will read about the exceptions. You probably know a great deal about both regular and irregular verbs because you are already an experienced speaker and writer of English. However, you will need to learn about the irregular verbs you are unsure of.

19.1 Regular Verbs

Verb forms show that an event is taking place in the present, took place in the past, or will take place in the future. These verb forms are called *tenses.*

Regular verbs form tenses in a regular, consistent way.

All verbs have four principal parts. These parts are used to form the different tenses.

PRINCIPAL PARTS OF THREE REGULAR VERBS			
Present	**Present Participle**	**Past**	**Past Participle**
pick	(am) picking	picked	(have) picked
ask	(am) asking	asked	(have) asked
smile	(am) smiling	smiled	(have) smiled

The *present (pick)* is the simplest form. Endings are added to it to form the other principal parts. The *present participle (picking)* is formed by adding *-ing* to the present. (If the present ends in *e*, the *e* is dropped.) A form of the helping verb *be* comes before the present participle. The *past (picked)* is formed by adding *-ed* or *-d* to the present. (If a verb already ends in *e,* simply add a *-d.* If not, add *-ed.*) The *past participle* is formed by combining the past with a form of the helping verb *have (have picked).*

You can see all four of the principal parts of a regular verb in the following sentences.

EXAMPLES: I use a tape recorder. (Present time)

I am using a tape recorder. (Present time)

I used a tape recorder. (Past time)

I have used a tape recorder. (Past time)

I will use a tape recorder. (Future time)

EXERCISE A: Using Regular Verbs. Copy the sentences below, supplying the correct form of each verb in parentheses.

EXAMPLE: I (finish) reading that book last week.
I finished reading that book last week.

1. A few weeks ago, my friend (recommend) a book to me.
2. While I was on vacation, I (start) to read it.
3. It tells of a family that is (live) in Connecticut.
4. They will (witness) the start of the American Revolution.
5. One son has joined the army, but the rest of the family has (stay) at home.
6. The parents have (remain) loyal to England.
7. Everywhere, patriots are (complain) about the British.
8. Many patriots have even (create) committees.
9. I have (learn) some history from this book.
10. I will (suggest) this novel to another friend.

EXERCISE B: More Work with Regular Verbs. Copy each sentence, supplying the correct form of the verb in parentheses.

1. Scientists have (explore) many underground caves and caverns.
2. They have (photograph) numerous interesting rock formations.
3. Rock formations resembling flowers have (develop).
4. I am (learn) about these fabulous interiors.
5. I have already (learn) about how caves are formed.

DEVELOPING WRITING SKILLS: Using Regular Verbs in Sentences. Write ten sentences telling about the activities of one of your friends. Use some form of each of the following verbs: *start, wait, call, act, help, joke, like, share, walk,* and *play*.

19.2 Irregular Verbs

Most verbs are regular. They form the past and past participle in a regular, consistent way by adding *-ed* or *-d* to the present. A small number of verbs do not follow this regular, consistent pattern. These verbs are called *irregular verbs.*

An irregular verb does not form the past or past participle by adding *-ed* or *-d* to the present.

The chart below lists the principal parts of a number of irregular verbs that have the same past and past participle.

IRREGULAR VERBS WITH THE SAME PAST AND PAST PARTICIPLE			
Present	**Present Participle**	**Past**	**Past Participle**
bring	(am) bringing	brought	(have) brought
build	(am) building	built	(have) built
buy	(am) buying	bought	(have) bought
catch	(am) catching	caught	(have) caught
get	(am) getting	got	(have) got *or* (have) gotten
have	(am) having	had	(have) had
lay	(am) laying	laid	(have) laid
lead	(am) leading	led	(have) led
lose	(am) losing	lost	(have) lost
pay	(am) paying	paid	(have) paid
sit	(am) sitting	sat	(have) sat
spin	(am) spinning	spun	(have) spun
sting	(am) stinging	stung	(have) stung
swing	(am) swinging	swung	(have) swung

EXERCISE: Using Irregular Verbs. Copy each sentence substituting the past or past participle for the verb in parentheses.

EXAMPLE: Last week Michelle (buy) a new jacket.
Last week Michelle bought a new jacket.

1. Andrew had (catch) enough trout to feed our entire family.
2. Have you (get) the postcard I sent you from Florida?
3. Rita (lead) the way and Paula followed.
4. Now that I have (pay) for this tape, I can give it to you.
5. The storyteller (spin) a tale of romance and adventure.
6. I (lose) the ticket.
7. José (swing) the bat, hit the ball, and ran to first base.
8. Mrs. Scott has (buy) a new coat.
9. Eddie (have) good news waiting for him when he got home.
10. My father (bring) a guest home to dinner.
11. The club members (pay) for the costumes.
12. Our team won the first game and (lose) the second.
13. Have you (bring) your guitar?
14. It seems that you have (catch) a cold.
15. Dan has (build) three model airplanes this year.
16. Last summer a bee (sting) me on the thumb.
17. Dina has (buy) this brand of toothpaste before.
18. Phil (sit) in the orchestra during the first part of the performance.
19. The nurse had (lay) out the instruments for the doctor.
20. Has the gate (swing) shut?

DEVELOPING WRITING SKILLS: Using Irregular Verbs. Write an advertisement for a "new" cereal. Include some form of at least five of the following verbs: *buy, get, say, pay, have, build, lay,* and *sit.*

19.3 More Irregular Verbs

For some irregular verbs, the *present,* the *past,* and the *past participle* are the same. One verb that follows this pattern is *spread.* Its principal parts are listed in the chart below.

Present	Present Participle	Past	Past Participle
spread	(am) spreading	spread	(have) spread

EXAMPLES: The messengers spread the news each day.

The messengers are spreading the news.

The messengers spread the news of last month's victory.

The messengers have spread the news.

The chart below lists the principal parts of other irregular verbs like *spread.*

IRREGULAR VERBS WITH THE SAME PRESENT, PAST, AND PAST PARTICIPLE			
Present	**Present Participle**	**Past**	**Past Participle**
bid	(am) bidding	bid	(have) bid
burst	(am) bursting	burst	(have) burst
cast	(am) casting	cast	(have) cast
cost	(am) costing	cost	(have) cost
cut	(am) cutting	cut	(have) cut
hurt	(am) hurting	hurt	(have) hurt
let	(am) letting	let	(have) let
put	(am) putting	put	(have) put
read	(am) reading	read	(have) read
rid	(am) ridding	rid	(have) rid
set	(am) setting	set	(have) set

EXERCISE: Using Irregular Verbs Correctly. Complete the answer to each question by using a form of the underlined verb.

EXAMPLE: Are you setting the table for dinner?
No, I ______ it an hour ago.
set

1. Are you cutting any more trees in this area?
   No, I ______ enough trees here.
2. Did your mother let you stay up for the second half of the program?
   She ______ me, but I fell asleep.
3. Are you putting more paper in the machine?
   No, I have ______ in enough.
4. Does your arm still hurt?
   No, it isn't ______ me anymore.
5. Is the collar ridding the dog of fleas?
   Yes, it has ______ him of most of them already.
6. Are you reading the magazine on the table?
   No, I have already ______ it.
7. Has the director cast the parts for the play?
   No, he is ______ them tomorrow.
8. Do you think that your balloon will burst?
   No, my balloon ______ yesterday.
9. Do oranges cost less this week?
   No, they ______ about the same as last week and the week before.
10. Are you bidding twenty-five dollars for the velvet-covered chair?
    Yes, I have already ______ fifteen dollars, but I will offer more.

DEVELOPING WRITING SKILLS: Using Irregular Verbs in a Summary. Write a paragraph summarizing the things you did yesterday. Use some form of each of the following verbs: *cost, read, put, let, cut,* or any other verb from the chart on the preceding page.

19.4 Other Irregular Verbs

Some verbs make a number of vowel and consonant changes in order to form their principal parts. To see how these verbs change, examine each one of them in the chart below.

VERBS THAT CHANGE IN A VARIETY OF WAYS			
Present	**Present Participle**	**Past**	**Past Participle**
be	(am) being	was	(have) been
begin	(am) beginning	began	(have) begun
choose	(am) choosing	chose	(have) chosen
do	(am) doing	did	(have) done
draw	(am) drawing	drew	drawn
drink	(am) drinking	drank	(have) drunk
drive	(am) driving	drove	(have) driven
eat	(am) eating	ate	(have) eaten
fly	(am) flying	flew	(have) flown
give	(am) giving	gave	(have) given
know	(am) knowing	knew	(have) known
lie	(am) lying	lay	(have) lain
ring	(am) ringing	rang	(have) rung
rise	(am) rising	rose	(have) risen
sing	(am) singing	sang	(have) sung
speak	(am) speaking	spoke	(have) spoken
swim	(am) swimming	swam	(have) swum
take	(am) taking	took	(have) taken
tear	(am) tearing	tore	(have) torn
throw	(am) throwing	threw	(have) thrown
write	(am) writing	wrote	(have) written

EXERCISE: Selecting the Correct Forms of Irregular Verbs. Choose the correct verb from the choice given in parentheses.

EXAMPLE: Sandra has (began, begun) to speak.
begun

1. My brother (drove, drived) to Canada during the summer.
2. Have you (flown, flew) on a 747?
3. The late bell had already (rang, rung) when I arrived.
4. Jim and Eric (swam, swum) ten laps in the pool.
5. Today I must (choose, chose) a partner in science class.
6. Ellen has (tore, torn) up the scrap paper.
7. He caught the ball and (threw, throwed) it to the pitcher.
8. The class had (knew, known) about the picnic for a week.
9. The balloon (rose, rised) high over our heads.
10. We (began, begun) our campaign for class president.
11. The student (did, done) a report on John Paul Jones.
12. Our class has (wrote, written) to our state senator.
13. The performers danced and (sang, sung) for us.
14. In the past, he (be, was) captain of the team.
15. Have you (gave, given) your suggestions to Miriam?
16. The principal has (spoken, spoke) to us about safety.
17. We (ate, eat) first and then went to the theater.
18. Cindy and Dan have (took, taken) a photography course.
19. Earlier in the afternoon, Sarah (lay, lain) down to rest.
20. I have (drank, drunk) the apple juice.

DEVELOPING WRITING SKILLS: Using Irregular Verbs in Sentences. Write ten sentences telling about some of the ways you have changed since last year. Use some form of each of the following verbs: *speak, know, write, eat, begin, choose, take, do, throw,* and *give.*

Skills Review and Writing Workshop

Using the Right Verb

CHECKING YOUR SKILLS

Copy each sentence below using the correct past or past participle form of the verb shown in parentheses.

EXAMPLE: Yesterday we (buy) new knapsacks.
Yesterday we bought new knapsacks.

1. Andy and I have (look) at backpacking equipment.
2. Some boots (cost) more than fifty dollars.
3. After examining sleeping bags, we (choose) one filled with goose down.
4. Andy (examine) the cotton tents, and I (inspect) the nylon ones.
5. Other backpackers have (teach) us about basic safety.
6. Last week they (let) us see their packs and frames.
7. We have (find) that it is important to be in good physical condition.
8. Andy and I have (be) jogging each morning.
9. We have (pay) close attention to experienced backpackers.
10. Last month we (begin) to make plans for our first trip.

USING USAGE SKILLS IN WRITING

Writing a Letter

You are in charge of a shelter for homeless animals. It is your job to place the animals in good homes. So you are going to write a letter to a farmer you know suggesting that he adopt two dogs. When you write this letter, there are two things to consider: first, how the dogs will help the farmer; second, how the farmer will benefit from adopting the dogs.

Remember that you are asking a favor, so be polite. Present all the arguments you can think of in favor of the farmer adopting the dogs, but don't push him too hard. Be sure your verbs are correct and that you are using the proper tenses.

Chapter 20

Using Verbs to Show Time

What is the difference between the sentence *Donna climbs the mountain* and the sentence *Donna has climbed the mountain*? It is the difference between *now* and *then*—a difference in time. Writers and speakers use verbs not only to show actions but also to show time. They can discuss what is happening now; they can re-create what happened in the past; and they can say what will happen in the future. All of this can be done by changing the form of the verb.

Verbs have different forms to show time. You already use these forms in your speaking and writing. When you write, you need to be particularly careful to use verbs correctly. As you learn more about the different verb forms, you will learn to correct sentences or phrases that do not sound quite right.

This chapter explains how verbs use tense to show time. Several tenses, such as the present, past, and future, are described. As you study these tenses, you will see that the way you use them largely determines the meaning of your sentences.

20.1 The Present, Past, and Future Tenses

Verbs have a number of different forms that tell when actions happen. These verb forms are called tenses.

A tense tells whether the time of a verb is in the present, past, or future.

English verbs have six basic tenses. This section tells about three of them: (1) present, (2) past, and (3) future.

One way to learn all of the forms of a verb is to conjugate it. A *conjugation* is a listing of the forms of a verb in a particular tense. It shows how the verb changes when it is used with different pronouns, such as *I*, *you*, or *it*.

PRINCIPAL PARTS OF *START*			
Present	**Present Participle**	**Past**	**Past Participle**
start	starting	started	started

CONJUGATION OF THE PRESENT, PAST, AND FUTURE TENSES OF *START*		
	Singular	**Plural**
Present	I start you start he, she, it starts	we start you start they start
Past	I started you started he, she, it started	we started you started they started
Future	I will start you will start he, she, it will start	we will start you will start they will start

Present Tense. The present tense shows actions that happen in the present. This tense is also used to show actions that occur regularly (every week, each day, or all the time).

EXAMPLE: I study science.

The dancers practice every day.

Barbara and Dan enjoy the seashore.

To form the present tense, use the present form. But when the verb follows the pronoun he, she, or it (or a noun that can replace these pronouns), add *-s* or *-es* to the present.

EXAMPLES: He takes me to the movies.

It seems strange.

Roberta brushes the dog each week.

Past Tense. The past tense shows actions that happened in the past. Regular verbs form the past tense by adding *-ed* or *-d* to the present. Irregular verbs change in other ways. The past tense forms of irregular verbs must be memorized. *See* becomes *saw; do* becomes *did;* and so on.

EXAMPLES: We discussed the problem.

My cousin offered to help us.

Audrey paid for the tickets.

Henry spoke to us before lunch.

Future Tense. The future tense shows actions that will take place in the future.

EXAMPLES: Caroline will begin the meeting.

Dr. Brown will join us later.

Sandra will arrive tomorrow.

Notice that the helping verb *will* is used before the present to form the future tense.

EXERCISE A: Using the Present, Past, and Future Tenses. Copy each sentence. Rewrite the verb in parentheses, using the tense shown next to it.

EXAMPLE: He (come–past) into the living room.
He came into the living room.

1. She (run–present) around the track every day after school.
2. We (discuss–past) our plans for the weekend.
3. The boat (sail–future) as soon as the cargo of machinery is loaded.
4. Natasha (enjoy–past) listening to the music.
5. He (like–present) musical comedies.
6. I (lend–future) you my new leather jacket.
7. These arguments (convince–future) you that I am right.
8. Although the car is old, it (run–present) well.
9. The shopper (ask–past) to see the manager.
10. The man in the corner (play–present) lead guitar in the band.

EXERCISE B: Identifying the Present, Past, and Future Tenses. Identify the tense of the underlined verb in each of the following sentences.

EXAMPLE: Almost everyone <u>likes</u> to hear a story.
present

1. When I <u>hear</u> a story, I use my imagination.
2. Storytelling <u>existed</u> before written history.
3. A good story <u>will have</u> action and drama.
4. Many tales <u>hold</u> my interest.
5. I <u>listened</u> to the legend of King Arthur many times.
6. My friend <u>prefers</u> the "trickster" tales from Africa.
7. The librarian <u>read</u> us fantasies by Tolkien.
8. We <u>will practice</u> storytelling this year.
9. First we <u>choose</u> a story we like.
10. We <u>will look</u> for folktales, myths, or legends.

EXERCISE C: More Work with the Present, Past, and Future Tenses. Identify the tense of the underlined verbs below.

EXAMPLE: Blue jays are interesting.
present

1. Blue jays have many unusual habits.
2. A jay will steal nuts from a squirrel.
3. First it frightens the squirrel by flying in circles above it.
4. The frightened squirrel drops the nut and quickly runs away.
5. The jay will dig up a nut buried by a squirrel.
6. Jays make both pleasant and unpleasant sounds.
7. Its unpleasant shriek will warn other animals of danger.
8. We spotted a bird with blue-and-white wings and tail.
9. It had a blue crest on its head and wore a black collar.
10. The bird we observed was a blue jay.

DEVELOPING WRITING SKILLS: Using Different Tenses. Use any five verbs given below in three different sentences for each. In the first sentence use the present tense. In the second sentence use the past tense. In the third sentence use the future tense. (You will write a total of fifteen sentences.)

1. live
2. want
3. play
4. see
5. believe
6. pretend
7. think
8. cook
9. drink
10. fix
11. start
12. read
13. take
14. follow
15. lift
16. open
17. drive
18. give
19. smell
20. close

20.2 The Present Perfect Tense

The present perfect tense shows actions that began in the past and continue to the present. It also shows actions that began and ended in the past.

EXAMPLES: I have sat here for over an hour now.

Irene and Laura have returned the tent.

To form the present perfect tense, use *have* or *has* as a helping verb with the past participle.

EXAMPLE: I have started my woodworking project.

The chart below shows the conjugation of the verb *return* in the present perfect tense. Notice that the third-person singular form is *he (she, it) has returned.*

THE PRESENT PERFECT TENSE OF THE VERB *RETURN*	
Singular	**Plural**
I have returned	we have returned
you have returned	you have returned
he, she, it has returned	they have returned

While the present tense shows what is happening in the present, the present perfect tense shows what has already begun in the past but may be continuing into the present. Compare the following sets of sentences.

PRESENT: Martin waits for his turn.

Alice wants to become a doctor.

They ask for permission to take photographs.

PRESENT PERFECT: Martin has waited for his turn.

Alice has wanted to become a doctor.

They have asked for permission to take photographs.

EXERCISE A: Using the Present Perfect Tense. Copy each sentence below changing each underlined verb to the present perfect tense.

EXAMPLE: Many people buy bicycles.
Many people have bought bicycles.

1. American and foreign companies produce bicycles.
2. The bicycle helps people travel from place to place.
3. Bicycles often last a lifetime.
4. My doctor recommends bicycling to keep fit.
5. I appreciate the ease of bicycle riding.
6. People pause to chat when they see me resting.
7. Al delivers newspapers, using his bike.
8. Some enthusiasts enter the yearly bicycle race.
9. Others attempt bicycle polo.
10. I find friends through my local bicycle club.

EXERCISE B: More Work with the Present Perfect Tense. Change each underlined verb to the present perfect tense.

1. Our club prints a newsletter.
2. We mail it to our members.
3. Many readers write comments to our editor.
4. The editor prints some of them.
5. Several reporters develop feature articles.
6. We use photographs in our newsletter.
7. A poet gives us original poems.
8. I memorize some of these poems.
9. I do the crossword puzzle on the back page.
10. The editor files a copy of each issue in the office.

DEVELOPING WRITING SKILLS: Using the Present Perfect Tense in Sentences. Write a brief paragraph about an activity you do regularly. Use present tense verbs. Rewrite the paragraph changing the verbs to the present perfect tense.

20.3 The Present and Past Progressive

The progressive forms of the tenses show continuing action.

The Present Progressive. The present progressive shows continuing action that is taking place in the present.

To form the present progressive, use the present tense of the verb *be* as a helping verb with the present participle.

THE PRESENT TENSE OF THE VERB *BE*	
Singular	**Plural**
I am	we are
you are	you are
he, she, it is	they are

The following examples show how the present progressive is used in sentences.

EXAMPLES: I am telling the truth.
We are studying American history.
Mary is watching the football game.

The Past Progressive. The past progressive shows continuing action that took place in the past.

To form the past progressive, use the past tense of the verb *be (was* or *were)* as a helping verb with the present participle.

EXAMPLES: I was standing in line for a ticket.
He was planning a party.
The students were singing a song.

EXERCISE: Using the Present and Past Progressive. Copy each sentence, changing the verb in parentheses as directed.

EXAMPLE: Alan (describe–present progressive) his trip.
Alan is describing his trip.

1. Ann (look–present progressive) for someone to interview.
2. Barbara (write–present progressive) about a sad memory.
3. I (worry–past progressive) about being on time.
4. We (imagine–past progressive) how it looked.
5. They (join–present progressive) the drama club.
6. Tom (move–present progressive) to Michigan.
7. I (arrange–past progressive) the papers on my desk.
8. They (enjoy–past progressive) the movie.
9. Terry (work–present progressive) on a computer program.
10. The librarian (tell–past progressive) about a new book.
11. Marie (admire–past progressive) the paintings.
12. We (begin–present progressive) to train the puppy.
13. He (follow–present progressive) my directions.
14. They (praise–past progressive) the cook.
15. I (take–present progressive) a walk in the woods.
16. We (lose–past progressive) the game when you arrived.
17. Dr. Morgan (expect–present progressive) a call.
18. I (wait–present progressive) for a reply to my letter.
19. We (laugh–past progressive) at the comedian's jokes.
20. Your story (become–present progressive) more interesting.

DEVELOPING WRITING SKILLS: Using the Present and Past Progressive. Describe a perfect day as if you were experiencing it right now. Use verbs in the present progressive. Start with *I am enjoying a perfect day.*

Skills Review and Writing Workshop

Using Verbs to Show Time

CHECKING YOUR SKILLS

Identify each underlined verb, using one of the following labels: present tense, past tense, future tense, present perfect tense, present progressive, or past progressive.

EXAMPLE: Mark has planned a camping trip.
present perfect tense

1. We sailed from New York to Southampton.
2. My friends and I have come to play in the tournament.
3. They were dancing, moving with the other dancers.
4. I observed the Big Dipper in the night sky.
5. Eddie always chooses vanilla ice cream.
6. The governors are meeting in Chicago.
7. They want to meet a celebrity.
8. Mrs. Powell teaches chemistry and natural science.
9. William is visiting his cousins in Ohio.
10. Susan will celebrate her twelfth birthday tomorrow.

USING USAGE SKILLS IN WRITING

Writing an Advertisement

You are planning to open an ice-cream parlor. Naturally you need someone to help you, so you are going to put an ad in the newspaper. Think about the kind of person you want to hire. What qualities are important to you? Try to be as exact as possible so the person who answers the ad will know what is expected of him or her. Explain that you now need someone to work part time after school and on Saturdays. But next summer you will want that person to work every day.

After you write your ad, read it over carefully. You want to put in as much information as you need to. But you don't want to have a lot of extra words because you are paying for each word! Proofread carefully, and check your verb tenses.

Chapter 21

Working with Troublesome Verbs

Do you *set* in a chair, or do you *sit* in it? Do you *lay* down when you take a nap, or do you *lie* down? Do you say *James done the assignment* or *James did the assignment?* According to standard English usage, you *sit* in a chair, and you *lie* down when you take a nap. You also say *James did the assignment.*

Pairs of verbs like *set* and *sit, lay* and *lie,* and *did* and *done* can be confusing. One problem people have is choosing the right verb. To make the right choice, you need to know what these verbs mean. That will help you express your ideas accurately. Another problem is remembering the principal parts of these verbs. If you know the principal parts by heart, you will find it easier to form the different verb tenses correctly.

This chapter will help you learn to use these troublesome verbs. First you will read about the three pairs of verbs: *did* and *done, lay* and *lie,* and *set* and *sit.* Then you will practice choosing the correct forms of these verbs and using these verbs in sentences and in a composition.

21.1 *Did* and *Done*

Did and *done* are both forms of the frequently used verb *do.*

Did **is the past form. It is used without a helping verb for actions that began and ended in the past.**

EXAMPLE: She did the drawings, and I did the paintings.

Done **is the past participle. It is always used with a helping verb, such as *have* or *has.***

EXAMPLES: We have done all the weeding in the garden.
Stan has done the sketch for our magazine cover.

The following chart shows the conjugation of two of the tenses of *do.*

CONJUGATION OF TWO TENSES OF *DO*	
Past Tense	**Present Perfect Tense**
I did	I have done
you did	you have done
he, she, it did	he, she, it has done
we did	we have done
you did	you have done
they did	they have done

If a sentence contains the past participle *done* without a helping verb, it is incorrect. To correct it, add a helping verb or change *done* to *did.*

INCORRECT: We done our best.

CORRECT: We have done our best.
We did our best.

EXERCISE A: Using *Did* and *Done.* Choose the correct verb from the two given in parentheses.

EXAMPLE: They have (did, done) all the filming in New York.

done

1. The flooding (did, done) more damage than the violent winds.
2. We have (did, done) what was necessary.
3. Our drama club (did, done) scenes from Shakespeare's play *Hamlet.*
4. Last summer I (did, done) a number of odd jobs at home.
5. David has (did, done) me a big favor.
6. On our trip, this car (did, done) twenty-five miles per gallon.
7. The mayor has (did, done) many useful things for this city.
8. No one has (did, done) the dishes.
9. We (did, done) this scene over seven times.
10. I (did, done) all I could.

EXERCISE B: More Work with *Did* and *Done.* Choose the correct verb from the two given in parentheses.

1. The magician (did, done) his act on the stage.
2. The runner has (done, did) a mile in less than four minutes.
3. She has (done, did) the problem on the blackboard.
4. The horse (done, did) badly in the race.
5. We (done, did) the work for you.

DEVELOPING WRITING SKILLS: Using *Did* and *Done* in Sentences. Write five sentences using *did.* Write about things that you have accomplished. Then write five sentences using *done* with a helping verb. Write about things that other people have accomplished.

21.2 *Lay* and *Lie*

Lay and *lie* are two different verbs with different meanings.

***Lay* means "to put or place something."**

PRINCIPAL PARTS OF *LAY*			
Present	**Present Participle**	**Past**	**Past Participle**
lay	(am) laying	laid	(have) laid

When the verb *lay* is used in a sentence, it takes a direct object.

EXAMPLES: Sue usually lays her books (DO) in the hallway.

The builders are laying the foundation (DO) for the house.

They laid their suitcases (DO) next to ours.

I have laid my glasses (DO) on the desk.

***Lie* means "to rest in a reclining position." Another meaning for *lie* is "to be situated."**

PRINCIPAL PARTS OF *LIE*			
Present	**Present Participle**	**Past**	**Past Participle**
lie	(am) lying	lay	(have) lain

Lie does not take a direct object. It can, however, be followed by an adverb or a prepositional phrase.

EXAMPLES: The capital city lies west of here.

Your report is lying on my desk.

I lay in the hammock all afternoon.

The trunk has lain in the attic for years.

EXERCISE A: Using *Lay* and *Lie*. Choose the correct verb.

EXAMPLE: Grandma is (lying, laying) down in her room.
lying

1. Melissa usually (lays, lies) her knapsack in the corner of her room.
2. I (lay, lain) under this tree for hours.
3. The photographer (laid, lay) his equipment down very carefully.
4. Marsha (lays, lies) on the beach, listening to music.
5. I am (laying, lying) your mail on your desk.
6. The shovel (lay, laid) untouched in the garden.
7. Where have you (laid, lain) your hat?
8. Rolling hills (laid, lay) everywhere I looked.
9. Canada (lays, lies) to the north of the United States.
10. Sharon (laid, lay) her book aside and went out.

EXERCISE B: More Work with *Lay* and *Lie*. Choose the correct verb.

1. Bob is (lying, laying) on the floor, reading a mystery novel.
2. Who has (lain, laid) this calculator on my dresser?
3. The dog (lay, laid) near his master.
4. I have (laid, lain) awake for hours.
5. We are (laying, lying) new carpet in this room.
6. He often (lays, lies) on the floor for hours.
7. The treasure (laid, lay) buried in the backyard.
8. We were (lying, laying) our designs out on the easels.
9. We (laid, lay) our gear down.
10. Henry is (lying, laying) his rock collection here.

DEVELOPING WRITING SKILLS: Using *Lay* and *Lie* in Sentences. Write five sentences using the verb *lay* and five sentences using the verb *lie.* Use all of the verb forms shown on page 176.

21.3 *Set* and *Sit*

Set and *sit* look and sound similar, but their meanings are different.

***Set* means "to put something in a certain place."**

PRINCIPAL PARTS OF *SET*			
Present	**Present Participle**	**Past**	**Past Participle**
set	(am) setting	set	(have) set

Set is followed by a direct object.

EXAMPLES:

DO
We set the clock ahead one hour.

DO
This group is setting a trend in music.

DO
The teacher set the chairs in a circle.

DO
They have set their notebooks on the bookcase.

***Sit* means "to be seated" or "to rest."**

PRINCIPAL PARTS OF *SIT*			
Present	**Present Participle**	**Past**	**Past Participle**
sit	(am) sitting	sat	(have) sat

Sit does not take a direct object. Instead, it is often followed by an adverb or a prepositional phrase, as in the following sentences.

EXAMPLES: We sit in groups to plan our projects.

Paul is sitting with Tim and Mario.

Carmen and Claude sat in the orchestra.

We have sat here for an hour.

EXERCISE A: Using *Set* and *Sit*. Choose the correct verb.

EXAMPLE: Felicia usually (sits, sets) in the first row.
sits

1. Mr. Randolph (set, sat) the projector on a table in the back of the room.
2. Tommy (sets, sits) next to me in English class.
3. The trophy is (setting, sitting) on my mantel for everyone to see.
4. Bill (set, sat) on the porch for hours.
5. The storekeeper is (setting, sitting) jars on the shelf.
6. When we play badminton, I (set, sit) the net up.
7. Eva is (sitting, setting) the books in a pile.
8. I have (set, sat) your wet umbrella in the hallway.
9. We (sat, set) on the carpet and listened to a fascinating story.
10. The statue (sits, sets) on top of a mountain.

EXERCISE B: More Work with *Set* and *Sit*. Choose the correct verb.

1. Ted was (sitting, setting) on the sidelines.
2. Karen (sat, set) at our table during lunch.
3. Wanda (set, sat) her packages on the chair.
4. We are (setting, sitting) all the boxes together.
5. My father usually (sits, sets) on this chair.
6. Daniel (set, sat) his suitcase in the baggage rack.
7. We are (sitting, setting) the chairs on stage.
8. Joan has (sat, set) at her desk for hours.
9. Who is (setting, sitting) over there?
10. Janet (sat, set) her plants in the sunshine.

DEVELOPING WRITING SKILLS: Using *Set* and *Sit* in Sentences. Write a paragraph describing your classroom. Then tell how it could be rearranged. Use at least three different forms of the verbs *set* and *sit*.

Skills Review and Writing Workshop

Working with Troublesome Verbs

CHECKING YOUR SKILLS

Read each sentence. If the underlined verb is used correctly, write *correct*. If the verb is used incorrectly, rewrite the sentence, using the correct form.

EXAMPLE: Are your parents setting in the bleachers?

Are your parents sitting in the bleachers?

1. They done it!
2. What have they done?
3. The teachers set down and made plans for a team.
4. They will set rules for us to follow.
5. This afternoon the coach will sit several soccer balls on the field so that we can play with them.
6. None of us will lie around then.
7. We are sitting here waiting for the game to begin.
8. Have they did the work on the field?
9. They are setting the boundaries of the field today.
10. They are lying the center line down first.

USING USAGE SKILLS IN WRITING

Writing a Report

You are an architect. You have been asked to come to school and look at the building. Write a report about the changes you want to make. Your report will have two sections. The first section will describe the school building the way it is now. The second section will describe the way the school building will be organized after you make your changes.

Make all the changes you wish, but don't forget to add a sentence or two explaining why you think each change is needed. Many people are going to read this report, so make sure all your verbs are correct. Proofread carefully.

Chapter 22

Using Pronouns

Read the following three sentences about Peter Cooper, paying particular attention to the words in italics: "Peter Cooper designed and constructed the first steam locomotive in the United States. *He* raced *his* locomotive against a car pulled by a horse. Many people believed *him* when he claimed that railroads would be an important means of transportation."

What do you notice about the words in italics? Each of these words takes the place of *Peter Cooper,* a proper noun. The three words are pronouns, words that refer to nouns.

Personal pronouns, such as *he, his,* and *him,* have different forms that tell how the pronouns are being used. Personal pronouns can be subjects *(he),* objects *(him),* or words showing ownership *(his).*

This chapter will tell you more about these three groups of personal pronouns. Each group does a different job when used in a sentence. In this chapter you will learn about each group. Then you will practice using the pronouns correctly.

22.1 Subject Pronouns

Pronouns have different forms to show how they are being used.

A subject pronoun is used as the subject of a sentence.

SUBJECT PRONOUNS	
Singular	I, you, he, she, it
Plural	we, you, they

When a sentence has a single subject, it is easy to select the right subject pronoun. However, when a sentence has a compound subject, it is more difficult to choose the right pronoun.

EXAMPLES: Fred and I [not me] volunteered to feed the animals.

Edward and he [not him] led the parade.

To choose the correct pronoun when the subject is compound, say the sentence to yourself with only the pronoun as the subject. Omit the other words in the subject. Say the sentence with each pronoun you think might be correct. Choose the one pronoun that sounds correct.

EXAMPLE: Ken and (I, me) joined the debating club.

Omit the words *Ken* and *and.* Try each of the pronouns with the rest of the sentence. "*Me* joined the debating club" does not sound right. "*I* joined the debating club" does. Now try another example.

EXAMPLE: (He, him) and (I, me) went to the zoo.

"*Him* went to the zoo" does not sound right; "*He* went to the zoo" does. "*Me* went to the zoo" does not sound right; "*I* went to the zoo" does. So "*He* and *I* went to the zoo" is correct.

EXERCISE A: Identifying the Correct Subject Pronoun. Select the correct subject pronoun from the two in parentheses.

EXAMPLE: Dr. Turner and (he, him) performed the experiment.

he

1. Ruth and (I, me) will be on television.
2. Either Erica or (her, she) will check the calculations.
3. The Hendersons and (we, us) are amateur golfers.
4. Neither the manager nor (them, they) like the idea.
5. You and (me, I) can change the tire.
6. Mr. Miller and (he, him) agreed to try the product.
7. Both Julia and (her, she) took piano lessons.
8. Our rivals and (we, us) are well matched.
9. The Rangers or (they, them) play here today.
10. Roy and (he, him) wrote to their state senator.

EXERCISE B: More Work with Subject Pronouns. Select the correct subject pronoun from the two in parentheses.

1. The travel agent and (they, them) planned the trip.
2. The visitors and (us, we) admired the building.
3. You and (she, her) will enjoy the new exhibit.
4. Fred and (me, I) began a small newsletter.
5. The fireman and (he, him) checked the building.
6. Teresa and (me, I) spend time in the greenhouse.
7. Douglas and (they, them) made the rules.
8. You and (she, her) worked well together.
9. The fifth graders and (we, us) organized the book fair.
10. Phil and (he, him) took pictures of old houses.

DEVELOPING WRITING SKILLS: Using Subject Pronouns in Sentences. Write ten sentences with compound subjects. Use one or more of the following subject pronouns in each sentence: *I, you, he, she, it, we,* and *they.*

22.2 Objective Pronouns

The objective pronouns are *me, you, him, her, it, us, you* (plural), and *them.*

Objective pronouns are used as (1) direct objects, (2) indirect objects, and (3) objects of prepositions.

Direct Object. An objective pronoun used as a direct object appears with an action verb and answers the question *Whom?* or *What?*

EXAMPLE: The hostess greeted <u>her</u>.

Indirect Object. An objective pronoun used as an indirect object appears with an action verb and a direct object. It answers the question *To or for whom?* or *To or for what?*

EXAMPLES: My friend told <u>me</u> a story.

The heavy rain and winds caused <u>them</u> many problems.

Object of a Preposition. An objective pronoun can also be the object of a preposition.

EXAMPLE: Our club voted for <u>him</u>.

Sometimes objective pronouns are part of a compound object. To determine the correct pronoun in this kind of sentence, use the pronoun by itself without the rest of the compound.

EXAMPLE: The hostess asked Marie and (she, her) for help.

First try the pronoun *she* without the rest of the compound direct object *(Marie and).* "The hostess asked *she* for help" does not sound right. Now try the pronoun *her.* "The hostess asked *her* for help" does sound right. The correct sentence is "The hostess asked Marie and her for help."

EXERCISE A: Identifying Objective Pronouns. Choose the correct pronoun from the two given in parentheses. Then tell how it is being used.

EXAMPLE: The carpenter told (we, us) a story.
us indirect object

1. An enthusiastic volunteer spoke to Gerald and (me, I).
2. The librarian reserved (she, her) a copy of the book.
3. The pianist played a song for Larry and (we, us).
4. Marcia went to the museum with (him, he) and his mother.
5. The manager showed Martha and (me, I) around the plant.
6. Stephen drew Sheila and (she, her) a portrait.
7. The guide showed (them, they) around the campus.
8. Mrs. Fitzpatrick had a friendly talk with (they, them).
9. Mr. Turner reminded Mary Louise and (we, us) of the time.
10. Everyone laughed except Linda and (me, I).

EXERCISE B: More Work with Objective Pronouns. Write the correct pronoun and tell how it used in the sentence.

1. Sue saw Joan and (she, her) at the stables.
2. Andrew offered John and (me, I) a ride on his bicycle.
3. You told Mark and (us, we) the wrong answer.
4. Joseph showed (he, him) the ranch.
5. The scouts didn't notice the birds above (they, them).

DEVELOPING WRITING SKILLS: Using Objective Pronouns in Sentences. Write ten sentences about unusual things that could happen. Use one of the following pronouns in each sentence: *me, you, him, her, it, us,* and *them.*

22.3 Possessive Pronouns

Possessive pronouns have a special job in sentences.

Use the possessive forms of personal pronouns to show ownership.

Some possessive pronouns come before nouns.

EXAMPLE: My tape recorder is at home.

Other possessive pronouns are used by themselves to show ownership. These pronouns do not come before nouns.

EXAMPLE: The white car is theirs.

THE POSSESSIVE PRONOUNS			
Used Before Nouns		**Used by Themselves**	
my	its	mine	its
your	our	yours	ours
his	their	his	theirs
her		hers	

Never use an apostrophe when writing a possessive pronoun.

INCORRECT: Their's is the best plan.

The notebook on the chair is her's.

CORRECT: Theirs is the best plan.

The notebook on the chair is hers.

A common error with possessive pronouns is to use an apostrophe after *it.* The possessive of *it* is *its. It's* means "it is."

CONTRACTION: I think it's a pine tree.

POSSESSIVE PRONOUN: Place the package on its side.

EXERCISE: Using Possessive Pronouns. Copy each sentence substituting a possessive pronoun for each blank.

EXAMPLE: This baseball is ______ .

This baseball is ours.

1. This briefcase is mine, but that briefcase is ______ .
2. ______ is the house with the green shutters.
3. ______ cousin is a wonderful athlete.
4. We gave the nursery school ______ picture books.
5. Barbara said that this scarf is ______ .
6. My soup is very hot. Is ______ ?
7. Please hand me ______ umbrella.
8. Have all the students in the class finished ______ reports?
9. The Nelsons borrowed our fan. ______ is broken.
10. Tommy said ______ mother was going to Ohio.
11. ______ father told me about the first trip to the moon.
12. Neil Armstrong and "Buzz" Aldrin landed ______ spacecraft.
13. ______ was an adventure of importance.
14. ______ trip was so successful that others have since followed.
15. Scientists in ______ country had never studied moon rocks.
16. The moon is ______ close neighbor.
17. ______ light comes from the sun, just as ours does.
18. ______ weight would be less on the moon than on the earth.
19. The moon's atmosphere is different from ______ .
20. Astronauts must carry ______ own supply of air.

DEVELOPING WRITING SKILLS: Using Possessive Pronouns in Sentences. Write a brief paragraph comparing your family to someone else's. Use at least five different possessive pronouns.

22.4 Using Different Pronoun Forms

In this chapter, three different forms of personal pronouns have been described: subject pronouns, objective pronouns, and possessive pronouns. These forms are called *cases.* Each case has different uses.

Use the cases of pronouns correctly.

Subject pronouns are said to be in the *nominative case.* Nominative case pronouns are used as subjects and as *predicate pronouns.* Predicate pronouns generally appear with some form of the linking verb *be.* They help identify the subjects of sentences.

PREDICATE PRONOUNS: The person in charge is she.

The culprit was I.

The other uses of each case of personal pronouns are more fully described in the first three sections of this chapter. The chart below summarizes the information contained in those sections.

THE THREE CASES OF PERSONAL PRONOUNS AND THEIR USES

Cases	Pronoun Forms	Uses
Nominative	I, you, he, she, it, we, they	Subject Predicate Pronoun
Objective	me, you, him, her, it, us, them	Direct Object Indirect Object Object of a Preposition
Possessive	my, mine, you, yours his, her, hers, its, our, ours, their, theirs	To Show Ownership

EXERCISE A: Identifying Different Pronoun Cases. Identify the case of each underlined personal pronoun.

EXAMPLE: He asked me to walk the dog.
nominative

1. They took a new route to school.
2. Daniel sent me a letter.
3. Can you come to my party?
4. Marilyn led them across the street.
5. The musician who will be playing is he.
6. The dancer hurt her leg.
7. It was they who presented the awards.
8. Our neighbor cuts the grass twice a week.
9. My mother read me an article from the evening newspaper.
10. Everyone went swimming except Kevin and him.

EXERCISE B: More Work with Pronoun Forms. Identify the case of each underlined personal pronoun.

1. He often draws cartoons.
2. The baby grasped her bottle.
3. They rehearsed the skits all morning.
4. Michelle sent us a greeting card.
5. The students who are going to Washington are they.
6. Gordon gave Nancy and her some flowers from his garden.
7. The person who will speak to us is she.
8. The auditorium is ours for the afternoon.
9. I have known Bert and him since we were in kindergarten.
10. The photographer showed them some cameras and lenses.

DEVELOPING WRITING SKILLS: Telling About Pronoun Cases. Write a paragraph explaining the uses of the nominative case. Include examples of each use.

Skills Review and Writing Workshop

Using Pronouns

CHECKING YOUR SKILLS

Choose the correct pronoun from the two in parentheses.

EXAMPLE Rosa and (she, her) read the autobiography of Artur Rubinstein.

she

1. His sisters and (him, he) played the piano.
2. Artur could listen to melodies and play one or more of (they, them) by ear.
3. An uncle recognized (his, his') special talent.
4. Of all the Rubinstein children, it was (he, him) who was a musical genius.
5. His work is preserved for (us, we) on tapes and records.
6. (His', His) was an active career as a concert pianist.
7. His wife inspired him; it was (she, her) who encouraged him to perfect his playing.
8. He made many recordings. These recordings made (he, him) more popular than ever.
9. The Rubinsteins became American citizens in 1946. (Their, They're) decision was made after World War II.
10. Does your record collection contain recordings by Rubinstein? (Ours, Our's) does.

USING USAGE SKILLS IN WRITING

Writing About Your Favorite Subject

Think about the subjects you study in school. Which one do you like best now? Did you always like it best? Write a paragraph about why you like that subject. If you enjoy two subjects equally well, mention them both.

Remember that sometimes you like things because you can do them well. But you may like doing something even though you can't do it well. Proofread. Check your pronouns carefully.

Chapter 23

Making Words Agree

Which of these sentences is correct: *The kittens are lively* or *The kittens is lively?* You probably picked the first sentence. This sentence is correct because the subject *(kittens)* and the verb *(are)* agree in number. Both the subject and the verb are plural.

The parts of a sentence must match up in several ways. One of these ways is that singular subjects are used with singular verbs and plural subjects are used with plural verbs. Another way that sentence parts match up is that pronouns must agree with the words they stand for or refer to.

This chapter gives more information about agreement between the parts of a sentence. You will learn about agreement of subjects and verbs, pronouns and verbs, and pronouns and the words they replace. You will also practice making sentences agree and writing original sentences that are correct and consistent. Finally, you will practice your skills by writing a composition with sentences that agree.

23.1 Subjects and Verbs

Subjects are either singular or plural. Singular subjects refer to one person, place, or thing. Plural subjects refer to more than one. Verbs, too, are either singular or plural. Singular subjects take singular verbs. Plural subjects take plural verbs.

Singular and Plural Subjects. Many subjects are nouns. Most singular nouns can be made plural by adding *-s* or *-es*. Some, however, like *woman,* form their plurals differently.

SINGULAR NOUNS: cup, telephone, tax, church, woman

PLURAL NOUNS: cups, telephones, taxes, churches, women

Singular and Plural Verbs. Present-tense verbs have both singular and plural forms. Third-person singular verbs end in *-s,* while plural verbs do not. This is just the opposite of nouns that form their plurals by adding *-s.*

The chart shows how an *-s* is added to the third person singular form of the verb *look.*

PRESENT TENSE VERB FORMS	
Singular	**Plural**
I look	we look
you look	you look
he, she, it looks	they look

Agreement. The subject and verb in a sentence must agree in number.

Use a singular subject with a singular verb.

Use a plural subject with a plural verb.

SINGULAR SUBJECT AND VERB: Terry wants a bicycle.

PLURAL SUBJECT AND VERB: They want a bicycle.

EXERCISE A: Making Subjects and Verbs Agree. For each sentence, write the verb that agrees with the subject.

EXAMPLE: Many animals (live, lives) in tropical forests.
live

1. Plants (grow, grows) thickest along the edges of tropical forests.
2. The tropical forest (remain, remains) warm and humid.
3. The trees (grow, grows) year round.
4. The branches (reaches, reach) over one hundred feet.
5. This level (is, are) called the canopy.
6. Orchids (hang, hangs) from the branches of trees.
7. Some forest animals (glides, glide) through the air from branch to branch.
8. A gibbon (swing, swings) through the treetops.
9. Many insects (live, lives) on rotting jungle wood.
10. Birds (flies, fly) around these forests during the day.

EXERCISE B: More Practice Making Subjects and Verbs Agree. Write the verb that agrees with the subject.

1. The elderly man (sit, sits) in the easy chair, talking to a friend.
2. The boys (watch, watches) the craftsman make a chair.
3. Katherine and Thomas (laugh, laughs) at the amusing story.
4. That successful author (plan, plans) to write another novel.
5. The artist (thinks, think) about the colors she will use.

DEVELOPING WRITING SKILLS: Writing Sentences with Subjects and Verbs That Agree. Write ten sentences about your neighborhood. Make sure the subjects and verbs agree.

23.2 Compound Subjects and Verbs

A *compound subject* is two or more subjects that share the same verb. They are connected by conjunctions such as *and, or,* or *nor.*

A number of rules can help you choose the right verb to use with a compound subject.

COMPOUND SUBJECTS
Robert and Jennifer draw well.
Tulips or daffodils bloom in this spot.
Neither snow nor hail is expected today.

When a compound subject is connected by *and,* the verb that follows is usually plural.

EXAMPLE: English and science are my favorite subjects.

There is an exception to this rule. If the parts of a compound subject are thought of as one person or thing, the subject is singular and takes a singular verb.

EXAMPLE: Bacon and eggs is my favorite breakfast.

When two singular subjects are joined by *or* or *nor,* use a singular verb. When two plural subjects are joined by *or* or *nor,* use a plural verb.

SINGULAR: A cat or a dog makes a good pet.

PLURAL: Neither children nor adults like to wait in lines.

When a compound subject is made up of one singular and one plural subject joined by *or* or *nor,* the verb agrees with the subject closer to it.

SINGULAR SUBJECT CLOSER: Neither the gloves nor the softball is in the closet.

PLURAL SUBJECT CLOSER: Neither the softball nor the gloves are in the closet.

EXERCISE A: Making Compound Subjects and Verbs Agree. Write the verb that agrees with the subject of each sentence.

EXAMPLE: Sam and Randy (is, are) examining the globe.
are

1. Land and water (is, are) drawn to scale on a globe.
2. On a globe or a map, an inch or a centimeter (stand, stands) for a much larger unit of measurement.
3. Neither these globes nor this map (show, shows) my street.
4. Valerie and Katy (measure, measures) distance on a globe.
5. Maps and globes (has, have) different uses.
6. Either the globe or the maps (belong, belongs) here.
7. Neither bridges nor airports (is, are) labeled on the map.
8. Bill or John (has, have) the map that shows products.
9. The atlas or a few globes (is, are) helpful to us.
10. The scientists or their assistants (use, uses) this map.

EXERCISE B: More Practice with Compound Subjects and Verbs. Write the verb that correctly completes each sentence.

1. Rob or Fred (plays, play) basketball after school.
2. The teacher or the students (explain, explains) the display to visitors.
3. Neither Grace nor Kirk (remember, remembers) the name.
4. A laboratory and an office (is, are) on the first floor.
5. Beef and broccoli (is, are) a popular Chinese dish.

DEVELOPING WRITING SKILLS: Writing Sentences with Compound Subjects. Write ten sentences about different people, places, or things. Begin each sentence with a compound subject. Make sure the compound subject and the verb agree.

23.3 Pronoun Subjects and Verbs

Indefinite pronouns refer to people, places, or things in a general way.

When an indefinite pronoun is the subject of a sentence, it must agree with the verb.

INDEFINITE PRONOUNS				
	Singular		**Plural**	**Singular or Plural**
anybody	everyone	nothing	both	all
anyone	everything	one	few	any
anything	much	other	many	more
each	neither	somebody	others	most
either	nobody	someone	several	none
everybody	no one	something		

Indefinite Pronouns That Are Always Singular. Indefinite pronouns that are always singular are used with singular verbs.

EXAMPLE: Everyone is ready.

Indefinite Pronouns That Are Always Plural. Indefinite pronouns that are always plural are used with plural verbs.

EXAMPLE: Both of my suitcases are in the closet.

Indefinite Pronouns That Are Either Singular or Plural. Some indefinite pronouns can be either singular or plural. To decide on the number, look for the noun that the pronoun refers to. If the noun is singular, the pronoun is singular. If the noun is plural, the pronoun is plural.

EXAMPLES: All of my money is gone.

All of these gifts are for you.

EXERCISE A: Making Pronoun Subjects and Verbs Agree. Write the verb that agrees with the subject.

EXAMPLE: Both of my parents (practice, practices) law.
practice

1. All of our courts (is, are) part of our government.
2. Many of the tax cases (goes, go) to a tax court.
3. Few of the cases (get, gets) to the Supreme Court.
4. Everything usually (begins, begin) in a lower court.
5. Everybody on the Supreme Court (vote, votes) on the cases to review.
6. One of the members (serves, serve) as Chief Justice.
7. Each of the Justices (has, have) an office and a staff.
8. No one (expect, expects) every case to be reviewed.
9. One of the requirements for a review (is, are) time.
10. Anybody without money (apply, applies) as a poor person.

EXERCISE B: More Work with Pronoun Subjects and Verbs. Write the form of the verb that agrees with the subject.

1. Someone from the office (call, calls) every day.
2. Either of the girls (deliver, delivers) the newspaper.
3. Each of the men (catch, catches) fish in the lake.
4. Somebody (write, writes) a daily progress report.
5. Others (admire, admires) his courage.
6. Nobody (want, wants) to travel so far in one day.
7. Most of the viewers (admire, admires) the magician.
8. Neither of the pieces (belong, belongs) to this game.
9. Anything about birds (interest, interests) me.
10. Much of the collection (look, looks) new.

DEVELOPING WRITING SKILLS: Writing Sentences with Pronoun Subjects and Verbs. Use each of the following indefinite pronouns as the subject of a sentence: most, others, nothing, everyone, one, other, several, most, few, and much.

23.4 Pronouns and Antecedents

An *antecedent* is the word that a pronoun stands for.

Use a singular pronoun with a singular antecedent.

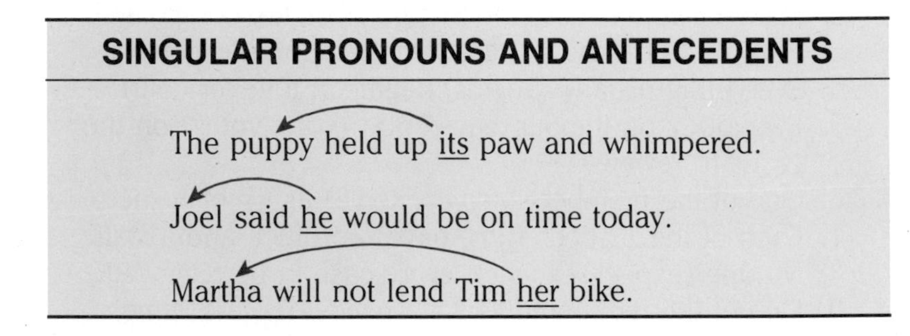

SINGULAR PRONOUNS AND ANTECEDENTS

The puppy held up its paw and whimpered.

Joel said he would be on time today.

Martha will not lend Tim her bike.

Use a plural pronoun with a plural antecedent.

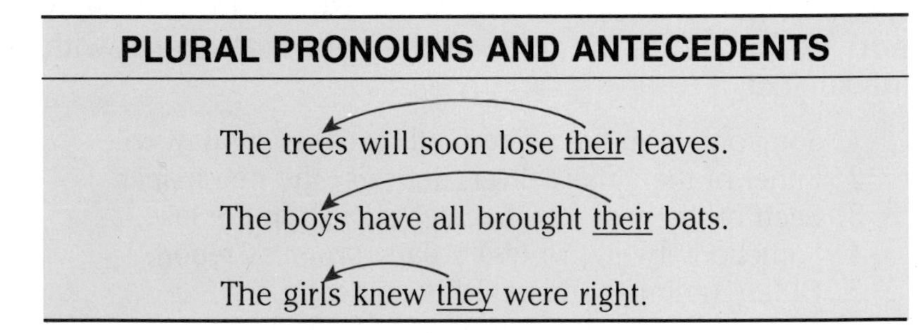

PLURAL PRONOUNS AND ANTECEDENTS

The trees will soon lose their leaves.

The boys have all brought their bats.

The girls knew they were right.

Two special rules are used for compound antecedents.

Use a singular pronoun with two or more singular antecedents joined by *or* or *nor.*

EXAMPLE: Andrew or Keith gives his report today.

Use a plural pronoun with two or more singular antecedents joined by *and.*

EXAMPLE: Joyce and Robert showed their father the drawing.

EXERCISE A: Making Pronouns and Antecedents Agree. Copy each sentence, filling in the blank with a pronoun that agrees with its antecedent.

EXAMPLE: Jake trained ______ dog to do tricks.
Jake trained his dog to do tricks.

1. The astronomers said that ______ were studying storms on Mars.
2. My coat is clean, but Julie must take ______ coat to the cleaners.
3. Rachel and Donald told about ______ trip to the museum.
4. The woman related ______ story to the police.
5. Neither Fred nor Anthony brought ______ baseball bat.
6. Joan and Linda started ______ science project.
7. Mary always leaves ______ umbrella in the hallway.
8. Either Paul or Claude takes ______ turn next.
9. When Bill and Debbie play tennis, ______ use lightweight rackets.
10. Either Kenneth or Alan brought ______ camera.

EXERCISE B: More Work with Pronouns and Antecedents. Copy each sentence, filling in the blank with a pronoun that agrees with its antecedent.

1. Abby asked ______ father if she could keep the hamster.
2. Did Jed and Ethan find ______ pet gerbil?
3. Either Maria or Janet will give ______ recital today.
4. The boy still remembers when he got ______ dog.
5. Neither Sue Jones nor Brenda Smith takes ______ cat outside.

DEVELOPING WRITING SKILLS: Using Pronouns and Antecedents in Sentences. Write ten sentences about famous people. Use a pronoun and an antecedent in each sentence.

Skills Review and Writing Workshop

Making Words Agree

CHECKING YOUR SKILLS

Copy each sentence below, choosing the correct verb or pronoun from the choice in parentheses.

EXAMPLE: Everyone in the relay race (stand, stands) behind this line.

Everyone in the relay race stands behind this line.

1. The ambassador (travel, travels) to several countries.
2. Either James or Chris (feed, feeds) the animals.
3. A robin or a cardinal (sing, sings) outside my window.
4. France and Holland (is, are) interesting countries.
5. The chart (show, shows) the population growth of the United States over the past century.
6. Either Ellen or Yvonne will perform (their, her) gymnastic routine.
7. Both of the boys (build, builds) model airplanes.
8. Neither the roses nor the apple tree (blooms, bloom) this early in the spring.
9. Most of my friends (ride, rides) horses.
10. Neither Tom nor Dave can remember (his, their) lines.

USING USAGE SKILLS IN WRITING

Writing History

The coins you have in your pocket may be older than you are. Make up a short history of one of those coins. Imagine at least two people who had the coin before you. How did they get it? Did they save it for a while or did they spend it right away? What did they buy? How did buying that object change their lives? Use your imagination.

Proofread to see that all subjects and verbs, and all pronouns and antecedents, agree.

Chapter 24

Using Adjectives and Adverbs

Many of the choices you make are probably made after comparing one thing with another. For example, you may select one apple because it looks riper than another. You may request a particular time for a meeting because it is more convenient than another time. Or you may buy a particular radio because it has the best sound of all the radios you have played. In each of these cases, one item is compared with one or more other items.

Adjectives have different forms for making comparisons. For instance, one apple looks *ripe;* another looks *riper;* and a third looks the *ripest* of all.

Adverbs, too, have forms for making comparisons. For instance, one person swims *fast;* another swims *faster;* and a third swims the *fastest* of all.

This chapter tells more about using adjectives and adverbs to compare. You will learn about the three degrees of comparison—the positive, the comparative, and the superlative. In addition, there are exercises to help you practice using these forms.

24.1 Using Adjectives to Compare

Adjectives are often used to compare people, places, or things. The form of the adjective to use depends on the kind of comparison.

There are three degrees of comparison—the positive, the comparative, and the superlative.

POSITIVE: This room is large.

I am short.

COMPARATIVE: This room is larger than the bedroom.

I am shorter than Rita.

SUPERLATIVE: This is the largest room in the house.

I am the shortest person in my family.

The *positive degree* is used when one noun or pronoun is described. Only one item is involved. The *comparative degree* is used when two items are being compared. The *superlative degree* is used when three or more items are being compared.

Most one- and two-syllable adjectives form the comparative by adding *-er* and the superlative by adding *-est.*

DEGREES OF COMPARISON FORMED BY ADDING *-ER* AND *-EST*		
Positive	**Comparative**	**Superlative**
funny	funnier	funniest
great	greater	greatest
heavy	heavier	heaviest
loud	louder	loudest

Notice that adjectives that end in *y* (such as *funny* and *heavy* often change the *y* to *i* before adding *-er* or *-est.*

EXERCISE A: Forming the Degree of Comparison of One- and Two-Syllable Adjectives. Make a chart showing the positive, comparative, and superlative forms of each adjective listed below.

EXAMPLE: thick

Positive	Comparative	Superlative
thick	thicker	thickest

1. kind
2. mean
3. rich
4. shiny
5. cloudy
6. white
7. tall
8. big
9. young
10. wild
11. strong
12. old
13. soft
14. plain
15. pretty
16. bright
17. sweet
18. cold
19. smooth
20. sad

EXERCISE B: More Work with Degrees of Comparison of One- and Two-Syllable Adjectives. Make a chart showing the positive, comparative, and superlative forms of each adjective listed below.

1. high
2. angry
3. slow
4. sharp
5. small
6. new
7. hard
8. nice
9. healthy
10. dull

DEVELOPING WRITING SKILLS: Using Adjectives to Compare. Write a brief paragraph in which you compare two or three real or imaginary products. For example, you could compare two kinds of computer games or two breakfast cereals. Use at least five adjectives in their comparative or superlative forms. Underline each adjective you use.

24.2 Using Adjectives with *More* and *Most*

Besides adding *-er* and *-est* to adjectives, there is another way adjectives change to show comparison.

***More* and *most* can be used to form the comparative and superlative degrees of many adjectives.**

Although short adjectives tend to use *-er* and *-est,* many use *more* and *most*. Some use only *more* and *most.*

***More* and *most* can be used with many one- and two-syllable adjectives.**

EXAMPLE: This book is more moving than that one.

With some adjectives you can use either *-er* and *-est* or *more* and *most* to form the comparative and superlative degrees. With other adjectives, adding either *-er* or *-est* produces an awkward-sounding word. When you are not sure of which form to use, try *-er* or *-est.* Say the word aloud. If it sounds awkward use *more* or *most* instead.

Adjectives with three or more syllables use *more* or *most* to form the comparative and superlative degrees.

EXAMPLES: Your magazine is more interesting than mine.
His scheme is the most ingenious of all.

SOME ADJECTIVES REQUIRING *MORE* AND *MOST*

Positive	Comparative	Superlative
comfortable	more comfortable	most comfortable
expensive	more expensive	most expensive
generous	more generous	most generous
terrible	more terrible	most terrible

EXERCISE A: Using Adjectives with *More* and *Most*. Use *more* and *most* to form the comparative or superlative form of each adjective shown in parentheses.

EXAMPLE: This trip was (enjoyable) than the last one.
This trip was more enjoyable than the last one.

1. From there we had the (magnificent) view of all.
2. This hotel is (luxurious) than the new one.
3. Sue bought furniture that is (modern) than ours.
4. Angela's solution is the (sensible) one of all.
5. This assignment is the (difficult) one so far.
6. She is the (responsible) baby sitter I know.
7. This is the (interesting) film I have ever seen.
8. A blue sofa would be (attractive) than a gray one.
9. His paintings are (colorful) than hers.
10. This is the (thoughtful) report in the class.

EXERCISE B: More Practice Using Adjectives with *More* and *Most*. Follow the directions in Exercise A.

1. Our new buses are (comfortable) than our older ones.
2. This is the (exciting) building in town.
3. The book describes the (incredible) events of our time.
4. Who is the (famous) scientist—Franklin or Einstein?
5. That was the (outrageous) story I have ever heard.
6. Peter is (enthusiastic) about skateboarding than I am.
7. Margaret's arguments are (convincing) than Jack's.
8. Last Thanksgiving was the (eventful) holiday I remember.
9. The almond cake is their (delicious) dessert.
10. This magazine is (interesting) than that one.

DEVELOPING WRITING SKILLS: Using Adjectives with *More* and *Most*. Write five sentences with adjectives in the comparative degree using *more* and five with adjectives in the superlative degree using *most.*

24.3 Using Adverbs to Compare

Adverbs also have three degrees of comparison.

POSITIVE: Bob tries hard.

COMPARATIVE: Bob tries harder than Marty.

SUPERLATIVE: Bob tries the hardest of all.

The positive degree is used to describe only one action. The comparative degree is used when two actions are being compared. The superlative degree is used when three or more actions are being compared.

Most adverbs of one-syllable form the comparative by adding *-er* and the superlative by adding *-est.*

The chart below shows a number of these adverbs.

DEGREES OF COMPARISON FORMED BY ADDING *-ER* OR *-EST*		
Positive	**Comparative**	**Superlative**
high late	higher later	highest latest
fast soon	faster sooner	fastest soonest

Most adverbs of two or more syllables, especially those ending in *-ly,* use *more* to form the comparative and *most* to form the superlative.

DEGREES OF COMPARISON FORMED BY ADDING *MORE* OR *MOST*		
Positive	**Comparative**	**Superlative**
rapidly	more rapidly	most rapidly
clearly	more clearly	most clearly
confidently	more confidently	most confidently

EXERCISE A: Forming the Comparative and Superlative Degrees of Adverbs. Make a chart showing the positive, comparative, and superlative degree of each adverb listed below. Add *-er* or *-est* to adverbs whenever possible. When necessary, use the words *more* and *most.*

EXAMPLE: fast

Positive	Comparative	Superlative
fast	faster	fastest
politely	more politely	most politely

1. plainly
2. low
3. safely
4. recently
5. quickly
6. deep
7. nearly
8. lively
9. hastily
10. definitely

EXERCISE B: More Work with the Comparative and Superlative Degrees of Adverbs. Make a chart showing the positive, comparative, and superlative degree of each adverb listed below. Follow the advice given in Exercise A regarding the use of *-er* or *-est.*

1. softly
2. silently
3. long
4. briefly
5. suddenly
6. hard
7. firmly
8. short
9. carefully
10. distantly

DEVELOPING WRITING SKILLS: Using Adverbs to Compare Actions. Write a brief paragraph describing how three people perform the same activity. For example, you could describe how people speak, play a game, cook, or work on a project. The people you describe can be real or imaginary. In your paragraph, use at least five adverbs in their comparative or superlative forms. Underline each adverb.

Skills Review and Writing Workshop

Using Adjectives and Adverbs

CHECKING YOUR SKILLS

Copy each sentence below, using the form of the modifier indicated in parentheses.

EXAMPLE: The hurricane winds became (weak—comparative).

The hurricane winds became weaker.

1. A hurricane covers a (large—comparative) area than a tornado.
2. The (calm—superlative) part is called the "eye."
3. The (hard—superlative) rains occur around the eye.
4. Winds move (rapidly—superlative) around the eye.
5. Hurricane winds can move (fast—comparative) than 200 miles an hour.
6. Water can be (dangerous—comparative) than these winds.
7. Many of our (interesting—superlative) views of hurricanes are from satellite photographs.
8. A hurricane advances (slowly—comparative) than it swirls.
9. One of the (terrible—superlative) hurricanes occurred in Galveston, Texas, in 1900.
10. The (urgent—superlative) job after the storm was to build shelters.

USING USAGE SKILLS IN WRITING

Writing a Comparison

Write a paragraph comparing two people you like very much. Describe the way they look, talk, and move, even the way they dress. Think about the way they are when they are with you. Are they funny? Are they helpful? Ask yourself why you like them and why you like to be with them.

Check your work carefully. Have you used adjectives and adverbs effectively and correctly?

Working with Troublesome Modifiers

You probably use most adjectives and adverbs with little difficulty. Using modifiers is important because they add detail to speaking and writing. They help make communication clear. For example, if you play the piano, do you play *well* or *badly?* It is the modifier that gives you the answer.

Some frequently used modifiers can be troublesome. For instance, is it correct to say *I play bad* or *I play badly?* (In this case, the answer is *I play badly. Badly* is an adverb, and an adverb is needed to modify the verb *play.*)

To understand troublesome modifiers, you must learn which word in each pair is an adjective and which word is an adverb. Then when a sentence requires either an adjective or an adverb, you will know which word to use.

This chapter tells about two pairs of troublesome modifiers. First, the modifiers *bad* and *badly* are explained. Then the modifiers *good* and *well* are explained. The exercises in this chapter will give you practice using all of these modifiers

25.1 Using *Bad* and *Badly*

You will not confuse *bad* and *badly* if you remember that one is an adjective and that the other one is an adverb.

***Bad* is an adjective. It is used with linking verbs.**

The three examples in the following chart show bad used correctly.

BAD WITH LINKING VERBS

LV
My TV reception is bad.

LV
The latest news sounds especially bad.

LV
That new lavender dress looks very bad on you.

In each of the sentences above, the adjective *bad* follows a linking verb and describes the subject of the sentence. Other linking verbs that *bad* may follow are *appear, become, feel, grow, remain, seem, smell, stay, taste,* and *turn.*

***Badly* is an adverb. It is used with action verbs.**

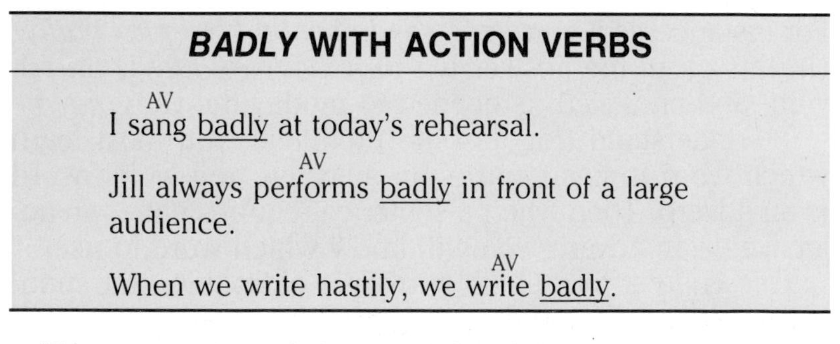
BADLY WITH ACTION VERBS

AV
I sang badly at today's rehearsal.

AV
Jill always performs badly in front of a large audience.

AV
When we write hastily, we write badly.

To summarize, if the modifier follows a linking verb and describes the subject, use *bad.* If the modifier follows an action verb and describes it, use *badly.*

EXERCISE A: Using *Bad* and *Badly*. Write the correct modifier—*bad* or *badly*—for the verb in each sentence below.

EXAMPLE: The report on the radio sounded (bad, badly).
bad

1. This new style of baggy pants looks (bad, badly) on me.
2. Paul draws portraits (bad, badly).
3. The magician performed (bad, badly).
4. The new perfume smells (bad, badly) to me.
5. This detergent cleans (bad, badly).
6. This fabric wrinkles (bad, badly).
7. My brother cooks (bad, badly).
8. My new blueberry dessert creation tastes (bad, badly).
9. After ten days the cream turned (bad, badly).
10. In spite of her lessons, Mary plays (bad, badly).

EXERCISE B: More Practice Using *Bad* and *Badly*. Write the modifier that correctly fits each verb.

1. During his illness, Henry looked (bad, badly).
2. The plumber repaired the sink (bad, badly).
3. In the afternoon the weather turned (bad, badly).
4. I felt (bad, badly) when I forgot your birthday.
5. Because she hurried, she wrote (bad, badly).
6. We had problems because we planned the trip (bad, badly).
7. The new method of farming works (bad, badly).
8. The visibility at the airport remained (bad, badly).
9. This painting looks (bad, badly) in this spot.
10. These candles flicker and smoke (bad, badly).

DEVELOPING WRITING SKILLS: Using *Bad* and *Badly* in Sentences. Write five sentences using *bad* with various linking verbs. Then write five sentences using *badly* with action verbs.

25.2 Using *Good* and *Well*

Good and *well* are used differently in sentences. *Good* is always an adjective, but *well* can be either an adjective or an adverb. To decide which word to use, you must think about the meaning of the sentence and how the word is being used.

***Good* is an adjective. It is used with linking verbs.**

***GOOD* WITH LINKING VERBS**
The soft wool feels (LV) good.
That pizza smells (LV) good.
All of his mystery novels have been (LV) good.

***Well* can be an adverb or an adjective. When *well* is an adverb, it is used with an action verb.**

WELL AS AN ADVERB: Your sister sings (AV) well.

The outfielders have been hitting (AV) well.

Jennifer speaks (AV) Spanish well.

When *well* is an adjective, it is used with a linking verb and usually refers to a person's health.

WELL AS AN ADJECTIVE: You look (LV) well now that your cold is gone.

My parents both are feeling (LV) well.

This morning I felt (LV) well enough to go for a walk.

EXERCISE A: Using *Good* and *Well.* Write the correct modifier—*good* or *well*—for the verb in each sentence below.

EXAMPLE: Our first baseman hits (good, well).
well

1. During practice Arlene skated (good, well).
2. Your poster looks (good, well) here.
3. After a summer at the lake, I will swim (good, well).
4. Tony is very talented; he sings (good, well).
5. The sandwiches here taste (good, well).
6. Although it is old, this table looks (good, well).
7. Anna had been sick but now seems (good, well).
8. All winter he stayed (good, well).
9. The rolls you are baking smell (good, well).
10. When Peter plays the violin, it sounds (good, well).

EXERCISE B: More Work with Using *Good* and *Well.* Write the correct modifier—*good* or *well*—for the verb in each sentence below.

1. We searched the room (good, well).
2. During the show, the children listened (good, well).
3. These flowers smell (good, well).
4. This cheese tastes (good, well) to me.
5. When he became (good, well), he returned to work.
6. This wood burns (good, well) in our fireplace.
7. As a campsite, this spot looks (good, well).
8. The breezes feel (good, well) after our day in the sun.
9. Hats look (good, well) on you.
10. Those fresh muffins smell (good, well).

DEVELOPING WRITING SKILLS: Using *Good* and *Well* in Sentences. Write five sentences using *good* and five sentences using *well.*

Skills Review and Writing Workshop

Working with Troublesome Modifiers

CHECKING YOUR SKILLS

In many of the sentences below, the modifiers *bad, badly, good,* and *well* are used incorrectly. Rewrite each incorrect sentence so that the troublesome modifier is used correctly. If the sentence is correct, just write the word *correct*.

EXAMPLE: That young boy paints good.
That young boy paints well.

1. When I am tired, I sing bad.
2. I can see the fireworks good from here.
3. This unusual combination of foods tastes badly.
4. Your weekend plans sound good.
5. This electric saw cuts good.

USING USAGE SKILLS IN WRITING

Writing a Character Reference

At the end of the last chapter you wrote a comparison of two people you like. Imagine that one of those people has been interviewed for a job as a teacher. Now he or she has asked you to write a character reference. A character reference explains why you think someone should get a particular job.

Before you write, ask yourself what qualities the person has that would make him or her a good teacher. Is the person intelligent? Is he or she good at explaining things? Does he or she like children? Is the person reliable so you know he or she would come to school every day? When you write the character reference, you might also include information about how long you have known the person, since that would make you a good judge of his or her abilities. Be sure your character reference is neat and clearly organized. Proofread to see that all modifiers have been used correctly.

Solving Special Problems

A sentence such as *I am more happier now* is incorrect. What is wrong with it? It contains two forms that compare—*more* and *happier.* Not only is it unnecessary to use two forms of comparison in a sentence, it is also incorrect. A double comparison is not acceptable in standard speech or writing.

The sentence *We have not told nobody the news* contains another usage problem. This sentence also has two forms that do the same job—the two negative words, *not* and *nobody.* In a negative statement, only one negative word is needed. Double negatives are not acceptable in standard English.

This chapter tells more about these two special usage problems—double comparisons and double negatives. You will find an explanation of each of these problems. You will also find exercises that will give you practice correcting the problems. Finally, you will be asked to write a composition applying what you have learned in this chapter.

26.1 Avoiding Double Comparisons

Adjectives and adverbs are often used to compare people, places, or things. There are two basic methods for making this kind of comparison. Both of these methods are correct.

To form the comparative degree, use either the suffix *-er* or the word *more.* Do not use both.

It is incorrect to use both methods of comparison together. This error is called a *double comparison.*

INCORRECT: Asia is more larger than North America.

Stan looks more happier today than yesterday.

It is more stormier today than Friday.

Karen speaks more louder than Tanya.

CORRECT: Asia is larger than North America.

Stan looks happier today than yesterday.

It is more stormy today than Friday.

Karen speaks louder than Tanya.

There are also two basic methods of comparing three or more people, places, or things.

To form the superlative degree, use either the suffix *-est* or the word *most.* Do not use both.

Double comparisons are always incorrect.

INCORRECT: This is the most simplest solution.

Mr. Finch is the most kindest man I know.

Ted is the most fastest runner.

She writes the most longest letters.

CORRECT: This is the most simple solution.

Mr. Finch is the kindest man I know.

Ted is the fastest runner.

She writes the longest letters.

EXERCISE A: Avoiding Double Comparisons. Most of the sentences below contain double comparisons. Rewrite these sentences correctly. Write *correct* if there are no errors.

EXAMPLE: This pony is more healthier than that one.
This pony is healthier than that one.

1. The planet Venus is more closer to us than Neptune is.
2. Here is our most newest model.
3. Of all these gems, this is the most rarest.
4. This car uses gasoline the most efficiently.
5. We heard the most oddest sound before the big storm hit.
6. My dog is more smaller than yours.
7. We began our work earlier than usual.
8. Robert calculates more faster than Alan.
9. The more older model still runs well.
10. Mahogany logs burn longer than pine.

EXERCISE B: More Practice Correcting Double Comparisons. Rewrite correctly each sentence that contains a double comparison. Write *correct* if there are no errors.

1. Now that the summer tourist crowd is gone it is more quieter.
2. The vegetables sold at the stand here are the most freshest.
3. He smiled and acted more friendlier than before.
4. Betty worked the most hardest during those two weeks.
5. I awoke more later than my brother.

DEVELOPING WRITING SKILLS: Using Comparisons in Sentences. Write five sentences comparing two objects and five sentences comparing three objects. Use the comparative and superlative degrees.

26.2 Avoiding Double Negatives

Negative words are words such as *not, no,* and *never.* They deny or say *no*. Although it was once considered correct to use two or more of these negative words in one statement, that is no longer true. Today a *double negative* is considered an error.

A statement needs only one negative word to give it a negative meaning.

Many different words can signal a negative meaning. The chart below lists a number of negative words as well as the contraction *n't,* which stands for *not.*

NEGATIVE WORDS				
never	nobody	no one	not	nowhere
no	none	nor	nothing	n't

To correct a statement with a *double negative,* make one of the negative words positive.

CORRECTING DOUBLE NEGATIVES	
Double Negative	**Corrected Sentence**
She would not speak to nobody.	She would not speak to anybody. She would speak to nobody
John hasn't touched none of his dinner.	John hasn't touched any of his dinner. John has touched none of his dinner.
I never go nowhere on Sunday afternoons.	I never go anywhere on Sunday afternoons. I go nowhere on Sunday afternoons.

EXERCISE A: Correcting Sentences with Double Negatives. Rewrite each sentence to correct the double negative.

EXAMPLE: We haven't tried none of these programs.
We haven't tried any of these programs.

1. We hadn't never realized that Theodore wrote so well.
2. I can't never remember that incident.
3. Ann hasn't said nothing about her new job.
4. This ice cream isn't sold nowhere else.
5. There isn't room nowhere for this table.
6. They aren't taking none of these rumors seriously.
7. I wouldn't never make that journey alone.
8. The court hasn't heard no testimony yet.
9. The storyteller didn't tell none of the old legends.
10. I haven't told nobody about your discovery.

EXERCISE B: More Practice Correcting Double Negatives. Rewrite each sentence below to correct the double negative.

1. The visitors don't want no publicity.
2. The end isn't nowhere in sight.
3. Our newspaper hasn't printed nothing about the event.
4. We can't agree on no location for the meeting.
5. The committee didn't select nobody as chairperson.
6. They aren't giving none of the popcorn to us.
7. Marilyn doesn't study no foreign language.
8. We never saw nobody enter the house.
9. The children didn't hear nothing about the disaster.
10. He never had no formal education.

DEVELOPING WRITING SKILLS: Using Negative Words in Sentences. Write ten sentences using negative words. Avoid double negatives.

Skills Review and Writing Workshop

Solving Special Problems

CHECKING YOUR SKILLS

Each sentence below contains either a double comparison or a double negative. Rewrite each sentence correctly.

EXAMPLE: I want a more smaller dog than that one.
I want a smaller dog than that one.

1. Grandfather hasn't never arrived before noon.
2. Virginia never complains about nothing.
3. The most nearest post office is a mile away.
4. Your cousins haven't never met my parents.
5. Susan finished more sooner than you did.
6. Jacqueline is the most strongest girl in our class.
7. We haven't seen none of her drawings yet.
8. Cleo didn't tell nobody she was leaving.
9. This is the most hardest jigsaw puzzle I ever completed.
10. Please push the chairs more closer together.

USING USAGE SKILLS IN WRITING

Writing a Character Reference for Yourself

You have always wanted to be president of your club. Now that may be possible. But first you have to win an election. You are running against a fellow who is smart and popular. Also, he wants to win as much as you do. So you have decided to write an article in the club newspaper explaining why everyone should vote for you.

Before you write, decide what you want to tell people about yourself that will convince them to vote for you. If you think you have an advantage over your opponent in some area, then include that in your piece. Remember, you want to present the strongest possible argument. Proofread your piece carefully. Have you avoided double comparisons and double negatives?

UNIT III

Mechanics

Chapter 27

Using Capital Letters

Several words are capitalized in the sentence *During the winter Nancy, Marie, Hal, and I skate on Crystal Lake and Lake Charles.* Some of these words name specific people. Other words name specific places. The capital letters indicate that these are important words in the sentence.

Another use of capital letters is to signal the beginning of a sentence. When you have several sentences following one another in a paragraph, capital letters can help you separate sentences. They help to indicate when you can pause in your thinking and reading to sort out ideas.

Capital letters have a number of different uses. Besides indicating the beginning of sentences and the names of specific people and places, capital letters are used to point out specific things. These things can be holidays like Mother's Day or documents like the Constitution. Capital letters are also used to show the specific titles of people, such as Governor Cuomo, or of things, such as the book *Julie of the Wolves.* Finally, capital letters are used in parts of letters. This chapter gives information about each of these uses of capital letters.

27.1 Capitals for Sentences and the Word *I*

One important use of capital letters is to indicate the beginning of a sentence.

Always capitalize the first word of a sentence.

EXAMPLE: He visited the historical landmark.

Some sentences include a person's exact words. These words are called a *direct quotation.*

Capitalize the first word of a direct quotation when it is used as part of a larger sentence.

EXAMPLES: He said, "Here is my coin collection."
"Hawaii," she said, "is made up of islands."

When a quotation is interrupted, the last part of the quotation is not capitalized. In the last example above, the words *she said* interrupt the direct quotation "Hawaii is made up of islands." The word *is,* in the second part of this quotation, is not capitalized.

***I* is always capitalized.**

EXAMPLE: The librarian knows I am interested in astronomy.

EXAMPLES OF CAPITALS FOR SENTENCES AND *I*
Nancy enjoys science-fiction novels and stories. (Capitalize the first word of a sentence.)
Ed asked, "Who brought the bats?" (Capitalize the first word of a direct quotation within a larger sentence.)
I know I can learn to ski well if I practice enough. (I is always capitalized.)

EXERCISE A: Supplying Capital Letters. Rewrite each sentence below using capital letters when necessary.

EXAMPLE: the two rival teams were playing hockey.
The two rival teams were playing hockey.

1. all twelve hockey players were skating briskly early in the morning.
2. there was one player i began to watch closely.
3. i said to my dad, "watch number 27."
4. he was swinging at the puck.
5. my dad asked, "do you think he will score?"
6. "yes," i replied, "i do."
7. instead, the player passed the puck to a teammate.
8. i yelled, "that was a great pass!"
9. i saw the forward shoot the puck into the net.
10. he scored a goal.

EXERCISE B: More Work with Capital Letters. Rewrite each sentence below using capital letters when necessary.

1. a few people were waiting at the bus stop.
2. the teacher asked, "did your experiment work?"
3. i decided i should revise my story.
4. answer the question.
5. i remember the first day i went to school.
6. they asked her to show how to use the machine.
7. i think i can finish this book by tomorrow.
8. Tim said, "this new chair is very comfortable."
9. the cabin attendant announced, "fasten your seatbelts."
10. our science laboratory is an interesting place.

DEVELOPING WRITING SKILLS: Using Capital Letters Correctly. Write ten sentences about a place you know well. Make sure each sentence begins with a capital letter and that the word *I* is always capitalized.

27.2 Capitals for Names of People and Places

A capital letter indicates the name of a specific person (Helen Keller) or a specific place (Kansas City).

Capitalize the name of a specific person.

EXAMPLES: Pearl Buck, H. G. Wells

Notice that a person's initials are capitalized.

The names of specific places also begin with capital letters.

Capitalize the name of a specific place.

The chart shows some of the kinds of specific places that take capitals.

CAPITALS FOR SPECIFIC PLACES	
Streets	Warren Street, Carlton Avenue, Bleecker Street
Cities	Baltimore, London, Memphis, Tokyo
States	Arizona, Florida, Hawaii, Idaho
Nations	Italy, Canada, France, Peru
Continents	North America, Asia, Africa, Antarctica
Deserts	the Sahara Desert, the Negev Desert
Mountains	Mount Everest, the Rocky Mountains
Regions	the Great Plains, the Appalachian Highlands
Islands	the Canary Islands, the Fiji Islands
Rivers	the Mississippi River, the Amazon River
Lakes	Lake Michigan, Great Salt Lake, Lake Erie
Bays	Hudson Bay, Baffin Bay, Biscayne Bay
Seas	the Black Sea, the Mediterranean Sea, the North Sea
Oceans	the Atlantic Ocean, the Arctic Ocean

EXERCISE: Using Capitals for Names of People and Places. Rewrite each sentence, using capital letters when needed.

EXAMPLES: gerald r. ford was born in omaha, nebraska.
Gerald R. Ford was born in Omaha, Nebraska.

1. madeline spencer spent a month in greece last summer.
2. great bear lake is located in canada.
3. The snake river is over 1,000 miles long.
4. Dr. John s. Knickerbocker's office is at the end of main street.
5. In 1519 hernando cortés discovered mexico.
6. mount kilimanjaro is in africa.
7. victoria c. woodhull ran for President in 1872.
8. The book Antoinette has been reading is by j. r. r. tolkien.
9. lake george is a popular vacation spot.
10. stan laurel and oliver hardy made comic films.
11. The rocky mountains stretch across much of north america.
12. lake erie is more than 9,000 miles long.
13. west virginia and kentucky have large deposits of coal.
14. The second largest river in europe is the danube.
15. atlanta and denver are capital cities.
16. The largest lake in africa is lake victoria.
17. levi hutchins invented the alarm clock.
18. james l. plimpton designed the first roller skates.
19. harriet tubman helped slaves escape to freedom.
20. charles lindbergh was the first person to fly solo across the atlantic.

DEVELOPING WRITING SKILLS: Using the Names of People and Places in Sentences. Write ten sentences, using the name of a specific person or place in each sentence.

27.3 Capitals for Names of Specific Things

In addition to capitalizing the names of specific persons and places, you should also capitalize the names of specific things.

Capitalize the names of specific things.

The chart below lists a number of categories of specific things.

CAPITALS FOR SPECIFIC THINGS	
Historical Periods and Events	the Renaissance, the Battle of Lexington
Historical Documents	the Constitution
Days and Months	Monday, December
Holidays	Memorial Day, Arbor Day
Organizations and Schools	the Antique Airplane Club, Jamaica High School
Government Bodies	the Senate, Congress
Political Parties	the Democratic Party
Races	Caucasian, Mongoloid
Nationalities and Languages	Colombian, Canadian
Monuments and Memorials	the Washington Monument, the Lincoln Memorial
Buildings	the World Trade Center
Religious Faiths	Christianity, Judaism, Islam, Hinduism
Awards	the Nobel Prize
Air and Sea Craft	the China Clipper, Old Ironsides

Space and Land Craft	Apollo 2, the Metroliner

Unlike other specific times, the names of the seasons of the year are not capitalized. Write *spring, summer, fall* (or *autumn*), and *winter.*

EXERCISE: Using Capitals for the Names of Specific Things. List each specific thing requiring capitals in the sentences below. Add the necessary capital letters.

EXAMPLES: On july 4, 1776, congress accepted the declaration of independence.

July, Congress, Declaration of Independence

1. Our class is learning about the constitution.
2. The lions club will sponsor a picnic next saturday.
3. the mayas and the aztecs lived in mexico.
4. Fernando speaks english, spanish, and italian.
5. The sears tower in chicago, illinois, is 1,450 feet high.
6. Pearl Buck won the nobel prize.
7. washington's birthday is celebrated in february.
8. Rae sailed along the coast of maine on the mattie.
9. we visited carpenter's hall and independence hall.
10. The maplewood school is open monday through saturday.
11. The candidates from the republican party will speak here on tuesday.
12. The golden kite award was presented to M. E. Kerr.
13. skylab 2 gave american astronauts a chance to spend more time in space than ever before.
14. The first sunday after labor day is grandparent's day.
15. The treaty of versailles was rejected by the senate.

DEVELOPING WRITING SKILLS: Using Names of Specific Things in Sentences. Write ten sentences. In each sentence, include the name of a specific thing from the following categories: days, months, holidays, school clubs, nationalities, languages, religious faiths, monuments, awards, space and land craft. Capitalize that item.

27.4 Capitals for Titles of People

Whether or not a title of a person is capitalized often depends on how it is used in a sentence.

Capitalize a social or professional title before a person's name or in direct address.

BEFORE A NAME: Today, Governor Brown spoke about taxes.

DIRECT ADDRESS: Tell us, Governor, about the new program.

SOME OTHER SOCIAL AND PROFESSIONAL TITLES	
Social	Sir, Mister, Miss, Madame, Mesdames
Professional	Congresswoman, Senator, Governor, Mayor, Secretary of the Treasury, Attorney General, Professor, Doctor, Attorney, Judge, Reverend, Father, Rabbi, Bishop, Sister, Private, Lieutenant, Sergeant, Corporal

Capitalize a title showing a family relationship when it is used before a person's name or when it is used in direct address.

BEFORE A NAME: I sent an invitation to Aunt Alexandra.

DIRECT ADDRESS: I mailed you an invitation, Grandpa.

Capitalize a title showing a family relationship when it refers to a specific person, except when it follows a possessive noun or a possessive pronoun.

REFERS TO A SPECIFIC PERSON: Ask Grandmother her opinion.

FOLLOWS A POSSESSIVE: I'll ask my grandmother.

EXERCISE A: Using Capitals for Titles of People. Copy the following sentences, adding capital letters when necessary.

EXAMPLE: The new course is taught by professor Cooper.
The new course is taught by Professor Cooper.

1. The commander of the ship is captain Jones.
2. Last spring, doctor Martin traveled abroad.
3. At night aunt Bonnie reads mysteries.
4. Today ambassador Burton made the announcement.
5. This soup, cousin Jane, is really delicious.
6. I asked grandmother Smith to show me her album.
7. What is your position on education, governor?
8. The speaker, rabbi Stern, talked about Israel.
9. The officer, captain Lee, was in charge.
10. Is uncle George visiting for the weekend, mother?

EXERCISE B: More Practice Capitalizing Titles of People. Write each sentence, adding capital letters when necessary.

1. Every year uncle Jack has a backyard barbecue.
2. He asks dr. Henderson, his neighbor, to help.
3. Then aunt Irene sends out invitations.
4. Her cousin, judge smith, usually comes.
5. One of the regular guests is coach Ryan.
6. He and aunt Irene organize a volleyball game.
7. My dad's lawyer, attorney Stevens, always plays.
8. His team played a team led by grandpa Max.
9. I wasn't sure grandfather would play.
10. Grandpa, however, scored more points than cousin Ralph.

DEVELOPING WRITING SKILLS: Using Titles of People in Sentences. Write ten sentences. In five of these sentences include different social or professional titles. In the other five sentences include titles that show different family relationships.

27.5 Capitals for Titles of Things

Capitals are used in titles of things.

Capitalize the first word and all other key words in the titles of books, newspapers, magazines, short stories, poems, plays, movies, songs, paintings, and sculptures.

All the words in a title are capitalized except articles *(a, an, the)* and prepositions and conjunctions that are only two, three, or four letters long. Even these short words are capitalized when they begin a title.

TITLES OF WRITTEN WORKS AND WORKS OF ART	
Books	A Tale of Two Cities
Newspapers	the Fort Worth Star-Telegram
Magazines	Popular Mechanics
Short Stories	"The Bet"
Poems	"Birches"
Plays	Death of a Salesman
Movies	The Sting
Songs	"Walkin' in the Rain"
Paintings	Three Musicians
Sculptures	Bird in Space

Capitalize the title of a school course when it is followed by a number or refers to a language.

EXAMPLES: French
History 420
Algebra II

Otherwise, school subjects are not capitalized.

EXAMPLE: I have social studies, music, and science this morning.

EXERCISE A: Using Capitals for Titles of Things. Copy the following titles, adding capital letters as necessary. Keep the underlining and quotation marks as shown.

EXAMPLE: the sound of music
The Sound of Music

1. the good earth
2. "spring fever"
3. "sounds of silence"
4. mathematics 103
5. mona lisa
6. national geographic
7. the poseidon adventure
8. french
9. "the split cherry tree"
10. "the lady or the tiger?"
11. the los angeles times
12. science digest
13. "the rain in spain"
14. life with father
15. my fair lady
16. animal farm
17. the pearl
18. history 570
19. the crucible
20. "the circuit"

EXERCISE B: More Practice Using Capital Letters for Titles of Things. Follow the directions for Exercise A.

1. algebra II
2. the way we were
3. the new york daily news
4. the devil and daniel webster
5. when the legends die
6. "the most dangerous game"
7. island of the blue dolphins
8. "the fun they had"
9. treasure island
10. "the road not taken"
11. latin
12. the sunflowers
13. the outsiders
14. a raisin in the sun
15. "the base stealer"
16. the red pony
17. a star is born
18. fiddler on the roof
19. "mother to son"
20. popular computing

DEVELOPING WRITING SKILLS: Using Titles of Things in a Paragraph. Write a paragraph about the kind of books or movies you enjoy. Include at least three titles.

27.6 Capitals in Letters

Several parts of friendly letters are capitalized.

In the heading, capitalize the street, city, and state and also the month of the year.

HEADING: 17 Chestnut Street
Newton, Massachusetts 02162
May 29, 1987

In the salutation, capitalize the first word, any title, and the name of the person or group mentioned.

SALUTATIONS: My dear Susan, Dear Uncle Steve,

In the closing, capitalize the first word.

CLOSINGS: Your friend, Affectionately, Love,

Notice how capitals are used in this friendly letter.

83 Spring Road
Princeton, New Jersey 08540
June 1, 1987

Dear Jennifer,

Have you packed all your things for camp? This year I'm taking some extra batteries so that I don't have the same catastrophe I had last year. It was lucky you were with me!

I can't wait to go swimming in the lake. I'm hoping to improve my swimming so that I can make the swim team.

I can't wait to see you. Say hi to your parents for me.

Love,
Sarah

EXERCISE A: Using Capitals in Letters. Rewrite the parts of letters shown below, adding capital letters as needed.

EXAMPLE: dear arnold
Dear Arnold

1. 128 hollings drive
   freeport, maine 04033
   april 20, 1987
2. 418 tremont avenue
   atlanta, georgia 30339
   september 15, 1987
3. dear uncle bill,
4. my dear sister,
5. sincerely,
6. affectionately,
7. 43 tenth street
   berkeley, california
   94710
   august 10, 1985
8. 225 highland street
   canton,
   massachusetts 02021
   may 14, 1987
9. greetings, marcia,
10. fondly,

EXERCISE B: More Practice Using Capitals in Letters. Rewrite the parts of letters shown below, adding capital letters as needed.

1. 46 lincoln avenue
   hancock, new
   hampshire 03449
   february 16, 1987
2. 791 central avenue
   bloomington, indiana
   47401
   august 23, 1987
3. hello, george,
4. howdy, mindy,
5. love,
6. yours truly,
7. 347 willow road
   san antonio, texas
   78216
   december 7, 1987
8. 86 kirkland street
   portland, oregon
   97223
   june 15, 1987
9. dear aunt karen,
10. your friend,

DEVELOPING WRITING SKILLS: Using Capitals in Letters. Write a letter with a heading, salutation, and closing to a friend. Tell about something interesting you have been doing at home or in school.

Skills Review and Writing Workshop

Using Capital Letters

CHECKING YOUR SKILLS

Copy each sentence below, adding capital letters as needed.

EXAMPLE: uncle harry reads the chicago tribune.
Uncle Harry reads the Chicago Tribune.

1. charles l. dodgson, the author of alice's adventures in wonderland, used the pen name lewis carroll.
2. henry fonda won an academy award for the film on golden pond.
3. the newport bridge connects newport and jamestown, two cities in rhode island.
4. i told mother, "thanksgiving day is always on a thursday."
5. attorney general stevens was praised by governor watkins.
6. aunt ann and uncle bill visited us on new year's day.
7. "the magic shop" is a story by h. g. wells.
8. i began the letter like this: dear grandpa.
9. my sister studies spanish, history III, geometry, science, and english.
10. lake superior, located in north america, has an area of 32,483 square miles.

USING MECHANICS SKILLS IN WRITING

Writing Dialogue

You and your friend are planning a trip. You want to travel around the United States, but your friend wants to go to Europe. Imagine the conversation you are going to have before you resolve this problem! Write the conversation.

Decide where you would like to travel in the United States and why you want to see particular places. Imagine the places in Europe your friend wants to see. You can have one person interrupting the other once in a while. Proofread, and check that you used capital letters correctly.

Chapter 28

Using Abbreviations

The following items have something in common: *Dr., Prof., Blvd., RI, qt.* Do you know what it is? How are they similar? Each of them is an abbreviation or shortened form of a word. The complete words are *Doctor, Professor, Boulevard, Rhode Island,* and *quart.*

Abbreviations are useful because they save time and space. People generally use them when they write notes or lists. Sometimes abbreviations are used on maps or charts. Most abbreviations are not acceptable in essays and reports such as you write for school. Their main use is in notes, lists, memos, and other kinds of casual writing. It is important to know when it is acceptable to use abbreviations and when it is not.

This chapter gives more information about abbreviations. It tells about abbreviations used for titles of people, names of places, times, dates, and measurements. Examine the charts provided in each section and refer to them as you complete the exercises.

28.1 Abbreviations for Titles of People

Social and professional titles are often abbreviated. The abbreviations of most professional titles, however, are used more in informal than in formal writing.

An abbreviation of a social or professional title used before a person's name begins with a capital letter and ends with a period.

Social Titles. The chart below shows several abbreviated social titles followed by proper names.

ABBREVIATIONS OF SOCIAL TITLES	
Singular	**Plural**
Mr. Arnold	Messrs. Jones and Black
Mrs. Henshaw	Mmes. Gold and Tucker
Mme. Dupont	Mmes. White and Anderson

Professional Titles. Abbreviations of professional titles are used mainly in informal writing. The following chart presents several of these titles.

ABBREVIATIONS OF SOME PROFESSIONAL TITLES				
Governmental	Rep.	Representative	Gov.	Governor
	Sen.	Senator	Treas.	Treasurer
	Sec.	Secretary	Pres.	President
Military	Pvt.	Private	Corp.	Corporal
	Lt.	Lieutenant	Maj.	Major
	Gen.	General	Sgt.	Sergeant
Professional	Dr.	Doctor	Atty.	Attorney
	Prof.	Professor	Rev.	Reverend
	Sr.	Sister	Hon.	Honorable

EXERCISE: Using Abbreviations for Titles of People. Rewrite each sentence, substituting an abbreviation for each title.

EXAMPLE: Doctor Beck gives me a yearly checkup.
Dr. Beck gives me a yearly checkup.

1. The lecture was given by Professor Judith Rogers.
2. General Robert E. Lee led the Confederate forces.
3. The bill is sponsored by Senator Ralph Lee.
4. Madame Duchamp held a news conference.
5. My cousin, Corporal Andrew Fleming, was promoted.
6. Secretary Jane Benson wrote the report.
7. Attorney M. S. Lewis examined the contract.
8. I have an appointment with Mister Benjamin Adler at 10 a.m.
9. Major Thomas Hodges made an inspection of the camp.
10. Representative Cynthia Miller was re-elected.
11. My grandfather knew the late Governor Nelson Rockefeller of New York.
12. The health clinic is run by Sister Anne.
13. Lieutenant Marilyn Howe explained the procedures to us.
14. He asked Private Theodore Morales for a demonstration.
15. President Jimmy Carter served one term.
16. A report was made by Treasurer Angela Rivera.
17. Representative Ida Lewis is a Republican.
18. The Reverend William McConnell met with local officials.
19. The Honorable Muriel Bradley is a federal judge.
20. Messieurs Henry Abbott and James Alvarez are partners.

DEVELOPING WRITING SKILLS: Using Abbreviated Titles. Write ten sentences about real or imaginary people. Use an abbreviated title in each sentence.

28.2 Abbreviations for Names of Places

Abbreviations for the names of places are generally used only in informal writing, such as lists, or in addresses.

An abbreviation for the name of a place that is used before or after a proper noun begins with a capital letter and ends with a period.

The abbreviation is always part of a proper name. It helps name a specific place.

EXAMPLES:	Foster Ave.	Pikes Pk.
	Water Edge Dr.	Times Sq.
	Plymouth Rd.	Whitehouse Ct.
	Acadia Natl. Pk.	Hylan Blvd.
	Mt. Fuji	Pan American Hwy.
	Wexford Ter.	Wake Is.
	Suffolk Co.	Ft. Ticonderoga

The chart below lists common abbreviations for places.

COMMON ABBREVIATIONS FOR PLACE NAMES

Ave.	Avenue	Mt.	Mountain
Bldg.	Building	Pen.	Peninsula
Blvd.	Boulevard	Pk.	Park, Peak
Co.	County	Pl.	Place
Ct.	Court	Rd.	Road
Dr.	Drive	Rte.	Route
Ft.	Fort	Sq.	Square
Hwy.	Highway	St.	Street
Is.	Island	Ter.	Terrace
Jct.	Junction	Tpk.	Turnpike

EXERCISE: Using Abbreviations for the Names of Places. Write the abbreviation for each underlined word in the following sentences.

EXAMPLE: The highest point on Lookout Mountain is 2,126 feet.
Mt.

1. I would like you to meet me at 7:00 p.m. at 415 Lovett Boulevard.
2. Spain and Portugal make up the Iberian Peninsula.
3. The Confederates captured Fort Sumter in 1861.
4. To get to Joseph's house, follow Kings Highway to Birch Street.
5. A concert will be held in Central Park.
6. My dentist is located on Livingston Avenue.
7. Montauk Point is on eastern Long Island.
8. The school on Fremont Terrace has a large gym.
9. Where is the Jefferson County Courthouse?
10. That theater is on Fordham Road.
11. The Saltonstall Office Building is 396 feet high.
12. The address of my new home is 14 Garland Drive, Akron, Ohio.
13. A jumping-frog contest is held in Calaveras County.
14. My uncle's office is on Campbell Place.
15. We took Route 95 because it is the fastest way to get home.
16. My aunt's house is on Barrows Court.
17. The ferry to Casco Island leaves every hour.
18. Our hotel in New York City was near Union Square.
19. The New York Stock Exchange is on Wall Street.
20. Independence Historical Park is in Philadelphia.

DEVELOPING WRITING SKILLS: Using Abbreviations in Sentences. Write directions from your house to a friend's house. Use at least two of the following abbreviations: Rd., Ave., Hwy., Dr., Ct., Pk., Blvd., Rte., and St.

28.3 Abbreviations for Names of States

Use Postal Service abbreviations for the names of states when you address envelopes. On envelopes, these abbreviations are followed by ZIP codes.

Capitalize both letters in Postal Service abbreviations of states. No period follows these abbreviations.

POSTAL SERVICE ABBREVIATIONS FOR NAMES OF STATES

AL	Alabama	MT	Montana
AK	Alaska	NE	Nebraska
AZ	Arizona	NV	Nevada
AR	Arkansas	NH	New Hampshire
CA	California	NJ	New Jersey
CO	Colorado	NM	New Mexico
CT	Connecticut	NY	New York
DE	Delaware	NC	North Carolina
FL	Florida	ND	North Dakota
GA	Georgia	OH	Ohio
HI	Hawaii	OK	Oklahoma
ID	Idaho	OR	Oregon
IL	Illinois	PA	Pennsylvania
IN	Indiana	RI	Rhode Island
IA	Iowa	SC	South Carolina
KS	Kansas	SD	South Dakota
KY	Kentucky	TN	Tennessee
LA	Louisiana	TX	Texas
ME	Maine	UT	Utah
MD	Maryland	VT	Vermont
MA	Massachusetts	VA	Virginia
MI	Michigan	WA	Washington
MN	Minnesota	WV	West Virginia
MS	Mississippi	WI	Wisconsin
MO	Missouri	WY	Wyoming

The example below shows how to use Postal Service abbreviations and ZIP codes when you address an envelope.

RETURN ADDRESS

Carlos Becerra
19 Green Street
Matawan, N.J. 07747

MAILING ADDRESS

Michael Decker
13 Wells Avenue
Hastings, NE 68901

EXERCISE: Using Abbreviations for Names of States. Write the Postal Service abbreviation for each state listed below.

EXAMPLE: New Hampshire NH

1. South Carolina
2. Louisiana
3. Pennsylvania
4. Georgia
5. New York
6. Kentucky
7. Wyoming
8. Tennessee
9. Michigan
10. Colorado
11. Missouri
12. Alabama
13. Utah
14. Delaware
15. North Dakota
16. Virginia
17. Indiana
18. Maine
19. Ohio
20. Kansas

DEVELOPING WRITING SKILLS: Using Abbreviations for Names of States to Address Envelopes. Draw three envelopes on your paper. Write both a return address and a mailing address for each of these envelopes. Use a different state abbreviation for each of your addresses.

28.4 Abbreviations for Time and Dates

Abbreviations are frequently used in informal writing for both time and dates.

Abbreviations for time begin with small letters and are followed by periods.

The chart shows some common abbreviations.

COMMON ABBREVIATIONS OF MEASURES OF TIME					
sec.	second(s)	hr.	hour(s)	mo.	month(s)
min.	minute(s)	wk.	week(s)	yr.	year(s)

A.M. and *P.M.* are abbreviations for *before noon* and *after noon.* They can be written with either capital or small letters.

EXAMPLE: My English class begins at 9:15 a.m.
Dinner will be served at 7:00 P.M.

Abbreviations of the days of the week and months of the year begin with capitals and end with periods.

ABBREVIATIONS OF DAYS AND MONTHS					
Days		Months			
Sun.	Sunday	Jan.	January	July	July
Mon.	Monday	Feb.	February	Aug.	August
Tues.	Tuesday	Mar.	March	Sept.	September
Wed.	Wednesday	Apr.	April	Oct.	October
Thurs.	Thursday	May	May	Nov.	November
Fri.	Friday	June	June	Dec.	December
Sat.	Saturday				

EXERCISE A: Abbreviating Time and Dates. Write the abbreviation for each item listed below.

EXAMPLES:	Sunday, January 15, 1987	seventeen months
	Sun., Jan. 15, 1987	17 mo.

1. Wednesday, April 15, 1970
2. Monday, February 22, 1982
3. Thursday, September 30, 1920
4. eleven o'clock in the morning
5. Tuesday, March 9, 1976
6. fifteen minutes and twenty-two seconds
7. seventeen weeks
8. three hours, five minutes, and seventeen seconds
9. one hundred years
10. twenty-five minutes
11. Wednesday, September 25, 1985
12. five minutes past nine o'clock in the morning
13. three months
14. ten seconds
15. seven o'clock in the evening

EXERCISE B: More Practice Abbreviating Time and Dates. Write the abbreviation for each item listed below.

1. Friday, October 3, 1980
2. three o'clock in the afternoon
3. Monday, January 1, 1945
4. Sunday, December 11, 1977
5. Saturday, November 8, 1956
6. three weeks
7. thirty-seven minutes
8. five hours, twelve minutes, and eight seconds
9. fifty-five seconds
10. Saturday, May 18, 1985

DEVELOPING WRITING SKILLS: Using Abbreviations of Time and Dates. Make a list of important events in your life. Use abbreviations for time and dates.

28.5 Abbreviations for Measurements

Two systems of measurement are used in this country—traditional measurements and metric measurements.

Abbreviations of traditional measurements begin with small letters and end with periods.

EXAMPLE: Add 2 tbsp. of baking soda. (two tablespoons)

I rode 5 mi. on my bicycle this morning. (five miles)

In the following chart, notice that the abbreviation for *Fahrenheit* is capitalized. This is an exception to the rule.

TRADITIONAL MEASUREMENTS					
in.	inch(es)	tsp.	teaspoon	dr.	dram(s)
ft.	foot, feet	tbsp.	tablespoon	oz.	ounce(s)
yd.	yard(s)	pt.	pint(s)	lb.	pound(s)
mi.	mile(s)	gal.	gallon(s)	F.	Fahrenheit

Abbreviations for metric measurements begin with small letters but do not end with periods.

The abbreviations for *liter* and *Celsius* are exceptions to this rule. They both have capital letters as their abbreviations.

METRIC MEASURES					
mm	millimeter(s)	mg	milligram(s)	L	liter(s)
cm	centimeter(s)	g	gram(s)	C	Celsius
m	meter(s)	kg	kilogram(s)		
km	kilometer(s)				

EXAMPLE: Draw a line 2 m long.

EXERCISE A: Using Abbreviations for Measurements. Write the abbreviation for each item listed below. Use a numeral with each abbreviation.

EXAMPLES: twenty miles five degrees Fahrenheit
20 mi 5°F.

1. three feet, six inches
2. thirty yards
3. three teaspoons
4. twelve ounces
5. two pounds, three ounces
6. six centimeters
7. ten milligrams
8. twelve degrees Celsius
9. eleven kilograms
10. fifteen meters

EXERCISE B: More Practice Using Abbreviations for Measurements. Write the abbreviation for each item listed below.

1. three and one half inches
2. eighty-two degrees Fahrenheit
3. two tablespoons
4. four gallons
5. one pint
6. eight grams
7. two millimeters
8. four liters
9. seventeen degrees Celsius
10. thirty-five kilometers

DEVELOPING WRITING SKILLS: Writing Abbreviations for Measurements. Write ten informal sentences giving instructions on how to make something or cook a dish. Be sure to use an abbreviation for a measurement in each one.

Skills Review and Writing Workshop

Using abbreviations

CHECKING YOUR SKILLS

Write the abbreviation for each underlined word or phrase in the following sentences.

EXAMPLE: A statue seventeen feet tall commemorates George Washington. 17 ft.

1. A meeting took place on Monday, February 4, 1985.
2. Governor Anderson met with Senator Kelly.
3. We met in the Tyler Building on Atlantic Boulevard.
4. These officials met for two hours and ten minutes.
5. The meeting began at 9:30 in the morning.
6. They made a statement for the voters of Minnesota.
7. The new program has the support of the President.
8. Government leaders plan to discuss these plans in more detail with citizen groups from Cook County.
9. Although the temperature was ninety-one degrees Fahrenheit, the officials smiled enthusiastically.
10. The group is scheduled to meet again in March.

USING MECHANICS SKILLS IN WRITING

Writing a Synopsis of a TV Show

Your cousin is going to miss her favorite TV show. You have agreed to watch it and write down exactly what happened. You plan to take notes quickly and then write your notes neatly. Use abbreviations for the characters: Professor Steele, Doctor Gonzalez, Governor Jackson, Mister Manchester. It starts in Mister Manchester's home in New York. Everyone is discussing the disappearance of Private Drake. He disappeared Sunday, April 5, and hasn't been heard from since his phone call at ten o'clock yesterday morning.

Invent what happens when Detective Rogers arrives. Be sure your abbbreviations are correct. Proofread carefully.

Chapter 29

Using End Marks and Commas

How would you punctuate this string of words? *Please deliver the tomato soup chicken salad corn bread and fruit I ordered.*

There are a number of possible ways. First, the sentence could read *Please! Deliver the tomato soup, chicken salad, corn bread, and fruit I ordered.* Or, with a change in punctuation, it could read *Please deliver the tomato, soup, chicken, salad, corn, bread, and fruit I ordered.* Punctuation can make a difference in meaning.

Correct punctuation helps make the meaning of a sentence clear. It does this by telling the reader when to pause briefly and when to come to a full stop. It also tells whether a sentence is meant to make a statement, ask a question, make a command, or show surprise.

This chapter tells about four different punctuation marks—the period, the question mark, the exclamation mark, and the comma. You should read, study, and practice using these four marks. Notice how these marks are used in the books, newspapers, and magazines you read.

29.1 Periods

A period indicates the end of a sentence or abbreviation.

Use a period to end a declarative sentence.

A declarative sentence makes a statement of fact or opinion.

DECLARATIVE SENTENCE: Ocean water is always moving.

Use a period to end an imperative sentence.

An imperative sentence gives a direction or command.

IMPERATIVE SENTENCE: Finish reading the chapter.

Use a period to end a sentence that contains an indirect question.

An indirect question reports a question but does not ask it. It does not give the speaker's exact words.

INDIRECT QUESTION: Mae asked me whether I could stay.

Use a period after many abbreviations and after initials.

ABBREVIATIONS: Gov. Gen. Mrs. St. Rd. Ave.
Ala. Vt. N.Y. Fla. Conn.
Nebr. E.B. White Robin F. Brancato

WHEN TO USE A PERIOD	
With a Declarative Sentence	Mauna Loa is an active volcano.
With an Imperative Sentence	Show me your report.
With an Indirect Question	Susan asked me when to begin.
With an Abbreviation	Dr. Lee gave me an injection.

EXERCISE: Using Periods. Copy the following sentences taken from a notebook, adding periods when necessary.

EXAMPLE: Napoleon was about 5 ft, 4 in tall
Napoleon was about 5 ft., 4 in. tall.

1. Napoleon Bonaparte was born in Corsica on Aug 15, 1769
2. He was quickly promoted from Pvt to Corp to Sgt
3. "The Little Corporal" was his nickname
4. In battles, he attacked the enemy at its weakest point
5. He expanded his empire by warfare
6. At one time his empire included almost all of Europe
7. On Apr 11, 1814, he gave up his throne
8. His final defeat was at the Battle of Waterloo
9. He died in 1821 on the island of St Helena
10. Some historians have questioned the cause of his death
11. Mr Wyman belongs to a stamp club in Wilmington, Del
12. Mrs Callaghan asked me when I started my stamp collection
13. Look at the color and ink on these stamps
14. This stamped envelope is postmarked Philadelphia, Pa
15. Ed asked whether a magnifying glass was needed
16. I bought this magnifying glass on Willow Ave
17. A dealer on Spruce St sold me these stamps
18. The stamps are from Eng, Fr, and Ger
19. To remove a stamp from an envelope, soak it in water
20. The face of Dr Walter Reed is on a commemorative stamp

DEVELOPING WRITING SKILLS: Using Periods in a Paragraph. Write a paragraph about an important event in your life. End each declarative sentence, imperative sentence, and indirect question with a period.

29.2 Question Marks

A question mark follows a sentence that asks a question.

Use a question mark after an interrogative sentence.

An interrogative sentence asks a *direct question.*

INTERROGATIVE SENTENCES: Who was the first woman governor**?**

When does history class begin**?**

Sometimes a single word or brief phrase is used to ask a direct question. Such a question is punctuated as if it were a complete sentence, since the words left out are easily understood.

Use a question mark after a word or phrase that asks a question.

EXAMPLES: Dr. Roberts called a meeting. Why**?**

(Understood: Why did Dr. Roberts call a meeting?)

He claims this invention is original. In what way**?**

(Understood: In what way is it original?)

The following chart shows the different kinds of questions and the different ways of punctuating them.

QUESTIONS AND HOW TO PUNCTUATE THEM
Direct Question in a Complete Sentence: Use a question mark. (How old is Steven**?**)
Direct Question in an Incomplete Sentence: Use a question mark. (How tall**?**)
Indirect Question: Use a period. (I asked Steven where he was born**.**)

EXERCISE: Using Question Marks. Copy the sentences below, adding the missing question marks and periods.

EXAMPLE: She asked me to list the U.S. Presidents But why

She asked me to list the U.S. Presidents. But why?

1. Have you read "Charles," by Shirley Jackson
2. When did Edgar Allan Poe and Charles Dickens meet Why
3. The capital of Brazil was moved from Rio de Janiero to Brasilia When
4. How large is the planet Jupiter
5. Were you able to see the comet
6. Can you meet with me tomorrow Where
7. How did they choose a student representative
8. Who recited the poem by Walt Whitman
9. Marie Curie discovered radium When
10. If we leave early, we will have time to stop at the zoo
11. Who is expected to win the long jump
12. Arthur will speak to us about computers At what time
13. Carol said there is a rehearsal this afternoon Where
14. What new records have been purchased for the library
15. One of the building plans was accepted Which one
16. Who left this message for me Why
17. Did you meet a journalist when you visited the newspaper
18. When will we talk about the class trip With whom
19. Which of these pictures do you like best Why
20. Can you think of a way to solve this problem How

DEVELOPING WRITING SKILLS: Writing Questions. Write ten questions about a person, place, or thing. Use some complete sentences and some words or phrases following a complete sentence.

29.3 Exclamation Marks

An exclamation mark indicates strong feeling or emotion, including surprise.

Use an exclamation mark to end an exclamatory sentence.

The following are typical exclamatory sentences.

EXCLAMATORY SENTENCES: I don't believe it!
I'm leaving!
What a wonderful idea!
We won the game!

Use an exclamation mark after an imperative sentence that gives a forceful or urgent command.

IMPERATIVE SENTENCES: Get me some water!
Stay right here!
Move back!
Don't close that gate!
Stop, thief!

Remember that only imperative sentences containing forceful commands are followed by an exclamation mark. Mild imperatives are followed by a period.

Use an exclamation mark after an interjection expressing strong emotion.

An interjection is the part of speech that expresses feeling or emotion. In each example below, the first word is the interjection.

INTERJECTIONS: Wow! That was a great throw.
Hey! Grab this package.
Oh! Look what I found.
Great! You did that well.

EXERCISE A: Using Exclamation Marks. Copy each item below, adding the necessary exclamation marks.

EXAMPLE: I knew it
I knew it!

1. Listen to me
2. On your mark Get set Go
3. Deliver this message immediately
4. What a wonderful idea
5. Sit down
6. Oh This is truly a surprise.
7. Hey It's not time to begin.
8. Be still
9. Never I cannot agree.
10. Goodness You must consider the consequences.

EXERCISE B: More Practice Using Exclamation Marks. Copy each item below, adding the necessary exclamation marks.

1. Ah I've found it.
2. Look out
3. Hurray We finished first.
4. Wow We saw a really magnificent view.
5. Open the window at once
6. Super That's an extraordinary idea.
7. Drop that ball
8. Impossible This report can't be true.
9. Get out
10. What a ridiculous story

DEVELOPING WRITING SKILLS: Using Exclamation Marks to Show Strong Feelings. Write a short scene from a play in which two characters show strong feelings. Use exclamation marks after exclamatory sentences, after sentences giving strong commands, and after interjections.

29.4 Commas in Compound Sentences

One major use of the comma is to separate two simple sentences that are joined by a coordinating conjunction. The two joined sentences form a compound sentence.

Use a comma and a coordinating conjunction to separate the two simple sentences that form a compound sentence.

The following chart shows how a compound sentence is built. The two simple sentences must be related in meaning.

THE COMPOUND SENTENCE		
SIMPLE SENTENCE	COORDINATING CONJUNCTION (and, but, for, nor, or, so, yet)	SIMPLE SENTENCE

The comma in a compound sentence is followed by one of the following conjunctions: *and, but, for, nor, or, so,* or *yet.* Notice how commas and conjunctions are used in the examples below.

COMPOUND SENTENCES: Tommy and Arlene will play badminton**,** and Felicia will keep score.

The concert was over**,** but no one wanted to leave.

Katy can stay here for the summer**,** or she can visit her relatives in Iowa.

If the two simple sentences in a compound sentence are short, the comma may be omitted.

COMPOUND SENTENCE WITHOUT A COMMA: Randy cut and I pasted.

I phoned but no one answered.

EXERCISE A: Using Commas in Compound Sentences. Copy each of the following sentences, putting in commas where needed.

EXAMPLE: A husky is a large dog but a sheepdog is larger.
A husky is a large dog, but a sheepdog is larger.

1. I turned on the light for it was getting dark.
2. I think we should take a vote but Alan wants to wait.
3. We can stay and explore or we can return tomorrow.
4. I explained the procedure but they didn't understand.
5. Anna wants to join the art club for she loves to paint.
6. Terry calls once a week but Bill telephones every day.
7. Alice was shy so Barbara did all the talking.
8. Summer has arrived yet the days are still chilly.
9. We can walk to the park or we can take our bicycles.
10. They did not seem confused nor did they ask for help.

EXERCISE B: More Practice Using Commas in Compound Sentences. Copy each of the sentences, putting in commas where needed.

1. I trained my dog to sit but Bob never trained his dog.
2. Our dog is a mongrel for his parents were different breeds.
3. Our dog seems intelligent yet he can't do many tricks.
4. Mark's dog lives outdoors so Mark keeps the doghouse warm.
5. Bring your dog on the picnic or leave him with your dad.

DEVELOPING WRITING SKILLS: Using Commas to Punctuate Compound Sentences. Write ten compound sentences. Use a comma and one of the following conjunctions to join each part: *and, but, for, nor, or, so, yet.*

29.5 Commas in Series

Sometimes a sentence lists a number of items. When three or more items are listed, the list is called a *series.* The items in the series are separated by commas.

Use commas to separate a series of words or a series of phrases.

The items in a series may be single words or groups of words.

SERIES OF WORDS: My favorite vegetables have always been peas, carrots, beets, and asparagus.

At school we study English, mathematics, history, and French.

Edward is a star player in softball, hockey, and soccer.

SERIES OF PHRASES: I shall spend the evening doing my homework, studying for a test, getting my clothes ready for tomorrow, and reading a book.

I searched under the table, along the wall, and behind the sofa for the missing shoe.

My house is located past the post office, opposite the school, and before the highway.

Notice that each of the items except the last one in these series is followed by a comma. The conjunction *and* or *or* is added after the last comma.

If each item in a series is followed by a conjunction, commas are not needed. The conjunctions separate the items.

EXAMPLES: I visited castles and museums and forts.

We can swim or row or jog this morning.

EXERCISE A: Using Commas with Items in a Series. Copy each sentence below, adding commas where they are needed.

EXAMPLE: Redwoods pines and firs are all needleleaf trees.

Redwoods, pines, and firs are all needleleaf trees.

1. Memphis Nashville and Chattanooga are cities in Tennessee.
2. We met the writer producer and director of the television show.
3. As John made the winning shot, the fans gasped cheered and began shouting his name.
4. We must have volunteers who are willing to supply soda to cook hamburgers and to prepare a salad.
5. They could not decide whether to take their vacation in June in July or in August.

EXERCISE B: More Practice Using Commas with Items in a Series. Copy each sentence below, adding commas where they are needed.

1. From my window I can see pigeons sparrows robins and starlings.
2. I wrote folded and sealed the letter without remembering to enclose the pictures.
3. We walked along the waterfront past the marina and beyond the shops.
4. Boston has harbors public parks and historic places to visit.
5. Alex Patty Chris and Ian are all planning to visit Susan after she moves to Detroit.

DEVELOPING WRITING SKILLS: Writing Sentences with Items in a Series. Write ten sentences about things to do, things to see, or things to listen to. In each sentence, include three or more words or phrases in a series.

29.6 Commas with Introductory Words and Phrases

When a sentence begins with an introductory word or phrase, the word or phrase is generally separated from the rest of the sentence by a comma.

Use a comma after an introductory word or phrase.

EXAMPLES: Yes**,** the newspaper has arrived.

Kim**,** we need your help.

Surrounded by a crowd**,** the celebrity smiled graciously.

During his last visit**,** he asked many interesting questions.

To get to the turnpike**,** turn left at the light.

The chart below gives additional examples of commas used after introductory words and phrases.

USING COMMAS WITH INTRODUCTORY WORDS AND PHRASES	
Introductory Words	Well**,** how shall we begin?
	Jane**,** please read that page aloud.
	No**,** we already have too many magazines.
Introductory Phrases	Besides camping and hiking**,** Dave also canoes.
	To play in the band**,** you must be willing to practice.
	Waiting in the rain**,** we were furious that she was so late.

EXERCISE A: Using Commas with Introductory Words and Phrases. Copy the sentences below, placing a comma after the introductory words and phrases.

EXAMPLE: After six weeks of training she began a new job.

After six weeks of training, she began a new job.

1. Yes I am concerned about saving the whales.
2. Because of the bad weather we will need to cancel the game.
3. At every club meeting Mary asks for suggestions.
4. Oh I do have one more thing to say.
5. Leaning on the podium Mr. Price spoke to the students.
6. Henry will you read your story to me?
7. According to the latest report our play was a success.
8. In the new book I found three stories that I already had read.
9. True this is a priceless collection of jewels.
10. On their vacation in Mexico City they took three hundred pictures.

EXERCISE B: More Practice Using Commas with Introductory Words and Phrases. Follow the directions in Exercise A.

1. Well we are all very glad that the mystery is solved.
2. With the talent on our team how can we lose?
3. No I have not seen the newly designed airplane.
4. Mr. James please tell me about your trip to Italy.
5. Seeing the play for the first time we were impressed.

DEVELOPING WRITING SKILLS: Writing Sentences with Introductory Words and Phrases. Write ten sentences describing what you think homes of the future will be like. Use an introductory word or phrase in each sentence.

29.7 Commas with Interrupting Words and Phrases

Some sentences contain words or phrases that interrupt the flow of the sentence. They should be set off from the rest of the sentence by commas.

Use commas to set off interrupting words and phrases from the rest of the sentence.

The commas indicate that these words could be left out and the sentence would still make sense.

Words That Name a Person Who is Being Addressed. Interrupting words tell who is being spoken to.

EXAMPLE: Look**,** Nat**,** at what we did last week.

Words That Rename a Noun. Words that rename a noun give additional information about it.

EXAMPLE: His present**,** a camera**,** is just what he wanted.

Common Expressions. Writers often use certain expressions to indicate that they are expressing an opinion, a conclusion, or a summary.

EXAMPLE: The game**,** I believe**,** starts at three o'clock.

The following chart gives further examples of how commas are used with interrupting words and phrases.

USING COMMAS WITH INTERRUPTING WORDS AND PHRASES	
To Name a Person Being Addressed	Why**,** Mr. Kane**,** are you doing that?
To Rename a Noun	Daniel Boone**,** an American pioneer**,** helped build the Wilderness Trail.
To Set Off a Common Expression	The offer**,** however**,** came too late.

EXERCISE A: Using Commas with Interrupting Words and Phrases. Copy each sentence, adding commas where necessary.

EXAMPLE: Dover the capital of Delaware is a shipping port.

Dover, the capital of Delaware, is a shipping port.

1. This dance Eleanor is one of my favorites.
2. Venice the famous Italian city has over 150 canals.
3. What we should remember of course is our purpose.
4. When Bobby is the next baseball game?
5. Walt Disney an American cartoonist created Mickey Mouse.
6. This new invention will I believe save you time.
7. Your garden Mrs. Tyler looks very well planned.
8. My parents are however more enthusiastic than I am.
9. They are visiting Laura my cousin in Arizona.
10. Please Phil try to get here earlier tomorrow.

EXERCISE B: More Practice Using Commas with Interrupting Words and Phrases. Copy each sentence, adding commas where necessary.

1. Bill Lee a left-handed pitcher won more than one hundred games.
2. Here is a book Natalie about the Olympics.
3. Jan Morris a travel writer described her trip to Vienna.
4. Many items that you packed John are really not necessary.
5. His fans no doubt will be eager to hear his recording.

DEVELOPING WRITING SKILLS: Using Interrupting Words and Phrases in Sentences. Write ten sentences about different hobbies. Use one of the following interrupting words or phrases in each sentence: true, in fact, for example, I think, it seems, after all, I believe, in my opinion, a popular pastime, a leisure-time activity.

29.8 Commas in Letters

Commas are used to punctuate the heading, the salutation, and the closing of a friendly letter.

In the heading of a friendly letter, use a comma between the city and the state. Use another comma between the number of the day and the number of the year.

HEADING: 1402 Croydon Street
Princeton**,** New Jersey 08540
February 15**,** 1987

Use a comma after the salutation in a friendly letter.

SALUTATION: Dear Lucy**,**

Use a comma after the closing of every letter.

CLOSING: Sincerely yours**,**

The following brief letter illustrates the above rules.

162 North Maple Avenue
Herndon, Virginia 22070
April 10, 1987

Dear Stacie,
Thank you very much for your kind present. I hope you enjoyed the party as much as we enjoyed having you here.
See you soon!

Your friend,

Marion

EXERCISE A: Using Commas in Letters. Copy each heading, salutation, and closing. Add commas where necessary.

EXAMPLE: Dear Arlene
Dear Arlene,

1. 211 Old Country Road
   Pearl River New York 10965
   December 7 1987
2. Dear Ellen
3. Your friend
4. Fondly
5. Dear Uncle Ted
6. 753 Water Street
   Danbury Connecticut 06810
   June 10 1982
7. My dear Michelle
8. Bye for now
9. 27 Commerce Street
   Dallas Texas 75240
   January 9 1987
10. Love

EXERCISE B: More Practice Using Commas in Letters. Copy each heading, salutation, and closing. Add commas where necessary.

1. 22 Park Lane
   Phoenix Arizona 85029
   August 3 1985
2. Yours truly
3. 320 Market Street
   Plainview New York 11803
   March 28 1984
4. Dear Mr. Tyler
5. Sincerely
6. Dear Melanie
7. My dear Aunt Jo
8. With love
9. Your nephew
10. Dear George

DEVELOPING WRITING SKILLS: Using Commas in a Letter. Write a short friendly letter to a real or imaginary friend. Include a heading, a salutation, and a closing.

29.9 Commas in Numbers

Numbers of one hundred or less and numbers made up of two words (for example, three thousand) are generally spelled out. Other large numbers (for example, 8,463) are written in numerals. Commas make large numbers easier to read.

Use commas with numbers of more than three digits.

To place the comma correctly, count three digits from the right. The comma is placed after the third digit.

EXAMPLES: a population of 247**,**867

an area of 3**,**615**,**122 square miles

Commas are also used with a series of numbers.

Use commas between three or more numbers written in a series.

EXAMPLE: Read pages 123**,** 124**,** and 125 carefully.

Notice that numerals are used for chapter numbers even though they are under one hundred. Not all large numbers are punctuated with commas.

Do not use a comma with ZIP codes, telephone numbers, page numbers, years, serial numbers, or house numbers.

NUMBERS WITHOUT COMMAS
ZIP code: Jamaica, NY 11432
Telephone number: (617) 532-7593
Page number: page 1002
Year: the year 2010
Serial number: 026 35 7494
House number: 1801 Houston Street

EXERCISE A: Using Commas in Numbers. Copy each sentence below, adding commas where necessary. If no commas are needed, write *correct.*

EXAMPLE: The area of Belgium is 11779 square miles.
The area of Belgium is 11,779 square miles.

1. Thomas Jefferson inherited 2750 acres of land.
2. The ZIP code for Parson, West Virginia, is 26287.
3. Kentucky has 12161 acres of forested land.
4. My telephone number is (203) 691-3155.
5. The serial number on the toaster is 716 025.
6. One acre equals 43560 square feet.
7. There were 3707000 children born in 1983.
8. This quote is on page 1317 of the reference book.
9. Mount McKinley in Alaska is 20320 feet high.
10. It cost $40948900 to build the Empire State Building.

EXERCISE B: More Practice Using Commas in Numbers. Follow the directions for Exercise A.

1. To call the hardware store, dial 524-5600.
2. The Statue of Liberty weighs 450000 pounds.
3. The references are listed on pages 22 23 and 24.
4. Each year 42515800 people visit our national parks.
5. The earth is an average of 92900000 miles from the sun.
6. In 1906 an earthquake shook San Francisco.
7. The highest mountain peak in South America is 22834 feet.
8. The Pacific Ocean is 64186300 square miles.
9. An article about Benjamin West begins on page 1116.
10. The World Trade Center in New York is 1350 feet high.

DEVELOPING WRITING SKILLS: Using Large Numbers in Sentences. Write a paragraph about a real or imaginary place. Use five or more large numbers in your paragraph.

Skills Review and Writing Workshop

Using End Marks and Commas

CHECKING YOUR SKILLS

Periods, question marks, exclamation marks, and commas have been left out of the sentences below. Rewrite the conversation, putting in the correct punctuation.

EXAMPLE: Dad: Who is ready to hear some good news
Dad: Who is ready to hear some good news?

Dad: Let's plan a trip to Cape Cod
Mom: Are you serious
Dad: I am definitely serious or I would not be studying this travel brochure
Ann: Terrific What a fabulous idea
Dad: We could visit Provincetown Hyannis and Wellfleet
Mom: I'll need some time to walk along the beach to see the sights and to shop for souvenirs
Dad: I'll make the reservations and you can plan a schedule
Ann: Well Dad when do we leave
Dad: How would July 10 suit you both
Mom: That's impossible I have 10001 things to do in order to get ready

USING MECHANICS SKILLS IN WRITING

Writing an Instruction Manual

Write an instruction manual on a machine you have invented. First, decide what you have invented. Think about something you would like to invent that would make your life better in some way. Next, decide how it works.

You could organize the manual in the following way: First, does the person with your invention have to do anything, such as put the whole thing together? Are batteries needed? Then explain how to operate the invention. Be sure your instructions are clear, and proofread for correct use of end marks and commas.

Chapter 30

Using Other Punctuation Marks

Could you understand a sentence if it were missing some of its punctuation? You probably could understand some sentences, but try this one: *Did Carla say I'm learning how to swim?* It's somewhat understandable, but it's also somewhat confusing. Who is learning how to swim? Is it Carla, or is it the person asking the question?

Here is one way to make the sentence more understandable: *Did Carla say, "I'm learning how to swim"?* In this case, it's Carla who is learning to swim. Here is another way to write the same sentence: *"Did Carla say I'm learning how to swim?"* In this case, it's the speaker who is learning how to swim.

Maybe now you can see why people are so concerned about punctuation. It helps writers to write clearly and it guides readers through written material.

This chapter tells about five different punctuation marks: the semicolon, the colon, the quotation mark, the hyphen, and the apostrophe. As you learn to use these marks, put them to work in your own writing.

30.1 Semicolons

Sometimes two independent clauses are so closely connected in meaning that they make up a single sentence, rather than two separate sentences.

Use a semicolon to connect two independent clauses that are closely connected in meaning.

If the two independent clauses do not seem to make up a single sentence, they should be punctuated as separate sentences, with periods.

EXAMPLES: Bill says the glass is half full**;** Betty says it's half empty**.** (two independent clauses closely connected in meaning)

Bill and Betty always see things differently**.** Betty has been working on a paper about television news**.** (two separate sentences)

Sometimes you will have a choice whether to use a semicolon or a period to punctuate independent clauses. Either punctuation mark will be correct. If you are not sure which to use, you should use a period.

The following chart gives more examples of independent clauses so closely connected in meaning that a semicolon should be used between them.

INDEPENDENT CLAUSES PUNCTUATED BY SEMICOLONS
I don't want pancakes; I want waffles.
I'll wash the car; you hose it down.
I hardly swung at all; the ball just leaped off my bat.
This book is over eight-hundred-pages long; it's much too long for me.

Remember that the two independent clauses must be closely related if they are to be connected by a semicolon.

EXERCISE A: Using Semicolons. Write each sentence below, adding a semicolon where necessary.

EXAMPLE: Benjamin Franklin was a printer he ran a newspaper in Philadelphia.

Benjamin Franklin was a printer; he ran a newspaper in Philadelphia.

1. We are going to stop at the museum it is presenting an exhibit on African art.
2. These books are about the American Revolution they were written by Esther Forbes.
3. Daniel is a serious photographer he has taken hundreds of photographs.
4. The stories she told me were fascinating they were about her childhood.
5. You are invited to my graduation come to the school auditorium on Friday at 7:30 p.m.

EXERCISE B: More Practice Using Semicolons. Write each sentence below, adding a semicolon where necessary.

1. The movie was entertaining the characters and the plot held my interest.
2. Sunday afternoon is my favorite time I listen to music with my friends.
3. This committee wants to know your opinions let us hear from you.
4. These rooms are quite similar they are both used for conferences.
5. There is a concert in the park tonight an orchestra will play the "1812 Overture."

DEVELOPING WRITING SKILLS: Using Semicolons in Your Own Writing. Write ten sentences about things you have done in the past month. In each sentence use a semicolon to join two independent clauses.

30.2 Colons

A colon (:) is a punctuation mark with a number of uses.

Use a colon after an independent clause in order to introduce a list of items.

The independent clause that comes before the colon often includes the words *the following, as follows, these,* or *those.*

EXAMPLES: Students may study any of the following languages: French, German, Spanish, Italian, or Latin.

Our tour will take us to three states: Maine, New Hampshire, and Vermont.

My favorite pastimes are these: photography, fishing, and reading.

Do not use a colon after a verb or a preposition.

INCORRECT: Veronica always orders: soup, salad, and dessert.

CORRECT: Veronica always orders soup, salad, and dessert.

Simply removing the colon from the incorrect sentence above would make it correct.

SOME ADDITIONAL USES OF THE COLON		
To Separate Hours and Minutes	3:15 p.m.	9:45 A.M.
After the Salutation in a Business Letter	Gentlemen: Dear Miss Robinson:	
On Warnings and Labels	Warning: The ice is thin. Note: Shake before using. Caution: Children playing.	

EXERCISE A: Using Colons. Rewrite each of the items below, adding colons where needed.

EXAMPLE: We visited three Canadian cities Calgary, Edmonton, and Winnipeg.

We visited three Canadian cities: Calgary, Edmonton, and Winnipeg.

1. The works of three poets will be featured in the magazine this month Edna St. Vincent Millay, William Carlos Williams, and Robert Frost.
2. We play on the following dates May 15, May 18, or May 21.
3. The three dives I am able to perform are these the cannonball, the backward somersault, and the jackknife.
4. I left the beach at 430 p.m. and arrived at Grandmother's house at 645 p.m.
5. Caution Do not set or store container where temperature exceeds 120° F.
6. The movie can be seen at the following times 145, 330, and 515.
7. When you tour Wyoming, be sure to see these places Yellowstone National Park, Fort Laramie, and Devils Tower National Monument.
8. Choose a book about one of these topics animals, conservation, or oceanography.
9. The first three United States Vice Presidents were the following John Adams, Thomas Jefferson, and Aaron Burr.
10. Dear Ms. Wilson

DEVELOPING WRITING SKILLS: Using Colons. (1) Write two sentences each of which includes a list requiring a colon before it. (2) Write a sentence that includes a list which should not have a colon before it. (3) Write a sentence that gives the time of day in hours and minutes. (4) Write a warning or label with a colon.

30.3 Quotation Marks in Direct Quotation

A *direct quotation* conveys the exact words that a person wrote, said, or thought.

Use quotation marks to enclose a person's exact words.

A direct quotation is often accompanied by words such as *he said* or *she replied.* These words, which may fall at the beginning, middle, or end of a quote, identify the speaker.

Introductory Words. When words that identify the speaker come right before a direct quotation, they are followed by a comma.

EXAMPLE: Jay said**,** **"**I have permission to interview the coach**."**

Interrupting Words. When words that identify the speaker come in the middle of a quoted sentence, each part of the interrupted quotation is enclosed in quotation marks. The first part of the quotation ends with a comma followed by quotation marks. The interrupting words are also followed by a comma.

EXAMPLE: **"**I have permission**,"** Jay said**,** **"**to interview the coach**."**

Concluding Words. If the words that identify the speaker are placed at the end of a direct quotation, the quoted material is followed by a comma, question mark, or exclamation mark placed inside the final quotation marks.

EXAMPLES: **"**From whom did you get permission**?"** the teacher asked**.**

"Throw home**!"** the shortstop yelled to the third-baseman**.**

EXERCISE A: Using Quotation Marks in Direct Quotations. Write each sentence below, adding commas and quotation marks where necessary.

EXAMPLE: This is a picture of my mother said Carol.
"This is a picture of my mother," said Carol.

1. Sam asked Do you want to go to the baseball game?
2. This movie Robin said is really exciting.
3. Pick up these puzzle pieces immediately! Mom ordered.
4. Miss Harris added We are going to have to work quickly.
5. This building is a city landmark Jeff explained.
6. Do not the museum guide warned touch the displays.
7. When can I see your science project? Steve asked.
8. Please read me another story pleaded the child.
9. Captain Lee said My next voyage will be to the Bahamas.
10. Simone asked Did you just get home?

EXERCISE B: More Practice Using Quotation Marks with Direct Quotations. Write each sentence below, adding commas and quotation marks where necessary.

1. John suggested We could drive to Sturbridge for the day.
2. What activities have been planned? Emily inquired.
3. Bruce thought This Brazilian jazz group is wonderful.
4. The new schedule announced Marilyn will begin tomorrow.
5. I can Stephen volunteered come an hour early to help.

DEVELOPING WRITING SKILLS: Writing Sentences with Direct Quotations. Write ten sentences. In each one tell what a character in a book or movie might say after visiting your school.

30.4 Quotation Marks with Other Punctuation Marks

Commas, periods, question marks, and exclamation marks are often used with quotation marks.

Place commas and periods inside final quotation marks.

EXAMPLES: "Our class trip is this Tuesday**,**" said Janet.

Matthew added, "We are leaving very early**.**"

Place a question mark or exclamation mark inside the final quotation marks if it is part of the quotation.

EXAMPLES: Beth asked, "How far is Quebec from Montreal**?**"

George shouted to Harry, "Run as fast as you can**!**"

Each sentence above is declarative. That is, each makes a statement by reporting what someone said. Nevertheless, neither ends with a period. Since a sentence cannot have two final punctuation marks, the punctuation needed for the direct quotation stands alone, inside the quotation marks.

CORRECT: Dan asked, "When can I get a pet**?**"

INCORRECT: Dan asked, "When can I get a pet**?**"**.**

Place a question mark or exclamation mark outside the final quotation marks if the mark is not part of the quotation.

EXAMPLES: Who said, "We have nothing to fear but fear itself"**?**

Don't say, "I doubt that it will work"**!**

EXERCISE A: Using Quotation Marks with Other Punctuation Marks. Copy each sentence, adding commas, periods, question marks, and exclamation marks where needed.

EXAMPLE: I was annoyed when you yelled, "I'm staying here"

I was annoyed when you yelled, "I'm staying here!"

1. "Aunt Martha called while you were in school" said Lynn.
2. Marissa volunteered, "I can help you in math"
3. Ruth asked, "Why did you choose that bicycle"
4. The policeman shouted, "Go back to your houses immediately"
5. I was thrilled when he said, "You can leave now"
6. Why did Marie say, "Kim should be treasurer"
7. How did Ira know I wrote, "Ira took the cookies"
8. Howard muttered, "I can explain why I'm late"
9. Jack wondered, "When did the Johnsons move here"
10. "Take your time" advised the teacher.

EXERCISE B: More Practice Using Quotation Marks with Other Punctuation Marks. Copy each sentence below, adding the missing punctuation marks.

1. "Please bring me the evening paper" said Paul.
2. Don't you dare say, "I didn't do it"
3. The detective blurted out, "This case is extraordinary"
4. Thea inquired, "How much longer will I have to wait"
5. The waitress asked, "What would you like to order"

DEVELOPING WRITING SKILLS: Writing Sentences with Quotation Marks and Other End Marks. Write ten sentences, each with a direct quotation. Use commas, periods, exclamation marks, and question marks to end your direct quotations.

30.5 Quotation Marks for Dialogue

A dialogue is talk between two or more people.

In dialogue, start a new paragraph to signal a change of speaker.

A new paragraph signals that a different person is speaking.

EXAMPLE: "William!" Erica shouted to her brother. "You better get up and feed the dog."

"All right," William groaned, "I'm coming."

"And hurry. Champ looks mighty hungry."

"I said all right, Erica," William snapped. "C'mon, Champ, breakfast time."

"William," said their mother, in another room, "you'll find the dog food in the large pantry. I moved it out of the cupboard. And don't forget your own breakfast, dear."

The following chart presents some of the guidelines to follow when writing dialogue.

GUIDELINES FOR WRITING DIALOGUE
1. Follow the general rules for using quotation marks, capital letters, end marks, and other punctuation marks.
2. Start a new paragraph with each change of speaker.
3. When a speaker utters two or more sentences without interruption, put quotation marks at the beginning of the first sentence and at the end of the last sentence.

The last guideline is illustrated in the following examples.

INCORRECT: Bob said, "Let's play chess." "I'm ready for a few good games with you."

CORRECT: Bob said, "Let's play chess. I'm ready for a few good games with you."

EXERCISE A: Using Quotation Marks in Dialogue. Turn the numbered sentences below into a dialogue. Add any missing punctuation marks and start a new paragraph whenever the speaker changes.

EXAMPLE: (1) Are you all right? he asked.
(2) I'm fine I replied.

"Are you all right?" he asked.
"I'm fine," I replied.

(1) Tomorrow announced Mom is Open School Night. (2) How can I find your classroom? (3) It's on the third floor I replied. (4) Walk in the front door, turn left, and go up three flights. (5) The room number is 307. (6) Will any of your work be on display? Mom asked. (7) Yes I said our writing folders will be on our desks. (8) The story I wrote about our cat is my best piece of writing. (9) Mom slowly inquired Is there anything I should know before I go? (10) Honestly I protested you don't need to worry.

EXERCISE B: More Practice Using Quotation Marks in Dialogue. Follow the directions for Exercise A.

(1) Fred, are you busy? Naomi asked. (2) No, why? replied Fred. (3) Well, I'm planning a surprise party for Barbara, and I could use your help. (4) What would you like me to do? asked Fred. (5) Two things, answered Naomi. (6) First, I was hoping you would design the invitations. (7) And second, it would be a real help if you would keep Barbara out of the house while I decorate. (8) You can count on me said Fred. (9) Terrific! said Naomi enthusiastically. (10) I am totally Fred responded at your service.

DEVELOPING WRITING SKILLS: Writing a Dialogue. Write a dialogue in which one person tries to persuade another person to try something new. Write ten lines.

30.6 Underlining and Quotation Marks in Titles

Many titles and names are either underlined or enclosed in quotation marks. Underlining is used only in handwritten or typewritten material. In printed material italic (slanted) print is used instead of underlining.

Underline the titles of long written works, movies, television and radio series, paintings, and sculptures. Also underline the names of specific vehicles.

KINDS OF TITLES THAT ARE UNDERLINED	
Written Works	
Books	The Outsiders, The Good Earth
Plays	The Miracle Worker, Pygmalion
Magazines and Newspapers	Newsweek, USA Today
Other Artistic Works	
Movies	Gone with the Wind, Star Wars
Television Series	Hill Street Blues
Paintings and Sculptures	Christina's World, The Thinker
Names of Specific Vehicles	
Aircraft	the Spirit of St. Louis
Ships	the Queen Mary
Trains	the Yankee Clipper
Spacecraft	Discovery

Use quotation marks around titles of short written works and other short artistic works.

KINDS OF TITLES THAT ARE ENCLOSED IN QUOTATION MARKS	
Written Works	
Stories	"The Most Dangerous Game"
Chapters	"The First Americans"
Articles	"Meet a Mystery Writer"
Other Artistic Works	
Episodes	"Foreign Territory" (the second episode of To Serve Them All My Days)
Songs	"Memory"

EXERCISE: Using Underlining and Quotation Marks. Each sentence below contains a title or name that needs to be underlined or enclosed in quotation marks. Write the title or name on your paper and punctuate it correctly.

EXAMPLE: In class we are reading the novel Johnny Tremain.

Johnny Tremain

1. I shall see the musical comedy My Fair Lady.
2. Mr. Greene flew to France on the Concorde.
3. I am going to subscribe to USA Today.
4. The painting The Dream is shown in this book.
5. Lizard Music is the title of an amusing book.
6. I am reading the chapter entitled The Chase.
7. Today we will hear the next episode, The Way Out.
8. Flowers for Algernon is an unusual story.
9. Who starred in the movie Gone With the Wind?
10. Ursula LeGuin wrote the book Wizard of Earthsea.

DEVELOPING WRITING SKILLS: Using Titles in Sentences. Write ten sentences. Include a different title in each.

30.7 Hyphens in Numbers and Words

Hyphens have a number of uses with numbers and words.

Use a hyphen when you write the numbers *twenty-one* through *ninety-nine.*

EXAMPLES: seventy-eight thirty-five forty-six

Use a hyphen when you use a fraction as an adjective but not when you use a fraction as a noun.

EXAMPLES: This glass is two-thirds full. (adjective)

Two thirds of the members were present. (noun)

Hyphens in Words. Hyphens are also used to separate certain words from the prefixes and suffixes attached to them.

Use a hyphen after a prefix followed by a proper noun or a proper adjective.

EXAMPLES: pre-Columbian pro-British mid-August

Use a hyphen in words with the prefixes *all-*, *ex-*, and *self-* and the suffix *-elect.*

EXAMPLES: all-American ex-President

self-conscious mayor-elect

Use a hyphen when you write some compound nouns.

Compound nouns are written in three different ways: as single words, as separate words, or as hyphenated words. When in doubt, check a dictionary.

SINGLE WORDS: flashlight passageway

SEPARATE WORDS: rocking chair time clock

HYPHENATED WORDS: ten-year-olds mother-in-law

EXERCISE A: Using Hyphens in Numbers and Words. Rewrite each of the sentences below, adding hyphens where necessary. If no hyphens need be added, write *correct.*

EXAMPLE: A music festival will be held in mid July.
A music festival will be held in mid-July.

1. There are twenty six amendments to our Constitution.
2. Sue was given an award as best all around athlete.
3. Antarctica occupies one tenth of the world's land area.
4. My uncle operates his own business; he is self employed.
5. The social studies test was one half written and one half oral.
6. The senator elect held a victory party.
7. There is much pro British feeling where we spent our vacation.
8. Bill is less self conscious than he used to be.
9. The ex President wrote a book about politics.
10. Our library has more than five hundred volumes.

EXERCISE B: More Practice Using Hyphens in Numbers and Words. Rewrite the sentences below, adding hyphens where necessary. If no hyphens need be added, write *correct.*

1. The singer recorded some all time favorites.
2. The movie theater was three fourths empty.
3. Two thirds of the year has already passed.
4. The population of Finland is over four million.
5. The law was passed during the pre Reagan years.

DEVELOPING WRITING SKILLS: Using Hyphenated Words. Write ten sentences about subjects of interest to you. In each sentence use a hyphen within a number or a word.

30.8 Hyphens at the Ends of Lines

When you cannot avoid dividing a word at the end of a line, the following is the chief rule to follow.

Divide a word only between syllables.

EXAMPLE: Marcia seems to have taken my advice seriously.

Check in a dictionary if you are unsure how a word is divided into syllables. Looking up the word *seriously,* for example, would show that its syllables are *se-ri-ous-ly.*

The following chart presents four other rules for dividing words.

FOUR OTHER RULES FOR WORD DIVISION
1. Never divide a one-syllable word.
2. Never divide a word so that one letter stands alone at the end of a line or the beginning of the next.
3. Never divide proper nouns or proper adjectives.
4. Divide a hyphenated word only after the hyphen.

If the rules make it impossible for you to fit a word at the end of a line, simply move the word down to the next line.

The examples below and on the next page illustrate the rules in the chart.

INCORRECT: John finished the race first.

CORRECT: John finished the race
first.

INCORRECT: The soup tastes too salt-
y.

CORRECT: The soup tastes too
salty.

INCORRECT: Most of the work was done by Joanne.

CORRECT: Most of the work was done by
Joanne.

INCORRECT: You have no good reason to be self-conscious.

CORRECT: You have no good reason to be self-
conscious.

EXERCISE: Using Hyphens to Divide Words. Use a hyphen to show how you would divide each word listed below if it were to occur at the end of a line. If a word cannot be broken, simply rewrite the word. If you are not sure of how to divide a word, look up the word in a dictionary.

EXAMPLE: quarter
quar-ter

1. perform
2. agent
3. group
4. enormous
5. handbook
6. unicorn
7. concern
8. bring
9. overheard
10. overdue
11. glance
12. dolphin
13. ticket
14. equality
15. open-ended
16. lunch
17. lion
18. step-son
19. addition
20. view

DEVELOPING WRITING SKILLS: Dividing Words at the Ends of Lines. Write ten sentences about things that are fun to do. Make each sentence at least two lines. Divide the last word in line one of each sentence so that part of the word is on line one and part of the word is on line two. Use a dictionary to check the syllables in each word you divide.

30.9 Apostrophes Used to Show Ownership

An apostrophe is used with singular or plural nouns to show ownership or possession.

To form the possessive of a singular noun, add an apostrophe and an *-s.*

EXAMPLES: the doctor's advice — the dog's bowl
Nat's decision — the girl's bicycle

Some singular nouns already end in *-s.* With a few exceptions, most of these nouns also add an apostrophe and an *-s.*

To form the possessive of a singular noun that ends in *-s,* add an apostrophe and an *-s.*

EXAMPLES: James's jacket — his boss's idea
Bess's desk — our class's display

The exceptions are words and phrases that would have too many *s* sounds in a row. Try saying *Ulysses's travels.* It makes sense to drop one of the *s* sounds and to use instead *Ulysses'* travels, which is much easier to say.

Most plural nouns already end in *-s.* These nouns form the possessive by simply adding an apostrophe.

To form the possessive of plural nouns that end in *-s,* add an apostrophe.

EXAMPLES: the officers' club — the witnesses' testimonies

Some plural nouns do not end in *-s.* They form the possessive the same way singular nouns do.

To form a possessive of a plural noun that does not end in *-s,* add an apostrophe and an *-s.*

EXAMPLES: The men's store — the women's committee
the trees' leaves — the students' newspaper

EXERCISE A: Using Apostrophes to Show Ownership. Write the possessive form of each underlined noun.

EXAMPLE: The judge remarks were lengthy.
judge's

1. The artist latest painting sold for $10,000.
2. The boss office is down the hall.
3. As I came closer, I could hear Sharon voice.
4. The children singing and playing were delightful.
5. All of the rooms ceilings are fifteen feet high.
6. The mouse squeak could be heard from afar.
7. Mr. Smith calls himself the people candidate.
8. A sign hung in the window of my father store.
9. I shall read two of Charles Dickens books.
10. This baseball has ten players autographs on it.

EXERCISE B: More Practice Using Apostrophes to Show Ownership. Write the possessive form of each underlined noun.

1. The scientist argument was very convincing.
2. Hercules adventures are extremely varied.
3. Have you seen Mr. Wallach coin collection?
4. The women decision was to begin a monthly newsletter.
5. Bess baked bread is the best I have ever tasted.
6. The youngsters ages are six, ten, and twelve.
7. Several designers fashions are on display in the department store.
8. Doris cousin ran along the shore.
9. The audience applauded the musician performance.
10. The mice cage is kept in the science laboratory.

DEVELOPING WRITING SKILLS: Using Nouns to Show Ownership. List the possessive form of five singular and five plural nouns. Use each possessive noun in a sentence.

30.10 Apostrophes in Contractions

A contraction is a word or a combination of two separate words written in a contracted (shortened) form.

Use an apostrophe in a contraction to show where one or more letters have been omitted.

Contractions are used in informal speech and writing. You can often find contractions in the dialogue of stories and plays. Contractions create the feeling of real-life speech.

EXAMPLE: "I'll bring in all the packages."
"Fine. I'd help, but I'm late already."

The chart lists the most commonly used contractions.

COMMONLY USED CONTRACTIONS	
aren't (are not)	couldn't (could not)
isn't (is not)	didn't (did not)
wasn't (was not)	don't (do not)
weren't (were not)	doesn't (does not)
hasn't (has not)	shouldn't (should not)
haven't (have not)	won't (will not)
hadn't (had not)	wouldn't (would not)
can't (cannot)	
I'll (I will)	she'll (she will)
you'll (you will)	we'll (we will)
he'll (he will)	they'll (they will)
I'm (I am)	we're (we are)
you're (you are)	they're (they are)
he's (he is)	who's (who is)
she's (she is)	where's (where is)
it's (it is)	Patty's (Patty is)

EXERCISE A: Using Apostrophes in Contractions. Write the contractions that can be used in place of the underlined words in the sentences below.

EXAMPLE: The music was not loud enough.
wasn't

1. He is writing a mystery story.
2. Natalie asked if we will take care of her dog.
3. They have not heard of a musicologist.
4. Maria has not met our friend Simon.
5. They will probably ask us to come along.
6. Who will volunteer to act as secretary?
7. Where is the latest edition of the newspaper?
8. I am sure we will stop at the Air and Space Museum.
9. Earl speaks Spanish, but he cannot speak French.
10. The attorneys are not sure how long the trial will last.

EXERCISE B: More Practice Using Apostrophes in Contractions. Write the contraction that can be used in place of the underlined words.

1. I think you will enjoy reading this novel.
2. I would like to make some suggestions.
3. The tour does not include a stop at the Alamo.
4. It is important for you to consider the alternatives.
5. They do not want to attract a large crowd.
6. I think you would enjoy seeing San Francisco.
7. Please tell Larry that I will be late.
8. Diane could not remember the time they arrived.
9. She will probably send us a letter with all the details.
10. Who is going to begin the discussion?

DEVELOPING WRITING SKILLS: Using Contractions in a Dialogue. Write a dialogue in which one person shows another person how to do something. Use at least ten contractions to give your dialogue the feel of real people talking in a natural way.

30.11 Avoiding Problems With Apostrophes

Even good writers must sometimes pause to figure out whether to write *its* or *it's*, *theirs* or *there's*, *whose* or *who's*, or *your* or *you're*. It is helpful to remember the following guideline.

It's, *there's*, *who's*, and *you're* are contractions for *it is*, *there is*, *who is*, and *you are*.

EXAMPLES: It's now seven o'clock. (*It is* now seven o'clock.)

There's Fred. (*There is* Fred.)

Who's bringing the food? (*Who is* bringing the food?)

You're a good sport. (*You are* a good sport.)

It's, *theirs*, *whose*, and *your* are possessive forms of *it*, *they*, *who*, and *you*.

EXAMPLES: Uncle Bert's old car stalled when its engine overheated.

Is it our turn or theirs?

Whose dog is that?

Your friend Tom just phoned.

Another rule that may help is the following.

Do not use an apostrophe with any possessive personal pronouns.

Notice in the chart below that no apostrophes are used with *your*, *hers*, *its*, *ours*, and *theirs*.

POSSESSIVE PERSONAL PRONOUNS					
my	your	his	hers	our	their
mine	yours	her	its	ours	theirs

EXERCISE A: Using Apostrophes Where Necessary. Rewrite each sentence with the correct choice of the two given in parentheses.

EXAMPLE: May I borrow (you're, your) pencil?
May I borrow your pencil?

1. (Who's, Whose) joining the team?
2. The best science exhibit was (there's, theirs).
3. Jane felt that (her's, hers) was the better party.
4. (It's, Its) not too late to try out for the team.
5. Carlos, give us (you're, your) opinion, please.
6. I know (who's, whose) pet this is.
7. (Our's Ours) was the best dance routine.
8. Now the sun is at (it's, its) highest point in the sky.
9. Look, (there's, theirs) the house I was born in.
10. Maybe (you're, your) right after all.

EXERCISE B: More Practice Using Apostrophes Where Necessary. Rewrite each sentence with the correct choice of expression.

1. Let's follow this stream to (it's, its) source.
2. (Who's, Whose) idea was it to camp here?
3. The highest grades were Phil's and (her's, hers).
4. (You're, Your) victory clinched the tournament for us.
5. (There's, Theirs) was the greatest accomplishment.
6. I think I know (who's, whose) responsible for this.
7. Bob mowed her lawn first and then (our's, ours).
8. They say (you're, your) a good pianist.
9. Who said, "(There's, Theirs) no business like show business"?
10. This flower has lost (it's, its) sweet smell.

DEVELOPING WRITING SKILLS: Writing Sentences with Contractions and Possessive Personal Pronouns. Use each of the following words in a sentence of your own: it's, its, there's, theirs, who's, whose, you're, your, hers, and ours.

Skills Review and Writing Workshop

Using Other Punctuation Marks

CHECKING YOUR SKILLS

Semicolons, colons, quotation marks, underlining, hyphens, and apostrophes have been left out of the article below. Rewrite the article, adding the missing punctuation.

EXAMPLE: Were with you, Alberts supporters shouted.
"We're with you," Albert's supporters shouted.

(1) On Thursday at 145 p.m., a student committee announced the results of the election for president of the senior class at Highland High School. (2) The winner, Albert Jones, received eighty seven votes, while his opponent, Sylvia Masters, received seventy nine votes it was a close election.

(3) The new president said, Im very happy. (4) Ill do my best to serve all the students.

(5) When interviewed afterward, Albert was reminded that he had made the following promises longer lunch breaks, more playtime, and frequent class trips. (6) When, the reporter asked, can we expect to see these changes?

(7) Just wait till Im in office! boasted Albert. (8) Alberts supporters nodded in approval.

USING MECHANICS SKILLS IN WRITING

Writing an Essay

Everyone studies grammar. Some people like it and some people don't. But just about everyone understands that it is important to know what the rules of grammar are and how to use those rules. There are, of course, people who don't think grammar is important. Here's your chance to convince them they are wrong. Write an essay explaining why grammar is important. As you write, try to observe all the rules of grammar that you know. This will show that knowing *how* to write well *does* help you write well.

UNIT IV

Composition

The Writer's Techniques

Chapter 31

The Writing Process

There is nothing mysterious about writing. Writing is a skill that anyone can learn. It is a process that includes certain steps.

If you were going to build a house, you would follow a process made up of certain specific steps. First you would buy a lot and measure it. Then you would design a floor plan to show where every room would go. You would start building by laying the foundation. Then you would add the floors, walls, and windows. You would install insulation, electrical wiring, and plumbing. Finally, you would add the roof, gutters, and paint the outside of the house.

You would not try to build the house all at once. And you would not try to perform the steps out of order. You could not install the roof, for instance, before the walls and floors were in place.

Many young writers, however, make the mistake of trying to start writing immediately, before going through the initial stage of planning and organizing what they will write. Then they wonder why they cannot think of anything to say. Even the best, most experienced writers need to organize their thoughts first. If you follow the steps of the writing process, you will be able to put together a successful composition.

31.1 Prewriting

The first step in the writing process is the prewriting stage. This is the planning that you do before you start to write. The prewriting stage itself can be broken down into a series of steps. In prewriting, you explore ideas, choose a topic, determine your audience, decide on a purpose, select a main idea, support your main idea, and organize the supporting information.

Complete all the steps of prewriting before you begin to write.

The following chart lists and explains the basic steps that you will follow in prewriting.

THE STEPS OF PREWRITING	
Exploring ideas	First, explore ideas for writing topics using such techniques as brainstorming, free writing, and journal writing.
Choosing a topic	From your list of ideas, choose one topic that is narrow and specific enough for you to cover it in the space available.
Identifying your audience	Decide who will be your potential readers—teachers, students, parents, or those who share a particular interest.
Determining your purpose	Decide whether your purpose will be to inform, to persuade, or to entertain.
Selecting a main idea	In a complete sentence state the most important idea of your paper.

Supporting your main idea	Support your main idea with examples, details, or incidents.
Organizing your supporting information	Organize your supporting information in chronological order, spatial order, or order of importance.

You should begin your prewriting with exploring ideas for a topic. The best topic is probably one that you are interested in and know something about. So review your interests, opinions, preferences, skills, and experiences for possible topics. Books, television programs, and school courses are other good sources of ideas. To jog your memory, try asking yourself questions like those in the following chart.

QUESTIONS FOR INTERVIEWING YOURSELF

1. What hobbies or sports do I enjoy?
2. What special skills do I have?
3. What subjects do I know best?
4. What topics arouse my curiosity? What would I like to learn about?
5. What do I like to talk about with my friends?
6. Has anything unusual happened to me recently?
7. Have I read any books or seen any television programs about interesting topics?
8. What interesting topic have I read about in newspapers?
9. What interesting or unusual experience have I heard about from friends or relatives?
10. What things have been on my mind lately?

One useful technique for producing ideas is called brainstorming. In brainstorming, you simply take a sheet of paper and write down everything that comes into your head.

STEPS IN BRAINSTORMING

1. Choose any general topic that comes to mind and write it on your paper.
2. Starting from your general topic, let your mind roam freely and write down all the ideas that come into your head.
3. Don't reject any ideas because they seem silly or unusable; write down every topic you think of without judging how good it is.
4. Try to break down broad topics into smaller ones. Look at the smaller topics and see if they can be broken down into even smaller ones.
5. When you have filled a page, stop. If you run out of ideas, consider trying another broad topic.

Notice that two of the broad topics have been broken down into smaller ones in the sample below.

SAMPLE BRAINSTORMING LIST

Topic: Music

Styles of music	Types of music
jazz	orchestral music
rock	choral music
folk	chamber music
classical music	opera
country-western	Famous composers
Rock groups	Electronic music
Solo singers	Wind instruments
Taking piano lessons	Brass
Playing in the school band	Strings

A variation of the brainstorming technique is free writing. In free writing, you choose a certain length of time to write or a certain number of pages to fill. For example, you might decide to write for twenty minutes or for three pages. Then you write without stopping until your time is up or your pages are filled. When you have finished your free writing, set it aside for a while. Then reread it and decide whether it contains any useful ideas for writing topics.

To guide you in brainstorming, you may want to use a method that newspaper writers use to develop a story. It is known as the "five W's" method. The five W's are the questions Who? What? When? Where? and Why? (Sometimes a sixth question, How?, is included.) The method is a good way to work with a general topic that appeals to you but does not lead to any specific ideas you can write about.

For example, if the general topic music occurred to you, you might get stuck at that point and be unable to think of anything to say about it. You could then use the five W's and come up with something like the following:

Who? Me
What? Practicing the clarinet
When? Every day for at least thirty minutes
Where? At home
Why? To improve my technique

By asking these five specific questions, specific ideas were suggested. A writer could then think about them to arrive at a specific subject to write about.

Another method of stimulating brainstorming ideas is to write the letters of the alphabet down the left side of your paper. Then try to think of at least one idea about your topic for each letter of the alphabet. Your list might resemble the following example.

A: Music appreciation; arpeggios
B: Band music, band concerts; brass instruments
C: Clarinet playing; country-western music; composers
D: Disk jockeys

Another way of producing ideas for writing topics is keeping a journal. When you keep a journal, you record your everyday experiences. Usually, you also record your thoughts and feelings about these experiences.

Most journal writers keep a special notebook for journal entries and try to write in it every day or at least every week.

The following is an example of a journal entry that might suggest writing topics.

> *November 20.* Band practice this afternoon. First we rehearsed "The Star-Spangled Banner." It's beginning to sound pretty good. Then we read through "White Christmas" and some traditional carols for the Christmas concert. Ouch! Quite a few wrong notes. We're not very good at sight reading. Mr. Schwartz gave us some suggestions for individual practice. He said we should play the difficult sections slowly, over and over.

The writer of this journal entry might look it over in the future and decide to write a story about how a concert comes about. An essay describing how embarrassed a musician can feel when he or she first attempts to play a new piece is another possibility.

Chapter 40, "Personal Writing," discusses journal writing in more detail. As you reread your journal, you may find that it contains good ideas for writing topics.

Instead of a journal, you may want to keep a file of possible writing topics. Jot down ideas that interest you. Take notes on the books you read. Cut out and save magazine or newspaper articles.

When you have a long list of ideas for possible writing topics, you will need to focus your ideas. Your goal is to choose a topic that can be discussed fully in the space available. The more specific your topic, the more effectively you can cover it in a short paper.

You may be assigned a general topic by your teacher. Or you may arrive at a broad topic through some type of brainstorming. Either way, it is up to you to narrow down the topic. One good way is by brainstorming. Another way is to do some reading on the topic. A third way might be to discuss the topic with friends. A detailed brainstorming list now will help you think of details to write about later.

The chart below lists several broad topics and gives suggestions for narrowing them down.

NARROWING DOWN A TOPIC	
Broad Topic	**Narrower Topics**
Health	Nutrition eating a balanced diet the best sources of vitamins Exercise working out jogging
Animals	Wild animals endangered species Pets goldfish parakeets training a pet
Hobbies	Collecting stamps comic books

When you write, what you say about your topic and how you say it will depend on whom you are writing for. Will your audience be your teacher, your classmates, your parents, or the readers of the local newspaper?

When you have thought about your audience, you should be able to state your purpose—to inform, to persuade, or to entertain.

PURPOSES FOR WRITING	
Purpose	**Description**
To inform	To describe a process or object To narrate an event To tell how to do something.
To persuade	To make readers accept an opinion
To entertain	To tell an amusing or interesting story

The following chart shows how similar topics may vary according to audience and purpose.

AUDIENCES AND PURPOSES FOR WRITING TOPICS		
Topic	**Audience**	**Purpose**
Techniques of practicing a musical instrument	Fellow musicians	To inform
Why playing music is more fun than listening to it	Classmates who do not play instruments	To persuade
What happened on the band's concert tour	All classmates	To entertain

Stating your audience and purpose clearly will help you decide what details to include and what kind of language to use.

Now that you have chosen your topic, audience, and purpose, you are ready to state your main idea and decide how to support it. Your main idea is a statement, usually a sentence, that sums up the point of your composition. In a paragraph, your main idea will be stated in the topic sentence. In a longer paper, your introductory paragraph will probably state your main idea.

There are many types of supporting information. They include examples, details, and incidents.

SUPPORTING A MAIN IDEA	
Examples	Examples can explain, illustrate, or elaborate on a main idea.
Details	Details can describe an object or event and make an idea seem more vivid.
Incidents	One or more incidents may illustrate a main idea.

Chapter 34, "Looking at Paragraphs," discusses these types of supporting information and will also help you in your writing.

When you have listed all your supporting ideas, you will need to decide how to organize them. Your decision will be based on the nature of your topic. It may also depend on your audience and purpose. Three ways of organizing support are in chronological order, in spatial order, and in order of importance.

Chapter 35, "Looking at Paragraph Organization," shows how to organize supporting information in these three ways.

EXERCISE A: Exploring Ideas and Selecting a Topic. Explore ideas for a topic for a short paper. Use one of the brainstorming techniques described earlier in this section to think of specific ideas that you might use for a topic. Choose one topic that is narrow enough to be discussed fully in a brief composition of one or more paragraphs.

EXERCISE B: Choosing an Audience, Purpose, and Main Idea. Start with the topic you chose for Exercise A. Select an audience for whom you will write the paper. Now state your purpose in writing—to inform, to persuade, or to entertain. Finally, write a sentence that expresses the main idea that you want to get across to your audience.

DEVELOPING WRITING SKILLS: Preparing to Write Your Paper. Brainstorm for information to support the main idea you have chosen. Decide what kind of supporting information you will use and how you will organize it. Number the ideas in the order in which you will mention them. Or rewrite them in a simple outline which will organize your ideas. Save your notes for use later in this chapter.

31.2 Writing

When you have chosen your main idea and arranged your supporting information, you can begin to write. The first version of your paper is called the first draft. One mistake that beginning writers make is to think that a good writer can simply sit down, start writing, put everything down on paper, and then stop, with all work done. The last section made it clear that planning should precede writing. And the planning should be systematic. Even good and experienced writers usually have to go through all the steps that make up prewriting. When they have done so, then they can write their first draft.

Write a first draft based on all the prewriting work you have done.

You will rewrite your first draft at least once. But remember: The better your first draft, the less time you will have to spend rewriting it. This does not mean that you should take pains over spelling every word correctly or using perfect grammar. It means that you should try to get all that you want to say down on paper. And it means that supporting information should be in the order you have planned on using. Polishing your sentences, correcting errors in grammar or spelling, and other such changes will be taken care of in the third stage of writing: revising.

Working from your prewriting notes, write your paper in the order you have planned. You will probably want to begin by stating your main idea. Your main idea should be followed by your supporting information—examples, details, or incidents. You should mention your supporting information in the order that you have chosen for it. There is still time to change your mind, however. You may decide that a different order would be better. And, of course, you may think of more supporting information. If so, do not hesitate to add it.

The chart on the following page offers guidelines for writing a first draft.

WRITING A FIRST DRAFT

1. Start with your main idea and list of supporting information.
2. Mention your supporting ideas in the order that you have chosen—chronological order, spatial order, or order of importance.
3. Feel free to change the order of ideas if listing them in another order seems more logical.
4. Add appropriate examples, details, or incidents that come to mind.
5. Delete any supporting information that seems unrelated to your main idea.
6. Keep your audience and purpose—to inform, to persuade, or to entertain—in mind as you write.

If you have done your prewriting thoroughly, you should have no trouble writing a first draft. If you get stuck, go back to your prewriting notes. You may need to repeat one of the prewriting steps. Perhaps you will need to brainstorm for more supporting information. Or you may have to change your main idea to make your topic broader or narrower.

EXERCISE: Writing a First Draft. Working with the prewriting notes that you made for the exercises in Section 31.1, write a first draft of a short paper. Refer to the chart in this section for a suggested procedure. If you get stuck at any point, review the steps of prewriting. You may need to repeat one or more of those steps to get your writing moving ahead.

DEVELOPING WRITING SKILLS: Planning and Writing a Short Paper. Go back to your prewriting notes from Section 31.1. Choose another main idea, an audience, and a purpose. Brainstorm for supporting information, and write a first draft of a short paper about this main idea.

31.3 Revising

The third stage in the writing process is revising. Revising involves two kinds of changes: rewriting for sense and editing for word choice and sentence variety. This stage is often neglected. But it is just as important as the other two. Every first draft can be improved by careful revision. So it is essential that you allow time for the revising stage.

Revise your paper, first for sense and then for specific words and sentences.

When you have finished writing your first draft, put it aside for a time before you start to revise it. That way you will be rereading it from a fresh perspective. You may want to ask a friend to read your paper and comment on it.

The following chart lists several suggestions for rereading.

SUGGESTIONS FOR REREADING
1. Wait for an hour or so, or even longer, before you reread your first draft.
2. Read the first draft aloud to yourself and listen for problems.
3. Read the first draft to someone else. Ask your listener to point out sentences that are awkward or hard to understand.
4. Ask another person to read the first draft aloud while you listen for weak or confusing ideas.
5. Have someone else read your draft silently and then comment on the ideas.

Whether you are reading your draft to someone else, or someone is reading it aloud to you, you may feel a little embarrassed. Fight this feeling. Concentrate on what you have written, not on your feelings about it.

The first time you reread, watch for problems of sense. Check to see that there is enough supporting information and that it is arranged in logical order. The following chart lists questions to ask when rereading a first draft for sense.

REVISING FOR SENSE
1. Is the main idea stated clearly?
2. Is there enough supporting information? What examples, details, or incidents could be added?
3. Is any of the supporting information unrelated to the main idea?
4. Would the ideas be clearer if they were arranged in different order?

After you have revised your paper for sense, reread it again. This time, check for word choice and sentence style. Your goal is to make sure that you have expressed yourself as clearly as possible.

The following chart lists questions to ask when rereading a paper for words and sentences.

EDITING WORDS AND SENTENCES
1. Have I used the clearest, most specific words to express my ideas?
2. Have I used language appropriate for my audience?
3. Is the meaning of each sentence clear?
4. Have I used a variety of sentence lengths and structures?

Chapter 32, "Improving Your Use of Words," discusses how to choose the right word to say exactly what you mean. Chapter 33, "Improving Your Sentences," explains how to use a variety of sentence styles to make your writing more interesting and graceful.

On the following page is an example of a revised draft of a section of a composition on learning to play a musical instrument.

Every musician knows that practice is important. But not every music student knows how to make the most of ~~his or her~~ practice time, You need to follow certain steps. ~~Having a good teacher is important, especially at the beginning.~~

Good habits are easy to continue, Bad habits are hard to break. You need to develop good habits from the beginning. ~~Proper~~ posture is important; you cannot play ~~properly~~ if you slouch. Be sure you know the correct way to hold and finger your instrument. If you play a wind instrument, you will need to work on proper breath control.

Once you know the fundamentals, you can practice to improve your technique, tone, intonation (pitch), and interpretive ability. You should practice at least thirty minutes a day. Practice regularly.

Warm up by playing scales and arpeggios, or broken chords. Since most of the music you will play will be based on major or minor scales, memorizing ~~the~~ scales will make you a better sightreader and enable you to learn new music faster. So ~~play~~ exercises based on scales and arpeggios.

Playing scales and arpeggios very slowly will improve your intonation. Play octaves and triads, and listen to how well in tune you ~~are~~. Practice sustained tones for at least five minutes.

Etudes teach both interpretation and technique. So your first goal will be technical mastery. Spend the last fifteen minutes play etudes, If you run into a difficult passage, stop and make an excercise out of it. Slow it dow, change the rhythmic pattern, practice the passage over and over until you can play it ~~with facility~~.

The final step in revising is proofreading. When you proofread, you check for mechanical errors—mistakes in spelling, grammar, punctuation, and capitalization.

SUGGESTIONS FOR PROOFREADING
1. Look for sentence errors, such as fragments, run-on sentences, and misplaced modifiers. 2. Make sure all your subjects and verbs agree. 3. Make sure you have used correct pronouns. 4. Check for errors in capitalization. 5. Be sure you have used periods, commas, semicolons, apostrophes, and other punctuation marks correctly. 6. Use your dictionary to check the spelling of doubtful words.

If you find only a few errors, correct them right on the final copy. If you find many errors or a few major ones, however, recopy the passage and proofread it again.

Remember that you must be alert for errors when you proofread your own writing. Because you know what you meant to say, it is easy to "read through" your mistakes.

EXERCISE A: Revising Your First Draft. Revise the first draft that you wrote for the exercise in Section 31.2. Revise first for sense and then for word choice and sentence variety.

EXERCISE B: Proofreading Your Revised Version. Proofread your revised version carefully. Make a clean final copy.

DEVELOPING WRITING SKILLS: Revising and Proofreading a Short Paper. Revise and proofread the first draft that you wrote for "Developing Writing Skills" in Section 31.2. Then make a clean final copy.

Writing Workshop: The Writing Process

ASSIGNMENT

Topic My State

Form and Purpose A composition that informs, persuades, or describes

Audience Visitors vacationing in your state

Length Two to three paragraphs

Focus After narrowing the topic to one specific aspect of your state, present your main idea in a topic sentence. Then give details, facts, and examples that support your main idea.

Sources Books, magazines, newspapers

Prewriting Narrow your topic by choosing a specific aspect of your state that interests you and can be covered well in two or three paragraphs. Decide on your purpose and write a main idea. List supporting details in an order that fits your purpose.

Writing Use your notes to write a first draft.

Revising Use the checklists on pages 306 and 307 to revise your paper. Then prepare a final copy.

Improving Your Use of Words

When you speak, you want people to understand what you say. If your listeners do not understand you, your words have been wasted. When you write, the same thing is true. The purpose of your writing is to communicate something to your readers. If listeners or readers do not understand you, it is possible that you have not chosen your words carefully enough.

Using the right words not only makes your meaning clearer, it also makes your writing much more vivid. Your readers will want to read further. For example, the sentence *Some animals are very intelligent* conveys little information or interest. However, the sentence *Chimpanzees have learned to use sign language to "talk" to humans and other chimpanzees* is clear and specific. Many people would be interested in reading more.

In this chapter you will learn to use action words to express ideas clearly and forcefully. You will learn to choose specific words to create vivid word pictures. And you will practice avoiding slang and replacing it with more appropriate language.

32.1 Using Action Words

To express action in your writing, it is important to use verbs well. Choosing the right verbs can make the difference between strong and weak writing.

Some verbs are action verbs. An action verb describes an action performed by someone or something. *Run, jump,* and *dive* are action verbs. Other verbs are linking verbs. A linking verb links the subject with another word in the sentence. *Be, become,* and *seem* are linking verbs. Action verbs usually state ideas more vividly than linking verbs.

Use action verbs to express ideas clearly and forcefully.

You will still use linking verbs in your writing, but you should try to replace them with action verbs whenever possible.

LINKING VERB: My cousin *is* a teacher at the state university.

ACTION VERB: My cousin *teaches* at the state university.

REPLACING LINKING VERBS WITH ACTION VERBS
Sentence with a Linking Verb
My sister was the winner of an award from the science department.
Sentence with an Action Verb
My sister won an award from the science department.
Sentence with a New Action Verb
My sister earned an award from the science department.
Sentence with Different Wording
The science department gave my sister an award.

EXERCISE A: Using Action Verbs. Rewrite each of the following sentences using the action verb in parentheses.

EXAMPLE: Joe was the leader of the search party. (led)
Joe led the search party.

1. The field goal meant the end of the game. (ended)
2. My cousin is a worker in a toy factory. (works)
3. The loud music was painful to my ears. (hurt)
4. African farmers are hopeful that it will rain. (hope)
5. Wilma was excellent in the high jump. (excelled)
6. The radio was a distraction for me. (distracted)
7. Our weather seems pleasant to most visitors. (pleases)
8. The satellite is in orbit around the earth. (orbits)
9. She was responsible for selling the car. (sold)
10. The ape was frightening to the children. (frightened)

EXERCISE B: More Work with Action Verbs. In each sentence, change one of the words into an action verb, introduce a new action verb, or change the wording so an action verb can be introduced.

1. Bad weather was the ruin of our plans.
2. Ants are a bother to picnickers.
3. Budget cuts are a threat to school sports.
4. The dance company gave a performance at our school.
5. The neighbors were angered by our loud music.
6. The children became tired of playing on the swings.
7. The letter was received in six weeks.
8. Many members of the audience were bored by the speaker.
9. Biology was taught by Ms. Chung last year.
10. Several houses were destroyed by the tornado.

DEVELOPING WRITING SKILLS: Using Action Verbs in Your Own Writing. Write ten sentences using action verbs to describe people performing specific actions.

32.2 Using Specific Words

Clear, specific words can create pictures in the minds of readers.

Choose specific nouns, verbs, adjectives, and adverbs.

VAGUE WORDS	SPECIFIC WORDS
The restaurant served good food.	The steakhouse served fresh salads and tender steaks.
Some birds went into the water.	Hundreds of penguins plunged into the icy Antarctic Ocean.
The horse made it over the fence.	The black stallion cleared the six-foot fence effortlessly.

Unless you use specific nouns, your sentences may mean little to your readers.

VAGUE: The *animals* searched for *food.*

SPECIFIC: The *dolphins* searched for *fish.*

Using specific verbs can make your word pictures much more lively.

VAGUE: The mountain goat *got* across a crevice.

SPECIFIC: The mountain goat *sprang* across a crevice.

Using specific adjectives and adverbs can also make your writing clearer and more lively.

VAGUE: My new sports car is *colorful.*

SPECIFIC: My new sports car is *bright red.*

VAGUE: She did the somersault *well.*

SPECIFIC: She did the somersault *flawlessly.*

EXERCISE A: Choosing Specific Words. Replace the underlined words with more specific ones.

EXAMPLE: Mrs. Smith gave us food.

Mrs. Smith served us ham and cheese sandwiches.

1. I caught a big fish.
2. Sandy did well on the test.
3. The guard saw a man leaving the building.
4. I am reading a good book.
5. Some gazelles moved across the plain.
6. The plants in our garden are growing.
7. Sondra and Walter bought some things at a store.
8. The music sounded strange.
9. Flowers covered the area.
10. The poor weather is depressing.

EXERCISE B: More Work with Specific Words. Find the vague words in each sentence. Replace them with more specific words.

1. I see an unusual animal over there.
2. Her room looked nice.
3. Juan told a story about some people.
4. A colorful bird flew along the road.
5. Our car moved along the road.
6. We served an interesting dessert to our guests.
7. While we were away, someone took some things.
8. Bill is going out West for a while.
9. Marlene made a machine.
10. A person was walking around the place.

DEVELOPING WRITING SKILLS: Using Specific Words in Your Own Writing. Write a brief paragraph using specific words to create a vivid picture of an incident.

32.3 Avoiding Slang

Slang is language that is too casual for most writing. Although it may be acceptable in conversation, it is not considered standard English.

Avoid slang in your writing.

Watch for slang in the sentences you write. If you use words and expressions that only young people use, those expressions are probably slang. Replace them with clearer, more acceptable words. The following examples show how slang can be replaced by standard language.

SLANG: My sister *digs* skiing.

REVISED: My sister *enjoys* skiing.

SLANG: The test will be a *piece of cake.*

REVISED: The test will be *easy.*

SLANG: We *freaked out* when the band appeared.

REVISED: We *cheered loudly* when the band appeared.

The following chart gives more examples of slang expressions followed by standard ones.

REPLACING SLANG WITH STANDARD ENGLISH

Slang Expression	Standard English Expression
far out	unusual, strange
flunk	fail
groovy	enjoyable, excellent
gross out	disgust
hassle	annoy, harass
laid back	relaxed, easy-going
rap	talk, converse
square	old-fashioned, conventional
turkey	fool
with it	up-to-date

EXERCISE A: Finding and Replacing Slang. Find the slang word or expression in each sentence. Rewrite the sentence using more appropriate English.

EXAMPLE: Let's split before it's too late.
Let's leave before it's too late.

1. My brother totaled his car in the accident.
2. I hope you'll make the scene at the football game.
3. Abstract art is too far out for me.
4. We'll stay in town if we can find a place to crash.
5. Waiting in line to buy tickets is a drag.
6. Horror films give me the creeps.
7. Maria told her younger brother to bug off.
8. The band members hammed it up on stage.
9. Rounding the final turn, the horses looked bushed.
10. Mr. Harris was ripped off by a dishonest car dealer.

EXERCISE B: More Work with Slang. Find the slang word or expression in each sentence. Rewrite the sentence using more appropriate English.

1. Several boys were hanging out in front of the theater.
2. Eddie went ape when we splashed cold water on him.
3. Unfortunately, Phyllis bombed on the test.
4. The class trip was a gas.
5. Her last play wowed the critics.
6. I've studied ballet, but it just isn't my bag.
7. Cleaning fish grosses me out.
8. Larry told the curious children to get lost.
9. You'll flip over this new record.
10. It was an extremely long race, but all the runners hung in there.

DEVELOPING WRITING SKILLS: Avoiding Slang in Your Own Writing. Write five sentences that contain slang. Then replace the slang with standard English.

Skills Review and Writing Workshop

Improving Your Use of Words

CHECKING YOUR SKILLS

Rewrite the following paragraph, substituting specific and lively words for vague and weak ones. Replace slang with acceptable expressions.

(1) Australia has some of the most far-out animals in the world. (2) Most of the world's marsupials (mammals whose young develop in an external pouch instead of inside the mother's body) live there. (3) The kangaroo is a fun marsupial. (4) The cute little koala is another. (5) Then there are the birds. (6) The ostrich is the largest of all birds and can run like crazy when it doesn't have its head stuck in the sand. (7) The cassowary is smaller but is also fast, and it has been known to kill people. (8) Neither of these crazy birds can fly. (9) And there's the duckbilled platypus, which can't decide whether it's a bird or a mammal. (10) It's really weird. (11) Some great-looking tropical fish swim in the waters around the Great Barrier Reef. (12) But divers who see a fin above the water know they should beware: It could be either a groovy dolphin or an ungroovy shark.

USING COMPOSITION SKILLS

Choosing the Right Words

Turn back to Exercise A in Section 32.2. Choose one of the sentences that you rewrote to make them more specific. Use your revised version of the sentence as the beginning of a paragraph. Before you begin writing, jot down some ideas about what you would like to say in the paragraph.

Now write your first draft. Try to use as many action words as possible. Do not use slang.

After you have written your draft, reread it. Will your exact meaning be clear? Have you used standard, appropriate English? Write a neat final version, and proofread your work.

Chapter 33

Improving Your Sentences

Composition students are sometimes embarrassed by the sound of their own writing. Listening to one of your writing assignments read aloud to the class can be as painful as the sound of chalk squeaking on a blackboard.

If the sound of your writing is unpleasant, it may be because all your sentences begin and end the same way. When every sentence in a paragraph is the same length, the paragraph usually sounds monotonous. When the sentences are short and choppy, they tend to sound babyish. When most of the sentences contain nothing more than a subject, verb, and complement, they sound dull and lifeless. When several separate ideas are combined into one long sentence, the sentence generally is awkward and confusing.

In this chapter, you will study several methods of improving your writing by varying your sentence style. You will practice combining two or more short sentences into one. You will learn to add details to lengthen a short, choppy sentence. And you will learn to separate a long, rambling sentence into shorter sentences.

33.1 Sentence Combining

A passage with too many short sentences can sound choppy and monotonous. It is a good idea to combine some of these short sentences so that your writing will include sentences of various lengths. This will make your writing smoother and easier to follow.

Combine two or three short, choppy sentences into one longer sentence.

For instance, the two short sentences below sound monotonous. They could easily be combined into one sentence, however, without changing their meaning in any way.

TWO SHORT, CHOPPY SENTENCES:	The Ledbetters went hiking in the Appalachian Mountains. The Jacksons also went hiking in the Appalachian Mountains.
ONE LONGER SENTENCE:	The Ledbetters and the Jacksons went hiking in the Appalachian Mountains.

The single sentence means exactly the same as the two shorter sentences and sounds much smoother.

There are several ways to combine two short sentences. One way is to form one sentence with a compound subject.

COMBINING TWO SENTENCES BY USING A COMPOUND SUBJECT
Glorida Rodriguez is running for class president. Bill Johnson is also running for class president.
Glorida Rodriguez and Bill Johnson are both running for class president.

Another way of combining two sentences is to form a single sentence from them using a compound verb with a single subject.

COMBINING TWO SENTENCES BY USING A COMPOUND VERB

My little brother sat at a roadside stand. He sold lemonade to passing drivers.

My little brother sat at a roadside stand and sold lemonade to passing drivers.

Sometimes two short, choppy sentences can be combined into one compound sentence.

FORMING A COMPOUND SENTENCE

The bell rang. Sandra ran to her next class.

The bell rang, and Sandra ran to her next class.

Or two sentences can be combined to make a complex sentence.

FORMING A COMPLEX SENTENCE

Bill served sodas. Janice entertained the guests.

Bill served sodas while Janice entertained the guests.

Turning one sentence into an appositive phrase is a simple, effective way of combining two short sentences.

USING AN APPOSITIVE PHRASE

Ms. Torres used to teach at Elmwood High School. She is our new science teacher.

Ms. Torres, our new science teacher, used to teach at Elmwood High School.

Making a prepositional phrase out of a short sentence is another good way to combine two sentences.

USING A PREPOSITIONAL PHRASE
A German shepherd barked at Tim and me as we walked across the street. The dog was in our neighbor's front yard.
A German shepherd in our neighbor's front yard barked at Tim and me as we walked across the street.

A good way to combine two short, choppy sentences is to change one of the sentences into a participial phrase.

USING A PARTICIPIAL PHRASE
Coach Harvey waited for an upset. He watched the game very intently.
Waiting for an upset, Coach Harvey watched the game very intently.

EXERCISE A: Combining Sentences. Using any of the sentence-combining techniques you have just learned about, combine the sentences in each of the following items.

EXAMPLE: We sat on the beach. We watched the sun rise.
Sitting on the beach, we watched the sun rise.

1. Joe parked the car. He carried the groceries into the house.
2. Janice and Terry ran indoors. They were drenched from the sudden rain shower.
3. The exhibit was a success. The bake sale was a success too.
4. I usually arrive early at school. I enjoy walking in the morning.
5. Marty had a pet snake. It lived in a glass tank in Marty's bedroom.
6. Mr. Wilson paints landscapes. He sells them at the Community Art Center.

7. The Rangers tasted victory. It was the first time this season.
8. Two famous ball players were the surprise guests. They were guests at our awards banquet. The banquet was held Friday.
9. The bank robber was disguised. She looked like a policeman. She escaped unnoticed into the crowd on the sidewalk.
10. The walrus looks clumsy. It appears sluggish. It is quite agile in the water.

EXERCISE B: More Work with Combining Sentences. Combine the sentences in each of the items.

1. Mother ordered flowers for the party. The flowers were delivered next door by mistake.
2. The tool shed stays warm during the winter. It has good insulation.
3. Thomas Jefferson was the third President of the United States. He helped to write the Declaration of Independence.
4. Stephanie wants to buy a new stereo. She wants to get a personal computer. She needs a new bicycle first.
5. The beaver slapped the water with its tail. It swam away. It swam down the river.

DEVELOPING WRITING SKILLS: Using Sentence Combining to Rewrite a Paragraph. Rewrite the following passage using sentence-combining techniques.

A permanent space station is possible. It could happen by the end of this century. There would be scientific laboratories on board the space station. Solar panels would power the laboratories. The solar panels would also power television monitors. Astronauts would be able to move freely. The astronauts would conduct experiments. They would analyze cloud formations on earth. They would examine tides. They would study weather patterns.

33.2 Adding Details to Sentences

Another way to improve short, choppy sentences is to lengthen them by adding details to the various parts of the sentence.

Enrich short sentences by adding details to the subject, verb, or complement.

The two sentences below illustrate how details can be added.

SHORT SENTENCE: Our barn caught fire.

WITH DETAILS ADDED: In the middle of the night, our old, empty barn caught fire.

The following chart shows three ways to add details to short sentences. In some sentences, you may use only one of these methods. In others, you may use two or three.

LENGTHENING SHORT SENTENCES BY ADDING DETAILS	
Adding Details to the Subject	
His car lay alongside the road.	Burned almost beyond recognition, his car lay alongside the road.
Adding Details to the Verb	
The swimmers dove into the water.	The swimmers dove with a great splash into the water.
Adding Details to the Complement	
We found a purse.	We found a worn, dusty purse filled with old coins.

EXERCISE A: Adding Details to Short Sentences. Rewrite each of the following sentences by adding the details in parentheses. Put them in where they best fit and where they seem most clear.

EXAMPLE: The sun blazed down. (summer, onto the beach)

The summer sun blazed down onto the beach.

1. We ate a picnic lunch. (under the trees, of sandwiches and sodas)
2. The tree swayed in the wind. (its leaves rustling, outside my window)
3. They studied. (every night, afraid of failing their math test)
4. Birds perched in a cage. (large gilded, enormous multicolored)
5. We jumped and ran. (hearing a loud crash, afraid that the roof would cave in)

EXERCISE B: More Work with Short Sentences. Rewrite each of the following sentences by adding at least two details.

1. Our kite soared.
2. We painted my room.
3. Pam spoke to my father.
4. Eileen and I rode our bicycles.
5. George saw a shape.

DEVELOPING WRITING SKILLS: Using Details to Improve a Paragraph. Rewrite the following passage by adding details. Remember that details can be added to the subject, verb, and complement.

Joe and I sailed in the regatta last week. We made a good team. We entered the yacht race. We sailed my grandfather's yacht. Joe and I had been practicing all summer. It was an exciting race. We finished second, close behind the winning boat. Ten other yachts finished behind us.

33.3 Shortening Rambling Sentences

Rambling compound sentences are as bad as too many short sentences. A long compound sentence that links several clauses with conjunctions such as *and* and *but* is known as a rambling sentence. Such a sentence should be split up into two shorter sentences.

Separate a rambling compound sentence into two or more shorter sentences.

Compound sentences are often useful, of course. It is only when too many ideas are strung together in the same sentence that the sentence becomes awkwardly long. For instance, the following sentence contains six independent clauses linked together with conjunctions.

RAMBLING SENTENCE: John tried to lift the box, *but* he couldn't, *and* then his uncles tried, *but* they couldn't lift it either, *and* then John's father and brother tried to lift the box, *but* not even they could lift it.

A sentence like the one above will sound better if it is split up into several shorter sentences. Read the sentence and look for the end of each complete thought. Then take out the conjunction that links that complete thought, or independent clause, with the clause that follows it. Replace the conjunction with a period, and begin a new sentence. In the sentence above, three conjunctions can be removed and replaced with periods.

SEVERAL SHORTER SENTENCES: John tried to lift the box, *but* he couldn't. Then John's uncles tried, *but* they couldn't lift it either. Finally, John's father and brother tried to lift the box. Not even they could lift it, however.

EXERCISE: Shortening Rambling Sentences. Rewrite each rambling sentence to make two or three shorter ones.

EXAMPLE: The cat stood up, and she jumped off the shelf, and she knocked over a vase.

The cat stood up. She jumped off the shelf and knocked over a vase.

1. My sister wanted to ride the roller coaster, but it was raining, so we couldn't, so we saw a movie instead, and on the way home we stopped for ice cream.
2. Uncle Henry bought a new car, and it looked sturdy, but it soon developed problems, and so he had to sell it.
3. Mix three eggs in a bowl and add half a cup of milk, and beat the ingredients, and dip slices of bread into the mixture, and then fry the bread on a griddle.
4. Connie's aunt sent her some money, so Connie decided to buy some clothes, so she took the bus downtown, and she bought a new ski jacket and boots.
5. Bill closed his eyes and swung the bat, and it connected with a crack, and he started running, and he just made it to second base a second before the throw.

DEVELOPING WRITING SKILLS: Rewriting Rambling Sentences. Rewrite the following passage by shortening rambling sentences.

I thought drive-in movies were a thing of the past, but we found one near our summer cottage, so naturally we asked Dad to take us, and he did, but none of us remembers what movie was playing, because first Monica made friends with the girls in the next car, and then Skip and I explored the grounds, especially between the car and the refreshment stand, where we also made some new friends, and Dad spent his time cleaning out the trunk of the car, and we all accomplished a lot that night.

Skills Review and Writing Workshop

Improving Your Sentences

CHECKING YOUR SKILLS

Rewrite the following paragraph so that there are no short, choppy sentences or long, rambling ones.

(1) Most insects develop by undergoing a series of changes. (2) This series of changes is called metamorphosis. (3) In incomplete metamorphosis, the insect begins as an egg, which hatches into a nymph, which is an immature form that looks much like the adult insect. (4) Except that it has no wings. (5) The nymph molts, or sheds its outer covering, several times until it becomes an adult. (6) In complete metamorphosis, there are four stages instead of three. (7) The egg hatches into a stage called the larva. (8) It looks like a worm. (9) The larva spends most of its time eating. (10) Its soft body molts several times as it expands. (11) When it enters the next stage, the larva stops eating and attaches itself to an object and becomes a pupa. (12) Sometimes, but not always, the larva spins a silken cocoon to cover its pupa stage. (13) Inside the pupa, the insect develops into an adult. (14) When it is full grown, the adult insect breaks the shell of the pupa and crawls out, and the adult looks different from the previous three stages, and so an ugly caterpillar may turn into a beautiful butterfly.

USING COMPOSITION SKILLS

Combining and Shortening Sentences

Turn back to Exercise B in Section 33.2. Choose one of the sentences that you rewrote by adding details. You will use this sentence as the beginning of a paragraph. Write your first draft, expanding and developing the idea expressed in the first sentence. Include as many details as you can.

Reread your paragraph and rewrite it by adding appropriate details. Write a final version, and proofread it carefully.

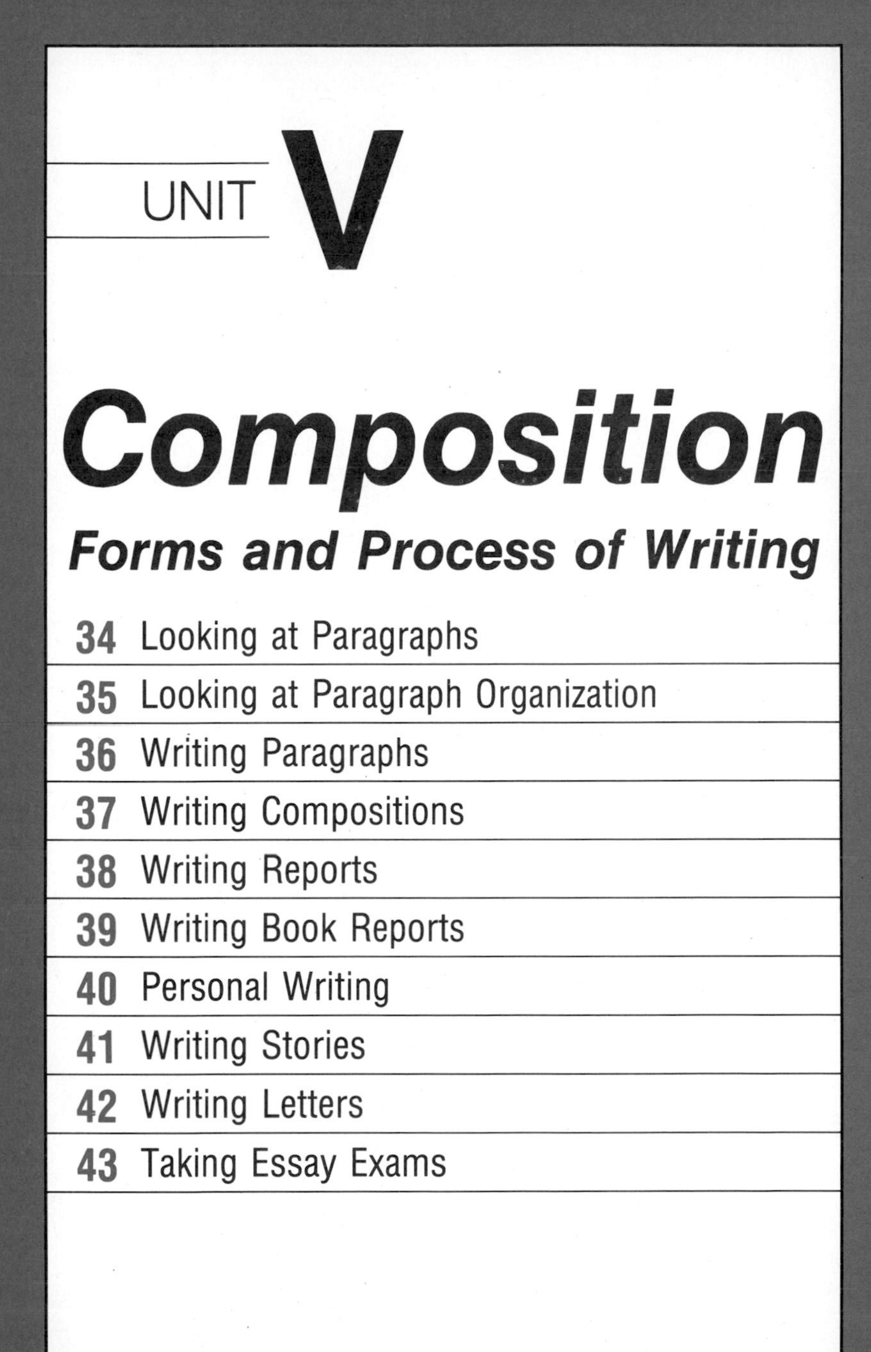

UNIT V

Composition

Forms and Process of Writing

Chapter 34

Looking at Paragraphs

A paragraph is a group of sentences linked by a single main idea. It is easy to recognize a paragraph because the first word of the first sentence is usually indented. But there are other features that can help you recognize a paragraph. One of the sentences usually expresses the main idea of the whole paragraph. The other sentences in the paragraph give more information about that main idea. They explain, support, or develop it.

In this chapter, you will learn to identify the sentence that expresses the main idea of a paragraph. And you will learn how to support that sentence by adding examples, details, or incidents.

34.1 Topic Sentences

The most important sentence in a paragraph is the topic sentence. It is often the first sentence of the paragraph, though it may be found elsewhere. Sometimes it may come at the end of a paragraph, or even near the middle.

The topic sentence of a paragraph expresses the main idea of the paragraph.

In the following paragraph, the first sentence is the topic sentence. The other sentences support it. By giving examples they explain and clarify the main idea.

Some species of fish have developed unusual adaptations to life underwater. The electric eel, for example, stuns or kills prey with a charge of electricity. It also uses electricity to navigate through murky waters. The archerfish shoots down insects with drops of water from its mouth. The deep-sea angler fish attracts smaller fish with a light-giving bulb that dangles in front of its mouth. The hammerhead shark, like all other sharks, has a keen sense of smell. The two nostrils on its hammer-shaped head allow it to smell prey at a great distance. The flying fish can escape enemies by leaping out of the water and gliding through the air on fins that resemble wings. The seahorse can anchor itself to coral or seaweed with its graceful, curved tail. The pancake-shaped flounder swims along the ocean floor camouflaged to match its surroundings. But perhaps the strangest adaptation of all is the lunglike organ that allows the African lungfish to survive out of water by breathing air.

If the topic sentence of this paragraph were removed, the idea that ties all the other sentences together would be missing. The paragraph would be made up of a number of statements about different kinds of fish. There would be no clear connection between the statements. With the topic sentence, it is clear how the statements fit together.

EXERCISE: Recognizing Topic Sentences. From each group of sentences find the topic sentence.

EXAMPLE: a. The judicial branch interprets the law.
b. The legislative branch makes laws.
c. The U.S. government has three branches.
d. The executive branch enforces the law.
The U.S. government has three branches.

1. a. For the cowboys who herded cattle on the cattle drives, life was hard.
   b. Indians were sometimes hostile.
   c. The cattle were likely to stampede.
   d. Cowboys had to live outdoors during bad weather.
2. a. Computers are used to regulate airplane traffic.
   b. Computers are an important part of modern life.
   c. Computers guide rockets and satellites.
   d. Computers calculate bank balances.
3. a. African elephants are larger than Indian elephants.
   b. African elephants have larger ears than Indian elephants.
   c. Female African elephants have tusks; female Indian elephants usually do not.
   d. There are several differences between African elephants and Indian elephants.
4. a. Newspapers provide much information.
   b. Newspapers advertise sales and job openings.
   c. Newspapers announce local events.
   d. Newspapers report national and international news.

DEVELOPING WRITING SKILLS: Supporting a Topic Sentence. Choose one of the topic sentences below and write three or four sentences that support it.

I have learned to expect the unexpected.
Sometimes an hour seems to last a year.
Things aren't always what they seem to be.

34.2 Supporting Topic Sentences with Examples

Once you have chosen a topic sentence for a paragraph, you need to develop and support it. Sometimes the best way to support a topic sentence is by examples.

Use examples to clarify or illustrate a topic sentence.

In the following chart, a topic sentence is given on the left. On the right, four examples illustrate the idea stated in the topic sentence. Notice how the examples make the idea come alive.

Topic Sentence	Examples
My fourteen-year-old sister is very strange.	She runs around the house in a bath towel. She eats pickles with milk. She sleeps with her pillow under her feet. She bites her toenails while watching TV.

The following is a paragraph outlined above. It was written by a sixth grader. The writer made the first sentence her topic sentence. Then she presented her examples.

My Sister

My fourteen-year-old sister is very strange. For one thing, she always runs around the house in a bath towel. For another, she eats pickles with milk and likes it. At night, when she goes to bed, she sleeps with her pillow under her feet. But maybe the best example of her strange ways is that while she watches TV she bites her toenails.—Liz O'Connor

EXERCISE A: Finding Examples to Support a Topic Sentence. Below are five sentences that could be used as topic sentences. Write each sentence on your paper, and below it write three examples that clarify, illustrate, or otherwise support it.

EXAMPLE: There are several good ways to earn spending money during summer vacation.

There are several good ways to earn spending money during summer vacation.

You can baby-sit for your neighbors' children.

You can take care of their pets if your neighbors go traveling.

You can mow lawns or wash cars.

1. Some of my favorite films are horror movies.
2. Some big cities have professional sports teams.
3. Many animals hide from enemies by using camouflage.
4. Strange creatures are found in my classes.
5. Rock stars sometimes look as if they came from other solar systems.

EXERCISE B: More Work with Examples. Follow the directions in Exercise A.

1. Young people's hobbies sometimes develop into careers.
2. There are several good, inexpensive ways of getting exercise.
3. Several kinds of fish are found in this lake.
4. Our state boasts some famous landmarks.
5. You can have different kinds of fun at a lake.

DEVELOPING WRITING SKILLS: Using Examples to Support a Topic Sentence. Choose one topic sentence from Exercise A or Exercise B. Write a paragraph using the examples that you listed.

34.3 Supporting Topic Sentences with Details

Sometimes the best way to develop or support a topic sentence is to include details.

Use details to give a clear, complete picture of the idea expressed in a topic sentence.

The following chart shows a topic sentence developed by details. The main idea is about a clown's costume. The details that describe the costume make the main idea seem clearer and more vivid.

Topic Sentence	Details
The clown had put on an amusing costume.	He was wearing enormous bright yellow shoes.
	He had stuck a red ball on the end of his nose.
	His suit was much too large for his body.

In the following paragraph, notice how the details support and expand on the topic sentence.

> The first annual sailing marathon took place in very rough weather. The National Weather Service had promised high waves and winds. For once, the prediction turned out to be right. Halfway through the race, heavy rain began to fall. It quickly became a downpour. The rain effectively blocked the sailors' view of the course. At the same time, swirling winds made it impossible for some of the boats to stay on course. The weather was so bad that most of the boats dropped out of the race.

EXERCISE A: Finding Details to Support a Topic Sentence. Below are five sentences that could be used as topic sentences. Write each sentence on your paper, and below it write three details that support it.

EXAMPLE: Our village is a typical New England village.

Our village is a typical New England village.

The houses along Main Street are covered with white clapboard.

At the end of the street is a church with a tall steeple.

Behind the church is a cemetery filled with weathered, forgotten tombstones.

1. At night, the deserted mansion looks ghostly.
2. His room was a total mess.
3. The woman looked like a witch.
4. The living room was well equipped for entertainment.
5. The fire seemed a monster eating up everything in sight.

EXERCISE B: More Work with Details. Follow the directions for Exercise A.

1. The members of the team wear unusual uniforms.
2. It was a storm such as I had never experienced before.
3. We left the spaceship and looked around at the planet.
4. It was a dinner fit for a royal wedding.
5. By morning, the snow had blotted out every familiar sight.

DEVELOPING WRITING SKILLS: Using Details to Support a Topic Sentence. Choose one topic sentence from Exercise A or Exercise B. Write a paragraph that develops it. Use the details that you listed for that sentence.

34.4 Supporting Topic Sentences with Incidents

Sometimes the best way to develop a topic sentence is by an incident—a brief story that illustrates the main idea. Most readers like stories, and a story is often an effective way to establish an idea.

Use an incident to support a paragraph's main idea.

The following chart shows how an incident can be used to develop a topic sentence.

Topic Sentence	Incident
A recent experience my mother had shows the importance of seat belts.	While she was driving to work one day, my mother's car was struck from behind by another car. Luckily, she was using her seat belt. Although the other driver suffered cuts and bruises, my mother was unhurt. The police told her that the belt may have saved her life.

In the paragraph below, a single incident develops the idea stated in the topic sentence.

Both ancient legends and modern tales mention rescues of human beings by dolphins. One old fisherman told of a sailboat that capsized near his village. The two men aboard were thrown into the rough sea. A dolphin swam over to them and waited for them to seize one of its flippers. The surprised sailors then rode the dolphin to a nearby cove where they could easily swim to shore.

EXERCISE A: Using an Incident to Develop a Topic Sentence. Below are five sentences that could be used as topic sentences. Choose one of the sentences and write a summary or outline of an incident that might be used to support it.

EXAMPLE: Mountain climbing can be dangerous.

On an expedition to Mount Everest in 1924, two English climbers attempted to reach the summit but were forced to turn back when one began seeing double from lack of oxygen.

1. It is easy to start a fire accidentally.
2. Animals have saved people's lives.
3. Amusement park rides make me ill.
4. Most television commercials insult viewers' intelligence.
5. Bad weather can spoil a person's plans.

EXERCISE B: More Work with Incidents. Below are five sentences that could be used as topic sentences. Choose one of the sentences and write a summary or outline of an incident that might be used to support it.

1. Students who do poorly in school may have trouble in later life.
2. Cats can be amusing pets.
3. Visiting another country is always an exciting experience.
4. Sometimes, if we wait a while, problems seem to solve themselves.
5. I have learned to expect the unexpected.

DEVELOPING WRITING SKILLS: Using an Incident in a Paragraph. Choose one of the summaries that you wrote in Exercise A or Exercise B and write a paragraph that includes the topic sentence and the supporting incident.

Writing Workshop: Looking at Paragraphs

ASSIGNMENT 1

Topic Meeting Someone from the Past

Form and Purpose A paragraph that informs readers and supports your opinion of someone

Audience Other students in a history class

Length One paragraph

Focus In your topic sentence, identify a person from the past and give the reason you would like to meet him or her. Then support your reason with specific details and examples.

Sources History books, encyclopedias, biographies

Prewriting Select someone from the past who interests you. Then research and take notes on his or her life.

Writing Using your notes, write a first draft of your paragraph.

Revising Make sure that your topic sentence clearly states your main idea and that the supporting sentences develop your main idea. Correct any errors in spelling, punctuation, and capitalization. Then prepare a final copy.

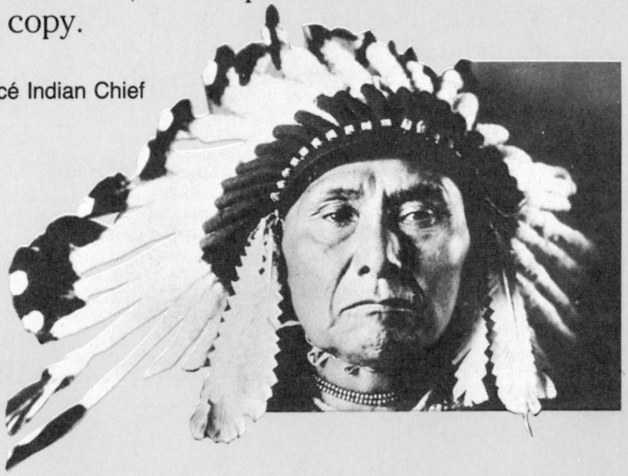

Chief Joseph, Nez Percé Indian Chief

ASSIGNMENT 2

Topic My Greatest Achievement

Form and Purpose A paragraph that explains and narrates a personal experience

Audience Relatives or friends

Length One paragraph

Focus Identify the achievement in a topic sentence. Then support your topic sentence with details of the incident.

Sources Personal experiences and feelings

Prewriting Decide on your greatest achievement. Then write notes about what happened and how you felt.

Writing Using your notes, write a first draft of your paragraph.

Revising Make sure that the details you included are arranged in the order they happened. Check for any errors in capitalization, punctuation, and spelling. Then prepare a final draft.

Topics for Writing: Looking at Paragraphs

The cartoon above may make you think of a topic sentence for a paragraph. If so, plan and write a paragraph. If not, choose one of the following topic sentences to develop into a paragraph.

1. A person can get into trouble by trying to impress other people.
2. It is important in life to have a sense of humor.
3. ____________________ really confuses me.
4. Sometimes life is stranger than fiction.
5. Being different can make a person feel lonely.
6. Thinking is sometimes painful.
7. Some days seem to drag on forever.
8. Change can be both an exciting and an upsetting experience.
9. To accomplish something important, it is often necessary to make a sacrifice.
10. Fear can cripple a person.

Looking at Paragraph Organization

In Chapter 34, you learned that a good paragraph is made up of sentences that support and develop one main idea. The main idea is expressed in the topic sentence of the paragraph. It is not enough, however, simply to present adequate support for the topic sentence. The support must be organized. Each sentence should lead naturally to the next.

The order in which sentences appear in a paragraph should depend on the topic. For some topics, you may want to present events in the order in which they occurred. For descriptions of places or objects, you may want to present details according to how they are arranged in space. For the effective presentation of an idea, you may want to give reasons arranged so that the more important ones follow the less important ones.

In this chapter, you will learn different ways of organizing a paragraph. You will practice arranging sentences in the order of events, in spatial order, and in order of importance.

35.1 Paragraphs That Follow the Order of Events

Suppose you were writing a paragraph about something that had happened. A logical way to proceed would be to tell what occurred first, what occurred next, and so on. A paragraph that followed the order of events would be in chronological order—the order of time.

Use chronological order to present clearly the unfolding of an event or the steps in a process.

Chronological order tells a story or describes historical events. You can also use it to describe how to do or make something.

The following outline for a paragraph shows a main idea developed in three chronological steps.

Main Idea	Steps
A surprise party for Joan	1. First, send invitations. 2. Then, get help from Joan's parents. 3. Finally, trick her into coming on time for the party.

Below is the finished paragraph. The words *first, then,* and *finally* emphasize the use of chronological order. Such words are called transitions.

I'm planning a surprise party for Joan. First, I'll send invitations to her other friends. I'll warn them to keep silent about the party. Then I'll make sure that Joan will be at my house on time by involving her parents in my plan. Finally, I'll trick her into coming to my house by telling her I have a new record. But when the door opens, everyone will jump out and shout, "Surprise!"

EXERCISE: Arranging Sentences in Chronological Order. Each group below contains a topic sentence and five supporting sentences. On your paper, arrange the supporting sentences in chronological order.

1. I've discovered a shorter way to get to school.
   a. When you get to Sam's house, make a left onto Cooper Lake Road.
   b. Once on Washington Avenue, you can easily see the school.
   c. Then, from Cooper Lake Road, make a right onto Washington Avenue.
   d. Walk down First Street until you reach Sam's house.
   e. First, go down Maple Street and turn right onto First Street.
2. The exploration of space has progressed greatly in this century.
   a. Robert Goddard launched the first rocket in 1926.
   b. Now, astronauts routinely enter space to gather scientific data and repair satellites.
   c. In 1969, the Apollo program was the first mission to put astronauts on the moon.
   d. In 1961, a Russian cosmonaut, Yuri Gagarin, orbited the earth in a spaceship.
   e. In 1968, three American astronauts orbited the moon ten times.
3. Take a golf stroke in one smooth motion.
   a. With your forearm straight, pull the club back.
   b. First, straddle the ball with flexed knees.
   c. Keep your head down during the stroke.
   d. With your eye on the ball, follow through the swinging motion and hit the ball.

DEVELOPING WRITING SKILLS: Writing a Paragraph with Chronological Order. Choose one of the groups from the Exercise above. Use it to write a paragraph in chronological order.

35.2 Paragraphs That Follow Spatial Order

A paragraph using spatial order groups things according to their physical location in space.

Use spatial order to present details according to their physical location.

For instance, a paragraph might describe a statue from top to bottom. Another paragraph might describe a landscape from near to far.

The following outline for a paragraph shows supporting details arranged in spatial order.

Main Idea	Details
The view from the hilltop	1. Above: the peaks of the White Mountains 2. Left: the setting sun 3. Below: a roaring waterfall 4. Nearby: another group of hikers sitting on a ledge

The finished paragraph describes the landscape in a spatial order that helps readers picture the scene. Notice how the transitions, such as *above us* and *to our left,* make clear how the viewer actually saw the details.

The view from the hilltop was spectacular. Above us, we could see the craggy peaks of the White Mountains. To our left, the sun was setting behind the green hills of Lawrence County. Almost directly below us, a roaring waterfall pounded the rocks, while on a nearby ledge sat another hiking group. Their voices could not be heard over the thundering water. How magnificent nature can be!

EXERCISE: Arranging Sentences in Spatial Order. Each of the three groups below contains a topic sentence following by four supporting sentences. On a sheet of paper, arrange the supporting sentences in a clear spatial order.

1. With two out, the Panthers got two hits and a walk and had the bases loaded.
   a. Ramirez was on second base, following Steiner's walk.
   b. Jones went to third base on Ramirez's hit.
   c. Logan stepped up to the plate.
   d. Steiner, having gotten an intentional base on balls, was on first.
2. Cape Cod is shaped very much like an arm bent at the elbow.
   a. Crossing the "shoulder" is the Cape Cod Canal.
   b. The quaint town of Chatham is located at the elbow of the Cape.
   c. Along the biceps lie such towns as Sandwich, Barnstable, and East Dennis.
   d. At the fist is Provincetown.
3. Scientists know that the earth is made up of a number of layers.
   a. The outside of the earth, the part we all see, is called the crust.
   b. Below the mantle is the outer core, which is thought to be about 1,380 miles thick.
   c. An inner core of solid iron and nickel is at the center of the earth.
   d. Beneath the crust is the mantle, which is about 1,800 miles thick.

DEVELOPING WRITING SKILLS: Writing a Paragraph with Spatial Order. Choose one of the groups from the Exercise above. Use it to write a paragraph with spatial order. Add transitions if they are needed to clarify the spatial relationships.

35.3 Paragraphs That Follow Order of Importance

Some paragraphs prove a point by beginning with the weakest ideas and presenting the strongest ones last.

Use order of importance to arrange examples, details, or reasons from least important to most important.

The following outline is for a paragraph whose purpose is to win support for national parks. Notice that the reasons build in strength from weakest to strongest.

Main Idea	Reasons
We should support and protect national parks.	1. Parks are places of relaxation. 2. Parks preserve natural wonders. 3. Animals are protected from civilization's threats. 4. Parks protect wilderness areas forever for all to enjoy.

Below is the finished paragraph. Notice how the transitions *furthermore* and *most of all* make the order clear.

Our national parks deserve our support and protection. They are great places for people to relax and to breathe good, clean air. Also, they preserve natural wonders for sightseers and offer recreation for campers. Furthermore, they protect animal populations from the threats of civilization. Most of all, national parks ensure that wilderness areas will always be available for everyone to enjoy.

EXERCISE: Arranging Sentences in Order of Importance. Each of the three groups below contains a topic sentence and four supporting sentences. On a sheet of paper, arrange the supporting sentences in order of importance.

1. Letter-writing is a better form of communication than telephoning.
   a. When you write a letter, you can take the time to express yourself better than you can when telephoning.
   b. It is often less expensive to write than to phone.
   c. By taking the trouble to write a letter, you pay the receiver a greater compliment than you would by phoning.
   d. Letter-writing develops your overall writing ability.
2. I think too much TV has been bad for my family.
   a. Finally, we constantly argue about what programs we will watch.
   b. Many of the programs that I watch are a silly waste of time.
   c. Also, TV keeps me from reading or doing my homework.
   d. It seems that my brothers and sisters and I hardly ever talk to each other in the evening.
3. I am hoping that my parents will buy the new front-wheel-drive Sniper sports car.
   a. The front-wheel drive makes the car safer on snowy or icy roads than rear-wheel-drive cars.
   b. A car with front-wheel drive is roomier than a rear-wheel-drive car of the same size.
   c. The Sniper is nice-looking.
   d. The Sniper offers outstanding gas mileage.

DEVELOPING WRITING SKILLS: Writing a Paragraph with Order of Importance. Choose one of the groups from the Exercise above. Use it to write a paragraph in which the supporting sentences are arranged in order of importance. Add transitions if necessary.

Writing Workshop: Paragraph Organization

ASSIGNMENT 1

Topic What Do the Contents of Your Refrigerator Tell You About Your Family?

Form and Purpose A paragraph that describes items in a spatial order

Audience A group of food storage designers

Length One paragraph

Focus Describe the contents of your refrigerator in spatial order. Use sensory words to describe each item. Conclude with a topic sentence summarizing how your refrigerator reflects your family's habits.

Sources Personal observations

Prewriting Study the subject, and decide on a specific spatial order. Then make notes about the contents.

Writing Using your notes, write a first draft.

Revising Review your paragraph, and add sensory words that will clearly describe each item. Proofread your paragraph and write a final draft.

ASSIGNMENT 2

Topic Skills Needed in a Particular Sport

Form and Purpose A paragraph that informs readers and is organized in order of importance.

Audience Coaches or physical education teachers

Length One paragraph

Focus In your topic sentence, state a main idea about necessary skills in the sport you selected. Then describe each skill, organizing your ideas in order of importance.

Sources Personal experience, books, magazines, TV sports programs

Prewriting Select a sport that interests you. Take notes about the skills needed to play that sport. Organize the skills in order of importance. Think of a main idea for a topic sentence.

Writing Using your notes, write a first draft of your paragraph.

Revising Check spelling, punctuation, and capitalization. Correct any errors, and write a final copy.

Topics for Writing: Looking at Paragraph Organization

The characters above are examining one of the first electric washing machines. If this suggests a writing topic to you, plan and write a paragraph. Other possible topics are listed below. Decide whether you will tell about your topic's importance or important features, describe it, or tell how it works. Then choose an appropriate method of organizing your paragraph.

1. Bicycle Pump
2. Telescope
3. Light Bulb
4. Fuse
5. Solar Cell or Panel
6. Camera
7. Ten-Speed Bike
8. Hang Glider
9. Wind Surfer
10. Gas Station Pump

Chapter 36

Writing Paragraphs

Sometimes the hardest part of writing a paragraph is choosing a topic. One way to make it easier is to choose a topic that you know something about. When you are writing about something you are familiar with, the paragraph almost writes itself.

Whatever your topic, you still need to plan the paragraph carefully. Careful planning will help you make sure that you have included all the information your reader needs. It will also help you eliminate information that is not related to your topic.

This chapter suggests ways to plan and write paragraphs. You will learn how to search your imagination and your memory for possible topics. You will learn how to break down topics so that they can be discussed in a single paragraph. You will use your imagination to decide what supporting information to include. And after you have written your paragraph, you will revise it at least once to make sure that it says exactly what you wanted to say.

36.1 PREWRITING: Planning Your Paragraph

Before you can write, you need to choose a topic. A good way to find a topic and supporting information is to brainstorm.

Brainstorm for topics; write a topic sentence; and then brainstorm for information to support the topic sentence.

To brainstorm, take a sheet of paper and write down all the topics you can think of. Let your mind range freely over your hobbies, interests, experiences, reading, and school courses. Don't worry about whether an idea is a good one. Write down everything that comes into your head. The longer your list, the better the chance that you will find a good topic.

After you have a list of possible topics, think about how each one could be written about. Try to break down the broader topics into smaller ones.

The chart below shows a sample brainstorming list. Notice that some of the ideas have been broken down to make them more suitable for a paragraph.

BRAINSTORMING FOR A PARAGRAPH TOPIC

Poisonous snakes

Lions

—Training lions for circuses

—Breeding lions in zoos

—Lions' social organization

—Lions' hunting skills

Computer software

Video games

Television shows

—The best news shows

—This season's new series

—How ratings are determined

Once you have chosen a topic, you must find a main idea. Ask yourself questions about the topic. "What should readers already know about this topic?" "Why might it interest them?" Your answers to such questions will lead to main ideas.

If you had chosen the topic Lions' Hunting Skills, you might ask yourself the following questions.

ASKING QUESTIONS TO FOCUS ON A MAIN IDEA

Questions	Possible Main Ideas
What do I want my readers to know about lions' hunting skills?	Lions are strong, intelligent hunters.
Why are people interested in lions?	People admire lions' strength and beauty. They are both fascinated and frightened by lions. People are hunters, too. Lion cubs are playful and appealing.
What is unusual about lions?	Lions are the only big cats that live in prides. Unlike other big cats, lions often hunt in groups.
How do lions hunt?	Lions hunt by stalking, alone or in groups. Lions find prey by using their keen senses of sight, smell, and hearing.
What kinds of animals do lions hunt?	Lions will eat anything they can catch. But most often they hunt herd animals such as zebras and antelopes.

Are lions good hunters?	When a single lion attacks, its prey may escape. So lions often increase their chances of catching prey when they hunt in groups.
What animals do lions hunt?	Lions hunt many kinds of African game. Two of their favorite prey are antelopes and zebras. A group of lions can hunt large animals that a single lion could not kill, such as buffaloes or giraffes. Lions have attacked domestic animals when game is scarce. Some lions have even attacked humans.
Which lions do the hunting?	Lionesses do most of the hunting, but male lions also kill prey. When a lioness kills an animal, the cubs and males come to eat the meat. Sometimes a male drives the lioness away until he has finished eating.

When you have a long list of supporting ideas, read through it several times. Make sure that you have enough good ideas for a paragraph. Cross out any unrelated or unnecessary ideas. Then decide whether you need to add any new information.

Now you need to arrange your supporting information in some logical order. Keeping your topic sentence in mind, look over the supporting information. Decide whether chronological order, spatial order, order of importance, or some other order would be most appropriate. Then arrange your supporting information in the order you have chosen.

After you have decided on the main idea of your paragraph, you can write a topic sentence. Although your main idea is already a complete sentence, it may not be the best possible topic sentence for the paragraph. So experiment with several different versions. For example, suppose you have chosen the main idea *The lion is a good hunter.*

POSSIBLE TOPIC SENTENCES

Main idea: The lion is a good hunter.

1. The lion is an excellent hunter.
2. The lion is an efficient hunter.
3. The lion is a careful, intelligent hunter.
4. The lion is a cruel, vicious hunter.

Once you have several topic sentences, you can choose the one you like best. For example, you might decide to use number 3 above because it is the most specific and the most accurate. In addition, you already have some sentences in your brainstorming list that support the idea.

Now that you have your topic sentence, you need to support it with examples, details, or incidents. To think of supporting information, you can use the brainstorming technique again. If you wish, you can ask yourself specific questions about your main idea and write down the answers. Or you can discuss your main idea with a friend to find out what kinds of questions a reader might ask. Write down as much information as you can. Some of it will be eliminated later, but a long list will help you choose the strongest and most relevant support.

If you wish, you can make an outline of the paragraph

you are going to write. Or you can simply number the items on your brainstorming list to show which you will cover first, which second, and so on.

EXERCISE A: Breaking Down Paragraph Topics. Each of the following five topics is too general for a single paragraph. Write each topic on your paper. Under each one, list three smaller, more specific topics on the main subject that would make good topics for paragraphs.

EXAMPLE: Relatives
—my older brother's funny behavior
—the camping trip with my cousins
—Aunt Sally's Thanksgiving dinner

1. Music
2. Sports
3. Vacations
4. Hobbies
5. Pets

EXERCISE B: More Work with Paragraph Topics. Choose one of the specific topics you thought of for Exercise A. Then do each of the following steps.

1. Think about the people who will be reading your paragraph. How much will your readers know about the topic?
2. Write down at least two questions about your topic.
3. Write a one-sentence answer to each question. These answers will be your possible main ideas.
4. Read over your list of possible main ideas and choose the one that best expresses what you would want to say in a paragraph.

DEVELOPING WRITING SKILLS: Beginning a Paragraph. Choose another specific topic from Exercise A, and carry out the steps in Exercise B.

WRITING: Creating the First Version 36.2

Now that you have decided on your topic sentence and supporting information, you are ready to begin writing. Start by writing a first version, or first draft, of your paragraph.

Using the topic sentence and support that you have arrived at by brainstorming, write a first draft of your paragraph.

Although you will rewrite your first draft at least once, you should approach the first draft as if it were the final version. The better your first draft, the less time you will have to spend revising it.

Use the ideas in the following chart as a guide while you write your first draft.

SUGGESTIONS FOR WRITING A FIRST DRAFT

1. Refer to your outline or your list of supporting information.
2. Write your paragraph in the logical order that you have chosen: the order of events, spatial order, or order of importance.
3. Feel free to change the original arrangement of ideas if necessary.
4. Add new examples, details, or incidents that may come to mind if they are appropriate.
5. Remove unrelated supporting information.
6. Use transitions to link ideas smoothly.
7. Always keep your readers in mind. Consider what they will want to know about the topic, and be sure that what you are writing will be clear to them.

If you were planning to write a paragraph about lions' hunting skills, your first draft might have some of the flaws of the following draft. Can you pick them out?

The lion is a careful intelligent hunter. Lions cannot run very fast; they have little endurance; they must catch prey by stalking. Jackals and hyenas try to steal meat from lions' kills. Vultures fly overhead, looking for leftovers. Lions hunt antelopes, zebras, and other animals. They often hunt at night. Lions live in groups called prides. Two or more lions may hunt together. A group of lions may fan out to surround a herd of animals. A lion at one end drives the animals toward the other lions, and the lions increase their chances of catching one of the animals. Lionesses do most of the hunting. Sometimes a male drives a lioness away from an animal she has killed, until he has finished eating.

In the next section, you will learn how to revise a first draft such as this one. You will learn to eliminate unrelated supporting information and make your writing clear and lively.

EXERCISE A: Writing a First Draft. Using the paragraph topic that you chose for Exercise B on page 358, write a topic sentence and a list of supporting information. If you wish, use the question-and-answer method to think of supporting ideas for the topic you have chosen. Then arrange the supporting information in some logical order and write a first draft of a paragraph about your topic.

DEVELOPING WRITING SKILLS: More Work with First Drafts. Choose another topic for a paragraph. Either select one of your own or use one of the topics that you selected for the Developing Writing Skills on page 358. Brainstorm for a main idea and supporting information. Then write a first draft of a paragraph.

REVISING: Creating the Final Version 36.3

Revising is an important step in the writing process. When you revise a paragraph, you make a final check of your topic sentence and supporting information to be sure that the paragraph is well organized. You eliminate unnecessary information. Also, you proofread the paragraph for mechanical errors in grammar, spelling, and punctuation.

Revise your paragraph by adding supporting information, taking out unrelated information, arranging your ideas in more logical order, and correcting grammar, spelling, and punctuation.

You may find that it helps to put your first draft aside for a time before revising it. That way you will be rereading it from a fresh perspective. Or you can ask a friend to read your paragraph and comment on it.

The following chart gives several other suggestions for rereading your work. You might try one or all four of the suggestions.

SUGGESTIONS FOR REREADING

1. Set your paragraph aside an hour or so while you do something else. Then go back and reread it. Read your paragraph aloud to yourself. Listen for confusing ideas and other weaknesses.
2. Read your paragraph to someone else. Ask the listener to give an opinion of it.
3. Have someone else read your paragraph aloud to you. Listen to the places where the reader has problems and for ideas that sound weak or confusing.
4. Have someone else read your paragraph silently and then comment on the ideas.

As you reread, you should watch for certain specific problems. For instance, the supporting information may fit together but the topic sentence may not seem to match the paragraph. In this case, you may have one of two problems. You may have written a topic sentence that is too narrow, or you may have written a topic sentence that is too general. A topic sentence that is too narrow covers only part of the supporting information in the paragraph. A topic sentence that is too general leads the reader to expect more information than you have included in the paragraph.

Suppose you were writing a paragraph about the farm products of Brazil. The following topic sentence would be too narrow because it suggests that the paragraph will be about coffee only.

TOO NARROW: Brazil is one of the largest producers of coffee in the world.

The next topic sentence is too general because it suggests that the paragraph will be about all types of products from Brazil.

TOO GENERAL: Brazil produces many types of farm, factory, and forest products.

The final topic sentence clearly indicates to a reader that the paragraph will focus on the farm products of Brazil.

CLEARLY FOCUSED: The farmers and ranchers of Brazil produce many good things to eat and drink.

To revise a topic sentence, reread your paragraph and check the supporting information against the topic sentence. If the topic sentence is too narrow, expand it to cover the information in the paragraph. If the topic sentence is too general, you must narrow it to fit the supporting information.

You should also notice other parts of your paragraph as

you reread it. In addition to possible problems with the topic sentence, there may not be enough supporting information relating back to the topic you have chosen. The paragraph may contain information that is not related to the topic sentence. Or the information may not be arranged in the most logical order to make your writing clear and understandable for your reader.

Use the following checklist of questions that will help you identify specific problems in the first draft you have written.

CHECKLIST FOR REVISING A PARAGRAPH

1. Does the main idea of the paragraph cover all the other ideas in the entire paragraph?
2. What examples, details, or incidents could you add to develop the topic sentence more fully?
3. Can you find any generalizations or any weak statements that should be replaced with specific supporting information?
4. Are there any pieces of supporting information that are unrelated to your topic sentence?
5. Would your ideas be clearer if they were arranged in a different order?
6. Could any transitions be added to help the reader follow your ideas?
7. What other changes in words or sentences would make your paragraph become clearer and more lively for your readers?

When you have revised your paragraph, copy it neatly in its final form. Then proofread it for mechanical errors. The checklist above points out the kinds of errors you should look for when proofreading your rewritten version.

CHECKLIST FOR PROOFREADING A PARAGRAPH

1. Are there any errors in sentence structure, such as fragments or run-ons, or are there any problems with modifiers?
2. Have you used verbs and pronouns and correctly?
3. Are there any errors in capitalization?
4. Have you used periods, commas, semicolons, apostrophes, and other punctuation marks where they are needed?
5. Have you checked the spelling of any words that do not look right or that you often misspell?

You may be able to correct most of the errors that you catch right on the final copy and still keep your writing neat. If, however, you find major errors or a large number of errors, you should recopy the paragraph and proofread it again.

Here is a final version of the paragraph about lions' hunting skills. It has been revised and proofread for errors.

> The lion is a careful, intelligent hunter. Lions cannot run very fast, and they have little endurance. So they must catch prey by stalking. Lions have keen senses of sight, smell, and hearing that help them find prey. They will stalk antelopes, zebras, or other animals silently and patiently. Lions often hunt at night, when they cannot be easily seen. By day, their tawny coat makes it easy for them to hide in the grass of the African plains. Lions are social animals that live in groups called prides. Two or more lions frequently hunt together. A group of lions may fan out to surround a herd of animals. Then a lion at one end drives the animals toward the other lions. In this way, the lions increase their chances of catching at least one of the animals in the herd.

If you compare this final version of the paragraph with the first draft on page 360, you will notice several changes. More supporting information about lions' keen senses has been added. The two sentences beginning "Jackals and hyenas . . . " have been deleted because they are not related to the main idea. And several spelling errors (pray, staking, their) have been corrected. Can you spot any other changes?

EXERCISE A: Revising a First Draft. Below is a first draft of a paragraph. Using the suggestions in this section for revising a paragraph, revise the first draft and write a final version of the paragraph.

My dog, Deirdre, is the nicest dog I have ever known. She never barks, She never jumps on the furniture or goes into rooms she is not supposed to enter. Except for the hair she sheds in summer, there is hardly a sign that we have a dog in the hous. We got deirdre because a man down the rode abandoned her. When we found her and returned her to the man, he said he did not want her any more. Deidre loves to be with people. She is friendly and playful with all. She is part German shepherd and part beagle. With me and my mom and dad, she is very loving. As soon as she sees me coming toward the house after school, she gets up on her hind legs and waves her front legs in greeting. When I come through the door, she licks my hands and face, Then she waits to be scratched and petted. She eats too much.

EXERCISE B: More Work with Revising. Using the suggestions in this section for revising a paragraph, revise the first draft you wrote for Exercise A on page 360. Then write a final version of the paragraph.

DEVELOPING WRITING SKILLS: More Work with Revising. Revise the paragraph you wrote for the Developing Writing Skills on page 360.

Writing Workshop: Writing Paragraphs

ASSIGNMENT 1

Topic A Persuasive Ad

Form and Purpose A paragraph designed to persuade a reader to buy a product

Audience Consumers

Length One paragraph

Focus State a positive opinion about an item or product in a topic sentence. Then, tell about the product, moving from the least to the most important feature.

Sources Advertisements, your imagination

Prewriting Select a real or imaginary item or a product. Brainstorm for ideas about its most important features. List those features in order of importance.

Writing Using your list, write a first draft of your paragraph.

Revising Use the checklist on page 363 to revise your paragraph.

ASSIGNMENT 2

Topic A Description of an Automobile

Form and Purpose A paragraph that describes an automobile

Audience A person who has never seen the automobile you selected

Length One paragraph

Focus Identify the automobile and its dominant impression in a topic sentence. Then describe its appearance in spatial order.

Sources Personal observations, television and magazine ads

Prewriting Select an automobile and make a list of descriptive details. Arrange those details in spatial order, front to rear.

Writing Using your list of details, write a first draft of your paragraph.

Revising Revise your paragraph using the checklist on page 363.

Topics for Writing: Writing Paragraphs

The photo above may suggest a writing topic to you. If so, plan and write a paragraph. If not, choose an item from the list below and research it in an encyclopedia or other reference book. Then write an historical paragraph about it.

1. Granola
2. Yo-Yo
3. Typewriter
4. Battery
5. Glue
6. Safety Pin
7. Ballpoint Pen
8. Nails
9. Yogurt
10. Sandwich

Chapter 37

Writing Compositions

If you can write a paragraph, you can write a composition, for a composition is made up of paragraphs. Paragraphs are the building blocks of compositions, as sentences are the building blocks of paragraphs.

Organizing a composition is much like organizing a paragraph. Although a composition is longer and somewhat more complicated than a paragraph, you will follow the same steps when writing one that you followed when writing paragraphs.

In this chapter, you will learn the basic parts of a composition, and you will see how each part functions to state or develop a main idea. You will brainstorm for possible topics, select a main idea, and brainstorm for supporting information. You will learn to organize your supporting information into separate paragraphs. You will write a rough draft of your composition. Finally, you will revise the composition to make it a polished and effective piece of writing.

37.1 Looking at Compositions

A composition resembles a paragraph on a larger scale. A paragraph is a group of sentences about one main idea. A composition is a group of paragraphs about one main idea. Because a composition is longer than a paragraph, however, it can cover a broader topic. A writer can discuss an idea in greater detail in a composition than in a paragraph.

A composition is a group of paragraphs organized around a single main idea.

Good organization is just as important in a composition as it is in a paragraph. Like a paragraph, a composition has several basic parts. Each part functions in a special way to present and support the main idea.

The first part of any composition is the title. A good title catches the reader's interest and introduces the general topic of the composition.

The first actual paragraph of the composition is the introduction: The introduction tells the reader what the composition will be about. It may give background information that will help the reader understand the composition better. Usually, the last sentence of the introduction states the main idea of the composition. So this sentence is similar to the topic sentence of a paragraph.

The introduction is followed by several body paragraphs. The body paragraphs discuss the main idea of the composition. Like the supporting information in a paragraph, the body paragraphs are organized in a logical order.

The last paragraph of a composition is the conclusion. The conclusion reminds the reader of the main idea, without repeating it in exactly the same words. It sums up the whole composition.

The chart on the following page explains in more detail how each part of a composition helps to present and develop the main idea.

THE PARTS OF A COMPOSITION	
Part	**Function**
Title	It catches the reader's interest. It gives a general idea of the topic.
Introduction: the first paragraph	It introduces the topic. It may give background information needed by readers to understand what follows. It makes the reader want to read the composition. It often tells the reader what to expect in the body paragraphs. The last sentence of the introduction often states the main idea of the composition.
Body Paragraphs: the middle of the composition	They present specific information that supports the main idea. Each body paragraph usually focuses on one part of the main idea. They are organized in a logical order.
Conclusion: the last paragraph	It reminds the reader of the main idea. It brings the composition to a close in a striking, memorable way, sometimes by adding some unusual information.

The title, introduction, body paragraphs, and conclusion all work together to present and support the composition's main idea.

In the following composition, notice how all the parts mentioned in the chart work together. Notice how the title points you toward the main idea of the composition. Then notice the different paragraphs and how each develops the main idea in a different way.

How to Be a Friend

Too many people want others to be their friends, but they don't give friendship back. That is why some friendships do not last very long. To have a friend, you must learn to be one. You must learn to treat your friend the way you want your friend to treat you. Learning to be a good friend means learning three rules: Be honest; be generous; be understanding.

Honesty is where a good friendship starts. Friends must be able to trust one another. If you do not tell the truth, people usually find out. If a friend finds out that you haven't been honest, you may lose your friend's trust. Good friends always count on one another to speak and act honestly.

Generosity means sharing, and sharing makes a friendship grow. You do not have to give away your lunch money or your clothes, of course. Instead, you have to learn how to share things you enjoy, like your hobbies and your interests. Naturally, you will want to share your ideas and feelings. These can be very valuable to a friend. They tell your friend what is important to you. By sharing them, you help your friend know you better.

Sooner or later everyone needs understanding and help with a problem. Something may go wrong at home or at school. Talking about the problem can make it easier to solve. Turning to a friend can be a first step in solving the problem. So to be a friend you must listen and understand. You must try to put yourself in your friend's place so you can understand the problem better.

No two friendships are ever exactly alike. But all true friendships have three things in common. If you plan to keep your friends, you must practice honesty, generosity, and understanding.

EXERCISE: Analyzing a Composition. Reread "How to Be a Friend." Then answer the following questions on the composition.

1. Where do you first discover what this composition is about?
2. How does the title catch the reader's interest?
3. What other title might have been used?
4. Where in the introduction is the main idea stated?
5. Find the sentence in the introduction that tells you the main idea of the whole composition.
6. How does the introduction prepare you for the body paragraphs?
7. How are the body paragraphs organized?
8. What is the main idea of each of the body paragraphs?
9. What information does the conclusion give you?
10. How does the conclusion recall the main idea?

DEVELOPING WRITING SKILLS: Writing a Response. Think about the ideas expressed in the sample composition, "How to Be a Friend." Then write a paragraph titled "Another Thought on Friendship." Either respond to the sample composition or present an idea of your own on how to be a friend. Be sure to follow the steps for writing a paragraph discussed in Chapters 34–36:

1. Write a topic sentence, stating the main idea of the paragraph.
2. Write the body of the paragraph, including evidence that supports the main idea.
3. Write a conclusion, summing up the paragraph.

37.2 Prewriting: Planning Your Composition

To choose a topic for a paragraph, you used the technique of brainstorming. You can use the same technique to choose a topic for a composition.

Brainstorm for topics. Narrow down those that are too broad to be covered in a single composition.

As you learned in Chapter 36, brainstorming means letting your mind roam freely and writing down whatever topics come into your head. Think about books you have read, something that happened at school, or one of your hobbies. Look through magazines, browse in a library, or talk about your ideas with someone else.

Do not try to sort out your ideas into good ideas and bad ones. Concentrate just on getting a list of possible topics. If a topic on your list seems too broad, however, try to break it down into several smaller topics. You need a topic that you can discuss in a composition of about five or six paragraphs.

Below is a sample brainstorming list of possible topics for a composition. Notice that most of the ideas have been narrowed down into smaller topics.

BRAINSTORMING FOR A COMPOSITION TOPIC

Endangered species of wildlife

Whales
—History of whaling
—Regulation of whale hunting
—Uses for whale oil and whalebone

Unusual pets
—Raising bees
—Building an ant farm
—Habits of gerbils

Radio stations
—A good rock station
—A good news station

When you have a list that includes several good topics, choose the one that interests you most. If you already know something about the topic, you will find it easy to write the composition. If not, you may have to do some reading in encyclopedias, magazines, or other sources before you can write about the topic.

The next step is to focus your composition topic by stating your main idea.

State the main idea of your composition in a single sentence.

Before you state your main idea, you need to think about your readers. Who will be reading your composition? How much do they know about your topic? What should they be told about it? Will they probably agree or disagree with your opinions? Is your audience a specific person or group? How old is your audience? Answering such questions will help you decide what aspect of your topic to focus on.

You should also give thought to the purpose of your composition. Do you want to describe something or tell a story? Do you want to explain something? Or do you want to persuade your readers to agree with your opinion on something?

When you have answered these questions, you should be able to write down several possible main ideas. It may be helpful to ask yourself questions that you think your readers might ask about the topic. Look at the chart on pages 355–356 in Chapter 36 to see the kinds of questions you might ask yourself.

Once you have a list of possible main ideas for your composition, choose the one you like best. Think about your readers and purpose as you experiment with several different ways of stating the main idea. Of course, you may want to revise your main idea later as the composition takes shape. Even so, having a main idea in mind will help you focus your ideas as you write the rest of your composition.

When you have chosen your main idea, you need to find examples, details, incidents, or reasons to support it. Use the brainstorming technique to think of supporting information.

Brainstorm for support of your main idea.

Again, ask yourself questions about your main idea and write down the answers. Try to think of examples, details, or incidents that will explain what you want to say. Or, if you want to persuade your readers, think of reasons that will make them agree with you. Write down as much information as you can. You will sort it out later.

When you have a list of supporting items, go over it and cross out unnecessary ones. Then organize the rest in an outline.

Organize your supporting information in the most logical order by making a simple outline of the body of the composition.

Use the suggestions in the following chart to help you decide what information to include and how to organize it.

ORGANIZING MAIN-IDEA SUPPORT

1. Go over your supporting items and cross out those unrelated to your main idea.
2. If some ideas are important but do not belong in the body of your composition, save them for the introduction or conclusion.
3. If you think of new ideas, add them to your list.
4. With your main idea in mind, put your supporting items in groups. Each group will form one body paragraph.
5. Decide on an order (chronological order, spatial order, order of importance, or some other logical order) for each of the body paragraphs.
6. Outline the body of the composition.

EXERCISE A: Brainstorming for Topics. Use the suggestions in this section to brainstorm a list of topics for a composition. Remember, while you are brainstorming, do not try to sort your ideas into good ideas and bad ideas. Just focus on trying to make a list of topics. Write down at least five possible topics. If any of your topics is too broad, break it down into smaller topics. Then choose one topic that you want to write about.

EXERCISE B: More Work with Topics. Using the topic that you chose for Exercise A, do each of the following steps.

1. Think about the people who will be reading your composition. How much will they know about the topic?
2. Write down three questions that your readers might ask about your topic.
3. Write a one-sentence answer to each question. These answers will be your possible main ideas.
4. Read your list of possible main ideas and choose the one that best covers what you want to say in your composition.
5. Experiment with several different ways of stating your main idea in a complete sentence. Then choose the one that seems best for your purpose.
6. Make a brainstorming list of supporting items for the main idea you have chosen.
7. Organize the supporting information after crossing out the items not related to your main idea.
8. Write an outline of the body of the composition.

DEVELOPING WRITING SKILLS: Planning a Composition. Carry out the eight steps of Exercise B for another topic of your choice. The topic can be one of the ones that you thought of while brainstorming in Exercise A. Or it could be a completely new topic.

37.3 Writing: Creating the First Version

Now that you have organized the supporting information that will go into your composition, you are almost ready to begin writing. But before you start to write, you must plan your introduction, conclusion, and title. Each plays a very important part in the final composition.

Think of ideas for your introduction, conclusion, and title. Then write your first draft.

Jot down ideas for your introduction. Try to think of the most interesting way to introduce your topic and get your readers' attention. Perhaps an unusual question, statement, or quotation would work. Check your brainstorming list for good ideas that you are not using in the body paragraphs. Your introduction should also give any background information your readers need to understand what follows. The last sentence of the introduction should state the main idea of the composition.

Jot down ideas for your conclusion. Try to think of a way to tie together all of the ideas expressed earlier. Your conclusion should refer to the original main idea but should not repeat it in exactly the same words. A good conclusion adds some unusual information or ends with a striking statement that stays in the reader's memory.

Finally, think about possible titles for your composition. The title should give readers a general idea about the topic of the composition. It should also make the audience want to read the composition. The title should catch the reader's attention. With these things in mind, write down two or three possible titles. You can make the final choice after you have finished writing the composition. Now you are ready to write your first draft. Use your notes for the introduction and conclusion and your outline of the body of your composition. You can also refer to the suggestions in the following chart.

SUGGESTIONS FOR WRITING A FIRST DRAFT OF A COMPOSITION

1. Use clear, specific language, and avoid slang. If you are explaining, be direct and exact. If you are persuading, be firm but reasonable.
2. Arrange the body paragraphs in the logical order that you have chosen. Check your outline of the body paragraphs often to remind yourself of the order you planned. But do not hesitate to change the order if that seems appropriate.
3. If good new information occurs to you, add it.
4. Take out unrelated supporting information.
5. Make sure that each of your body paragraphs has a topic sentence.
6. Connect the parts of your composition by using transitions where they are needed.

You will probably rewrite your first draft more than once. But you should approach it as if it were the final version. Write complete sentences and full paragraphs. Write as well as you can. The more work you put into the first draft, the less time you will have to spend writing the final version.

EXERCISE: Writing Your Introduction, Conclusion, and Title. Following the suggestions in this section, write an introduction, conclusion, and title for the composition you outlined in Exercise B or "Developing Writing Skills" on page 377.

DEVELOPING WRITING SKILLS: Writing Your First Draft. Following the suggestions in the above chart, write a first version of the composition you outlined in Exercise B or "Developing Writing Skills" on page 377.

37.4 Revising: Creating the Final Version

After you have written the first draft of your composition, you should revise it carefully. Follow the same basic steps that you used to revise a paragraph.

Reread your composition several times. Use a checklist to revise it. Make a final copy and proofread it carefully.

When you reread your composition, try to see it from a fresh perspective. You can follow the suggestions in Section 5.3 for rereading a paragraph. Set the composition aside for an hour or more before you reread it. Read the composition aloud to see whether you can hear any rough passages. Read it aloud to someone else, and ask your listener to try to spot problem areas. Or ask someone else to read the composition to you while you listen for problems. Discuss the comments and try to think of ways to improve the unclear passages or rough spots.

You should watch (or listen) for specific problems as you reread. You can use the following checklist to remind you of what to watch for.

CHECKLIST FOR REVISING A COMPOSITION

Title

1. Does the title give the general idea of the composition?
2. Does the title catch the reader's attention?

Introduction

1. Do the opening sentences catch the reader's attention?
2. Have you included any background information that the reader would need to understand what follows?
3. Does the main idea fit the composition?
4. Is the main idea expressed clearly?

Body
1. Are the body paragraphs in the best order?
2. Does each paragraph have a topic sentence?
3. Have you used good, strong support?
4. Should you take out any of the support?
Conclusion
1. Does the conclusion recall the main idea and tie the whole composition together?
2. Can the conclusion be made more effective?

During your first rereading, make any needed changes on the first draft. If you change the order of ideas, circle the ideas you are moving and draw arrows to the places where they belong. If transitions are needed to help readers follow your ideas, add them. Check to see if changes in words or sentences would make the composition clearer. When you have finished revising, make a final copy.

Proofreading the final copy is the last step. Read the composition silently and aloud. Look for mistakes you may have overlooked before and mistakes you may have added in recopying. Use the proofreading checklist for paragraphs on page 364.

EXERCISE: Revising Your Composition. Reread the first draft that you wrote for "Developing Writing Skills" on page 379. Using the checklist in this section, find and correct any weaknesses.

DEVELOPING WRITING SKILLS: Writing the Final Version. Write a final version of your composition. Proofread it using the checklist for proofreading a paragraph on page 364.

Writing Workshop: Writing Compositions

ASSIGNMENT 1

Topic A Talented Animal

Form and Purpose A composition that informs readers about an animal's talents

Audience Members of your science class

Length Four to six paragraphs

Focus In the first paragraph, introduce your subject and state a main idea about its talents. Then give facts, examples, and details about the animal's skills and how it uses those skills. With an interesting comment about the animal's talents.

Sources Books, encyclopedias, magazine articles.

Prewriting Brainstorm for a specific topic. If necessary, research your subject. Write a main idea and list supporting facts, examples, and details.

Writing Use your notes to write a first draft.

Revising Use the checklist on page 380 to revise your composition.

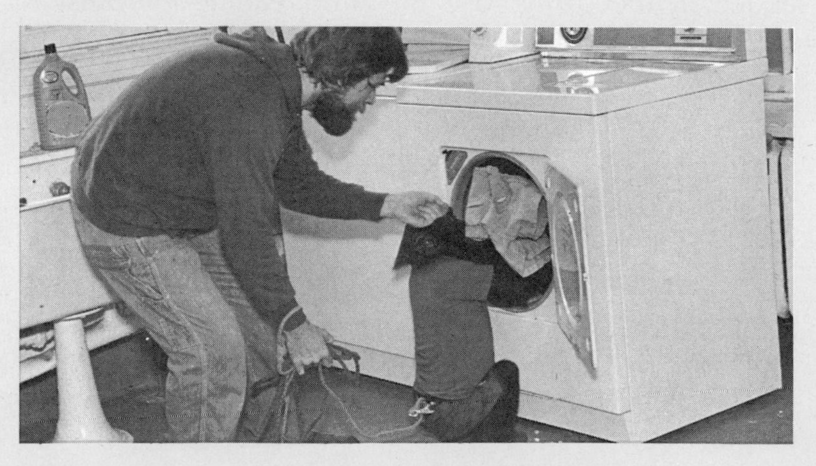

ASSIGNMENT 2

Topic Personal Health

Form and Purpose A composition that informs and/or persuades a reader about a personal health issue

Audience People seeking information about the health issue you selected

Length Four to six paragraphs

Focus State a main idea about personal health in the first paragraph. In the supporting paragraphs, develop subtopics with facts, details, and examples. Restate your main idea in the final paragraph and conclude with a strong statement about your topic.

Sources Books, health texts, encyclopedias, magazines

Prewriting Narrow your topic and decide on your main idea. Research your subject and decide on your specific purpose.

Writing Using your notes, write a first draft of your composition.

Revising Use the checklist on page 380 to revise your composition.

Topics for Writing: Writing Compositions

Christa McAuliffe

The photo above may suggest a writing topic to you. If so, plan and write a composition about your topic. If not, choose one of the related topics listed below.

1. What Is a Hero?
2. A Hero I Admire
3. A Popular Hero I Do Not Admire
4. Describing an Heroic Act
5. Popular Television Heroes: Are They Real?
6. A Villain Who Was Respected as a Hero
7. A Famous Hero from a Myth or Legend
8. A Hero Who Was Unpopular
9. A Memorable Film Hero
10. An Act of Personal Heroism

Chapter 38

Writing Reports

In many of your school courses, and possibly in your adult career, you will be asked to write reports. To write a report, you must consult outside sources. But you should combine the information you find in those sources with ideas of your own. Otherwise, you would simply be reciting a list of unrelated facts instead of presenting a logical, well-organized argument.

In structure, a report is similar to a composition. But, unlike a composition, a report relies on information from sources. So a report must include references to those sources, listed in a standard form.

In this chapter, you will study the important features of a report. You will learn how the sources used in preparing a report are listed. You will find out how to locate sources of information and how to take notes for a report. Finally, you will plan, organize, write, and revise a report on a topic you have chosen.

38.1 Looking at Reports

A report gives your readers information that you have found in books, magazine articles, and other sources. In a report, you use examples, details, and incidents from your reading to support your main idea.

A report uses information gathered from research to support an original main idea.

A report resembles a composition. It begins with a title. It has an introduction that states the main idea of the paper. It contains several body paragraphs that support the main idea. And it ends with a conclusion.

A report is like a composition, except for one important feature that a composition does not have: a list of the sources used to prepare the report. This list is called a bibliography.

Each part of a report has special functions.

THE PARTS OF A REPORT

Part	How It Works
Title	The title comes at the beginning othe report. —It catches the reader's interest. —It tells something about the report's topic.
Introduction	The introduction is the first part of the report. —It makes the reader want to read the report. —It includes a statement of the report's main idea.
Body Paragraphs	The body paragraphs form the middle of the report. —They present specific supporting information to develop the main point.

	—They present information and quotations gathered from sources. —They are organized in a logical order.
Conclusion	The conclusion is usually the final part of the report. —It reminds the readers of the main point of the report. —It ends the report smoothly with a final example or striking quotation.
Bibliography	The bibliography appears at the end of the report. —It lists sources in alphabetical order. —It includes for each entry information such as title, author's name, publisher, and copyright date.

When you write a report, you are relying on the facts or opinions of other writers. So you must be able to prove that those other writers actually wrote what your report says they did. The bibliography allows your readers to consult your sources and check your interpretation.

Your bibliography must include all the information your readers will need to find each source. For most sources, you will include the title, the author's name, and some information about where the source was published. The listing for each source is called a bibliography entry. Bibliography entries are arranged in an alphabetical list at the end of the report.

A report should include a bibliography that lists the sources used in the report.

The chart on the following page shows the proper form for bibliography entries. Note that for each entry every line after the first is indented. This makes it easier for the reader to pick out individual entries. Also note that an author's last name is given first.

SAMPLE BIBLIOGRAPHY ENTRIES	
Book (one author)	Lockley, Ronald M. *Whales, Dolphins, and Porpoises.* New York: W. W. Norton and Co., 1979.
Book (two authors)	Cousteau, Jacques-Yves, and Diolé, Philippe. *The Whale: Mighty Monarch of the Sea.* Translated by J. F. Bernard. Garden City, N. Y.: Doubleday and Co., 1972.
Magazine article	Ford, Anne. "Following a School of Whales." *Undersea Digest,* August 1985, p. 33.
Encyclopedia article	*The World Book Encyclopedia.* 1981 ed. "Whale."

The following is a report with a bibliography. Note that some of the quotations and statements are followed by references, in parentheses, to bibliography entries. They are a short form of the complete bibliographic references included in the bibliography itself. These parenthetical references show the reader the source of a direct quotation or of an original idea. They also might be used to show the source of information for an unusual fact or a specific fact involving numbers or dates.

Like a composition, this report has a title, an introduction, body paragraphs, and a conclusion.

Those Brainy Whale Families

Ask people what they know about whales. Most of them will say that whales are big. This is true. Whales are the largest animals in the world. Some blue whales have been more than 100 feet long and may have weighed as much as 200 tons (Small, *The Blue Whale,* pp. 32, 34). That is longer and heavier than the largest dinosaur was. Many people will say that the whale is a fish. This is not true. Whales are mammals. They give birth to live baby whales, called calves, and feed them milk. They breathe air through large blowholes on the tops of their heads. What most people don't know is how smart whales are. They are very intelligent and also have close family relationships.

Whales are so intelligent that they have their own "language" (Tinbergen, *Animal Behavior,* p. 42). They communicate with one another through clicks, rasps, and a variety of other strange noises. Of course, humans cannot understand the whales yet. Jacques Cousteau, an expert in undersea exploration, says that learning to understand the language of whales "is one of the most exciting challenges we have to face" (*The Whale,* p. 243). Scientists also have learned that whales use tricks to escape their enemies. Adult whales will lure predators away from mother whales and babies. Then they use their great speed to escape and return to the family.

"The family unit is the basis of a school of whales," says Cousteau (*The Whale,* p. 189). He has observed whales traveling in family groups, with mothers and other females caring for the young. The families protect their young calves for several years after they are born. When they grow up, the calves take their places as the adults in their families.

Scientists are still learning about whales. Someday, it may be possible to "talk" to whales—but not to one whale only. We will probably have to listen to the whole family.

BIBLIOGRAPHY

Cousteau, Jacques-Yves, and Diolé, Philippe. *The Whale: Mighty Monarch of the Sea.* Translated by J. F. Bernard. Garden City, N.Y.: Doubleday and Co., 1972.

McNulty, Faith. *The Great Whales.* Garden City, N.Y.: Doubleday and Co., 1974.

Small, George L. *The Blue Whale.* New York: Columbia University Press, 1971.

Tinbergen, Niko. *Animal Behavior.* New York: Time-Life Books, 1965.

The World Book Encyclopedia. 1981 ed. "Whale."

EXERCISE A: Reviewing Bibliography Entries. Listed below are some bibliography entries. Check each one to see if it is prepared according to the form shown in the chart on page 388. If you find any errors in the entries, be prepared to explain how to correct them.

1. Richard B. Morris, The American Revolution. New York: D. Van Nostrand Company, 1955.
2. Henig, Robin. "Eat Right and Live Longer." *Woman's Day*, February 8, 1983, pp. 135–142.
3. *We, the American Women: A Documentary History*. Millstein, Beth, and Bodin, Jeanne. Chicago: Science Research Associates, 1977.
4. *The World Book Encyclopedia*, 1981 ed., "Skiing."
5. Johnston, Moira. *The Last Nine Minutes*. Avon Books: New York, 1976.
6. Kuykendall, Ralph S., and A. Grove Day. *Hawaii: A History*. Englewood Cliffs, N.J.: Prentice-Hall, Inc., 1961.
7. Collins, Carol. *Hockey World*, January 1980, p. 56, "Safety First."
8. Ellis, William S. "Loch Ness: The Lake and the Legend." *National Geographic*, June 1977, pp. 758–779.

EXERCISE B: Examining a Report. Reread the report about whales. Then answer the questions below.

1. Which sentence states the main idea of the report?
2. What kinds of sources are used in the report?
3. How many entries does the bibliography contain?
4. In what order are the bibliography entries listed?
5. Find one more source of information about whales in your school or public library. Write a bibliography entry for this source.

DEVELOPING WRITING SKILLS: Writing a Response. Write a brief paragraph in which you tell why you would, or would not, like to learn more about whales.

Prewriting: Planning Your Report 38.2

The first step in planning a report is choosing a topic. Your teacher may have assigned you a topic. Or you may prefer to choose your own. Either way, it will be your job to make sure that the topic you write about is narrow enough to be covered in a brief report.

To choose your topic, start with the same brainstorming technique that you used in Chapters 36 and 37. Write down at least five possible topics that interest you. Before you choose one, however, you will have to know whether you can find enough information about it.

Choose a topic which interests you and for which you can find at least three good sources of information.

To find sources, go to the library. Look up your possible topics in the card catalog and in encyclopedias. These general sources will help you see how much information is available on the topics you are considering. Also, they will give you an overview of each possible topic. And they may help you narrow down a broad topic into a smaller one that can be covered in a report.

When you have chosen one topic that you want to write about, make a list of all the sources you plan to use. You can use 3″ × 5″ index cards for this list. Fill out one card for each possible source. Such cards are known as bibliography cards.

Make a bibliography card for every book, magazine article, or other source that you plan to use in preparing your report.

You may not actually use all the sources listed on your bibliography cards. And you may add additional sources as you do your research. Even so, by gathering together possible sources, you will gain a general idea about your topic.

Use the guidelines in the following chart to help you fill out your bibliography cards.

GUIDELINES FOR PREPARING BIBLIOGRAPHY CARDS

1. Use the library's card catalog or the sources themselves for information.
2. Fill out one index card for each source.
3. On each card, write all the information you will need for a bibliography entry.
4. For a book, include the library call number so you can find the book easily.

Below is an example of a bibliography card.

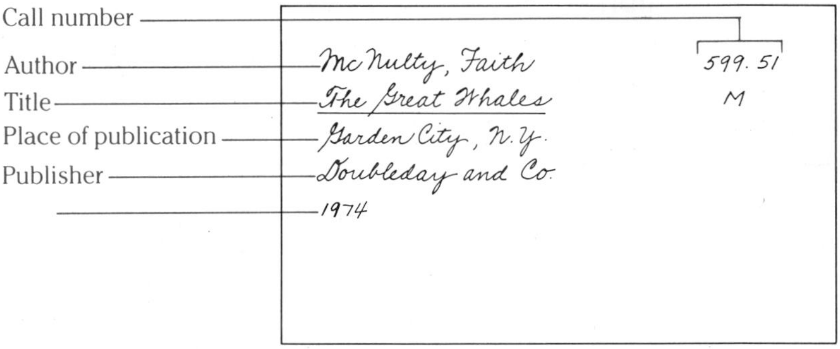

Call number	599.51 M
Author	McNulty, Faith
Title	The Great Whales
Place of publication	Garden City, N.Y.
Publisher	Doubleday and Co.
	1974

After you have filled out all your bibliography cards, you are ready to begin taking notes. By this time, you should be able to write down some questions about your topic. As you do your research, you will try to answer those questions. And you will try to focus on a main idea.

Make up a list of questions about your topic, and focus the topic into one main idea.

You can take your notes on 3″×5″ index cards. Use one note card for each source or for each idea that the source discusses. Since you will have many note cards, you will need to be able to sort them. So you should write a subject heading on each card.

Use these guidelines to prepare your note cards.

GUIDELINES FOR PREPARING NOTE CARDS

1. Take notes on 3″×5″ index cards. Use a separate card for each source or each idea that the source discusses.
2. In the upper left-hand corner of each card, write the author and title of the source. (You do not need to include complete bibliographical information on each note card.)
3. In the upper right-hand corner, write a heading that tells the subject of the information on the card.
4. Write each fact or idea on your card clearly, so that you will be able to understand it later. Put a page number after each piece of information.
5. Copy quotations word for word and put them in quotation marks. Include a page number for each quotation.
6. Keep the note cards from each source together, organized by subject headings.

You may want to begin your note-taking with general sources, such as encyclopedia articles. Focus on the main idea you have chosen. Ignore information that is not related to your main idea. Try to answer all the questions that you wrote.

The following are two sample note cards.

Subject heading

Cousteau and
Diolé
The Whale

Whale families

Exact quotation with page number

"The family unit is the basis of a school of whales." (p. 189)

Subject heading

George L. Small — Size of whales

The Blue Whale

Blue whale is largest animal that ever lived on earth, much larger than any dinosaur (p. 16)

Longest whale accurately measured was 106 feet (p. 32).

Whales difficult to weigh, but the largest whales may have weighed 400,000 pounds (p. 34)

Facts written in student's own words with page numbers

When you have finished taking notes, you will be ready to move on to the final planning step: organizing the report. Just as you did when you were planning a composition, you should arrange your ideas for the report in an outline.

Organize your report by arranging your ideas in an outline.

The four suggestions in the following chart will help you to organize your report. Using them in the order given will help you in your writing.

GUIDELINES FOR ORGANIZING A REPORT

1. Read over your note cards keeping your main idea in mind. Decide on what aspects of your main idea you will develop in your report. These aspects are called subtopics. In many reports, each of the subtopics represents one paragraph.
2. Group your note cards according to the subtopics you have chosen.
3. Decide on a logical order for presenting the subtopics in the report.
4. Write an outline that shows the organization of your subtopics and the organization of the supporting information under each subtopic.

EXERCISE A: Choosing a Topic for a Report. Brainstorm for possible report topics. Write down at least five topics. If any of the topics are too broad, break them down into narrower topics suitable for a brief report. In the library, check the available information for each topic. Choose a topic for which you can find at least three sources of information. Then fill out a bibliography card for each source.

EXERCISE B: Gathering Information for Your Report. Write down a main idea for your topic and three or four questions about it. Then use the guidelines in the chart on page 393 to take notes on the information in your sources.

DEVELOPING WRITING SKILLS: Organizing Your Report. Review your note cards and your main idea. Then follow the guidelines in the chart on page 394 to organize your report by arranging your ideas in an outline.

Writing: Creating the First Version 38.3

When you have your outline, you can start writing the report. First, jot down some ideas for your introduction and conclusion. And try to think of an interesting, appropriate title that hints at what is to come.

Using your outline and note cards, write a first draft of your report.

Begin your introduction, if you can, in an unusual, attention-catching way. Tell your readers what is interesting about your topic or why they should be concerned about it. As you did when writing a composition, consider who your audience is. What opinions might they already hold about your topic? What do they already know about the topic? Be sure to give them any background information they may need to understand the report.

In your conclusion, sum up all the ideas in the report. Remind your readers of your main idea and the subtopics in your body paragraphs. Do not repeat the same words you used before, however. If you can, end your conclusion with an unusual fact or a striking quotation. Your aim should be to make your readers remember your main idea, although they probably will forget most of the details you used to support it.

Now write your first draft. Even though you will revise it later, make your first draft as correct and complete as you can. Express your ideas in complete sentences and full paragraphs. The more time you spend writing your first version of the report, the less time you will have to spend on the final version.

Be sure that you present the information you have gathered accurately and honestly. This means understanding your sources and summarizing their contents fairly.

If you are using the exact words of any of your sources, be sure to enclose them in quotation marks. Give the author, title, and page number after the quote, in parentheses. Review the report in Section 7.1 to see how this is done.

You may decide to rephrase an idea in your own words. If the idea is an original one that is found in only one source, you still need to give credit to the source. Also, if you give your readers little-known facts or specific facts involving numbers or dates, you probably need to credit your source.

Take a moment to consider the title of your report. The title should give readers an idea about the topic of the report. It should also catch the reader's interest. Jot down two or three possible titles.

Now use the guidelines for writing a first draft of a report in the chart on the following page to help you write the first draft.

SUGGESTIONS FOR WRITING A FIRST DRAFT OF A REPORT

1. Reread your outline and note cards. Make notes for an introduction and conclusion.
2. Follow the order of your outline to organize the body of your report. You may change that order if necessary, however.
3. Make sure that each body paragraph has a topic sentence and that the supporting information is arranged in a logical order.
4. Be sure that every subtopic has enough supporting information. You may have to do more research to find supporting information.
5. Delete any information that is not directly related to the main idea or to any of the subtopics.
6. Give credit to your sources for direct quotations or original ideas.
7. Use transitions to connect the parts of your report.
8. Jot down two or three possible titles for the report. Then pick one.

EXERCISE: Preparing an Introduction and Conclusion. Make notes for an introduction and conclusion of the report you planned in Section 38.2. Make sure the introduction tells readers why they should want to read your report and provides any necessary background information they may need to follow your ideas. Be sure the conclusion sums up the ideas of the report and helps the readers remember your main idea.

DEVELOPING WRITING SKILLS: Writing Your Report. Using the note cards and outline you have prepared, write a first draft of your report, including an introduction, conclusion, and title.

38.4 Revising: Creating the Final Version

You will need to revise the first draft of your report at least once. In general, you should follow the same steps that you used to revise a composition. And you should prepare your bibliography now.

Revise your report using a checklist; write your bibliography; and proofread the whole report.

As you did when writing a composition, you may want to set your paper aside for a short time. And you may want to read parts of it to someone else. Your listener may be able to spot problems that you do not see because you are too close to the topic.

Now revise your introduction, body paragraphs, and conclusion. Write your bibliography on a separate page at the end of your report. The bibliography for the report on whales, in Section 38.1, is an example of the form you should use. Remember, bibliographic entries are listed in alphabetical order.

The questions in the following checklist will help you revise your report.

CHECKLIST FOR REVISING A REPORT

1. Is your title interesting and appropriate?
2. Does your introduction catch the reader's attention?
3. Does your introduction include all necessary background information?
4. Is your main idea stated in the best possible way?
5. Does your main idea have enough support?
6. Have you used only information that is related to the main idea?
7. Are your subtopics arranged in the best possible order?
8. Does each body paragraph have a topic sentence and enough supporting information?

9. Is each body paragraph in logical order?
10. Have you used transitions to connect your sentences and paragraphs smoothly?
11. Have you enclosed any direct quotations in quotation marks?
12. Have you given credit for all direct quotations, original ideas, and specific facts?
13. Does your conclusion remind the reader of the main idea without repeating it in the same words?
14. Does your bibliography include all the sources you used to prepare the report?
15. Are your bibliography entries written in the correct form and arranged in alphabetical order?

Finally, proofread your report and bibliography. Refer to Section 38.1 for correct bibliography form. Use the checklist for proofreading a paragraph on page 363 to proofread each paragraph of your report.

EXERCISE A: Revising Your Report. Reread the first draft that you wrote for "Developing Writing Skills" on page 397. Then use the checklist for revising a report to revise your first draft.

EXERCISE B: Revising With the Help of a Partner. Work with a partner to make final revisions on your report revised in Exercise A. Read portions of your report aloud to your partner. Discuss your partner's suggestions for revising your report and make those changes that you think improve it. When it is your turn to listen, concentrate closely. Make suggestions that you think will improve the report.

DEVELOPING WRITING SKILLS: Proofreading Your Report. Proofread the final version of your report, using the checklist for proofreading a paragraph on page 363.

Writing Workshop: Writing Reports

ASSIGNMENT 1

Topic Customs in a Different Culture

Form and Purpose A report that informs readers about cultural customs

Audience People attending a World Culture Fair

Length Four to six paragraphs

Focus Choose a culture that interests you. In your report, explore two or three of that culture's customs. Explain each by giving facts, details, and examples. Throughout your report, focus on what the customs you are discussing reveal about the people.

Sources Books, encyclopedias, magazines, television documentaries

Prewriting Before deciding on a specific topic, research various cultures. Narrow your topic to a specific culture. Continue your research, taking notes on bibliography cards. Use the checklist on page 392 to organize your notes.

Writing Using your notes, write a first draft of your report. Prepare a bibliography.

Revising The checklist on pages 398–399 will help you revise your report.

Market in Guatemala

Indonesia

ASSIGNMENT 2

Topic Unusual Events in Space

Form and Purpose A report that informs readers about an unusual astronomical event

Audience Readers of a magazine called *Space Mysteries*

Length Four to six paragraphs

Focus Narrow your topic to one unusual event. At the beginning of your report, introduce your topic and main idea. In your supporting paragraphs, give facts, examples, and details about the event; tell exactly what it is and why it is important and unusual. Conclude with a restatement of your main idea.

Sources Astronomy books, encyclopedia and magazine articles

Prewriting Research the subject and narrow your topic to one event. Continue your research, taking notes on bibliography cards. Then organize your note cards.

Writing Use your note cards to write a first draft. Prepare a bibliography.

Revising Use the checklist on pages 398–399 to revise your report.

Topics for Writing: Writing Reports

The cartoon above may indicate a writing topic to you. If so, research, plan, and write your report. Other topics related to past historical people, places, or events are listed below. If you prefer to use one of these topics for your report, you may have to narrow it first.

1. Alexander the Great's Accomplishments
2. The Mysterious Disappearance of a Prehistoric Animal
3. The Ice Age
4. Building the Great Wall of China
5. Major Causes of the American Revolutionary War
6. Nostradamus: Prophecies of the Future
7. The Strange Disappearance of the Roanoke Island Colony
8. Hiroshima and the First Atomic Bomb
9. Rome and Its Roads
10. Marco Polo and Emperor Kublai Khan

Chapter 39

Writing Book Reports

A book report is a special kind of report. When you write a book report, you do not use any sources except the book that you are reporting on.

You may already be familiar with book reports. In fact, when a friend asks, "Have you read any good books lately?" and you reply, "I'm reading a fascinating science-fiction novel about . . ." you are giving an informal, spoken book report. A written book report does basically the same thing. It gives the reader an idea of what a book is like and whether it would be enjoyable to read.

You can write a book report on any book, fiction or nonfiction. You can use different formats for book reports. But you should always try to include as much information as your readers need to decide whether to read the book.

In this chapter, you will learn the basic parts of most book reports. You will study several features of books that can be discussed in book reports. You will learn how to plan, write, and revise a book report. And you will write a report on a book that you have recently read.

39.1 Looking at Book Reports

A book report can be organized in many different ways. But most book reports have several things in common. A typical book report usually identifies the book, describes it briefly, and offers an evaluation of it.

A book report tells readers what a book is about and whether they are likely to enjoy it.

You can organize your book reports the same way you organized your compositions and research reports. You can start with an introduction, develop your ideas with several body paragraphs, and sum up the report with a conclusion. The following chart shows the function of each of these three basic parts of a book report.

BASIC PARTS OF A BOOK REPORT	
Part	**Function**
Introduction	The introduction covers basic information in one short paragraph. —It gives the title and author. —It tells what kind of book it is (for example, mystery, biography, or adventure novel). —It gives a short summary of the book.
Body paragraphs	The body paragraphs cover interesting features of the book. —Each paragraph presents a main idea about one of the features of the book (for example, a character, an incident, or the setting). —The main idea in each paragraph is supported with examples, details, and incidents from the book.

Conclusion	The conclusion offers an opinion about the book in one short paragraph. —It tells other readers whether the book is worth reading.

Your book reports will probably be one and one-half to two pages long. That will give you enough room for at least two body paragraphs. Each paragraph will focus on one feature of the book. It should have a topic sentence and be developed with supporting information. The following chart lists some of the features you may choose to write about.

FEATURES TO WRITE ABOUT IN A BOOK REPORT

Feature	What to Write About
Characters: The characters are the people in a story.	1. Your favorite or least favorite character 2. How a main character changes as the story moves along 3. Why a character is believable or unbelievable
Setting: The setting of a story is the time and place of the action.	1. How the setting plays an important part in what happens to the characters in the story 2. Why you would (or would not) like to live at the time and place of the story 3. How well the setting is described

Plot: The plot is the order of incidents in a story. It is often centered on a conflict that builds up to a high point, or a climax.	1. Which incident is the most memorable in the book 2. How interesting the plot is 3. How the author creates suspense in an incident
Theme: A theme is a central idea or general truth about life; it is the meaning, or point, of the story.	1. Something important that a character learns about himself or herself through the events in the story 2. How the book has changed your mind about something or made you see something in a new way 3. Why you agree or disagree with the view of life expressed by the story

The following book report is about the book *Friend Within the Gates*. Notice the main parts of the report and the features discussed in the body paragraphs.

Report on *Friend Within the Gates*

Friend Within the Gates by Elizabeth Grey is the true story of Edith Cavell, an English nurse who helped found a national nursing service in Belgium. When World War I began and the Germans invaded Belgium, Edith Cavell decided to remain there. Although Belgium was not her country, she thought of herself as a "friend within the gates (p. 103)," and she wanted to do everything she could to help. She and her nurses cared for wounded Allied soldiers, hid them from the Germans, and helped them escape across enemy lines to Holland. When the Germans found out what Edith Cavell had been doing, she was imprisoned, tried, and executed.

The eldest daughter of an English clergyman, Edith Cavell was taught from childhood that her first duty was to help others. She started early by caring for her younger sisters and brother and taking baskets of food to needy village families. Her parents, proud of their intelligent, hard-working daughter, somehow found the money to send Edith away to school. Being a governess—a teacher in a private home—was one of the few careers open to young women at that time. Edith decided to become one because it would allow her to pursue her goal of helping people. After several years as a governess to English families, she accepted a position in Brussels, which she had been offered because she could speak French. The light-hearted, fun-loving Belgians were very different from the English people she was used to, but she soon learned to love Belgium as her second home. Then she was called back to England suddenly to help nurse her sick father back to health. Edith now realized that her true calling was nursing. She trained at a hospital in London and eventually became a supervisor and teacher of nurses. But one day she was called back to Brussels. A group of Belgian doctors, impressed with the work of Florence Nightingale, were seeking an English nurse who could bring Belgian nursing up to English standards. Edith Cavell had founded several nursing schools when war broke out. A year later, in 1915, she was shot as a spy.

Edith Cavell was a woman of strong character and high principles. Her stern father had taught her the importance of duty, and her generous mother had shown her the joy of helping people less fortunate than she. Honesty was important to her. As a governess, she refused to tell callers that her employer was out when she actually was home but did not want to receive visitors. When the Germans questioned Edith Cavell about her activities, it never occurred to her to lie. In addition, she had great courage. She faced her death sentence bravely, saying, "I have seen death so often it is not strange or fearful to me (p. 180)."

Friend Within the Gates is an interesting portrait of a courageous woman. It shows how Edith Cavell's early life led up to her later career and her final heroic sacrifice. Elizabeth Grey also attempts to show how Edith's moral principles influenced her actions. It is difficult to know much about Cavell's thoughts and feelings, however. She was more interested in helping others than in talking about herself. Even her letters describe only events, not her reactions to them. *Friend Within the Gates* tells her story simply and well.

EXERCISE: Examining a Book Report. Reread the book report on *Friend Within the Gates*. Then answer the following questions.

1. What information about the book is given in the introduction?
2. What feature of the book does the first body paragraph focus on?
3. Name at least two examples, details, or incidents that are used to develop the paragraph on this feature.
4. What feature of the book does the second body paragraph focus on?
5. Name at least two examples, details, or incidents that are used to develop the paragraph on this feature.
6. Where is the setting (time and place) mentioned?
7. Where does the report offer an opinion of the book?

DEVELOPING WRITING SKILLS: Evaluating a Book Report. In a paragraph tell whether the report gives you a good idea of what *Friend Within the Gates* is like. Give reasons for your opinions.

Prewriting: Planning Your Book Report 39.2

The content of a book report comes mostly from the book itself, not from your head. So instead of brainstorming, you will take notes from the book to plan your report.

The chart on pages 405–406 discussed four features—characters, setting, plot, and theme. These features will appear in many types of books, especially biographies and fiction. However, books of other types may include other features. A nonfiction book about the solar system would have entirely different features. The chart below describes these features.

OTHER FEATURES TO WRITE ABOUT IN A BOOK REPORT

Feature	What to Write About
Explanatory Information: This includes specific facts and information presented by the author.	1. Whether the information was understandable to a non-expert 2. Certain pieces of information that were interesting or surprising 3. How the information gave you a new understanding of something
Ideas: This includes the opinions or concepts presented in addition to the specific facts and information.	1. How the author convinced you or changed your mind about something 2. How the book helped you think about something in a new way

Use the chart on pages 405 and 406 to help you select features to discuss. Skim through the book to find supporting information for each paragraph.

The following list of supporting information was prepared for the book report on *Friend Within the Gates.* The writer decided to discuss the theme of service to others and the main character, Edith Cavell.

LIST OF SUPPORTING INFORMATION FOR A BOOK REPORT	
Theme: A life of service to others	
Parents taught her to help others	Nursed her father
Carried food to poor families	Decided to become a nurse
Goal in life was service	Nursing service in Belgium
Became a governess	During World War I, helped Allied soldiers escape from the Germans
Worked for families in both England and Belgium	Executed in 1915 by Germans
Character: Edith Cavell	
Had high moral principles	Refused to lie and say her employer was out
Believed her duty was to help others	Was strict but fair
Had courage	Considered it her duty to help all people, not just English men and women
Was not afraid to die	
Was honest	
Told the truth when Germans accused her	

Arrange the supporting information in each paragraph in logical order. Decide on the order of the body paragraphs, and outline the whole report.

Decide what features of the book you want to discuss; write down supporting information for each feature; then arrange the supporting information logically.

At this stage you may also begin to jot down some ideas for your introduction and conclusion. Your introduction will probably include a summary of the book's main ideas or events. Your conclusion should give an evaluation that helps readers decide whether they want to read the book.

EXERCISE: Starting a Book Report. Choose a book you have read recently and select at least two features of the book to discuss in the body paragraphs. Remember that the features you choose may include characters, setting, plot, theme, explanatory information, or ideas.

DEVELOPING WRITING SKILLS: Planning a Book Report. On a blank piece of paper, jot down information you will use for your introduction. The introduction gives basic information about the book, such as title and author and what kind of book it is. It also briefly summarizes the book.

Then decide on a main idea for each of the features you have chosen to write about. Look through the book to find as many examples, details, facts, reasons, and incidents as you can that relate to your main ideas. List this information on your paper.

Finally jot down ideas for your conclusion. Remember the conclusion tells your readers whether or not you like the book. It explains your opinion in such a way as to persuade others.

39.3 Writing: Creating the First Version

After you have decided which features to write about and prepared your list of supporting information and a simple outline, you can write your first draft.

Use your outline and list of supporting information to write a first draft of your book report.

Your introduction should begin with the title, author, and type of book, such as mystery novel, adventure novel, science-fiction novel, or biography. The introduction should also include a summary of the book. Be careful not to include too much detail, however. Tell your readers only enough to interest them, not enough to spoil the story. Never give away a surprise ending.

The body of your book report should consist of several well-organized paragraphs. Each body paragraph should focus on one feature of the book. Each should have a well-written topic sentence and enough supporting information.

The conclusion of the book report will probably be the most difficult section to write. In the conclusion, you must offer your opinion of the book. But that opinion must be expressed in a full paragraph. Like any other paragraph, the conclusion must have a topic sentence and supporting information.

Your reason for recommending a book should be based on a strength of the book itself. You should not simply refer to one of your preferences. For example, you should not recommend a book by saying, "I liked this book because I like mystery stories." Instead, you might say, "The author builds up the events so that they seem believable and exciting." The chart of features to write about in a book report on pages 405–406 may give you some ideas about how you can support a recommendation of a book.

SUGGESTIONS FOR WRITING A BOOK REPORT

1. Refer to your outline and list of supporting information.
2. Give the title, author, and type of book in the introduction.
3. Include a brief summary of the entire book in your introduction.
4. Arrange the supporting information within each body paragraph in the order you have chosen. But feel free to change that order if necessary.
5. Make sure that every paragraph has an appropriate topic sentence.
6. If new, related information occurs to you, add it.
7. Take out unrelated supporting information.
8. Connect your ideas with transitions, both within paragraphs and between paragraphs.
9. Consistently use either the present or the past tense to describe the story.
10. Use quotation marks for direct quotations. Include page numbers in parentheses.

EXERCISE: Evaluating a Book. Outline the paragraph in which you will give reasons for your opinion of the book you selected. Make sure your opinion is based on the strengths or weaknesses of the book itself. Do not base your opinion of the book simply on your own preferences.

DEVELOPING WRITING SKILLS: Writing a Book Report. Using the outline and list of supporting information you prepared for the exercise in Section 39.2, write a first draft of a book report. Refer to the chart above on suggestions for writing a book report. The chart will help you make the first draft as effective as possible.

39.4 Revising: Creating the Final Version

After you have written the first draft of your book report, you should revise it carefully.

Use a checklist to revise your book report.

If you have time, you may want to set your report aside for a time so that you can read it with a fresh eye. Then revise it, checking for organization, completeness of supporting information, wording, grammar, spelling, and punctuation. You may even go back to the book and reread portions of it.

CHECKLIST FOR REVISING A BOOK REPORT
1. Have you mentioned the author, title, and kind of book in the introduction?
2. Have you given enough information about the contents of the book in your introduction?
3. Should you include more information from the book to support your main ideas about the features of the book that you are discussing?
4. Have you included any unnecessary information that you could take out?
5. Does every paragraph have a good topic sentence?
6. Are your ideas arranged in the most logical order?
7. Should any transitions be added between sentences or between paragraphs?
8. If you have used any direct quotations, are they accurate? Have you used quotation marks? Have you supplied page numbers?
9. Have you consistently used either the present or the past tense to describe the story?
10. Is your recommendation supported with reasons?

When you have finished revising your book report, make a clean final copy. Then proofread the final copy as you would any other report. On this final reading, look for mistakes you may have overlooked before. The proofreading checklist for paragraphs on page 339 can help you proofread each paragraph of your report.

EXERCISE A: Revising a Book Report. Use the checklist on page 414 to revise the book report you wrote for "Developing Writing Skills" in Section 39.3 on page 413.

EXERCISE B: Helping a Partner Revise a Book Report. Exchange book reports with someone in your class and follow these steps.

1. Use the questions in the exercise in Section 39.1 to examine the report. Read your partner's report carefully and then answer each question about it.
2. Use the checklist for revising on page 414 to evaluate the report. In the margins of the report, suggest further revisions. At the end write three or four sentences that comment on the strengths and weaknesses of the report. Revise your own report again, if necessary.

EXERCISE C: Writing the Final Version. Make a clean final copy of your book report and proofread it carefully for errors.

DEVELOPING WRITING SKILLS: Evaluating a Book Report. Read a book report (called a book review) in a newspaper or magazine. Answer the questions in the exercise in Section 39.1 about the report. Make notes about its strengths and weaknesses. Then write a paragraph in which you give your opinion of the report. Be sure to give reasons for your opinion.

Writing Workshop: Writing Book Reports

ASSIGNMENT

Topic A Review of a Collection of Children's Stories

Form and Purpose A report that summarizes, evaluates, and offers an opinion of a book

Audience Young readers

Length Two pages

Focus Begin by identifying the collection, its author, and telling what kinds of stories are included. Then explain two or three stories that you think reflect the quality of the collection. Conclude with an opinion and a recommendation.

Sources Collections of children's stories

Prewriting Read the collection. Select two or three stories. Make notes about the features of each story, using the checklist on pages 405–406 and 409 to guide you. Prepare an outline for your report.

Writing Follow your outline as you write a first draft.

Revising Revise your report using the checklist on page 414.

Chapter 40

Personal Writing

Book reports, reports on subjects you research in a library, and compositions on ideas or topics that do not relate to your own life are examples of impersonal writing. *Impersonal* simply means "not personal." When, however, you write about your own experiences, thoughts, and feelings, the result is personal writing.

There are different ways to write about one's own life and experiences. Poems are one way that many people express themselves. Autobiography—the story of one's own life—is another. In this chapter, you will learn about one of the most enjoyable and interesting forms of personal writing, journals.

40.1 Understanding Journals

People use journals to save and preserve their experiences. They do this by writing down not only events they have lived through but also their thoughts and feelings about those events. People who keep journals usually write in them either every day or at least a few times a week. Some journals cover many years in the writer's life.

Many famous and not-so-famous people have kept journals. People who traveled west on Conestoga wagons often recorded their experiencs in journals. Sailors at sea have also kept journals during their trips. Even youngsters in school have written of events and feelings in journals.

A journal is a continuing record of a person's experiences.

Journals are made up of entries. A *journal entry* is a piece of writing that is complete by itself. It may or may not relate to the entries that come before and after it. It can be as brief as a phrase or as long as several pages. Usually, it indicates clearly when the experience written about occurred. The following are three examples of journal entries.

Tuesday, March 2nd. I sat through the first ten minutes of math hoping Mr. Ferris wouldn't send me to the board to do a multiplication problem. I hate being called on like that, and I hate having to keep quiet and sit low in my seat so the teacher won't notice me when he's looking around for victims. Also, when you have to stand with your back to everyone, you get the feeling that any minute you're going to get it in the neck. Well, I got called on, but I worked out the problem just fine, and spent the rest of math relaxing in my seat and looking out the window.
Wednesday, March 3rd. Coach Durling had me play short center field in the softball game. A lot of action there.
Saturday, March 6th. I went to the zoo with Joey and his parents. It took a long time to get there and it was pretty crowded, but we had a great time anyway. I liked the el-

ephants best. One was getting a bath while we watched. He used his trunk to rinse himself off. One time, he squirted some water right at his keeper. We laughed. So did the elephant!

A journal may be written for the writer's eyes only or for other readers. Entries frequently present details about persons, places, things, and events to give the feeling of real experience. Some writers use journals to store up material for other kinds of writing, such as poems, stories, or essays.

EXERCISE: Examining a Journal Entry. Answer the following questions on the journal entries given on page 418 and above.

1. What seems to be the writer's purpose in the entry of March 2nd—to preserve an experience, to express thoughts and feelings about it, or to do both?
2. Which sentences record what happened in math class? Which express thoughts and feelings?
3. What seems to be the writer's purpose in the entry of March 6th?
4. Which sentences record what happened on the trip to the zoo? Which express thoughts and feelings?
5. In what way are these journal entries different from the kind of writing usually done for school?
6. Do the journal entries seem to be meant only for the writer's own eyes, or do you think the writer might show them to others?
7. How often did the writer make journal entries?
8. Does the second journal entry relate to the first one in any way?
9. Does the third journal entry relate to the others in any way?

DEVELOPING WRITING SKILLS: Using a Journal Entry Creatively. Write a brief story based on the first journal entry.

40.2 Keeping a Journal

Because a journal is so personal, there are really no "rules" of journal writing. However, the following guideline should be followed so that your journal will be a true journal, and not just a loose collection of jottings.

Write about your own experiences; include your thoughts and feelings; and follow chronological order.

One thing that you ought to do before starting a journal is to plan it. The following chart will help you do so.

PLANNING A JOURNAL
1. Decide on the purpose of the journal. Will you record daily experiences and events? Only important experiences and events? Will you be more concerned with ideas and feelings or with what happens?
2. Will you make entries in your journal every day, a few times a week, or only when you feel a strong urge to write?
3. Will you keep your journal in a loose-leaf binder, in some other kind of notebook, or in a book made specially for journal writing?
4. Will your journal be for your eyes only, or will you share it with others?

If you decide to keep a journal, you may come up against the common problem of getting started and deciding what to write. One way to overcome the problem is to use what are known as the "five W's." These are the questions Who? What? When? Where? and Why? By going through these questions when you want to write about some experience you have had, you will find that words start to come to you. For example, think again about the journal entries in Section 40.1. Consider the entry for

March 2nd. The writer might have used the five W's and gotten the following results.

WHO? Mr. Ferris, myself

WHAT? Getting called to the board to do a problem

WHEN? Math

WHERE? "

WHY? Nervousness, embarrassment

When you have answered as many of the five questions as you can, you can then brainstorm for details. The more details you can think of, the easier it will be to write an entry that captures your real experience.

You may be wondering whether a journal should be carefully written or not. It is certainly true that many journal writers pay no attenton to grammar, spelling, and the like. However, like so many other activities, keeping a journal will be more satisfying and rewarding if it is done properly and carefully. Legible, clean-looking entries in good English will make a journal you will be proud of and pleased with. In fact, many journals have been published as works of literature simply because the writers put care into them.

EXERCISE A: Planning a Journal. Answer the four questions in the chart on the preceding page in order to form a clear idea of the kind of journal you might keep.

EXERCISE B: Preparing an Entry. Think of some experience you have had that would be a good subject for a journal entry. Answer the questions Who? What? When? Where? and Why? Brainstorm for details.

DEVELOPING WRITING SKILLS: Writing a Journal Entry. Guided by your work in Exercises A and B, write a journal entry about the experience you have been thinking about.

Writing Workshop: Personal Writing

ASSIGNMENT 1

Topic Setting and Evaluating Personal Goals

Form and Purpose Journal entries that examine and evaluate personal goals

Audience Yourself

Length Daily journal entries written over a three-week period

Focus Set a goal at the beginning of each week. Write daily journal entries describing what you did each day to work toward accomplishing that goal. At the end of the week, review your journal entries and write a summary. Consider such questions as: Was your goal reasonable? Unachievable? Too easy? Do you underestimate or overestimate your abilities? Or neither?

Sources Yourself

Prewriting Brainstorm for personal goals that can be achieved over a one-week period.

Writing Record daily journal entries.

Revising Write a summary at the end of each week.

ASSIGNMENT 2

Topic Tracking Your Moods

Form and Purpose Journal entries that describe and explain emotional moods

Audience Yourself

Length At least one entry each day over a two-week period

Focus Write daily journal entries about a mood you felt during the day. In each entry, identify the mood, describe your exact feelings, and try to explain what brought on the mood.

Sources Yourself

Prewriting At the end of each day, identify a mood that you had. Think about exactly why the mood occurred.

Writing As you write each entry, concentrate on making a complete, exact description and explanation.

Revising At the end of two weeks, write a summary paragraph telling what you learned about yourself.

Topics for Writing: Personal Writing

The picture above may suggest a writing idea to you. If so, write about the topic in a daily journal. If not, choose one or more of the ideas below as a topic for a journal entry.

1. What I Would Do as President of the United States
2. Becoming a Professional Athlete
3. As a Billionaire, How I Would Help Others
4. Events I Would Change in History
5. Personal Fame in the Music Industry
6. A Year of Unlimited Travel
7. Places I Would Like to Have Been in Past History
8. Things I Would Change in the World
9. I Wish I Were My Own Parent
10. My Life as a Favorite Pet

Writing Stories

Most people enjoy reading stories. Writing stories can be fun, too. When you write a story, you can set your imagination free to create anybody or anything you want. You need not limit yourself to times and places with which you are familiar. And writing stories may help you understand and appreciate better the stories that you read.

In this chapter you will learn the basic features that most stories have in common. You will examine a typical story that has all of these features. You will learn how to plan a story by using your imagination to create characters and a situation for them. You will study various ways of bringing characters to life. Finally, you will write and revise a story of your own.

41.1 Looking at Stories

Most stories have certain features in common. A story usually has one main character, who is present throughout the story. A story usually has other characters, too. The actions of these characters generally affect the main character in some way—for good or bad. In a story, the main character faces a conflict, or problem, which is resolved in a series of incidents that form the plot. The plot builds up to a climax. The climax is the point at which the main character must make a decision and take action. And the story has a narrator, or storyteller. This can be a character in the story or it can be someone outside the story.

A story usually has a main character, other characters, a setting, a conflict, a plot, and a narrator.

The following chart defines these features in more detail. While reading the chart, think of examples of each feature from stories you have read.

FEATURES OF MOST STORIES	
Feature	**Definition**
Main character	Usually there is one important character who appears throughout the story. The main character acts, thinks, talks with other characters. The main character tries to solve problems.
Other characters	In addition to the main character, a story generally has several other characters. Some of the characters may work against the main character, and some may try to help the main character.

Setting	The setting of a story is the time it takes place (the year, the season, possibly the date and time of day) and the location where it takes place (the country, the town or city, the house and room).
Conflict	The conflict is a problem that the main character faces. The story usually describes how the main character solves or fails to solve the problem.
Plot	The plot is the order of incidents in the story. Usually the incidents in a story lead up to one main incident called the climax, when the conflict is settled.
Narrator	If the story has a first-person narrator, the main character or another character tells the story, using the words *I*, *me*, and *we*. If the story has a third-person narrator, someone outside the story tells the story, using the words *he, she, him, her, they,* and *them*.

As you read the following story, watch for each of these main features.

A Polished Performance

"Robert, my squire," called Sir Anthony one May morning, "make ready my armor, and polish my sword, spear, and shield. I must look my best in the tournament tomorrow."

"Yes, my lord," replied thc squire. "Straightaway."

Eagerly Robert ran across the castle's courtyard to the room where the weapons were kept. He would start with the fine Spanish sword of which his employer was so proud. But where was the sword? It was not in its accustomed place beside the knight's shield and spear. All the rest of the equipment was there, but the sword was missing.

Whenever Robert lost something, he tried to remember where he had seen it last. Now he sat down and thought about the sword. When had Sir Anthony last used it? Could it have been the last time there was a tournament? That had been several weeks before. Was it possible that the sword was still lying outside the castle gates?

Robert went out to the field to look for the sword. It was not long before he noticed it lying behind a bush. But when he picked it up, he gasped in surprise. The small bush had not protected the sword from the rain, which had been heavy that week. The steel blade was covered with rust.

The young squire was frightened. It was his responsibility to take care of the sword. What would Sir Anthony do if he found out that his squire had carelessly allowed such a valuable weapon to rust? But perhaps he would not find out, if Robert could polish the rust off the sword by the end of the day.

Robert spent the rest of the morning trying different ways to clean the sword. It seemed hopeless. The blade was as rusty as before. In despair, he hid the sword behind the bush again and walked off toward the river that flowed near the castle.

"Ho, Robert," called a voice. "Are you sick at heart, and think you to end your life here in this river?" It was John, another squire.

"Nay, my friend," replied Robert. "Yet I am sorrowful. For I have left Sir Anthony's sword out in the rain to rust, and I must polish it clean or he will send me away and find another squire."

"Have you cleansed it with vinegar?" John suggested.

"Aye."

"With mead?"

"Aye."

"With tallow?"

"Aye."

"With oil?"

"I have tried all of these," said Robert sadly. "Not even one of Merlin's potions could restore Sir Anthony's sword to its former beauty."

"You are wrong," said John. "For I know of a substance that will make the sword look new. Thomas uses it to polish utensils in the scullery."

Thomas was the head cook. An enormous hulk of a man, he despised all the squires, who were constantly stealing into the kitchen to snatch forbidden morsels.

"But how can I get this polishing substance?" asked Robert. "Thomas will not give me anything."

"If he will not give it, do not ask for it," replied John. "Simply take it. Come. I will run into the kitchen as if to steal some meat. While Thomas chases me, go into the scullery and take some of the polish. It is a white substance in a small pot."

They ran through the gates, across the courtyard, and into the corner of the castle that held the kitchen. They crept down the steps into the hot, dark room. John waved Robert toward the pot of polish and headed for a spit on which a boar was roasting. Robert quickly scooped up some polish. As he slipped out the door, he bumped into John, who was holding a boar leg dripping with fat.

"Hurry," John whispered.

Robert looked back to see Thomas's immense bulk filling the doorway.

"Hold, knaves!" cried the cook. "Come back here with that meat!"

The boys separated, and Thomas began to chase John, as planned. Robert ran out to the field where he had left the sword. Anxiously he began to polish it. To his relief, the polish worked. Soon the sword was gleaming like new.

Admiring his accomplishment, the young squire did

not notice the enormous figure behind him. Suddenly a booming voice startled him out of his concentration.

"I thought I would find you here, churl." Robert looked up to see Thomas standing over him. The cook's round, red face glistened with sweat.

"John escaped me, but I saw you heading out to this field and followed you easily. You shall pay for this, churl. On the morrow you shall serve as my scullion."

The next day, Sir Anthony defeated all his opponents in the tournament, but Robert was not there to watch the knight's triumph. Instead, he spent the day in the scullery, putting his newly acquired polishing skill to good use on Thomas's kitchen knives.

EXERCISE A: Examining a Story. Answer the following questions on "A Polished Performance."

1. Is a first-person or a third-person narrator used in the story?
2. What is the setting of the story?
3. Who is the main character?
4. What kind of person is the main character?
5. What details are included to describe the main character?
6. Who are the other characters in the story?
7. Which character or characters work against the main character?
8. Which character or characters try to help the main character?
9. What conflict does the main character face?
10. What is the climax of the story?
11. How is the conflict resolved?

EXERCISE B: Describing the Setting of a Story. Read the story again paying close attention to the details about the setting. Write a paragraph describing the setting of the story, using the details you have noted. Be sure to include details about time and location.

DEVELOPING WRITING SKILLS: Evaluating a Story. Write a paragraph in which you tell whether you liked "A Polished Performance," and why.

Prewriting: Planning Your Story 41.2

Before you can write a story, you must make certain decisions. You must choose a main character and probably some other characters, a conflct that the main character will face, a setting, and a narrator.

Choose a main character, a conflict, some other characters, a setting, and a narrator for your story.

Try to choose a main character who interests you. Your main character could be based on someone you know or on several people you know. You may get ideas from your reading or from experience you have had.

List details about the person, as in the following chart.

SKETCHING YOUR MAIN CHARACTER	
Details to Include	**Examples**
The character's name and age	Robert Thirteen years old
Physical characteristics	Tall, blond hair
The character's background	Squire of Sir Anthony, a knight Son of poor parents
The character's interests, personality, and behavior	Is enthusiastic and friendly Gets along well with almost everyone Is sometimes careless and forgetful

Also think about the conflict, or problem, that the character will face. Give the character a goal. Then decide who or what will act to prevent the character from achieving that goal. To overcome this problem and achieve the goal, the character should have to make a choice.

You should be able to state the conflict of your story in a few sentences. For example, the following chart shows the conflict for the story "A Polished Performance." The conflict includes a goal, a problem and a choice.

DEVELOPING A CONFLICT FOR A STORY	
Main Character	**Conflict**
Robert	As Sir Anthony's squire, Robert is responsible for keeping the knight's armor and weapons polished. But he carelessly leaves a sword out in the rain and allows it to rust. Robert must either find a way to clean and polish the sword or risk being punished and possibly dismissed.

Thinking about the conflict of your story will probably help you think of other characters. Most stories include both characters who work against the main character and characters who help the main character. You should write character sketches for all your characters, just as you did for the main character.

Another important part of your story is its setting—the time and place it occurs. For example, the setting of "A Polished Performance" is England in the Middle Ages. When planning a story, jot down as many details as you can about the setting. Try to imagine the scene as clearly as you can.

Decide whether your story will be told by a first-person narrator (an "I" who is a character in the story) or a third-person narrator (a speaker who is outside the story and refers to the characters as *he, she, they,* and so on). A first-person narrator can tell the reader his or her unspoken thoughts and feelings but cannot see into the minds of any other characters.

A third-person narrator is not part of the story. This narrator can see into the mind of at least one character and report that character's unspoken thoughts and feelings. Sometimes a third-person narrator reports the thoughts and feelings of all the characters.

The following passage could be written with either a first-person or a third-person narrator.

FIRST-PERSON AND THIRD-PERSON NARRATORS	
First Person	We ran across the courtyard to the corner of the castle that held the kitchen. The smell of roasting boar meat mingled with the stench of the rotting garbage piled outside. As we crept down the steps into the hot, dark kitchen, flies buzzed around our heads.
Third Person	They ran across the courtyard to the corner of the castle that held the kitchen. The smell of roasting boar meat mingled with the stench of the rotting garbage piled outside. As they crept down the steps into the hot, dark kitchen, flies buzzed around their heads.

When you have chosen your characters, conflict, setting and narrator, you will be ready to outline the plot of your story. The plot will consist of a number of incidents that build up to a climax. The climax is the point at which the main character must make a decision and take action.

Plot your story by deciding how much time it will cover, how many incidents it will have, and what will happen in the opening incident, the other incidents, and the climax.

Begin by deciding how much time your story will take—a few hours, a few days, or even longer. Does your main character need a few hours or a few days to struggle with and end the conflict? Or should your story take place over two or three weeks or even a year? A short time span is usually easier to handle and more dramatic than a long one.

Next, decide how many incidents the story will include. An incident is a scene or an important event. A story can have one incident that ends with the climax or a number of incidents leading up to the climax.

The opening incident of your story is very important. You should try to catch the reader's interest right away, perhaps by showing your main character doing something or speaking. And you should make the main character's goal and the conflict clear early in the story.

After planning the first incident, give some thought to the other incidents that lead up to the climax. How can you show the conflict growing? How can you show your main character dealing with the need to make a choice?

Finally, decide what the climax will be. What will happen? What decision will your main character make? What action will the character take? The decision and the action should fit the character. And they should decide how the conflict turns out.

List all of your incidents, including the climax, in a plot outline like the one that follows. You should describe each incident briefly.

PLOT OUTLINE FOR "A POLISHED PERFORMANCE"	
Time Covered	About twenty-four hours
Opening Incident	Sir Anthony asks Robert to polish his armor and weapons for a tournament to be held the next day. Robert realizes that he has left the sword out in the rain and that it has become rusty.

Second Incident	Robert asks John, another squire, for suggestions about how to clean the sword. The two boys work out a plan to steal some of the metal polish that Thomas, the cook, uses for kitchen utensils.
Third Incident	While Thomas is chasing John out of the scullery, Robert steals the metal polish and hurries off to the fields with it.
Climax	Thomas finds Robert just as he finishes polishing Sir Anthony's sword. As punishment, Robert has to work for a day in the scullery. He is not able to attend the tournament.

You may not follow your plot outline exactly. You may change, rearrange, or add incidents. But making a plot outline first will help you focus on the conflict and the action of your story.

An important part of most stories is dialogue. When you have your characters talk to one another, you are using dialogue.

Decide where you will use dialogue in your story.

Using dialogue is a good way to bring your characters to life. You will probably want to include dialogue at most or all of the important points in your story. Begin by deciding in which parts of the story you want the characters to speak. Mark your plot outline in those places.

When you begin to write the dialogue, be careful to set the scene for the reader. Also, make sure the reader can tell easily who is speaking. Use quotation marks to enclose the speakers' words and start a new paragraph for the words of each new speaker.

Dialogue should be lifelike. Have your characters speak in a way that they really would speak. To achieve this, you must pay attention to the words, expressions, and length of sentences of each speaker. For example, a child would not speak the same way as an adult.

To become more aware of speech differences, spend a few days paying special attention to the dialogues around you. Listen to your family at the dinner table, to your friends in the playground, or to the customers and salespeople in stores. Listening to real-life dialogues such as these will help you write dialogues in your story that are believable. After writing your dialogues, try reading them aloud with classmates playing each part. This will help you see whether real people might speak the words you have written.

Refer to the following chart when you start to write the dialogue for your story.

USING DIALOGUE IN A STORY
1. Decide where you want your characters to speak and mark these places on your plot outline.
2. Always set the scene briefly and make it clear who is speaking.
3. Make what the characters say and how they say it (the words, the length of the sentences, the expressions) fit their personalities.
4. Enclose all words spoken by characters in quotation marks. Begin a new paragraph with each new speaker.

EXERCISE A: Creating a Main Character. Think of a character for a story of your own. Give your character a name and an age. Brainstorm for other details about the character. Refer to the chart in this section for ideas if necessary. Write a brief character sketch of the main character.

EXERCISE B: Choosing a Conflict. Decide on a conflict for your story by following these directions.

1. Choose a goal for the main character.
2. Decide what will prevent the main character from reaching his or her goal.
3. State the conflict in a few sentences. Include the goal, the problem, and the choice the character must make.

EXERCISE C: Choosing Other Characters. Decide how many other characters you will have in your story. Write a brief character sketch of each character.

EXERCISE D: Choosing a Narrator. Decide who will tell the story: the main character or a third-person narrator. Write a short passage of the story using two different narrators. Then decide which one you will use.

EXERCISE E: Writing a Plot Outline. Make a plot outline of the story you have been planning in this section.

1. Decide how much time your story will cover.
2. Decide where the story will take place.
3. Decide how many incidents your story will have.
4. Write a brief summary of each incident, ending with a description of the climax of the story.

EXERCISE F: Analyzing a Story. Choose a story that is short and evaluate it. First, list details about the main character. Then state the conflict and determine the type of narrator. Next make a plot outine. Finally write a paragraph explaining how the story is put together.

DEVELOPING WRITING SKILLS: Planning Another Story. Follow the steps in Exercises A to E to plan another story.

41.3 Writing: Creating the First Version

Now that you have completed your outline, you are ready to write your first draft.

Use your plot outline and character sketches to write a first draft of your story.

As you write, concentrate on the action of the story. Try to avoid summarizing each incident. Instead, create a word picture of the action. Imagine that the events of the story are happening in front of you. Then try to re-create those events as a reader would see them.

A good way to make your story come alive is by using dialogue. Write as much dialogue for your characters as you can. Refer to your character sketches, and try to make your characters' speech reflect their personalities. Keep their ages and backgrounds in mind. A thirteen-year-old student, for instance, speaks differently from a college professor.

Connect the incidents in your story smoothly by using transitions between them. Your transitions should help the reader tell when and where each incident is happening. The transitions can be just a few words, such as *the next day* or *two hours later.* Or they can be sentences or short paragraphs that tell what has happened between incidents.

Your goal in writing a first draft should be a complete version of your story. You should not worry a great deal about fine points at this time. When you are revising the story, you will have a chance to polish your work.

When you have finished writing your story, think of a title for it. The title should hint at the conflict. It should make the reader want to read the story. But it should not give away the plot.

Use the suggestions in the chart on the next page to help you write your first draft.

WRITING A FIRST DRAFT OF A STORY

1. Refer to your outline of the plot of your story. Follow the order of the outline to arrange the incidents in the story.
2. Try to make your opening incident especially vivid and interesting to catch your readers' interest.
3. Be sure that the time and place of each incident in the story are clear.
4. Use transitions to connect incidents smoothly.
5. Try to make the story come alive for readers by creating word pictures of the incidents.
6. Instead of simply describing your characters, try to make the characters reveal their personalities through their words and actions.
7. When writing dialogue, try to make your characters speak in language that is natural for them.
8. To make sure that your characters are believable, show them speaking and acting consistently. Refer to your character sketches, and show each character acting as you would expect that character to act.
9. If you are using a first-person narrator, remember that the narrator cannot see into the minds of the other characters. If you are using a third-person narrator, you must decide whether the narrator can see into the minds of all or only some of the characters.
10. Try to choose an interesting, original title that suggests the conflict or plot of the story.

EXERCISE: Using Transitions. Briefly describe the time and place of each incident in the story you planned in Exercises A–E on pages 436–437. Write out the transitions you will use to connect each incident to the next.

DEVELOPING WRITING SKILLS: Writing Your Story. Write a first draft of the story.

41.4 Revising: Creating the Final Version

After you have written the first draft of your story, you should revise it carefully. As you reread the story, try to put yourself in your readers' place.

Examine your story from a reader's point of view to see ways of improving it.

Set your story aside for a while. When you reread it, pretend you are reading it for the first time. Read it aloud to yourself or to someone else. Ask your listener for comments and suggestions.

As you reread and discuss your story, pay special attention to the dialogue. Have you used enough dialogue to make the characters come alive? Do the characters speak in language that would be natural to them? Does a new paragraph introduce each new speaker? Is it always clear who is speaking?

Use the following checklist to revise your story.

CHECKLIST FOR REVISING A STORY

1. Does your title fit the story?
2. Does your story have a strong beginning that will catch readers' interest?
3. Will the setting be clear?
4. Can the reader form a clear picture of each character?
5. Do the characters' actions and thoughts show their personalities?
6. Is your dialogue natural and appropriate for each character?
7. Does your story move smoothly from incident to incident?
8. Could any transitions be added to make the time and place of each incident clear?

9. Is the ending of the story clear and believable?
10. Have you used the same narrator consistently throughout?

When you have finished revising your story, make a clean final copy. Then proofread the final copy for errors. Make sure you have used the correct punctuation in passages with dialogue. Quotation marks should come *after* commas, periods, question marks, or exclamation points. If a sentence ends with a question mark or exclamation point, do *not* add a period. Be sure to start a new paragraph with each speaker. The proofreading checklist on page 339 can help you proofread your story.

EXERCISE A: Revising Your Story. Reread, both silently and aloud, the first draft for a story that you wrote for "Developing Writing Skills" in Section 41.3. Use the checklist for revising a story to find weak spots in the story and make improvements in it. When you are satisfied with the story, make a clean final copy and proofread it.

EXERCISE B: Evaluating a Story. Exchange stories with someone in your class. Read your partner's story once for enjoyment. Then read it again to study the characters, conflict, plot, setting, and use of dialogue. Use the checklist for revising a story on page 440 and make notes in the margin where you think the story could be improved. Then write two or three sentences describing what you like and do not like about the story. Try to be as clear and helpful to your partner as possible. Finally, revise your own story once again using the comments that you received from your partner and your own ideas, and then proofread the final version.

DEVELOPING WRITING SKILLS: Writing the Final Version. Make a clean final copy of your story. Proofread.

Writing Workshop: Writing Stories

ASSIGNMENT 1

Topic Comic Book Characters and Stories

Form and Purpose A story that entertains readers

Audience Members of your writing class

Length Two to four pages

Focus Rewrite a comic book adventure story, developing your own plot and using descriptive language. Use dialogue to help bring the characters to life for your readers.

Sources Adventure stories in comic books or comic strips

Prewriting Find a comic book adventure story that interests you. Decide how you want to change the story. Then develop a plot outline for your version of the story.

Writing Follow your outline to write a first draft.

Revising Use the checklist on pages 440–441. Then prepare a final draft.

ASSIGNMENT 2

Topic Creating Creatures for Stories

Form and Purpose A story that entertains readers

Audience Young children at a storytelling festival

Focus Create a creature that you can use as a main character in a story. Your story should focus on a problem that the creature has or a problem that other characters have with the creature.

Sources Myths and legends, animal books, your imagination

Prewriting Create a creature. Then write a sketch for the creature and other main characters. Develop an outline of your plot.

Writing Use the sketches and plot outline to write a first draft. At some point, vividly describe your creature, and include dialogue throughout the story.

Revising The checklist on page 440–441 will help you revise the first draft. Then prepare a final, complete copy of your story.

Topics for Writing: Writing Stories

Gone with the Wind

A title of a story, book, poem, or film can lead to a story idea different from the original. If the above title suggests a story idea to you, plan and write your story. If not, borrow one of the titles below for your story.

1. "Last Night I Had the Strangest Dream"
2. "Rattlesnake Hunt"
3. "The Call of the Wild"
4. "The Country of the Blind"
5. "To an Athlete Dying Young"
6. "The Last Night of the World"
7. "Freedom"
8. "Traveling Through the Dark"
9. "The Most Dangerous Game"
10. "The Small Miracle"

Chapter 42

Writing Letters

A newspaper article once offered this advice: "Hang up and write a letter." But why write when it is so easy to phone? Among the many answers to this question are these: Sometimes you can reach a person only by letter; a phone call will not get through. Sometimes a letter is expected or required—as when people apply for a job or for admission to a school. Sometimes it is more thoughtful to write than to phone—as when you want to thank someone for a gift or an act of kindness. Sometimes you can express yourself better and more fully in a letter than by a phone call. And sometimes it is simply fun to write a letter.

In this chapter you will learn about the two basic kinds of letters, friendly letters and business letters. You will also learn how to reach out and touch someone—by writing.

42.1 Writing Friendly Letters

A friendly letter is a letter to a friend, an acquaintance, a family member, or anyone with whom you want to communicate in a personal, friendly way. It is like relaxed but polite conversation. Most friendly letters are made up of five parts.

The five parts of a friendly letter are (1) the heading, (2) the salutation, or greeting, (3) the body, (4) the closing, and (5) the signature.

The following thank-you letter is from a sixth grader to a guest speaker who visited the student's class.

11 Balint Drive
Yonkers, New York 10710
January 25, 1986

Dear Mr. Ellis,

Thank you very much for visiting our class and showing your slides of Morocco and Spain. I really enjoyed them, and they made learning about these countries more interesting. You sure are a terrific photographer.

It would be great if you could come and show us more slides in the future. Again, thank you for visiting our class.

Yours sincerely,

Laura Dickstein

In this letter, the *heading* gives the writer's address and the date when she wrote the letter. The *salutation,* or greeting, is "Dear Mr. Ellis" followed by a comma. The *body* is the main part, or message, of the letter. The *closing* ("Yours sincerely,") consists of the words that bring the letter to a close. *Cordially, Bye for now, Love, Your friend,* are some other commonly used closings. Closings begin with a capital letter and end with a comma. The *signature* is the name you sign at the end. You may use just your first name or a nickname when writing to a close friend.

Whenever you write a friendly letter, it is important to keep two things in mind: the purpose of your letter and the person who will be reading it, your audience.

The purpose of a friendly letter will often be one of the following: (1) to share personal news and feelings, (2) to send or to answer an invitation, or (3) to express thanks.

Keeping your audience in mind means thinking of your reader and what kinds of news that person would like to hear from you. If your purpose is to share personal news and feelings, ask yourself what funny or interesting happenings your reader might like to hear about. If you are sending an invitation, tell the date and time of the occasion or event, what the person should wear or bring, and any other important information that your reader will need to know to decide whether he or she will be able to attend the event. A thank-you letter will tell your reader that you appreciate something he or she did for you. The letter you read on page 446 is a typical thank-you note.

On the following page you will find a typical invitation. Note that the writer tells the reader the reason for the party, the place at which the surprise birthday party will be held, the day and date of the party, and the time. The writer also tells her friend what type of clothes to wear.

11 Balint Drive
Yonkers, New York 10710
May 18, 1986

Dear Heather,

I am planning a surprise birthday for Jerry at our house on Friday, June 7. I'd like everybody to get here by 3:30 – Jerry's arriving at 4:00.

Dress is casual. If you can bring a present, that would be nice. But make sure you bring yourself! Please let me know if you can come.

Your friend,
Judi

If you write your letter on stationery—as you should—you will probably have to fold it to fit it into the envelope. If you must fold the paper twice, follow the method shown in the diagram on the following page, making sure that you fold the paper neatly.

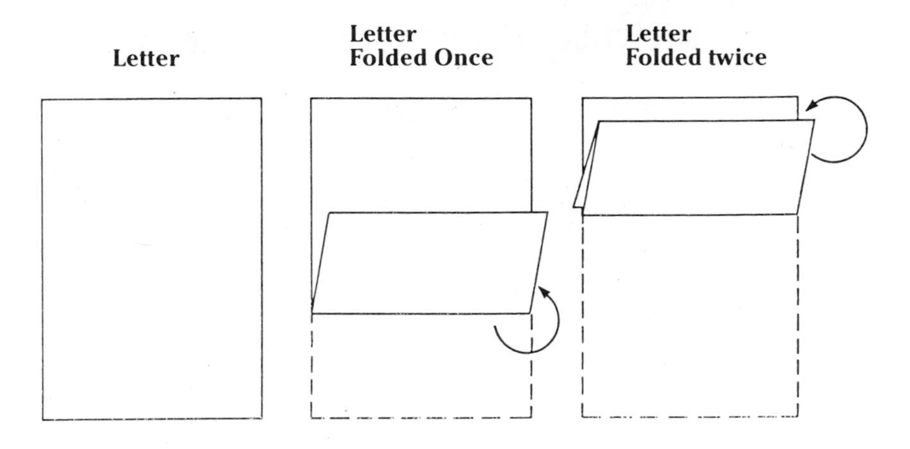

Address your envelope, being sure to include your return address. When addressed, your envelope should look like the following example.

Return address

Laura Dickstein
11 Balint Drive
Yonkers, New York 10710

Mailing address

Mr. Richard Ellis
8 Sandpiper Drive
West Nyack, New York 10994

EXERCISE: Sharing Personal News in a Letter. Write a letter to a friend with whom you have not spoken in a long time. Convey interesting news and your feelings about it. Make your friend want to write back. Prepare an envelope.

DEVELOPING WRITING SKILLS: Sending an Invitation. Write a letter of invitation to a real or imaginary friend. Prepare an envelope.

42.2 Writing Business Letters

Business letters are written for many different purposes—to order an advertised product, to apply for a job or for admission to a school, to express an opinion to a public official, and so on. They are somewhat different in form from friendly letters.

The six parts of a business letter are (1) the heading, (2) the inside address, (3) the salutation, (4) the body, (5) the closing, and (6) the signature.

These six parts can be seen in the following example.

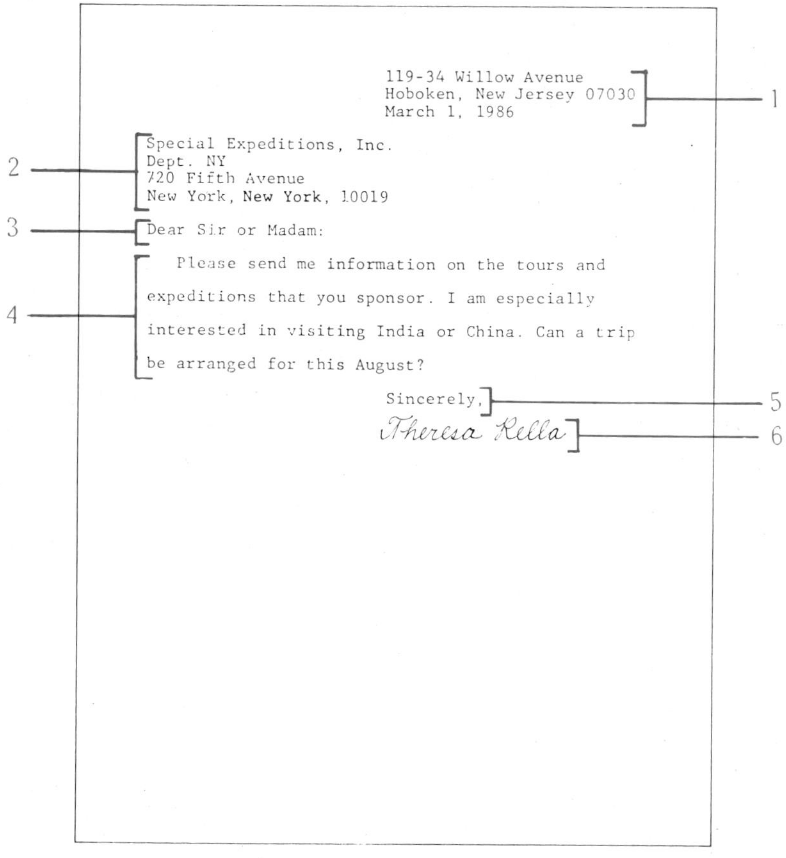

119-34 Willow Avenue
Hoboken, New Jersey 07030
March 1, 1986 — 1

2 — Special Expeditions, Inc.
Dept. NY
720 Fifth Avenue
New York, New York, 10019

3 — Dear Sir or Madam:

4 — Please send me information on the tours and expeditions that you sponsor. I am especially interested in visiting India or China. Can a trip be arranged for this August?

Sincerely, — 5

Theresa Rella — 6

As you can see from this example, the *heading* is exactly like that of a friendly letter: It gives the complete address of the writer—street address, town or city, state, and ZIP code. It also contains the date on which the letter was written.

The *inside address* is the address of the person or business to which you are writing. Friendly letters do not include inside addresses. The inside address begins with the name of the person or business, followed by the other details needed in a full address, such as office number, street address, town or city, state, and ZIP code.

The *salutation* is another point of difference between friendly and business letters: In a business letter, it should be a formal greeting followed by a colon. Here are examples of salutations for business letters.

SALUTATIONS: Dear Sir or Madam:
Gentlemen:
Dear Mrs. Jones:

The *body* should contain your message. The body of a business letter differs from that of a friendly letter in that it is usually briefer and more direct. It also has a more formal style of writing.

The *closing* begins with a capital letter and ends with a comma, like the closing of a friendly letter, but it should be more formal. Here are examples of closings for business letters.

CLOSINGS: Sincerely yours,
Very truly yours,
Cordially,
Sincerely,
Yours truly,

The *signature* is a business letter should also be formal. You should sign your full name, without, however, including any title, such as Mr. or Miss.

In writing a business letter, you should constantly think about your audience. You should try to make a good impression by following correct form, by being polite, and by being neat and accurate. Include all the necessary information as quickly and as simply as possible.

In addition to thinking about your audience, think about the results you want to achieve. State what you want clearly, and give the reader enough facts so that he or she can understand what you want.

One general rule applies to most of the business letters you will ever have to write.

When you write a business letter, follow the standards of business-letter writing.

The following chart presents the most important of these standards.

STANDARDS OF BUSINESS-LETTER WRITING

1. *Be polite.* In business-letter writing, as in business in general, politeness is the first requirement.
2. *Follow correct letter form.* The six basic parts of a business letter, described in Section 11.3, should appear in any business letter you write.
3. *Be brief and direct.* Most business letters are sent to people who do not have time to waste. By being brief and direct you are being polite and considerate.
4. *Be neat.* Since the physical appearance of a business letter matters, your letter and envelope should be free of smudges, careless erasures, and the like.
5. *Use business stationery.* Business stationery is usually white, 8½-by-11-inch paper, with matching envelopes.
6. *Double-check that you have included all necessary information.* Without all necessary information, a business letter is a waste of time.

The following letter meets all of these standards.

99 Bristol Knoll Road
Newark, Delaware 19711
December 1, 1986

Workman Publishing, Inc.
1 West 39 Street
New York, New York 10018

Dear Sir or Madam:

Please send me one copy of your 1986 Fishing Calendar. May I request that you send it C.O.D.? If you cannot do so, please let me know the cost of the calendar, including tax and handling, and I will send you a check.

Thank you for your attention to this matter.

Very truly yours,

Kenneth Robinson

EXERCISE: Using a Business Letter to Order a Product. Find an advertisement for a product that you can order by mail. Ignore any order coupon included in the ad, and write a business letter ordering the product. Make sure that your letter includes the six basic parts of a business letter. Check to see that you have followed the standards of business-letter writing given in the chart on the preceding page.

DEVELOPING WRITING SKILLS: Writing a Business Letter. Make up the name and address of a company, and write a business letter requesting its catalog of products. Use the sample letter as your model.

Writing Workshop: Writing Letters

ASSIGNMENT 1

Topic An Exotic, Imaginary Learning Experience

Form and Purpose A friendly letter that amuses and informs a reader

Audience A close friend

Length One to two paragraphs

Focus In your letter, tell a friend about an unusual and imaginary thing you learned to do. Be humorous, but informative. Conclude by asking your friend if he or she has had a similar experience.

Sources Your imagination

Prewriting Brainstorm for a list of imaginary, unusual learning experiences. Choose one and make notes about what it was, what happened, and what you learned.

Writing Use your notes to write a first draft.

Revising Check the position of all letter parts. Correct any errors in capitalization, punctuation, and spelling. Write a final draft of your letter.

ASSIGNMENT 2

Topic A Lemon of a Bike!

Form and Purpose A business letter that presents a complaint about a poorly made product

Audience The State Consumer Protection Agency

Length One to two paragraphs

Focus You and your parents bought a ten-speed bike that turned out to be very poorly made, but the dealer who sold it to you refuses to give a refund. In your letter to the State Consumer Protection Agency, tell when you bought the bike, give the dealer's name and address, and describe the problems you have had.

Sources Letters of complaint that appear in a newspaper column

Prewriting Write notes about problems you have had with the bike and the dealer. Organize your notes in a logical order.

Writing Use your notes to write a first draft.

Revising Check all letter parts and their positions. Correct any punctuation, capitalization, and spelling errors. Then prepare a final draft.

Topics for Writing: Writing Letters

The above cartoon may suggest an idea for writing a social invitation to an uncommon event. If so, plan and write that invitation to a friend. Include all of the necessary details in your invitation. If you wish, choose one of the social events which are listed below.

1. A Walking Catfish Marathon Race
2. A Football Game in the Mud Bowl
3. The Reunion Performance of a Great Band
4. A Film About What Will Happen Tomorrow
5. A Lecture to Young Writers—Being Delivered by a Character in a Book
6. A Demonstration Rally About Dogs' Inhumanity to Cats
7. A Trip Through the Earth's Core
8. A Dinner Party with a Famous Historical Figure
9. An Announcement: A Famous Athlete Retires Because He or She Makes Too Much Money
10. A Party Celebrating the Arrival of Other Beings from Outer Space

Chapter 43

Taking Essay Exams

Essay questions are a common feature of examinations. You have probably met with such questions before, and you can be sure that you will meet with them again. While no two essay questions are ever exactly alike, almost all have certain things in common. It is therefore possible to develop skills that can make it easier to answer almost any essay question you find on an exam—in whatever subject.

In this chapter you will learn about some of the challenges of essay questions. You will also learn about handling those challenges successfully. Above all, you will see that doing well on an essay exam is not simply a matter of "knowing the answer." It is as much a matter of putting to use test-taking skills that work—whatever the question, whatever the answer.

43.1 Understanding Essay Questions

One of the most common reasons for a poor grade on an essay exam is that the student did not understand the question. Often, however, this lack of understanding is due to the student's not reading the question carefully enough to understand it.

Do not begin to answer an essay question until you know exactly what it says.

EXAMPLE: How do we know what route the first Americans took to arrive in America? Answer this question in one or two paragraphs.

Some students might answer this question by telling that the earliest settlers in America traveled from Asia across the Bering Strait, between Siberia and Alaska. They might then go on to describe the first Americans' gradual movement through North, Central, and South America.

However, these students would not be answering the question! It says "*How* do we know . . . ?" A correct answer would tell about the evidence that scientists have used to figure out the route taken by the first Americans. Many of the students who gave the wrong answer would simply have not read the question carefully.

The following chart presents suggestions for understanding essay questions.

HOW TO READ AN ESSAY QUESTION
1. Read the question straight through to get a general sense of what it says.
2. Then reread the question two or more times to get a clear and exact sense of the information it is asking for. Notice words like *how, compare, describe, explain,* and so on.
3. Then ask yourself, *Just what is this question asking me to do?* Answer your own question in your mind, and check yourself against the test question.

EXERCISE A: Developing Essay-Test Skills. Read the essay question below carefully. Then read the answer that follows. Tell whether the student who wrote the answer seems to have read the question carefully.

> Why was it natural for ancient people to believe that the earth was the center of the universe and that the sun moved around the earth?
>
> In ancient Egypt, the people thought that the sun went around the earth. They believed that the sun god sailed a fiery boat across the sky and around the earth. The early Greeks also believed that a god made the sun circle the earth. But the Greek sun god rode in a chariot, instead of a boat.

EXERCISE B: Practicing Essay-Test Skills. Write two essay questions on subjects you studied recently. Have a partner try to answer your questions orally. You answer your partner's questions. Discuss whether you and your partner answered the questions that were asked.

EXERCISE C: Examining Essay Questions. Look through sections of your social studies, science, or other textbook that has essay questions. Use sections of the book that you have already studied. Select five essay questions from the book. Then follow these steps for each question:

1. Get a general sense of the question by reading it straight through.
2. Reread the questions to get a clear sense of exactly what it is asking for.
3. Ask yourself: What is this question asking me to do? Write a sentence in which you state in your own words exactly what the question asks of you.

DEVELOPING WRITING SKILLS: Evaluating Your Essay-Test Skills. Find a recent essay test you took. Explain whether or not you answered the question that was asked.

43.2 Writing Your Answers

The need to understand clearly what a question asks of you is one of the main differences between writing a composition at home and writing an essay answer on a test. Another main difference is the time pressure of a test.

Budget your time so that you can answer all test questions, including the essays.

Before you begin answering an essay question, figure out how much time you can spend on it. If, for example, the essay part of a test counts for 40% or 50% of the grade, plan to spend about half your time on the essay. When you know how you should budget your time, you can then tackle the question.

Work on an essay question in a systematic way.

Of all the time you will spend on the essay questions, about half should be spent planning the answers and half should be spent writing the answers and checking them over. The following chart presents the basic steps of writing an answer to an essay question.

ANSWERING AN ESSAY QUESTION
1. Brainstorm for, and list, the ideas and facts you will need to answer the question.
2. Arrange the ones you plan to use in a modified outline.
3. Write your essay following the outline.
4. Go over your answer for clarity and correctness in the writing. Make sure that you have actually answered the question.

EXERCISE A: Planning an Essay Answer. Brainstorm for the ideas and facts you would use to answer the following essay question. List your thoughts on a piece of paper. Allow yourself 20 minutes for this exercise.

Literature often presents characters who must face challenges, problems, or conflicts. From the stories, plays, or novels you have read, choose two such characters. Describe the challenge, problem, or conflict each character had to face. Tell whether they faced it successfully or not. And explain why the characters succeeded or failed. Give the title of the work in which each character appears.

EXERCISE B: More Work Planning an Essay Answer. Take the ideas and facts you listed in Exercise A and use them to put together a modified outline you can use to write an essay answer. (You might wish to write three short outlines, one for each character.)

DEVELOPING WRITING SKILLS: Writing an Essay Answer. Using the outline (or outlines) you made in Exercise B, write an essay that answers the question given above. When you have finished writing everything you want to say, reread the essay carefully. Ask yourself the following questions:

1. Have I written about three characters?
2. Have I described the challenge, problem, or conflict each had to face?
3. Have I told how the struggle turned out?
4. Have I explained why each character succeeded or failed?
5. Will my answer be clear to the teacher?
6. Are there errors in grammar, spelling, or punctuation?

Exchange papers with a partner and evaluate his or her essay answer. Make notes on a separate piece of paper of any places where the answer is unclear. Also note any places where the essay answer strays from answering the question. Discuss your notes with your partner and listen to your partner's notes on your essay answer. Finally, make any corrections that are needed.

Writing Workshop: Taking Essay Exams

ASSIGNMENT

Topic Answer this essay exam question: "Compare and contrast television and books as sources of entertainment and information."

Form and Purpose An essay that informs by comparing and contrasting

Audience Your English teacher

Length Two paragraphs

Focus In the first part of your answer, discuss similarities between television and books; in the second part, discuss differences between the two. Provide specific details to support your statements.

Sources Personal experiences and observations

Prewriting Brainstorm for similarities and differences. List them in a two-part modified outline.

Writing Use your outline to write your answer.

Revising Reread your essay to be sure that you clearly answered the question. Correct any errors in spelling, punctuation, and capitalization.

Unit

VI

Vocabulary and Spelling

Expanding Your Vocabulary

One of the most useful parts of your education is the development of a good vocabulary. By learning new words you will improve your reading, writing, speaking, and even thinking. Not only will you be better at these activities but you will get more enjoyment from them.

Perhaps the best ways of expanding your vocabulary are by reading good books and by having conversations with those who speak well. But there are other ways, too, and this chapter will introduce you to a few of them.

First, you will learn about two books that are especially helpful to everyone who wants a better vocabulary. They are the dictionary and the thesaurus. You may already know something about the dictionary. As for the thesaurus, it gives lists of words similar in meaning to the word you look up. It also lists words opposite in meaning to that word.

You will also learn how to work with words that are similar or opposite in meaning. You will learn about words that sound the same but are different in meaning and spelling. Finally, you will learn some ways to remember the new words that you meet.

44.1 Using a Dictionary and Thesaurus to Increase Your Vocabulary

The sure way to find out a word's meaning is to use a dictionary. When you read, you should have one nearby and turn to it whenever necessary.

Look up in a dictionary any word whose meaning you do not know and cannot figure out.

Another book you should be able to use is the thesaurus. A thesaurus lists words similar and opposite in meaning to a given word. If when writing you cannot think of the exact word to express your meaning, look up any similar word and you will probably find the word you need.

Use a thesaurus to find the exact word you need when you are writing.

The following is a thesaurus entry for *run.*

EXAMPLE: run, *n.* 1. (The act of running)—*Syn.* sprint, pace, bound, flow, amble, gallop, canter, lope, spring, trot, dart, rush, dash, flight, escape, break, charge, swoop, race, scamper, tear, whisk, scuttle, scud, flow, fall, drop.

USING A DICTIONARY AND A THESAURUS

1. Read with a dictionary nearby.
2. Look up in a dictionary any word whose meaning you do not know and cannot figure out.
3. Use a thesaurus when you are writing and cannot think of the word that expresses just what you want to say.
4. Use the thesaurus by looking up a word that is similar in meaning to the word you need but cannot think of.

EXERCISE A: Using a Dictionary and a Thesaurus. Look up the following words in a dictionary and write down the meaning of each. Then, look up each word in a thesaurus and write down three words similar in meaning to it.

EXAMPLE: edict an official public proclamation or order issued by authority
decree, proclamation, order

1. delirious
2. desist
3. endeavor
4. felony
5. inadequate
6. lucrative
7. malice
8. pomp
9. savory
10. stout

EXERCISE B: More Work with a Dictionary and a Thesaurus. Look up the following words in a dictionary and write down the meaning of each. Then, look up each word in a thesaurus and write down three words similar in meaning to it.

1. appliance
2. delude
3. general
4. hoodwink
5. jaunty
6. maze
7. notify
8. oust
9. quagmire
10. remote

DEVELOPING WRITING SKILLS: Using a Dictionary and a Thesaurus to Improve Your Writing. Look up the following words in a dictionary, and use each word correctly in a sentence. Then use a thesaurus to find a word similar in meaning to each of these words. Use each one of this second group of five words correctly in a sentence.

1. remote
2. optimistic
3. intrude
4. flatter
5. scent

44.2 Recognizing Synonyms, Antonyms, and Homonyms

Vocabulary growth means learning not only new words but also words that are similar in meaning.

Synonyms are words that are similar in meaning.

The four words in each of the following groups are synonyms. If you have read section 44.1, you know that even longer lists of synonyms can be found in a thesaurus.

EXAMPLES: old, aged, elderly, ancient
location, place, spot, section
connect, attach, unite, join

The more your vocabulary grows, the more you will also be aware of groups of words that are opposite in meaning.

Antonyms are groups of words that are opposite in meaning.

EXAMPLES: good, bad
fat, thin
order, confusion
praise, blame

You should also know that there are words people often confuse because they sound alike, even though they are spelled differently and have different meanings. Such words are called homonyms.

Homonyms are words that sound alike but have different meanings and different spellings.

EXAMPLES: there, their, they're
who's, whose
tale, tail
see, sea

SYNONYMS, ANTONYMS, AND HOMONYMS	
Synonyms	Words similar in meaning (finished, completed)
Antonyms	Words opposite in meaning (tall, short)
Homonyms	Words that sound alike but have different meanings and different spellings (bear, bare)

EXERCISE A: Recognizing Synonyms, Antonyms, and Homonyms. Identify each pair of words below as synonyms, antonyms, or homonyms.

EXAMPLE: smooth, rough
antonyms

1. attack, defend
2. permit, allow
3. big, huge
4. to, two
5. danger, safety
6. one, won
7. foolish, wise
8. waste, waist
9. announce, say
10. cheerful, sad

EXERCISE B: More Work with Synonyms, Antonyms, and Homonyms. Identify each pair of words below as synonyms, antonyms, or homonyms.

1. steal, steel
2. to, too
3. timid, shy
4. attempt, try
5. sharp, dull
6. generous, stingy
7. sun, son
8. speedy, rapid
9. rap, wrap
10. shallow, deep

DEVELOPING WRITING SKILLS: Using Synonyms, Antonyms, and Homonyms Correctly. Use each word below in a sentence. Look up in a dictionary any words you are unsure of.

1. stare
2. stair
3. two
4. too
5. praise
6. blame
7. practice
8. rehearse
9. dull
10. sharp

44.3 Remembering the New Words You Learn

It does little good to learn a new word unless you remember it. One good way to remember new words is to write them in a vocabulary notebook and review them from time to time.

Record in a vocabulary notebook each new word that you learn.

Fold each page of your notebook to make three columns. Head the first column *Words,* the second *Definitions,* and the third *Examples.* Write the new words you learn in the first column and their dictionary definitions in the second. Under *Examples,* you should write the sentences in which you found the words.

You might also divide your notebook into sections for the different subjects you are taking, plus an additional section for words from books that you read for pleasure. A typical vocabulary-notebook page would look as follows.

Chapter 3: Europeans Explore America

Words	Definitions	Examples
navigation	plotting a course at sea	Prince Harry improved navigation
colony	group of people in a distant land ruled by the government	Columbus set up the first Spanish colony in the New World
viceroy	an official who rules an area in the name of their native land of a monarch	The king put a viceroy in charge of the region

EXERCISE A: Using a Vocabulary Notebook. Prepare a vocabulary-notebook page using the directions on page 470. List the following words in the column headed *Words.* Look them up in the dictionary, and write their definitions in the second column. Under *Examples* use each word in a sentence that shows clearly the meaning of the word.

1. bleach
2. cartographer
3. disarm
4. germinate
5. hangar
6. indigent
7. kindle
8. literate
9. metallic
10. needy

EXERCISE B: More Work with a Vocabulary Notebook. As you read the following paragraph, look up the underlined words in a dictionary. Write the words, their definitions, and the sentences of the paragraph in which the words appear in a vocabulary notebook. Use the three-column arrangement explained on page 470.

Trout are important (1) game fish. They (2) thrive in cool, clear water. They normally (3) spawn in cold weather. Some rainbow trout (4) migrate from fresh water to the sea. They are called steelheads, because they take on a steely-blue color. Rainbows are (5) prized because they are beautifully colored and give a good fight. Another trout popular with (6) anglers is the brook trout. It has (7) olive and black markings on the back. The fins have dark brown and orange (8) mottlings. Rainbows and "brookies," as well as other varieties of trout, are often grown in (9) hatcheries. Today, thousands of lakes and streams are (10) stocked with hatchery trout.

DEVELOPING WRITING SKILLS: Using New Words. Look up the words *craving, devour, edible, appetizing,* and *nutritious.* Then use them in a brief paragraph on food.

Skills Review and Writing Workshop

Expanding Your Vocabulary

CHECKING YOUR SKILLS

Write each word and its definition, using a dictionary when necessary. Then state whether the words in each pair are synonyms, antonyms, or homonyms.

EXAMPLES: construct, disassemble
construct—put together
disassemble—take apart
antonyms

1. disclose, reveal
2. mongrel, cur
3. boar, bore
4. expensive, cheap
5. altar, alter
6. feeble, sturdy
7. pair, pare
8. grief, sorrow
9. tolerant, bigoted
10. request, petition

USING VOCABULARY SKILLS IN WRITING

Making a Comparison

In this exercise you will write a paragraph comparing two things. After you choose two things to compare, list either five pairs of synonyms or five pairs of antonyms. If your two subjects have more similarities than differences, you will list synonyms. If the subjects have more differences, you will list antonyms.

Write your paragraph, using the words you have listed. The paragraph should begin with an appropriate topic sentence. The other sentences in the paragraph should support the topic sentence.

Now revise your paragraph. Does your topic sentence sum up the whole paragraph, or is it too broad or too narrow? Is there enough support for the topic sentence? Are your sentences worded as clearly and forcefully as possible? When you have finished revising, proofread your paragraph.

Discovering Word Meanings from Context

In Chapter 44 of this unit, you learned that one way to discover the meaning of a word is to look up the word in a dictionary. Usually, you can be sure that you know what a word means when you have looked it up. The problem is that you may not always have a dictionary nearby. What do you do then when you come upon a word you don't know?

You should do something very much like what you have been doing automatically all of your life. Ever since you were very young, you have been hearing new words. You have learned what these new words mean by figuring out their meanings. You saw how they were used from the words and sentences around them, and you guessed or sensed their meanings.

The words and sentences around a word that help it to have a meaning are known as the word's *context.* In this chapter, you will learn how to use the context of a new word to get at its meaning.

45.1 Seeing Words in Their Contexts

In everyday life, every word you hear or read has a context. The context does a great deal to give meaning to a word. Unless you are aware of a word's context, you may not be able to understand what the word means.

When you think about the meaning of a word, think about the context in which it is used.

EXAMPLES: I could hardly bear the pain.

Bear the injured child into the ambulance.

The shelf can't bear the weight of those books.

What is the meaning of the word *bear*? It is impossible to give it one single meaning without seeing it in context. Look at these different uses of *bear*.

You can see that in the context of the first sentence, the word *bear* means "put up with" or "tolerate." In the context of the second sentence, the word means "carry." In the context of the third, it means "hold up" or "support." And of course in the context of the sentence *Bears can be very dangerous,* the word has yet another meaning.

The following chart sums up the main ideas about context presented so far.

CONTEXT
1. Context is the words and sentences that surround a word.
2. In ordinary speech and writing, every word has a context.
3. The context helps determine a word's meaning.
4. To understand what you read or hear, you may often have to think about the context in which a word is used.

Maybe you can already see a link between what you are learning about word contexts and vocabulary development.

EXERCISE A: Connecting Context and Meaning. Write the underlined word in each sentence below, and give its meaning. Use a dictionary, but let the context guide you to the definition that fits.

EXAMPLE: The forecast is for much precipitation in August.

precipitation rain

1. Fencing is an Olympic sport.
2. Dad bought fencing for our vegetable garden.
3. It is Stephanie's fault that we are late for the football game.
4. The referee called a fault on her serve.
5. The doctor told him to fast for twenty-four hours.
6. The boat was stuck fast between the rocks.
7. I think your wristwatch is two minutes fast.
8. My mother will book a hotel room with an ocean view.
9. In his pocket were a pen and a book of matches.
10. The captain's log revealed a lot about the ocean voyage.

EXERCISE B: More Work with Context and Meaning. Follow the directions in Exercise A for these five sentences.

1. Gum was seeping out of the wood.
2. The girl's job was to groom the horses.
3. The groom looked handsome in his tuxedo.
4. Sidney was asked to chair the meeting.
5. Mom likes to sit and write at her secretary.

DEVELOPING WRITING SKILLS: Understanding Context. Pick one of the following words and explain in a brief paragraph how it can mean different things in different contexts.

1. beat 2. star 3. hit 4. miss 5. fair

45.2 Using Context Clues to Find Word Meanings

When you read, you should try to figure out the meaning of an unfamiliar word from context. Even if you have a dictionary nearby, you should first make the effort to work out the meaning. Doing so will help you to remember the word in the future. Also, the more you practice figuring out word meanings, the easier it becomes.

Use context clues to figure out the meaning of a new word.

Context clues include the following: the words around the unfamiliar word, the sense of the sentence, and the sense of the entire paragraph or passage.

EXAMPLE: Winning a gold medal in the Olympics was the culmination of years of training and competition.

Culmination is a hard word for many readers. However, the reader who looks at the words around it in the above sentence and thinks about the meaning of what is being said can figure out the meaning of the word. If you had trained and competed for years, what would an Olympic gold medal mean to you? It would be the *result* of all your work, the *high point* of your athletic career. And "result" and "high point" are two meanings of *culmination.*

USING CONTEXT CLUES
1. Read the sentence carefully and focus on its overall meaning.
2. Look for clues in nearby words.
3. Guess the meaning of the problem word.
4. Reread the sentence, seeing if the guessed meaning fits.
5. If possible, check a dictionary.

EXERCISE A: Working with Context Clues. Figure out from context the meaning of each underlined word in the paragraph below. Write the word and its meaning.

EXAMPLE: All the weight the man has gained has made him obese.

obese very fat

William Shakespeare is generally (1) regarded as the greatest English writer. He is (2) revered the world over. His plays have been (3) staged for nearly four hundred years. His (4) sonnets are among the best poems ever written. Because his writings have delighted people all over the world, Shakespeare's appeal is (5) universal.

EXERCISE B: More Work with Context clues. Follow the directions in Exercise A for this paragraph.

The Amazon River's name (1) derives from the female warriors of myth called Amazons. When a Spanish (2) expedition up the river was attacked by warriors who were (3) apparently female, the Spaniards called their (4) foes Amazons. The river (5) spans a greater distance than that between New York City and San Francisco. Only the Nile River (6) surpasses it in length. But because of the hundreds of (7) tributaries that flow into it, the Amazon carries a greater (8) volume of water than any other river. Large ocean (9) vessels can sail more than half way up its 4,000-mile-long (10) course.

DEVELOPING WRITING SKILLS: Examining Context. In a brief paragraph, explain how the context of the following sentence could help a reader figure out the meaning of the underlined word. So many reports of UFO sightings have been proved false that I am skeptical about this latest report.

Skills Review and Writing Workshop

Discovering Word Meanings from Context

CHECKING YOUR SKILLS

Write the underlined word and its meaning as suggested by the context. Then write the word or words that were the most useful context clues.

EXAMPLE: Don't divulge the ending of the mystery story.
divulge   reveal   ending, mystery

1. Please discard that candy wrapper in the trash basket.
2. He is too young to enlist in the Armed Forces.
3. The police seized the culprits before they got away.
4. A strong wind carried the kite aloft.
5. Seeing the dog, the rabbit scurried away fast.

USING VOCABULARY SKILLS IN WRITING

Writing About Vacations

Look up the following words in a dictionary: *anticipation, commence, duration, jaunt, trek*. You will use these words to write a short paragraph about summer vacations. When you are sure of each word's definition, brainstorm for sentences that will bring out its meaning. Think of a topic sentence that will tie all the other sentences together.

Now write your paragraph. The first sentence will probably be your topic sentence. In the supporting sentences, you will use the five words listed above. You may want to include extra sentences to create smooth transitions.

To revise your paragraph, decide whether the context brings out the meaning of the five vocabulary words. Would a reader meeting these words for the first time be able to figure out their meaning? When you are satisfied with your paragraph, proofread it carefully.

Discovering Word Meanings from Word Parts

Many words are made up of word parts. The word *unfriendly*, for example, has three parts: *un-*, *-friend-*, and *-ly*. As you can see, the basic part of *unfriendly* is the word *friend*. The letters *un-* form what is known as a prefix. A prefix is one or more syllables added to the beginning of a word to form a new word. The *-ly* of *unfriendly* forms what is known as a suffix. A suffix is one or more syllables added to the end of a word to form a new word.

Prefixes and suffixes have meanings. If you learn the meanings of a fairly small number of prefixes and suffixes, what you know can help you figure out the meanings of a great many words. In this chapter, you will learn some of the most important prefixes and suffixes. You will practice using them to increase your vocabulary, and you will see how useful a knowledge of them can be.

46.1 Using Prefixes to Find Word Meanings

Knowing only a small number of prefixes can help you understand thousands of words.

Use your knowledge of prefixes to figure out the meanings of unfamiliar words.

Knowing, for instance, that the prefix *un-* means "not" will help you understand, or at least read more easily, a great many words such as the following.

EXAMPLES:	unadjustable	unbaked	unconvincing
	unadorned	unbleached	uncrowded
	unaided	unblemished	undefeated
	unavailable	unclaimed	undemocratic

The following chart presents some frequently used prefixes.

SEVEN COMMON PREFIXES			
Prefixes	**Meanings**	**Examples**	
anti-	against	anti- + -social	against society
mis-	wrong	mis- + -deed	a wrong act
non-	not	non- + -profit	not trying to earn a profit
pre-	before	pre- + -view	to view or show beforehand
re-	back, again	re- + -bound	to bound back
semi-	half, partly	semi- + -annual	happening every half year
trans-	over, across	transatlantic	spanning the Atlantic

EXERCISE A: Working with Prefixes. Using the chart on page 480, figure out the meanings of the underlined words in the sentences below. Write each word, and next to it write a word or phrase that defines it.

EXAMPLE: "As for Communism," I said, "I'm a nonbeliever."

nonbeliever   one who does not believe

1. Our class officers hold semimonthly meetings.
2. The magician made the vanished rabbit reappear.
3. I am reading a book about prehistoric life.
4. My young sister sometimes misbehaves.
5. Dad used to repair antiaircraft weapons.
6. Unlike Bob, Paul is completely nonathletic.
7. The photographer asked us to stand in a semicircle.
8. You should transplant that cactus into a larger pot.
9. My cousin Jill wants to reclaim the bike I borrowed.
10. Nonresidents of the village may not use the pool.

EXERCISE B: More Work with Prefixes. Follow the directions in Exercise A.

1. *Uncle Tom's Cabin* is a famous antislavery novel.
2. Did you misplace your pencil case?
3. A transoceanic voyage would be a wonderful experience.
4. Did you buy a pair of preshrunk jeans?
5. The engine of our car has been misfiring lately.
6. Vegetables are healthful nonfattening foods.
7. This store sells antifreeze at a reduced price.
8. An aquamarine is a semiprecious stone.
9. Weather conditions can affect radio transmission.
10. The sisters were reunited after years of separation.

DEVELOPING WRITING SKILLS: Using Prefixes. Write five sentences. In each, use a word beginning with one of the prefixes in the chart on the preceding page.

46.2 Using Suffixes to Find Word Meanings

A suffix is one or more syllables added to the end of a word to form a new word. Like a single prefix, a single suffix may be used to form hundreds of new words. Therefore, knowing only a small number of suffixes and their meanings can help you understand hundreds of words.

Use your knowledge of suffixes to figure out the meanings of unfamiliar words.

The very common suffix *-ly,* for instance, makes the word it is attached to mean "in a certain way." Thus, *swiftly* mean "in a swift, or rapid, way."

EXAMPLES: Jane sadly thought about the end of summer.

This math problem has me hopelessly confused.

The following chart presents some frequently used suffixes. Knowing them can make it easier to understand many of the hundreds of words that they are part of.

SEVEN COMMON SUFFIXES		
Suffixes	**Meanings**	**Examples**
-able (or -ible)	capable of being	love(e)- + -able
-ism	idea, belief, act	national- + -ism
-ist	believer, doer	violin- + -ist
-less	without	sound- + -less
-ly	in a certain way	smooth- + -ly
-ment	a result, act, fact, condition	state- + -ment
-tion (or -ion or -sion)	the act of, the state of being	creat(e)- + -ion

EXERCISE A: Working with Suffixes. Figure out the meanings of the underlined words in the sentences below. Write the words, and next to them write definitions in your own words.

EXAMPLE: His retirement surprised everyone.

retirement act of retiring or leaving a job

1. Penny is especially charitable at Christmas.
2. Bill is pleasant but somewhat humorless.
3. Sandy hopes to become a professional pianist.
4. Your reading comprehension needs improvement.
5. I admire the patriotism of our Olympic athletes.
6. The governor will make a statement later on.
7. We tried mightily to lift the boulder.
8. The words are too small to be readable.
9. The sky was clear and cloudless.
10. The election for officers will be held tomorrow.

EXERCISE B: More Work with Suffixes. Write the underlined words and next to them a word or phrase that defines them.

1. Is this desk movable?
2. Terrorism is a worldwide problem.
3. Nathaniel Hawthorne was an American novelist.
4. When our car wouldn't start, we all felt helpless.
5. The forest became oddly silent and still.
6. Bad weather may result in a postponement of the game.
7. The different news reports caused a lot of confusion.
8. My dog Deirdre lazily gnawed at her bone.
9. Maurice will be an excellent biologist.
10. Christianity is one of the world's major religions.

DEVELOPING WRITING SKILLS: Using Suffixes. Write five sentences. In each sentence, use at least one word that ends with one of the suffixes given in the chart.

Skills Review and Writing Workshop

Discovering Word Meanings from Word Parts

CHECKING YOUR SKILLS

Copy the following ten words, and underline the prefix or suffix in each. Alongside each word write the meaning of the prefix or suffix.

EXAMPLE: transcontinental
transcontinential across

1. misuse
2. Catholicism
3. senseless
4. treatment
5. nonviolence
6. redevelop
7. duplication
8. antitank
9. breakable
10. semiconscious

USING VOCABULARY SKILLS IN WRITING

Writing a Story

In this exercise you will write the beginning of a story about a winter day. Turn back to the prefix and suffix charts in this chapter. List one word that begins with each prefix and one word that ends with each suffix. Try to include words that might refer to winter or to winter activities.

Using as many of the words you listed as possible, write at least two or three paragraphs of a story. Each paragraph (except for dialogue) should have its own topic sentence.

To revise your story's beginning, make sure that you have established the setting and characters. Be sure that each descriptive paragraph has a topic sentence and enough supporting information. Enclose all dialogue in quotation marks, and begin a new paragraph with each new speaker.

Chapter 47

Learning More About Words

Most people do not think very much about the words they speak and write. They simply use words and take them for granted. However, words can be interesting in themselves. For example, take the word *sandwich.* In the eighteenth century, a certain English nobleman would have his servants bring him pieces of meat between slices of bread so that he could eat without interrupting his games and amusements. His title was the Earl of Sandwich. It is from him that the word *sandwich* comes.

Many of the other words you use every day come from foreign languages. German, French, Greek, Latin, Italian, Spanish, and Arabic are just a few of the many languages from which English has borrowed words. The fact that English has made use of words from so many languages makes it a very rich language. It also means that you, as a writer and speaker of English, have a broad number of words to choose from to make your ideas clear and interesting.

47.1 Looking into the Origins of Words

Consider a simple English sentence: *The raccoon ignored the sauerkraut but ate three crayons.* It sounds like English and it is English. But three of the words come directly from other languages. *Raccoon* is American Indian for scratcher. *Sauerkraut* is German for sour cabbage. And *crayon* is French for pencil.

Speakers of English are continually using words that originated in other languages. These words have all helped to make your language the rich and effective means of communication it is. The more you know about where English words come from, the better prepared you will be to understand and use your language.

Loanwords are foreign-language words that have become a part of the English language.

EXAMPLES: strudel, waltz, dachshund (German)
cigar, mosquito, vanilla (Spanish)
hallelujah, jubilee, sabbath (Hebrew)

The following chart lists some other foreign languages that have contributed words to English.

FOREIGN LANGUAGES CONTRIBUTING TO ENGLISH
French: marquis, viscount, duke, baron, carpenter
Scandinavian: birth, bloom, crook, sky, die
Dutch: boss, cookie, dope, snoop, waffle
Arabic: algebra, almanac, sugar, zero
Gaelic and Irish: shamrock, leprechaun, Tory, bog
Turkish: turban, coffee, kiosk, caviar
Portuguese: marmalade, flamingo, molasses, veranda
Japanese: shogun, kimono, tycoon, judo

47.1 Looking into the Origins of Words

Two of the most important languages that have contributed to English are Greek and Latin. Countless words you use or hear every day are made up of word parts that come from these two languages. The word *school,* for example, comes from the Latin word *schola,* which is based on a similar Greek word, *schole.* Knowing the origins and history of words makes you a better reader, writer, and speaker.

EXERCISE A: Exploring the Origins of Words. Using a dictionary that gives the origins of words, tell the foreign language that each of the following words comes from. You may have to check a list of abbreviations in the front or back of the dictionary to be able to read the languages. If more than one language is given, list the first one.

EXAMPLE: hero Latin

1. moose
2. loot
3. ski
4. courtesy
5. taco
6. hickory
7. item
8. pizza
9. Bible
10. exit

EXERCISE B: More Work with the Origins of Words. Follow the instructions given for Exercise A.

1. grammar
2. boomerang
3. postpone
4. chimpanzee
5. robot
6. cockroach
7. diameter
8. woodchuck
9. bayonet
10. piano

DEVELOPING WRITING SKILLS: Writing About Word Origins. Draw up a list of a dozen or more foods that you like or often eat. Look up the names of these foods in a dictionary that gives the origins of English words. Then write a paragraph about the names of these foods.

47.2 Exploring Changes in Language

One of the basic facts about language is that it changes. Some of the most important changes are those involving vocabulary.

Language changes by developing new words for new things and new meanings for old words.

Because new things come into the world, new words must be invented to express them.

EXAMPLE: meltdown—a defect in the cooling system of a nuclear reactor that leads to a radiation leak

This word entered the language along with nuclear power. Other changes that take place over the years may cause old words to change their meanings or take on new ones.

EXAMPLE: grammar—the study of the forms and structures of a language

Centuries ago, the word *grammar* meant "the study of Latin" or "all knowledge recorded in Latin." It had this meaning because the study of Latin was largely what school was about. It was only when English began to be taught in schools that *grammar* got the meaning it has for you.

The chart below presents a few of the words that have entered the language along with computers.

WORDS THAT GO WITH COMPUTERS
cursor: a video-screen pointer
glitch: a temporary failure to work right
input: information entered into a computer
interface: connection between a computer and a person
output: the information a computer produces
software: programs or information for a computer

EXERCISE A: Learning Newly Adopted Words. Look up the following words and write their meanings. Make sure you use a recent dictionary.

EXAMPLE: diskette software for computers

1. astroturf
2. biofeedback
3. clone
4. freeze-dried
5. gasohol
6. jet lag
7. joy stick
8. lowlife
9. microwave
10. turbocharger

EXERCISE B: More Work with Newly Adopted Words. Look up the following words in a recent dictionary and write their meanings.

1. anchorman
2. biodegradable
3. compactor
4. streetwise
5. gridlock
6. microfiche
7. microsurgery
8. quasars
9. spacewalk
10. space shuttle

DEVELOPING WRITING SKILLS: Using New Words. Choose any five of the words listed below, and use each in a sentence that shows the meaning of the word.

astroturf	freeze-dried	streetwise
clone	joy stick	spacewalk
microwave	anchorman	space shuttle

Skills Review and Writing Workshop

Learning More About Words

CHECKING YOUR SKILLS

Look up the following words in a dictionary. Define each word, and tell what you can about its origin.

EXAMPLE: abracadabra—magic spell; a word supposed to have magic powers. The word comes from the Greek word *abrasadabra,* a magic word used by an early religion group. Abrasax was the name of the group's god.

1. kosher
2. GIGO
3. zombie
4. ketchup
5. hooligan
6. tantalize
7. shampoo
8. macho
9. tepee
10. alphabet

USING VOCABULARY SKILLS IN WRITING

Writing a Letter

Using a recent dictionary, look up the following words: *Catch-22, fast-food, laser, microwave, user-friendly*. Be sure you understand their meaning and know how to use each one in a sentence. Take notes if necessary.

Write a brief letter to an imaginary friend. Include sentences that use the five words you looked up. Assume that your friend does not understand these five words. Be sure to use each word in a context that brings out its meaning.

Now revise your letter. Make sure you have used an appropriate heading, salutation, and closing. Make sure that the meaning of the five new words is clear. Finally, proofread your letter for spelling, grammar, and punctuation.

Developing Good Spelling Habits

Have you ever heard someone say, "I'm a bad speller"? Some people talk as if good spelling ability were something you are either born with or born without. While it may be true that some people have a better talent for spelling than others, it is also true that you can learn how to eliminate nearly all spelling errors from your writing. And learning how is not hard.

Spelling ability is not the most important thing in the world. Mistakes in spelling can cause you problems, however. Sometimes they will lower your grades. Other times they will get in the way of what you are trying to say. A reader may get tired of trying to read your writing if it contains too many careless mistakes.

Good spelling is a skill that you can learn easily. With a little effort and a regular program of spelling improvement, you can learn to spell words that have given you trouble in the past. Then you can avoid the problems caused by bad spelling.

This chapter will teach you how to use a dictionary and a spelling list to improve your spelling. There are other methods to improve spelling, but these two alone will prove very helpful.

48.1 Using a Dictionary to Check Your Spelling

If you have a dictionary with you when you write, you can almost make certain that your writing is free of misspelled words. Besides having a dictionary nearby, you must follow one all-important rule.

Look up any word whose spelling you are unsure of.

Here are a few examples of words often misspelled. Are they all correctly spelled here? Are you sure?

EXAMPLES: alot calendar cemetary

If you spotted the two incorrectly spelled words above, good for you! But the important thing is not just to know the words. The important thing is to know enough to look up their spelling if you are unsure. (In the case of these three words, you would find that *alot* should be spelled *a lot* and *cemetary* should be spelled *cemetery.*)

To check the spelling of a word you must already have an idea of how it is spelled. If you do not, the suggestions in this chart will be helpful.

FINDING HARD-TO-SPELL WORDS IN A DICTIONARY
1. On your paper write out several different possible spellings of the word.
2. Concentrate on figuring out the first letters of the word. (If you know them, you will probably find the word quickly.)
3. Check to see if your dictionary has a chart to help with unusual spellings.
4. If all else fails, look up a synonym of the word. Sometimes the word will appear in a definition of one of its synonyms.

48.1 Using a Dictionary to Check Your Spelling

EXERCISE A: Using a Dictionary to Check Spelling. Some of the following words are spelled correctly, and some are not. Use a dictionary to check the spellings of all the words. Then write out with correct spellings the words that are here spelled incorrectly.

EXAMPLE: accidently accidentally

1. scissors
2. exercize
3. neccesary
4. tomorrow
5. succede
6. library
7. labratory
8. neighbor
9. intresting
10. mathamatics

EXERCISE B: More Work Checking Spelling. Use a dictionary to check the spellings of the following words. Then write out with correct spellings the incorrectly spelled words.

1. Mississippi
2. Febuary
3. sophmore
4. eighth
5. hankerchief
6. rhythm
7. knowlege
8. college
9. believe
10. secretery

DEVELOPING WRITING SKILLS: Correcting Misspellings in a News Report. Imagine you are an editor whose job is to correct misspelled words in news reports. Rewrite the following paragraph to remove all misspellings.

Next Wendsday the basketball team meets Oakdale in our gymnazium. After a disapointing begining, Oakdale has won five strait games. Their captin, Dave Roby, has led Oakdale from eighth place to fourth in the legue by his consistant outside shooting and defensive play. According to Coach Markham, stopping Oakdale's aggresive offense will be the key to victory. Our team will have to find a way to stop there fast brake. If they get the ball up cort fast, we're in trouble.

48.2 Using a Spelling List

If you really want to improve your spelling, using a dictionary to find out or to check how a word is spelled is not enough. How often have you looked up a word, found the correct spelling, written the word properly—and then forgotten what you looked up? A good solution to this problem is a spelling list.

List in a notebook those frequently used words whose spellings give you trouble.

Reviewing such a list now and then will reduce the number of words that give you trouble. You may even find that you can remove words from the list faster than you have to add new ones.

Some of the hard-to-spell words you put into your list may have meanings that are unfamiliar to you. You should, therefore, make a list with one column set aside for the meanings of such words. The following list is an example of how your own list might look.

	WORDS	DEFINITIONS
	necessary	
	accessible	can be approached or entered
	Mississippi	
	spaghetti	

EXERCISE A: Developing a Spelling List. Look at how each word below is spelled. If you think it is spelled correctly, spell it that way on your paper. Otherwise, spell out the word as you think it should be spelled. Then check yourself with a dictionary. List any words you misspelled in your spelling list.

EXAMPLE: diemond
diamond

1. avenue
2. compleat
3. encouragment
4. expense
5. ninteenth
6. defeat
7. riligion
8. science
9. ninty
10. season
11. potatoe
12. sincerely
13. tomatoe
14. weapon
15. width
16. excape
17. medecine
18. cafeteria
19. pungtuation
20. Wensday

EXERCISE B: More Work with a Spelling List. Look at how each word below is spelled. If you think it is spelled correctly, spell it that way on your paper. Otherwise, spell out the word as you think it should be spelled. Then check yourself with a dictionary. List any words you misspelled in your spelling list.

1. absense
2. alphebet
3. antena
4. acquire
5. believe
6. bicycle
7. emptyness
8. machinery
9. personal
10. poizon

DEVELOPING WRITING SKILLS: Using Words from Your Spelling List in Sentences. Choose five words that you have added to your spelling list. Practice spelling them correctly by using each one in a sentence of your own.

Skills Review and Writing Workshop

Developing Good Spelling Habits

CHECKING YOUR SKILLS

Find the misspelled word in each sentence below. Check your answer in the dictionary and then write the correct spelling.

EXAMPLE: Chocolate cheesecake is my favorite desert.
dessert

1. Mrs. Wingdale sang the hymm admirably.
2. Pamela seldom discusses her personel life with anyone.
3. Would you like vegtable soup or clam chowder?
4. The recipe requires a spoonfull of honey.
5. The physician prescribed this medecine for Sal.
6. When did those colonies achieve their independance?
7. The principal's acceptence of my excuse surprised me.
8. The advertisement was for a Caribbean cruize.
9. Great herds of buffalo once romed these plains.
10. That vase is definitely not unbreakible.

USING SPELLING SKILLS IN WRITING

Describing the Future

Write a short essay about what life will be like in the twenty-first century. First, choose one of the misspelled words from the exercise above and use it to write a topic sentence for your essay. Then, use the other misspelled words to help you brainstorm for ideas about specific aspects of the future.

Now write your essay, beginning with your topic sentence. Try to use most of the words that were misspelled in the exercise above.

Revise your essay as usual. Check your dictionary to make sure you have spelled all words correctly.

Chapter 49

Using Spelling Rules

Learning a small number of spelling rules will help you spell correctly a great many words. This means that you will not have to use the dictionary so often. It also means that you will be able to write with greater confidence and ease. You will not have to pause over so many words and wonder whether you need to look them up.

In this chapter you will learn rules for forming plurals, for adding prefixes and suffixes to words, and for choosing between *ie* and *ei* in words containing those letters. There are other spelling rules, but the ones in this chapter are among the most important. Learn them and you will be on your way to becoming an outstanding speller.

49.1 Forming Plurals

Most nouns form their plurals according to a general rule.

To form the plurals of most nouns, add -s or -es.

Simply adding *-s* is the way most plurals are formed.

EXAMPLES: cat — cats
pencil — pencils

The following chart presents some rules for forming plurals with *-es*.

FORMING PLURALS WITH *-ES*

1. When a noun ends in *-s, -ss, -x, -z, -sh,* or *-ch,* add *-es* to form the plural. Examples: gas—gases, dress—dresses, ax—axes, buzz—buzzes, splash—splashes
2. When a word ends in a consonant plus *-y,* change *y* to *i* and add *-es.* Examples: pony—ponies, daisy—daisies
3. When a word ends in *-fe,* change *f* to *v* and add *-es.* Examples: life—lives, wife—wives
4. When a word ends in a consonant plus *-o,* add *-es.* Examples: potato—potatoes, tomato—tomatoes (Exceptions include musical terms, such as piano—pianos.)

Some nouns have what are known as *irregular plurals.* This means that their plurals are not formed according to the general rule stated above, for example, *man—men.*

EXAMPLES: man — men
woman — women
child — children

By using your language every day you will come to know when a noun has an irregular plural. If you are not sure just what the plural is, use the dictionary to find out.

EXERCISE A: Forming Plurals. Write the plural form of each of the following words. Use the rules on the previous page, but also check a dictionary when you are in doubt.

EXAMPLE: planet planets

1. bush
2. mouse
3. snake
4. fly
5. basketball
6. hero
7. knife
8. tooth
9. monkey
10. box

EXERCISE B: More Work with Plurals. Write the plural form of each of the following words. Use the rules on the previous page, but also check a dictionary when you are in doubt.

1. boy
2. lunch
3. goose
4. zebra
5. enemy
6. torpedo
7. solo
8. donkey
9. holiday
10. business

DEVELOPING WRITING SKILLS: Using Plural Nouns in a Paragraph. Write a paragraph in which you tell of a trip to a zoo (the trip may be real or imaginary). Use plural nouns to refer to the animals you saw. Check in a dictionary if you are unsure how to form any of the plurals you want to use. Include in your paragraph the plural forms of the following words from Exercises A and B above.

1. snake
2. monkey
3. goose
4. zebra
5. donkey

Using plurals, mention six or eight of the other animals you saw during your trip. Describe their appearance and how they behaved.

49.2 Adding Prefixes to Words

As you saw in Chapter 46, a prefix is one or more letters added at the beginning of a word to form a new word. Writers and speakers continually take words such as *fill,* add prefixes to them, and come up with other words, such as *refill.* So the following spelling rule is one you should know.

When a prefix is added at the beginning of a word, the spelling of that word stays the same.

EXAMPLES: mis- + -spell = misspell

re- + -act = react

un- + -finished = unfinished

All of the words in the following chart begin with prefixes. Notice that the spelling of the word to which the prefix is added is the same as it would be without the prefix.

WORDS BEGINNING WITH PREFIXES	
circumnavigate	circum- + -navigate
coexist	co- + -exist
depress	de- + -press
disservice	dis- + -service
immovable	im- + -movable
inaccurate	in- + -accurate
mismatch	mis- + -match
reenter	re- + -enter

The way the words in the chart are divided may help you to remember something very important to success in spelling. Big words *(circumnavigate)* often are made up of small words *(navigate)* and small word parts *(circum-)*. When you have to spell a long word like *circumnavigate,* first try to spell the small word and the small word part, or parts, that make it up.

EXERCISE A: Spelling Words with Prefixes. Make a new word out of each word below by using the prefix given in parentheses. Be sure you spell the new word correctly. Check the word in a dictionary if you are not sure of the spelling.

EXAMPLE: perfect (im-) imperfect

1. operate (co-)
2. compression (de-)
3. satisfaction (dis-)
4. polite (im-)
5. offensive (in-)
6. fortune (mis-)
7. elect (re-)
8. natural (un-)
9. author (co-)
10. fault (de-)

EXERCISE B: More Work with Prefixes. Make a new word out of each word below by using the prefix given in parentheses. Be sure you spell the new word correctly. Check the word in a dictionary if you are not sure of the spelling.

1. education (co-)
2. emphasize (de-)
3. qualify (dis-)
4. measurable (im-)
5. sincere (in-)
6. lead (mis-)
7. evaluate (re-)
8. pleasant (un-)
9. existence (co-)
10. form (de-)

DEVELOPING WRITING SKILLS: Using Words with Prefixes in Your Own Writing. Make up a word beginning with each prefix given below and use the word correctly in a sentence of your own. Do not use any of the words from the above exercises. Use a dictionary if you cannot think of a word for any given prefix. Also use the dictionary to make sure you spell the words correctly.

1. co-
2. de-
3. dis-
4. im-
5. in-
6. mis-
7. re-
8. un-
9. co-
10. de-

49.3 Adding Suffixes to Words

A suffix is one or more letters added at the end of a word to form a new word.

When a suffix is added at the end of a word, the spelling of the word often changes.

Just about every time you write, you will be using words with suffixes. Since such words often require you to pause and figure out their correct spelling, you should try to learn well the following rules.

SPELLING RULES FOR ADDING SUFFIXES

Rule 1. When a word ends in a consonant plus *-y,* change *y* to *i* before adding a suffix. (lazy, lazily)

Rule 2. When a word ends in a vowel plus *-y,* make no change before adding a suffix. (pay, payable)

Rule 3. When a word ends in *-e,* drop the *e* before adding a suffix beginning with a vowel. (adore, adorable)

Rule 4. When a word ends in *-e,* make no change before adding a suffix beginning with a consonant. (hate, hateful)

Rule 5. When a one-syllable word ends in a single vowel plus a single consonant, double the final consonant before adding a suffix beginning with a vowel. (pat, patted)

EXCEPTIONS TO RULE 1:	suffixes beginning with *i* (try, trying)
EXCEPTIONS TO RULE 2:	day, daily; gay, gaily
EXCEPTIONS TO RULE 3:	change, changeable; peace, peaceable
EXCEPTIONS TO RULE 4:	true, truly; argue, argument
EXCEPTIONS TO RULE 5:	words ending in *x* or *w* (mix, mixing; blow, blowing)

One good way to learn the rules and exceptions is to make up more examples that follow each one.

EXERCISE A: Spelling Words with Suffixes. Make a new word out of each word below by using the suffix given in parentheses. Be sure you spell the new word correctly. Check your words in a dictionary if you are unsure of the spelling.

EXAMPLE: happy (-ly) happily

1. fix (-ed)
2. try (-ed)
3. move (-able)
4. late (-ly)
5. meow (-ing)
6. greedy (-ly)
7. destroy (-ed)
8. use (-able)
9. tap (-ed)
10. mystery (-ous)

EXERCISE B: More Work with Suffixes. Make a new word out of each word below by using the suffix given in parentheses. Be sure you spell the new word correctly. Check your words in a dictionary if you are unsure of the spelling.

1. cry (-ing)
2. joy (-ous)
3. hungry (-ly)
4. love (-able)
5. true (-ly)
6. drop (-ed)
7. flow (-ing)
8. hope (-ful)
9. beauty (-fy)
10. toy (-ed)

DEVELOPING WRITING SKILLS: Using Words with Suffixes in Your Own Writing. Choose any five of the new words you made by following the directions in the exercises above. Use each word in a sentence of your own. Then write five more sentences. In each of these use one of the following words with the suffix given in parentheses.

Use the rules given on the preceding page to spell these words correctly. If you are still unsure of the right spelling, check a dictionary.

1. run (-ing)
2. health (-ful)
3. create (-ive)
4. tire (-ing)
5. delay (-ed)

49.4 Choosing Between *ie* and *ei*

Many people have trouble when they must spell a word containing the letters *ie* or *ei*. The following rules can help.

When a word has a long e sound, use *ie*.

When a word has a long *a* sound, use *ei*.

When a word has a long e sound preceded by the letter c, use *ei*.

EXAMPLES: belief (long *e* sound)
eight (long *a* sound)
ceiling (long *e* sound preceded by *c*)

SOME EXCEPTIONS TO THE *IE* AND *EI* SPELLING RULES	
either	seize
neither	friend

The next chart presents some of the many words that follow the rules.

COMMON *IE* AND *EI* WORDS		
Long e Sound: Use *ie*	**Long *a* Sound: Use *ei***	**Long e Sound Preceded by c: Use *ei***
achieve	eighty	deceive
believe	freight	perceive
field	neighbor	receive
grief	reign	receipt
piece	vein	

Try to think up more words that would fit in the chart above. Adding to the chart will help you memorize the rules.

EXERCISE A: Spelling *ie* and *ei* Words. On your paper write the incomplete word from each of the sentences below. Fill in the blanks with either *ie* or *ei.*

EXAMPLE: With effort you can ach __ __ ve your goal.
achieve

1. The sun came out after a br __ __ f shower.
2. Mr. O'Schaugnessy works on a fr __ __ ght train.
3. I'm the wide rec __ __ ver on the football team.
4. "Stop, th __ __ f!" the police officer cried.
5. Loretta is wearing a b __ __ ge sweater.
6. My cat gray Heathcliff w __ __ ghs about twelve pounds.
7. "Appearances," she said, "are sometimes dec __ __ ving."
8. Bill's drawing includes an apple p __ __ rced by an arrow.
9. Let's go look at the sailboats down by the p __ __ r.
10. Are there r __ __ ndeer in this zoo?

EXERCISE B: More Work with *ie* and *ei* Words. On your paper write the incomplete word from each of the sentences below. Fill in the blanks with either *ie* or *ei.*

1. S __ __ ze every opportunity to learn.
2. We were rel __ __ ved to hear that you were not injured.
3. This present is for my n __ __ ce.
4. If you throw the stick, Spot will retr __ __ ve it.
5. Mrs. White is __ __ ghty-one years old.

DEVELOPING WRITING SKILLS: Using *ie* and *ei* Words in Your Own Sentences. Choose any ten *ie* and *ei* words from the exercises above, and use each in a sentence of your own.

Skills Review and Writing Workshop

Using Spelling Rules

CHECKING YOUR SKILLS

Each of the following sentences contains one misspelled word. Find the word and spell it correctly on your paper.

EXAMPLE: We bought lettuce, ham, tomatos, bacon, and cheese.

tomatoes

1. These soldiers received praise for being true heros.
2. This shopping center was built to house as many as eighteen small busineses.
3. I believe this lovely little pond is still unamed.
4. We heard you were disatisfied with your grade on the test.
5. The canoe swerved crazyly down the rapids.

USING SPELLING SKILLS IN WRITING

Relating an Incident

Some of the following words are spelled correctly, and some are spelled incorrectly: *acheive, believe, donkies, dresses, holidays, moveing, pianos, potatos, reenter, tomatos*. Find the misspelled words and spell them correctly. Then choose one of the words and use it to write the topic sentence of a paragraph describing something that has happened to you recently.

In one or more paragraphs, tell the story of the incident, which may be real, imaginary, or a combination of both. You will probably want to arrange your paragraphs in chronological order.

Revise your paragraphs in the usual way. Rewrite topic sentences if necessary, and add any supporting information that may be needed. Make sure you have spelled all words correctly. Check your dictionary if you are not sure.

UNIT **VII**

Study and Research Skills

Chapter 50

Developing Study Skills

Study skills make it possible for you to learn. They provide you with ways of understanding and remembering what you study, read, or are taught. They also help you to apply what you learn. How well you do in school usually depends on your study skills.

Study skills are the habits or patterns that you follow in your school work. They include how you organize your time, how you take notes, how you use the library, and how you read a text book. They even involve how you read, write, speak, and listen.

Like most other skills, study skills need to be used regularly so that they become good habits. Turning skills into habits is not easy or fun. It is worthwhile, however, for the sake of doing work better and faster and getting higher grades.

In this chapter you will learn about three of the foundations of study skills. You will learn how to set up a study area, how to schedule study time, and how to find time for pleasure reading.

50.1 Setting Up a Study Area

A good place to study is the start of good study habits. You'll be spending a lot of time in your study area, so it should be set up properly.

Set up a study area where you can concentrate on your school work.

When choosing and equipping your study area, follow the guidelines listed below.

GUIDELINES FOR A GOOD STUDY AREA
1. Your study area should be the same every day.
2. It should be comfortable.
3. It should be free of constant interruptions.
4. It should be off-limits to other people.
5. It should be equipped with a desk or table and a chair.
6. It should be well lighted.
7. It should be equipped with all the tools needed for school work.
8. It should include a posted study schedule.

Your study area should be properly equipped with the "Definite Dozen" listed in the chart below.

THE DEFINITE DOZEN: MATERIALS FOR A HOME STUDY AREA	
pens and pencils	ruler
paper and notebooks	wastepaper basket
erasers	magic markers and crayons
tape	index cards
stapler and paper clips	manila folders
scissors	dictionary

EXERCISE A: Examining Your Study Area. On your paper, answer *Yes* or *No* to the following questions.

EXAMPLE: Does your study area allow you to concentrate completely on your work?

Yes.

1. Do you study in the same place every day?
2. Are you comfortable in the place where you study?
3. Do you study in a place where you are not interrupted?
4. Do others stay out of your study area when you are working there?
5. Do you have a desk or table and a chair to study at?
6. Is your study area well lighted?
7. Do you have a posted study schedule?
8. Is your study area neat and orderly?
9. Do you like being in your study area?
10. Does your study area make it easy for you to study properly?

EXERCISE B: Further Examination of Your Study Area. Answer *Yes* or *No* to the following questions.

1. Is your study area equipped with pens, pencils, and erasers?
2. Is it equipped with paper, notebooks, tape, and scissors?
3. Is it equipped with a stapler, paper clips, and a ruler?
4. Is it equipped with a wastepaper basket, magic markers, and crayons?
5. Is it equipped with index cards, folders, and a dictionary?

DEVELOPING WRITING SKILLS: Writing About Your Study Area. Write a paragraph in which you evaluate your place of study. Tell how your plan and place of study could be improved.

50.2 Scheduling Study Time

In order to improve your study habits, you need a plan for organizing your time.

Create a study schedule that you can follow every day. To draw up a study schedule, follow these directions.

SETTING UP A STUDY SCHEDULE

1. Divide time after school into half-hour segments.
2. Block out regularly scheduled after-school activities.
3. Block out your usual dinner hour.
4. Block out no more than one hour for television viewing.
5. Block out at least two hours for homework. Break this time into two separate segments.
6. Block out at least one half-hour before bed for pleasure reading.
7. Put your schedule on paper and attach it to your study area.

By following the guidelines listed above you should have a schedule that looks something like the sample below:

A SAMPLE STUDY SCHEDULE

3:30-4:00	After School Act.	6:00-6:30	Homework
4:00-4:30	" "	6:30-7:00	" "
4:30-5:00	Homework	7:00-7:30	Television
5:00-5:30	" "	7:30-8:00	" "
5:30-6:00	Dinner	8:00-8:30	Pleasure Reading

The most important thing about a schedule is this: You must follow it faithfully until it becomes a habit.

EXERCISE A: Preparing a Study Schedule. Write out the following statements filling in the blanks.

EXAMPLE: Without a study schedule, it is hard to organize (time).

1. A study schedule should be made up of segments a ______ long.
2. The first time segment should be for ______ activities.
3. About ______ hour a night may be set aside for TV watching.
4. You should schedule ______ segments for homework.
5. At least ______ hours should be scheduled for homework.

EXERCISE B: More Work Preparing a Study Schedule. Make up a realistic study schedule for yourself using a format like the one below. On each line fill in a half-hour time segment followed by an activity.

TIME	ACTIVITY
______	______
______	______
______	______
______	______
______	______
______	______
______	______
______	______
______	______
______	______

DEVELOPING WRITING SKILLS: Writing About Time Planning. Write a paragraph explaining why it is wise to plan how you should use your after-school time.

50.3 Finding Time to Read for Pleasure

Not everybody was meant to be a lover of books, and not everybody has the time to read. Nevertheless, for millions reading for pleasure is one of the great joys of life. But for beginning readers, reading may be more work than pleasure. It takes time for reading to become easy. It may take still more time for it to become enjoyable. The one way to make reading a pleasure and a joy is to make reading a habit.

Set aside time every day for pleasure reading.

Do you have time for pleasure reading during a typical day? Here are some pockets of time you might be able to find:

breakfast	on the school bus
free-reading time granted by a teacher during class	recess
	after-school hours
	the evening

No doubt you could pick out several times during your day when you have time for reading. The chief question for you may be how to find books you will enjoy. This chart presents some leads.

SOURCES OF TIPS FOR GOOD READING
Librarians, who can recommend books on what interests you
Friends who read and who share your interests
Reading lists in school books and in libraries
Bookstores, where you can usually browse or get suggestions
Television programs on interesting subjects also treated in books

EXERCISE A: Planning Time for Pleasure Reading. Below are some time periods when it may be possible for you to read for pleasure. List each one and state whether you do or do not use it for reading. For those you do not use, tell whether they *could* be used for reading. Explain what you might have to do to make it possible to read during that period.

EXAMPLE: Weekends—I use them for reading, usually in the mornings and late afternoons.

1. At home, before leaving for school
2. At the school-bus stop
3. During morning classes
4. During lunch period
5. Recess
6. During afternoon classes
7. After-school hours before supper
8. Evenings
9. Weekends
10. Other times

EXERCISE B: Further Planning for Pleasure Reading. On the preceding page, some leads for finding good books were given. For this exercise, think of ten (if possible) good books you have read that were not assigned by a teacher. List them, and for each tell what led you to read it—the suggestion of a librarian, teacher, or friend; the fact that you had read another book by the same author; etc.

DEVELOPING WRITING SKILLS: Writing About Reading. Write a paragraph in which you discuss your own experience as a reader. You might, for example, tell about some book you especially liked. Or you might describe what reading means to you—what pleasure you get from it or how it has enriched your life. You might even describe a plan for becoming a better reader.

Skills Review and Writing Workshop

Developing Study Skills

CHECKING YOUR SKILLS

Going by the information in this chapter, answer *true* or *false* for each statement below.

EXAMPLE: It is best to read for pleasure only three or four times a week.
false

1. Your study area should change from day to day.
2. An ideal study area would be one that other people stay out of.
3. If your study area does not include a desk, it should at least include a table and chair.
4. When making up a study schedule, you should not set aside time for watching television or pleasure reading.
5. In a good study schedule, the time set aside for homework will be a single unbroken segment in the late afternoon.

USING STUDY SKILLS IN WRITING

Describing a Goal

For each of the three areas of study skills covered in this chapter—setting up a study area, scheduling your study time, and reading for pleasure—write a sentence stating a goal that you can aim for to improve your own study habits. Select one of the sentences.

The sentence you have chosen will become the topic sentence of a paragraph. Use the rest of the paragraph to discuss how you will go about achieving the goal. Be sure to be clear and specific.

Now revise your paragraph. Is it organized in the best possible way? Have you left out any important information that might be included? Finally, proofread your paragraph for spelling, grammar, and punctuation.

Chapter 51

Developing Your Note-Taking Skills

"I can't seem to remember what I heard in class." "I sometimes forget what I have just read." Do you sometimes have these problems? You can reduce them if you take good notes when you read or listen.

The ability to take good notes is most important to success in school. In fact, the importance of note-taking increases as you progress from one grade to the next. A good notebook is like a second memory. It stores information so you can make it part of your real memory.

Really good note-takers are skilled readers and listeners. They can decide quickly what information should be recorded and what information can safely be left out. They listen or read so carefully and attentively that note-taking by itself becomes a kind of memorization. This is one reason why you should take your own notes and not copy them from your classmates.

In this chapter you will learn how to organize a notebook. You will also learn something about a skill very important to note-taking: outlining.

51.1 Organizing a Notebook

It is not hard to keep a good notebook. If you are thoughtful, careful, and plan ahead, you should be able to have a notebook that will be a real help to you when you are preparing for tests.

Keep your notebook organized, complete, and neat.

The following chart presents some suggestions for organizing a looseleaf notebook in a ringed binder.

HOW TO ORGANIZE A NOTEBOOK
1. Put plenty of looseleaf paper into your binder.
2. Use dividers to mark off sections for each subject that you take notes in.
3. Use gummed reinforcements around the paper holes to keep your notes from falling out.
4. Keep all notes in the same subject together.
5. Put in where they belong returned homework assignments and tests that may be useful for future studying.
6. Rewrite any notes that are sloppy or hard to read.

When you have been absent from class, ask your teacher to suggest how you can get the notes you missed. Your teacher may offer to supply them. Otherwise, you may have to ask a classmate. If you do, choose one who you know keeps a good, complete notebook.

Neatness is also important in note-taking. Not only must you be able to read what you have written but you should also want to have a notebook you can be proud of. A notebook may be thought of as a year-long project covering several subjects. If you can take pride in the notebook you have spent so many hours putting together, you will find it easier to take pride in the rest of your school work.

EXERCISE: Checking Up on Your Own Notebook. Answer the following questions by writing *Yes* or *No* on a piece of paper. The more questions you can honestly give a yes answer to, the better your notebook is.

EXAMPLE Do I keep my notes in a ringed binder?
Yes

1. Does it look as if I have enough paper in my notebook for each subject I take notes in?
2. Is my notebook divided up for all the subjects it covers?
3. Do I use gummed reinforcements to keep my notes from falling out?
4. Are my notes for each subject neat, orderly, and kept together?
5. Are returned homework papers and tests inserted next to the notes they relate to?
6. Have I gotten from my teacher or a classmate any notes I missed because of absence?
7. Are my notes clear and readable?
8. Is my notebook something to be proud of?
9. Are my notes good enough to be of real help when I am studying for tests?
10. Am I keeping a good enough notebook for me to feel that I can handle the rest of my school work equally well?

DEVELOPING WRITING SKILLS: Writing About Your Notebook. Write a brief paragraph with the title What My Notebook Reveals About Me. You should think about your answers to the questions in the exercise above and use the results to decide just how good your notebook is. Then imagine that someone who did not know you was looking over your notebook and forming an idea from it of the kind of student you are. What would this person think? After you have done this prewriting work, begin work on your paragraph.

51.2 Making Modified Outlines

A modified outline is a way of breaking down information so that you can remember it more easily. It is also a good way to organize ideas and information for a composition.

Use a modified outline to take notes on what you hear in class or read.

The outline that follows this brief paragraph is an example of how you might outline something you are reading. If you were reading a magazine article about the subject, your outline would contain many more details. If you were reading an entire book, you might make one or more outlines for each chapter.

Crazy Horse, chief of the Oglala Sioux Indians, was one of the greatest American Indians. It was he who led the Indians in the famous Battle of the Little Bighorn, sometimes known as Custer's Last Stand.

HEADING	Crazy Horse
	1. Chief of Oglala Sioux
DETAILS	2. One of greatest Indians
	3. Led Battle of Little Bighorn

The following chart gives some suggestions for outlining.

TIPS FOR MAKING MODIFIED OUTLINES

1. As you listen in class or read, ask yourself, "What is the subject I am hearing or reading about?"
2. A brief statement of the subject will be the heading of your outline.
3. Jot down details that contain useful information about the subject.

EXERCISE A: Making a Modified Outline. Follow the suggestions on the preceding page and outline the paragraph below.

The grizzly bears that used to be so common in the Canadian Rockies, the American Rockies, and Alaska are rapidly becoming an endangered species. Since these animals form strong attachments to their homes, they keep coming back to them and attacking humans to regain their space. To protect the humans, park rangers have had to destroy many grizzlies or send them to wilderness areas far removed from people. So, because of its special nature, the grizzly may be causing its own extinction.

EXERCISE B: More Work on Modified Outlines. Make a modified outline of the following paragraph.

Joe DiMaggio is one of the greatest baseball players who has ever lived. During his long career with the New York Yankees, he accomplished many things and earned many awards and honors. He was a member of eleven All-Star teams. He was voted the American League's Most Valuable Player three times. He achieved a lifetime batting average of .325. And in 1955, he was elected to the baseball Hall of Fame. His most famous accomplishment, however, is the fifty-six-game hitting streak he achieved in 1941. Some baseball experts regard the streak as an unbreakable record. But DiMaggio's greatness rests not just on one record but on his whole career.

DEVELOPING WRITING SKILLS: Writing a Paragraph from an Outline. Take either one of the two outlines you made for Exercises A and B and using only the details you jotted down write a paragraph. Then compare the paragraph you wrote with the one you outlined. Ask yourself: Does my paragraph have all the important facts presented in the original one?

51.3 Making Formal Outlines

A formal outline is a good way to organize a large amount of information. Whenever you are taking notes from a textbook or doing the prewriting work for a report, a formal outline can be a great help.

Use formal outlines to summarize chapters of textbooks and to prepare for the writing of a report.

The following is part of a formal outline of a chapter in a textbook on writing and producing a high-school newspaper.

The American Newspaper

I. Different Kinds and Purposes of Newspapers
    A. Different kinds of newspapers
        1. Daily newspapers
            a. Report local, national, and international news
            b. Offer "fresh" coverage of events
        2. Weekly newspapers
            a. Concentrate on local events
            b. Published in suburbs and small communities
        3. Ethnic newspapers
            a. For ethnic or cultural groups
            b. Often in foreign language
    B. Purposes of newspapers
        1. Informing readers on current events
        2. Helping readers live more comfortably
        3. Entertaining readers
        4. Informing government of public needs

What makes this outline formal is that the information is arranged in an orderly, systematic way. The order of importance of the different items of information is made clear by the use of numbers and letters and by the pattern of indentations.

In a formal outline, main ideas are shown by Roman numerals (I, II, III). The major details relating to each main idea are shown by capital letters (A, B, C). Minor details relating to major details are shown by regular numbers (1, 2, 3). If there are any subdetails relating to minor details, these are shown by small letters (a, b, c).

Not all formal outlines have minor details and subdetails. There may not be enough information to make it necessary to include them. However, a formal outline must always have at least two main ideas, and each main idea must have at least two supporting major details. (If the preceding formal outline had been given in its entirety, other main ideas, with their major and minor details, would have appeared.)

The following chart explains how to make a formal outline of a chapter in a textbook.

HOW TO MAKE A FORMAL OUTLINE

1. Make the chapter title the title of your outline. Center it on your paper or in your notebook.
2. Find the main ideas and give each one a Roman number. The largest headings within a chapter are probably the main ideas.
3. Find the major details that support a main idea and label them A, B, and so on. Any smaller headings that follow a large heading will represent the major details.
4. The sentences or paragraphs that follow a smaller heading contain the minor details. Assign regular numbers to the minor details that you pick out for your outline.
5. If you decide to support a minor detail with subdetails, assign small letters to the subdetails.

As in the sample outline, every new level of your outline should be indented. The numbers and letters line up as shown in the example and are punctuated with periods.

EXERCISE A: Working with Formal Outlines. In your notebook or on paper, copy the following partly completed outline on the material below. Then complete the outline.

The Central Nervous System

The central nervous system in a human being is made up of the brain and the spinal cord. The brain consists of three basic parts. The largest part is the cerebrum. It is divided into two halves. The left half controls the right side of the body; the right half controls the left side of the body. A second basic part of the brain is the cerebellum. It is found just beneath the back part of the cerebrum. It controls balance and coordination and affects posture. The third basic part is the brain stem. It consists of nerve fibers in a stalklike bundle. It links the cerebrum and the spinal cord.

The other main part of the central nervous system is the spinal cord. It is a nerve cord that connects the brain and the rest of the nervous system. It carries messages to the brain and back from the brain. The spinal cord is protected from damage by the small bones that make up the backbone.

The Central Nervous System

I. The brain
  A. Cerebrum
    1.
    2. Right half—controls left side of body
  B.
    1. Beneath back part of cerebrum
    2.
  C. Brain stem
    1.
    2.
II. The spinal cord
    1.
    2. Carries messages to and from brain
    3.

EXERCISE B: More Practice with Formal Outlines. Read the paragraphs below about California. Then copy the incomplete outline that follows into your notebook or on a separate sheet of paper. Complete the outline.

The Land and Climate of California

California's landscape is dramatic. Two tall mountain ranges cut through the area. The Coast Ranges hug the coast. The Sierra Nevada sit inland on the border of Nevada and Arizona. California's fertile central valley lies between these two ranges.

In northern California a great deal of rain falls. In the south, however, water is scarce. There much of the land is desert. Except in the high mountains, California enjoys mild temperatures all year.

The Land and Climate of California

I. The landscape
   A. Two mountain ranges
      1. Coast Ranges—along coast
      2.
   B.
II. Climate
   A. A great deal of rain in the north
   B.
   C.

EXERCISE C: Preparing a Formal Outline. Imagine that you are planning to write an autobiography, or story of your life. Prepare a formal outline to help you organize the information about your life.

DEVELOPING WRITING SKILLS: Making a Formal Outline. Make a formal outline of Section 50.3 of the last chapter. Suggestions: Use the title of the lesson as the title of your outline. Make the rule one main idea. Make the title of the chart a second main idea.

Skills Review and Writing Workshop

Developing Your Note-Taking Skills

CHECKING YOUR SKILLS

Read each statement below. If it is true, write *True* on your paper. If it is false or only partly true, write *False*.

EXAMPLE: A notebook should be organized and complete, but it need not be neat.
False

1. A notebook should be divided up according to subject, and notes in the same subject should be kept together.
2. If you are absent from a class, do not attempt to get the notes you missed.
3. When making a modified outline, you should try to pick out the main ideas to include, but ignore all details.
4. One basic difference between a modified outline and a formal outline is that a modified outline is more simple.
5. A good formal outline can consist of only one main idea supported by only one major detail.

USING STUDY SKILLS IN WRITING

Writing About Outlines

Plan a paragraph about why outlines are important and how they can help you take better notes. Refer to the information in this chapter and to your own classroom experience for ideas.

Write your paragraph. You will probably want to mention in what circumstances outlines can be used and what purposes they serve.

When you have finished writing your paragraph, revise it. Look for ways to make your paragraph clearer and more specific. Then proofread it carefully for spelling, grammar, and punctuation.

Chapter 52

Developing Your Critical-Thinking Skills

Do good readers believe everything they read? Probably not. They think about and judge it. They consider the author's purpose in writing. They ask themselves whether they can rely on what the author says. They think about what kind of information they are receiving.

Critical thinking means analyzing and judging. In this chapter, you will learn some important critical-thinking skills. You will learn how to tell the difference between fact and opinion. You will also learn how language can be used to control the way people respond to what they read or hear. Developing such skills will help make you a better—and more critical—thinker. Not only will you be able to read or listen more intelligently, you will be able to write and speak more effectively.

52.1 Separating Fact from Opinion

The first step in analyzing and judging information is to decide how reliable it is. You need to determine how much of it you can accept as true. To do this, you must be able to tell fact from opinion.

Learn how to tell the difference between fact and opinion.

A statement of fact is one that is either true or false. A statement of fact can be proved true or false by measurement, by observation, by consulting reliable reference books or other records, by scientific experiment, or by the word of an eyewitness or expert.

The following two sentences are examples of statements of fact.

FACT: Joe's brother is five feet ten inches tall.

FACT: It is raining now.

FACT: Plants need both water and sunlight to survive.

You could easily test the first statement by measuring Joe's brother. You could test the second statement by looking out the window and observing the weather. You could check the third statement by consulting books, performing experiments, or talking with an expert on the subject.

The following chart lists questions to ask yourself to help you identify a statement of fact.

RECOGNIZING STATEMENTS OF FACT
1. Can you test the statement by direct observation or measurement?
2. Can you test the statement by performing an experiment?
3. Can you test the statement by consulting reference books or other records?
4. Can you test the statement by consulting an authority—a witness or an expert?

Keep in mind that a statement of fact does not have to be true. We usually use the word *fact* to mean "something that is true." But a *statement of fact* merely means that what is said can be tested for truth or falsehood by measurement, observation, or the other ways mentioned in the chart. Therefore, the statement *The sun revolves around the earth* is a statement of fact, even though what is said is false.

A statement of opinion, unlike a statement of fact, cannot be proved either true or false. An opinion cannot be tested by observation. Some opinions express personal feelings or attitudes. Others express judgments based on facts. Still other opinions make predictions based on facts.

Although opinions cannot be proved true or false as statements of fact can be, not all opinions are equal. Opinions can be supported by facts. When you judge the opinions of others, look to see if facts are presented as support. Likewise, when you express your own opinions be prepared to support them with whatever relevant facts you can find. If you presented the opinion that American swimmer Mark Spitz was one of the greatest Olympic athletes, your opinion might mean little to someone who had never heard of Mark Spitz. It might mean little to someone who admired some other notable Olympian. But if you supported your opinion with the fact that Spitz won seven gold medals in the 1972 Olympic Games, your opinion would probably be accepted by many. And many others would at least see that it was a reasonable opinion.

The examples below illustrate the three types of opinions described above.

PERSONAL FEELING: Basketball is a fascinating and very exciting game.

JUDGMENT: Tall players have an advantage in basketball because it is easier for them to reach the basket.

PREDICTION: Joe's brother will make the high-school basketball team.

The first example is a purely personal statement, unsupported by any facts. The second opinion expresses a judgment based on fact. The third opinion is a prediction about the future. Although a prediction may be based on fact, it can be proved true only when the event actually happens.

The following chart lists questions to ask yourself to help you identify a statement as an opinion.

RECOGNIZING OPINIONS
1. Does the statement express a personal attitude or feeling?
2. Does the statement express a judgment?
3. Does the statement make a prediction about the future?

Much of what you read is a mixture of facts and opinions. A social-studies textbook, for example, may present a fact like the following: "The Communists joined the separate republics and formed the Union of Soviet Socialist Republics." Then the book may present an opinion: "Today the fifteen republics of the U.S.S.R. do not have enough independence to govern themselves well." A good reader should be able to spot which are statements of facts and which are statements of opinion.

EXERCISE A: Recognizing Fact and Opinion. Identify each of the following sentences as either a statement of fact or a statement of opinion. Keep in mind that the factual statements may be either true or false.

EXAMPLE: Mount Everest is the tallest mountain on the earth's surface.

Statement of Fact

1. Dogs make better pets than cats.
2. *The Adventures of Tom Sawyer* was written by Mark Twain.

3. No one should go skydiving.
4. Chocolate ice cream is better than butter pecan.
5. The elephant is the largest animal in the world.
6. The speed of light is about 186,000 miles per second.
7. It will rain tomorrow because a warm front is approaching.
8. Lincoln was the first President of the United States.
9. Science-fiction novels are better than mysteries.
10. The Atlantic Ocean is the largest ocean.

EXERCISE B: More Work with Fact and Opinion. Identify each of the following as either a statement of fact or a statement of opinion. Remember that statements of fact may be either true or false.

1. Bats are the only flying mammals.
2. Science is more interesting than history.
3. Water freezes at 32°F.
4. The California redwood is the tallest kind of tree in the United States.
5. Apples taste better than pears.
6. Ty Cobb was the greatest baseball player because his lifetime batting average is the highest of all time.
7. The cheetah can run faster than any other animal.
8. Babe Ruth hit 60 home runs in 1927.
9. After taking Mrs. Evans's course, you will be able to type 60 words a minute.
10. Our team is sure to win the ball game that we play next week.

DEVELOPING WRITING SKILLS: Evaluating Fact and Opinion. For each statement that you marked "fact" in Exercises A and B, tell whether the statement is true or false. If necessary, consult reference or other books on the subject. You might ask your teacher to help you choose a useful source. For each statement that you marked "opinion," tell whether the opinion is supported with facts.

52.2 Recognizing Uses of Language

Thinking critically also means noticing how words are used to express ideas. Words can be used to communicate clearly and honestly, or they can be used to trick and control readers or listeners.

Learn to identify different uses of language.

Word choices affect meaning. Most words have a basic specific meaning. But they may also suggest feelings and emotions. Often words with the same basic meaning have different tones, or emotional suggestions. For example, the words *walk, stroll,* and *trudge* all have the same basic meaning. But *stroll* suggests easy, pleasant walking; *trudge* suggests hard, unpleasant walking; and *walk* usually has no suggestions—it is neutral in tone.

In the following chart, the words in the left-hand column usually have a favorable tone. The words in the right-hand column usually have an unfavorable tone. And the words in the middle column are usually thought to be neutral in tone.

Favorable Tone	Neutral Tone	Unfavorable Tone
dine	eat	gobble
thrifty	economical	stingy
husky	heavy	fat
pass away	die	drop dead
calligraphy	handwriting	scribbling

EXERCISE A: Analyzing Word Choices. Tell whether the underlined word or words in the sentences below create a favorable or an unfavorable view of the person or thing described.

EXAMPLE: "Please keep your <u>mutt</u> out of our yard."
Unfavorable

1. Audrey babbles at me during our ride to school.
2. Audrey talks to me during our ride to school.
3. Most people think of Phil as ordinary.
4. Most people think of Phil as normal.
5. They have been observing that hippopotamus for a long while.
6. They have been gawking at that hippopotamus for a long while.
7. My friends like loud, garish clothes.
8. My friends like striking, colorful clothes.
9. Will is always high-spirited in class.
10. Will is always jumpy and fidgety in class.

EXERCISE B: More Work with Word Choices. Follow the directions for Exercise A.

1. The old woman laughed at my story.
2. The old woman cackled at my story.
3. I think that you are misrepresenting the truth.
4. I think that you are lying.
5. I think that your statement is inaccurate.
6. His home is the first one on the left as you come up Elm Street.
7. His shack is the first one on the left as you come up Elm Street.
8. That old woman is my neighbor.
9. That used up hag is my neighbor.
10. That mature woman is my neighbor.

DEVELOPING WRITING SKILLS: Revising for Fairness. Rewrite the following passage so that the person described is presented in a favorable way.

He barged into the room and plopped down in his seat. The sunlight glinted off his four-eyed mug. He babbled on and on at me. He was whining about how I always try to make music class fun for my friends and me. He's prejudiced against my easy-going and fun-loving personality.

Skills Review and Writing Workshop

Critical-Thinking Skills

CHECKING YOUR SKILLS

Read the following paragraph carefully. Identify the statements of fact and opinion in it. Then find examples of slanted language.

Our space program isn't getting enough support. In the 1960s we put a great deal of money into the "race for space" with the Soviet Union. The Apollo Project was the most exciting achievement in American history. Since then, our space program has been going downhill. The United States didn't even send a spacecraft to observe Halley's comet. Some unimaginative people say that the space program isn't worth what it costs. Anyone can see that that is nonsense. Where would we be without statellite TV transmissions, navigation signals, and weather forecasts? These tightfisted critics say that social problems on earth are more important. But no one is starving in this country, and our unemployment rate is lower than it has been in years. The space program deserves our support.

USING CRITICAL-THINKING SKILLS IN WRITING

Writing an Editorial

Imagine that you have been asked to write a newspaper editorial. Choose an issue about which you have an opinion. First, list the facts involved. Take notes on how they support your opinion. Also list opposing opinions, taking notes on how the facts support them.

Write an introductory paragraph that states your main idea. Then discuss the arguments for your point of view. Include an honest evaluation of the opposing viewpoints. Write a concluding paragraph that sums up your main idea.

Reread your editorial, revising it as necessary. Make sure that you have distinguished between fact and opinion. Be sure that you have presented all the facts, not just those that support your point of view.

Developing Your Reading and Test-Taking Skills

Good readers use different reading skills for different kinds of reading. They do not, for example, read a novel the same way that they read a cookbook. They do not read a cookbook the same way that they read a textbook.

You have been using textbooks for as long as you have been in school and you have probably already been using some of the reading skills they require. In this chapter, you will learn about some of the basic features of textbooks and how they can be used to make you a more skillful reader. You will also learn about something closely connected with textbooks—preparing for tests.

53.1 Reading Textbooks

Most textbooks have a number of features that help you in reading and studying.

Use the special features of your textbooks to improve your schoolwork.

SOME FEATURES OF TEXTBOOKS

1. The *table of contents* lists the units and chapters of the book and the pages where they begin.
2. The *index* lists alphabetically all the subjects covered in a book and tells the pages where information on them can be found. The index is in the back of the book.
3. The *glossary,* also in the back, lists and defines special terms you may have to look up.
4. Chapter *titles, headings,* and *subheadings* are printed in large, heavy type. they give you an idea of what you will be reading about. They divide the reading material into sections so that you can learn it more easily. And they help you to locate, preview, and review information.
5. *Questions* and *exercises* at the end of a chapter can be looked over before you read a chapter for hints of what to look for as you read. Afterwards, they can be used to help you retain what you have read.
6. *Pictures* and *captions* (information given next to or beneath a picture) can make ideas clearer or can enable you to use your imagination to enter more fully into the subject you are reading about. Sometimes pictures can express what words can not.
7. Chapter *introductions* arouse interest and make it easier for you to grasp main ideas.
8. *Summaries* offer a rapid review of what you have read and make it easier to remember main points and important information.

If you have not done so yet, take each of your textbooks and examine its special features. For example, read through the table of contents to get an idea of the range of material covered in the book. Find the glossary— do you see how it can help you with your reading assignments? Look over the headings. Why are some larger than others, or in a different color? Do the chapters have summaries? If they do, why might it be useful to read them *before* you read the chapters? These features and others are designed to make your reading and studying easier. It pays to take advantage of them.

EXERCISE: Examining the Features in Your Textbooks. Answer the following questions about either your science or social-studies textbook.

1. In a typical chapter, how many headings are there? How many subheadings? If you read over just the headings and subheadings, could you get at least a general idea of what the chapter is about?
2. Is there a chapter introduction? If there is, what seems to be its purpose?
3. How much could you learn about the contents of a typical chapter just by looking over the questions and exercises before reading the chapter?
4. Does your textbook have a glossary? If it does, look over a few words there and then look them up in a dictionary. Are the two entries similar?
5. Think of a topic covered in the book. Find out which is the faster way to find all the information on it—by using the index or by using the table of contents.

DEVELOPING WRITING SKILLS: Examining Pictures and Captions. Select one picture in your science or social-studies textbook. Study the picture and read the caption and surrounding text material. Then write a paragraph explaining how the picture illustrates or adds to the information provided in the text.

53.2 Preparing for a Test

Like it or not, success in school usually means success in taking tests. Since doing well on a test depends largely on good preparation, it is important for you to know how to prepare. Maybe the most important thing to know is what *not* to do.

Do not rely on last-minute cramming to prepare for a test.

Cramming for a test is like Christmas shopping on December 24th: It is an unpleasant chore, even a bore; and it spoils the thing it leads up to.

Tests may not often be fun, but they should leave you with the good feeling that you demonstrated real knowledge. They should not leave you with the feeling that the only thing you achieved was a number or letter at the top of a paper.

The following chart offers some suggestions that can make test-taking a satisfying experience, rather than a painful one. How many of them do you follow before an upcoming test?

PREPARING FOR A TEST

1. Review your notes or textbook chapter three times: the evening of the day when you took the notes, two days later, and the night before the test.
2. To find out what you do not know, make up questions covering the material you will be tested on, and write out the answers. Any problems you meet with will tell you where your knowledge is weak.
3. To memorize things, go over them repeatedly for at least several days before a test, and ask someone to quiz you on the material. Do your memorization work after you have done your other homework.
4. Use memorization tricks (words, rhymes, sentences, and so on) as a further aid to memory.

EXERCISE: Evaluating Your Test Preparation. To establish where you are strong and where you are weak in test preparation, answer *Yes* or *No* to the following questions. The more yes answers you have, the better your preparation is. A no answer indicates a weakness you should correct.

1. Do you review your notes the evening of the day that you made them?
2. Do you review them two days later?
3. Do you review them the night before a test?
4. To find out what you do not know, do you make up questions on the material that the test is likely to cover?
5. Do you write out answers to these questions and study the material you do not know?
6. To memorize things, do you go over them repeatedly for at least several days before a test?
7. Do you have someone quiz you on the material you have been memorizing?
8. Do you use memorization tricks?

DEVELOPING WRITING SKILLS: More Work with Test Preparation. Imagine that you had read and discussed the poem below in class and that you had to memorize it for a test to be given in one week. Write a paragraph explaining all the things you would do in the one week before the test to make sure you would know the poem. Base your answer on the material in this section.

The Eagle

He clasps the crag with crooked hands;
Close to the sun in lonely lands,
Ringed with the azure world, he stands. (azure = sky-blue)

The wrinkled sea beneath him crawls;
He watches from his mountain walls,
And like a thunderbolt he falls.
—Alfred Lord Tennyson

Skills Review and Writing Workshop

Developing Your Reading and Test-Taking Skills

CHECKING YOUR SKILLS

Read each of the following statements. If a statement is true, write *True* on your paper; if it is false, write *False*.

EXAMPLE: When preparing for a test, you should not ask others to quiz you on the material.
False.

1. You can find information on a subject by looking it up in the index of a textbook.
2. One purpose of chapter titles, headings, and subheadings is to give readers an idea of what they will be reading.
3. You can skip over pictures and captions because their only purpose is to decorate the pages they appear on.
4. Cramming may not be fun, but it is the best way to prepare for a test.
5. Memorization tricks are a waste of time.

USING STUDY SKILLS IN WRITING

Discussing Textbooks

Review the material in this chapter and plan a paragraph about how to use a textbook. Select an appropriate topic sentence and support it with details about using the parts of a textbook.

Write your paragraph. You will probably want to discuss the parts of a textbook in the order in which they appear, from table of contents to index.

When you have finished writing your paragraph, revise and proofread it carefully.

Chapter 54

Using the Library

A library is sometimes called "the place of a thousand doors." Just beyond these "doors" are a thousand adventures in imagination, a thousand discoveries of new knowledge, a thousand pathways to wisdom and wonders. And these doors open to all who can read.

All you need is the key—the ability to find the books that contain the wonders and wisdom and knowledge. This means knowing how the books and other materials in a library are organized. In this chapter, you will learn some of the basics of how libraries are organized and how a reader finds books. You can use the information in this chapter to help you take full advantage of both your school library and the public library.

54.1 Using the Card Catalog

The *card catalog* is the large cabinet whose drawers hold the information you need to find a book.

Use the card catalog to find a library book.

This is what a card catalog looks like:

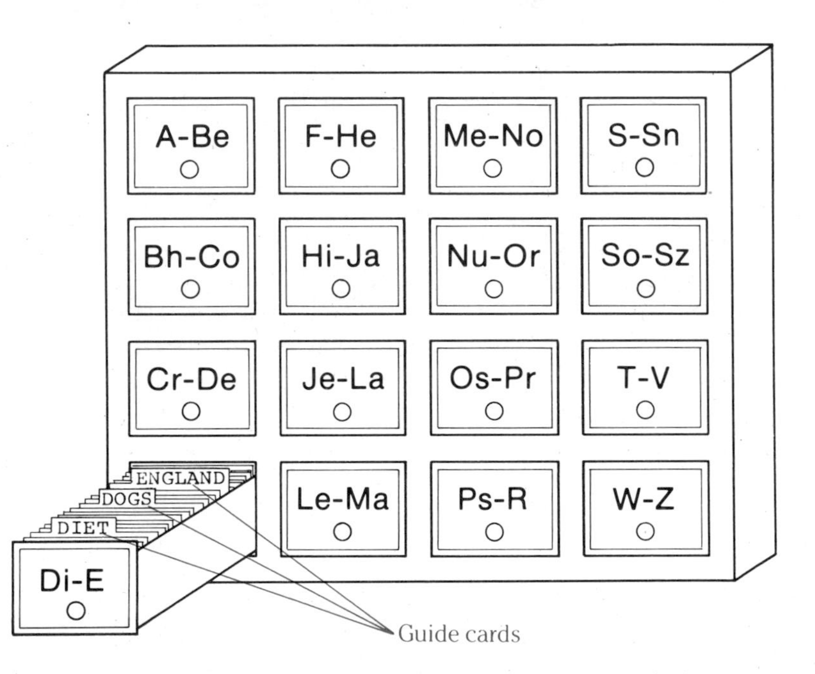

If you read the labels down the first line of drawers, down the second, and so on, you will see that the card catalog is in alphabetical order. Inside the drawers are cards, which are also in alphabetical order. The cards in each drawer fall within the part of the alphabet shown by the label.

These cards are called *catalog cards*, and there are three basic kinds: *author cards, title cards,* and *subject cards*. If you wanted to find a particular book, had forgotten its title, but knew that the author's name was David Hendin, you could look up "Hendin, David" in the card catalog. You would find a card that looks like this:

```
737.4     Hendin, David
He
            Collecting coins. New York
          Signet. 1978

          170 p.

          index
```

Author of book

This is an author card. Notice that the author's name appears above the other information.

Suppose you knew that the book you wanted was titled *Collecting Coins*. In that case, you would be able to look up that title and you would find a card that looks like this:

```
737.4     Collecting Coins
He
          Hendin, David. New York
          Signet. 1978

          170 p.

          index
```

Title of book

This is a title card. Notice that it is very much like an author card, except that the title of the book appears first.

Suppose that you were interested in finding a book on coins but did not have a particular title or author in mind. You could look up "Coins" and find a card that looks like this:

COINS — Subject of book

737.4 He — Hendin, David

Collecting coins. New York
Signet. 1978

170 p.

index

This is a subject card. Notice that the subject, coins, appears near the top, followed by the author's name, the title of his book, and other information. You would also find other subject cards headed "coins" alongside this one, and these other "coins" cards would list other books on the subject.

An actual catalog card, such as you would find in a school or public library, usually contains somewhat more information than any of the cards you have just been looking at. It might be more like the following one:

Subject — CATS

Author — Beadle, Muriel

Location symbol — 636.8 B

Title — The cat: history, biography, and behavior/Muriel Beadle; drawings by E. John Pfiffner. New York:

Publisher — Simon and Schuster,

Copyright date — (c 1977)

Number of pages — 251 p.:

Illustrations — ill.; 25cm.

Bibliography — Bibliography: p. 235-242.

Index — Includes index

On this subject card, the *location symbol* tells where the book is found on the shelves. The *copyright date* indicates how recent the book is. The abbreviation *ill.* means that the book has pictures or drawings. "Bibliography" tells you that the book contains a list of other books on the same subject. "Includes index" means that there also is an alphabetical listing of all topics covered in the book.

FEATURES OF LIBRARY ALPHABETIZING

1. The articles *a, an,* and *the* at the beginning of an entry are not part of the alphabetical order. For example, *The Magician* would be alphabetized under *M*.
2. Names of people are alphabetized by their last names.
3. Entries are alphabetized word-by-word.
4. Abbreviations are alphabetized as if they were spelled out as words. For example, *Mt. St. Helens* would be listed as if it were *Mount Saint Helens.*
5. Many libraries alphabetize last names beginning with *Mc* with last names beginning with *Mac*. For example, *McCall* would be listed as if it were *MacCall.*

EXERCISE: Working with Catalog Cards. Study the catalog card shown below. Then answer the questions that follow.

```
                MARSUPIALS

599.2       Rabinowich, Ellen
R               Kangaroos, Koalas & Other Marsupials
            New York: Watts, 1978

            An introduction to the characteristics
            and habits of various marsupials, the
            animals with pouches for young.
```

1. Is this an author card, a title card, or a subject card?
2. What is the title of the book that this card is for?
3. Does the card tell where the book can be found?
4. If you wanted another book by this author, under what letter in the catalog would you look?
5. Why does this card include the date 1978?

DEVELOPING WRITING SKILLS: Comparing Catalog Cards. Compare the above card with the subject card for CATS. What kinds of information are you given about the cat book that you are not given about the marsupial book? Write out your answer in a short paragraph.

54.2 Finding the Book You Want

Most books are classified as either *fiction* (novels and short stories) or *nonfiction*.

Books of fiction are arranged in alphabetical order by the last name of the author. An individual author's books are arranged in alphabetical order by the first words of the titles.

If you were looking for the novel *Charlotte's Web,* you could locate it easily, and without even using the card catalog, if you knew two things: that the author was E. B. White, and where the fiction section of the library was. You could then go to the fiction section, find the authors whose names begin with *W,* find E. B. White's books, find a title beginning with *C,* and thus find *Charlotte's Web*. If you did not know the author, you would have to look up the title in the card catalog to identify the author.

To find a nonfiction book, look it up in the card catalog and note its call number.

The *call number* is a combination of a number and one or more letters. It is found in the upper left corner of a catalog card and also on the spine of the book. To locate a book, you locate its call number on the shelves.

Most libraries indicate the range of call numbers found in each stack of shelves. So if, for example, you wanted a book with the call number 973.7/Be, you would go to the 900 shelves, find the 970's, and look for 973.7/Be.

Most libraries classify their nonfiction books by the *Dewey Decimal System*. In this system, books and their call numbers are divided into ten main groups.

DEWEY DECIMAL SYSTEM	
000–099	General works (such as encyclopedias)
100–199	Philosophy
200–299	Religion
300–399	Social sciences (such as economics)
400–499	Language (dictionaries, grammars, etc.)
500–599	Science (such as chemistry and biology)
600–699	Applied science (such as medicine)
700–799	Arts (such as music, painting, and dancing)
800–899	Literature (such as poetry and plays)
900–999	Geography and history (including biographies)

Knowing these ten Dewey decimal groups can make it easier to locate books. You are more likely to feel that you know where you are in a library if you know its general organization. You may even find it useful to remember some of the subgroups within the Dewey Decimal System. Knowing, for example that call numbers 920–929 are reserved for biographies can come in handy. If you like to read biographies, you can go straight to the 920's shelves and browse among all the true-life stories of interesting people. In this way you can find some very enjoyable books to read even though you entered the library with no particular book in mind. The Dewey Decimal System, therefore, is one of the keys to unlocking a library's treasures.

HOW TO LOCATE LIBRARY BOOKS

1. To find a novel or a book of short stories when you know the name of the author, go to the fiction section. Look for the author's name by alphabetical order and then the title.
2. When you do not know the name of the author, look up the title you want in the card catalog, note the author's name, and then proceed to the fiction section.
3. To find a nonfiction book, look up the title in the card catalog and note its call number. Look for the shelves where the range of call numbers includes the one you want. Go among the shelves and look for the call number.
4. If you cannot recall the title of a particular nonfiction book, look up the author in the card catalog and go through his or her author cards until you find the title you want and its call number. Then proceed to the shelves.
5. If you want a book on a particular subject, but do not have a title or an author in mind, look up the subject and see what suggestions the subject cards provide.

EXERCISE A: Finding Fiction. Arrange the following books of fiction in the order in which you would find them on the shelves of a library.

1. *Julie of the Wolves,* by Jean Craighead George
2. *The Lion, the Witch and the Wardrobe,* by C. S. Lewis
3. *Alice's Adventures in Wonderland,* by Lewis Carroll
4. *The Last Battle,* by C. S. Lewis
5. *Across Five Aprils,* by Irene Hunt

EXERCISE B: Working with the Dewey Decimal System. On your paper, copy the nonfiction titles listed below. Look at each title and decide which Dewey Decimal group it belongs to. Then next to the title write the call numbers of the group.

EXAMPLE: *Collected Poems of Edna St. Vincent Millay*

Collected Poems of Edna St. Vincent Millay 800–899

1. *A History of Ancient Greece*
2. *The New Columbia Encyclopedia*
3. *Art of the Dance*
4. *Asthma: The Facts*
5. *The Plays of Shakespeare*
6. *Ten Great Economists*
7. *The Bible in the Modern World*
8. *The Life of Emily Dickinson*
9. *Webster's New World Dictionary*
10. *Asimov on Chemistry*

DEVELOPING WRITING SKILLS: Writing About the Library. Imagine that you had to do a report on the topic Is There Life on Other Planets? Write a paragraph explaining how you would use the library to find the information you need. Tell what you would do first. Would you go to a librarian or to the card catalog? How would you use the card catalog? What kind of card would you probably first use? How would you then proceed?

Skills Review and Writing Workshop

Using the Library

CHECKING YOUR SKILLS

Number your paper from 1 to 5. Read each statement below carefully. If a statement is true, write *True* next to the appropriate number. If it is false, write *False* next to the appropriate number.

EXAMPLE: The card catalog contains information about only nonfiction books.
False

1. To find information about a particular book in the card catalog, you must know its title before you use the catalog.
2. In the card catalog, a subject card will tell you both the title and the author of a book on the subject you have looked up.
3. To find the novel *Penrod and Sam*, by Booth Tarkington, you would have to start with the card catalog if you did not know the author's name.
4. The Dewey Decimal classifications of one library are probably much different from the Dewey Decimal classifications of another library.
5. Fiction is classified with poetry and plays in the Dewey Decimal System.

USING STUDY SKILLS IN WRITING

Explaining How to Use the Library

In this exercise you will explain how to find in the library a book about whales called *Gentle Giants* by John Smith.

Write a brief paragraph giving several ways to look up the book in the library's card catalog. Also, tell where the book would probably be located in the library (its Dewey Decimal classification).

When you have finished writing your paragraph, revise and proofread it carefully.

Chapter 55

Working with Reference Books

If you have ever used an encylcopedia or a dictionary, then you are already acquainted with reference books. Reference books are not meant to be read as other books are. They are meant to provide information. You refer to them. You read *in* them. You do not read them from cover to cover.

For this reason, reference books are seldom taken out of the library. They are kept in a special reference section, and their spines often have an *R* in front of their call numbers. Some larger libraries even have a reference librarian who can direct you to those reference books that contain just the information you need.

Because these books are so useful, this chapter will prepare you to use some of the most important ones effectively.

55.1 Using Encyclopedias

Except for the dictionary, encyclopedias are the most frequently used reference books. You can find information on almost any subject. Sometimes the information will be more than enough for a school report. At other times, the information contained in the article you look up may not be enough for you. However, encyclopedias usually will tell you where you can find fuller information.

Use an encyclopedia for any of three purposes: (1) to get background information on a subject, (2) to learn basic facts about it, or (3) to find out where else to go for information.

The articles in an encyclopedia are arranged alphabetically. So are the volumes that make up the whole set. The following illustration shows the spines of the first six volumes of the popular World Book Encyclopedia.

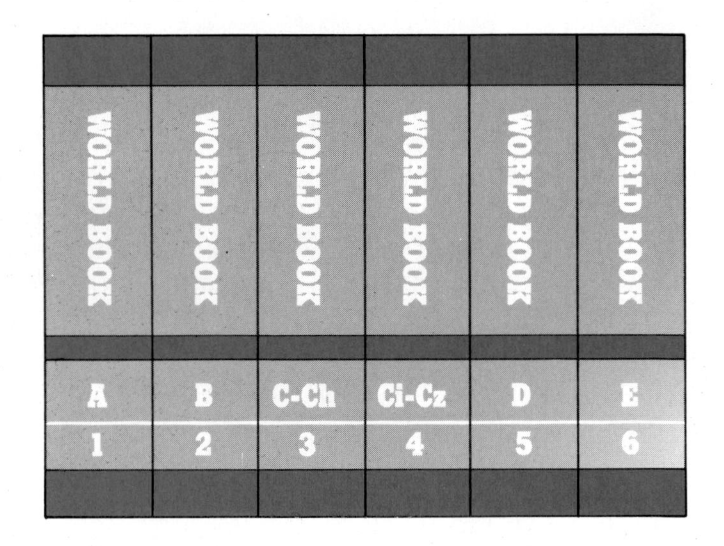

The major encyclopedias usually have an index. This is an alphabetical list of all subjects covered in the set. It indicates the articles where a subject is treated and the volume and page where the articles are found.

The following are some tips for using an encyclopedia effectively.

USING AN ENCYCLOPEDIA

1. Look up the subject under its most usual name. Sometimes there will be no article for the subject under the name you looked up, but there will be the direction *See*—, and another name for the subject will be given. Look that up.
2. Follow up the direction *See also* (followed by the name of a related subject). An article on a related subject will often provide useful information on the subject you are concerned with.
3. Some articles will be followed by a list of additional readings. These books or articles found in such a list should be useful when you need a thorough knowledge of a subject.
4. Look up your subject in the encyclopedia's index. Additional sources of information in the set may be found.

EXERCISE: Finding Information in Encyclopedias. Look up and read the article on your state in one of the following encyclopedias: *The World Book Encyclopedia Collier's Encyclopedia* the *Merit Students Encyclopedia* or the *Encyclopedia Americana*. Then, after following up any *See also* directions and checking the index, write a brief answer to the question: What information about my state does the encyclopedia provide besides the main article?

DEVELOPING WRITING SKILLS: Comparing Encyclopedia Articles. Look up a subject that interests you in any three of the encyclopedias (or others) listed in Exercise A. In a brief paragraph tell which encyclopedia article you liked the best, and why.

55.2 Using Other Reference Books

In addition to encyclopedias, there are a great many other reference books available in school and public libraries. Three of the most important other reference books are *almanacs, atlases,* and *biographical reference books*.

An almanac is a book of facts and statistics that people frequently want to know. It is made up largely of lists, tables, and charts. Most almanacs are updated every year.

Use an almanac to get a brief answer to a question involving facts or statistics.

EXAMPLES: What is the distance between Mercury and the sun?
(Answer: 36 million miles)

Who won the 100-meter dash for women in the 1960 Olympics?
(Answer: Wilma Rudolph, U.S.A.)

What is the tallest building in the United States?
(Answer: the Sears Tower, Chicago; 1,454′)

Facts and statistics such as these are all grouped under subject headings. These headings are alphabetized in the index. To find a fact or statistic, you must look in the index for the subject heading it is likely to be under. Often, it will be under more than one heading. For example, to find the population of a city you could look up *Cities* or *Population,* and you would find a page reference. Probably the two best-known almanacs are *The World Almanac and Book of Facts* and the *Information Please Almanac*. You will find it easier to use these almanacs if you look over their indexes to get an idea of their subject headings.

An atlas is a book of maps that offers much information about the countries of the world.

Use an atlas for information about the geography of a region.

The following chart lists some of the kinds of information found in a good atlas. Remember, however, that different atlases give different kinds of information.

KINDS OF INFORMATION FOUND IN ATLASES	
Climate	Population, including religious and ethnic groups
Natural resources	
Topography (surface features of the land)	Boundaries
	Cities, towns, villages
Agriculture	Historical changes
Industries	Trade routes

Maps that picture historical changes can give you a lively sense of how the world was affected by the movements and developments of the past.

The following chart lists some of the better known atlases. You will find historical atlases especially useful when you are studying history.

GENERAL AND HISTORICAL ATLASES
The Atlas of American History
Goode's World Atlas
The Hammond World Atlas
The National Geographic Atlas
Prentice-Hall Illustrated Atlas of the World
Rand McNally Historical Atlas of the World
World Book Atlas

Modern methods of communication and transportation have put every part of the world within reach of the individual. For this reason, atlases are more useful and important than ever before.

A biography is the story of a person's life. Biographical reference books provide information about famous or important people. Although a good encyclopedia will contain biographical information about a great many persons, you should be aware that most libraries have a number of reference books concerned only with biographical information. Sometimes these reference books are the handiest sources of information about people. At other times they may be the only sources of information.

Use biographical reference books to learn important facts about a person's life.

Biographical reference books are especially useful when you want to find out the following kinds of facts: the correct pronunciation of a person's name; dates of birth and death; the main dates and events of the person's life; or the main accomplishments.

The following chart lists some of the main biographical reference books usually available in libraries.

SOME BIOGRAPHICAL REFERENCE BOOKS

Current Biography. Published every month, this reference work prints short biographies of prominent living people. By looking up the person you are interested in in the index, you will find the month and year of the issue that contains the biographical information you seek.

Who's Who in America. Published every two years, this work provides facts and dates about famous Americans living at the time of publication. *Who Was Who in America* contains information about famous Americans who have died.

Webster's Biographical Dictionary. This one-volume work contains 40,000 brief biographies of famous people past and present.

McGraw-Hill Encyclopedia of World Biography. This work is made up of short articles about well-known people who are no longer living.

The following entry, from *Webster's Biographical Dictionary,* shows how brief the information in a biographical reference book tends to be.

Mad'-i-son (măd'*i*·s'n), Dolley, *nee* Payne. *Often spelled* Dolly. 1768–1849. American hostess, b. in Guilford Co., N.C.; m. John Todd, Jr. (1790; d. 1793), James Madison (1794). Famous Washington hostess while her husband was secretary of state (1801–09) and president (1809–17).

For a detailed, interesting-to-read account of a person's life, you would have to go to a full-length biography.

EXERCISE: Using Almanacs, Atlases, and Biographical Reference Books. Number your paper from 1 to 10. For each item below decide which of the three kinds of reference books covered in this section you would go to for information. Write *almanac, atlas,* or *biographical reference* on your paper.

1. the chief crops in Cuba
2. the baseball players in the Hall of Fame
3. rainfall in Brazil
4. the year Columbus died
5. how long Cleopatra ruled
6. the number of planes hijacked
7. China's natural resources
8. Paul McCartney's age
9. who discovered uranium
10. the state tree of Georgia

DEVELOPING WRITING SKILLS: More Work with Almanacs, Atlases, and Biographical Reference Books. Using the appropriate reference book for information, write a brief paragraph on one of the following subjects: Recent Developments in Space Exploration, The Route You Would Take for a Trip Around the World, or Was There a Real King Arthur?

Skills Review and Writing Workshop

Working with Reference Books

CHECKING YOUR SKILLS

For each of the statements below, write *True* or *False* on your paper.

EXAMPLE: Reference books can usually be taken out of the library.
False

1. An encyclopedia article will always provide enough information for a full report on any subject.
2. A "See also" direction in an encyclopedia article may lead you to additional information on your subject.
3. To find information in an almanac, you seldom need to use the index.
4. Different atlases contain different kinds of information.
5. Atlases never present historical information about a region.

USING STUDY SKILLS IN WRITING

Writing About Reference Books

In this exercise you will write a paragraph explaining how you might use certain reference books. First, choose a famous person whose life you would like to learn about. What kinds of reference books would you consult to find out about the life and achievements of this person? What information would you expect to find in each book? Review the material in this chapter for ideas.

Now write your paragraph. Begin by telling which book you would consult first and why you would do so. Then tell which book you would consult second and what you would use it for, and so on.

After you have written your paragraph, revise it. When you are satisfied with your revised paragraph, proofread it carefully for errors.

56

Using the Dictionary

If there is one book that stands out from all others in your education, that book is the dictionary. One of the main purposes of education is to learn how to use words to understand things, to think, to speak, and to write. The dictionary exists to help you achieve this purpose. Developing the habit of using a dictionary regularly can be a valuable study skill, one that can help you improve your school work.

In the first section of this chapter, you will learn the basic dictionary skill of looking up and finding words quickly. In the second section, you will learn about some of the different kinds of information you can get when you look up words. This chapter will help you see how you can use the dictionary both to increase your knowledge of words and to earn better grades.

56.1 Finding Words Quickly

The words in a dictionary are arranged in alphabetical order to make it easy to look them up.

Use letter-by-letter alphabetical order to find a word in a dictionary.

Letter-by-letter alphabetical order means strict alphabetical order. The other kind of alphabetical order is word-by-word. The card catalog in a library uses this other system. The following example shows the difference between the two.

LETTER-BY-LETTER: *news* before *New Testament*

WORD-BY-WORD: *New Testament* before *news*

In a dictionary, *news* comes before *New Testament* because the *s* in *news* comes earlier in the alphabet than the *T* in *Testament.*

Some dictionaries have a thumb index. This is a series of indentations labeled with letters along the edge of the book. A thumb index makes it easy to find the letter that begins the word you are looking up.

If your dictionary does not have a thumb index, the quickest way to find a letter is by the four-section approach. All this means is that the pages of a dictionary can be mentally divided up into four roughly equal sections by letter groups.

FOUR SECTIONS: ABCD EFGHIJKL
MNOPQR STUVWXYZ

If, for example, you want to look up a word beginning with *s,* you should turn to the fourth quarter of the dictionary to find the *s* words.

At the top of each page will be *guide words*. The guide word at the left tells you the first word on the page. The guide word on the right tells the last. These words make it easier to follow the alphabetical order and to find the page where the word you are looking for appears.

The following chart gives the steps you should follow to find words quickly in a dictionary.

HOW TO FIND WORDS QUICKLY
1. Use the thumb index or the four-section approach to get to the letter that begins the word you are looking up.
2. Use the guide words to find the page where the word appears.
3. Follow letter-by-letter alphabetical order to locate the word.

EXERCISE: Finding Words in a Dictionary. Copy each word below. Tell the section of the dictionary in which it is found (Section 1, A–D; Section 2, E–L; Section 3, M–R; Section 4, S–Z). Then give the guide words that appear at the top of the page in your dictionary.

EXAMPLE: timber

timber Section 4 tiger moth, timbre

1. lenient
2. entrench
3. roadrunner
4. Aegean
5. fernery
6. undulation
7. sedation
8. fissure
9. blotch
10. ornate

DEVELOPING WRITING SKILLS: Understanding Alphabetical Order. Write a paragraph explaining letter-by-letter alphabetical order. Use the following pairs of words as examples: fountainhead—Fountain of Youth; handsome—hand-me-down.

56.2 Understanding Main Entries

The words that make up a dictionary are called *entry words*. An entry word with all the information about it is called a *main entry*.

Learn to recognize and use the different kinds of information in a main entry.

There are different kinds of entry words. The following are some examples.

A SINGLE WORD: compensate

A COMPOUND WORD: echo chamber

AN ABBREVIATION: FBI, F.B.I. Federal Bureau of Investigation

A PREFIX: anti- against

A SUFFIX: -tion action, condition

A PROPER NOUN: Nicaragua

The following chart lists some of the different kinds of information found in main entires.

SOME DIFFERENT KINDS OF MAIN-ENTRY INFORMATION
1. How a word is spelled
2. Syllabification—how a word is divided into syllables
3. Pronunciation
4. The part, or parts, of speech of a word
5. Etymology—the origin and history of a word
6. Definitions—the different meanings a word can have

For words that can be spelled in more than one way, the entry word will be given in each of the correct spellings.

EXAMPLE: cat·a·log, cat·a·logue

When two spellings of an entry word are given, the first is often the more commonly used or preferred spelling. You should, however, check in your dictionary's introductory section to see whether the first spelling is in fact the preferred one. In some dictionaries it may not be.

In the last example, dots were used to divide the word *catalog* (or *catalogue*) into syllables. Dictionaries will use dots, spaces, or slashes (/) to show a word's syllabification. This is useful to you when you write, because you may need to know where to "break" a word when you come to the end of a line. The following chart presents some of the basic rules of word division in writing.

DIVIDING WORDS AT THE ENDS OF LINES

1. If you are not sure how a word may be divided by syllables, look it up in the dictionary.
2. Never divide a word so that a syllable of one letter comes at the end of a line (for example, *e-/ventuality*).
3. Never divide a word so that a syllable of one letter starts a line (for example, *vocabular-/y*).
4. Do not divide words of one syllable.

An entry word is followed by its pronunciation. This is indicated by a *phonetic alphabet,* a set of symbols that each represent a sound.

EXAMPLES: flew (flo͞o) Plato (plā′tō)
Odysseus (ō dis′yo͞os)

A pronunciation key in the front or back of the dictionary and often on the bottom of the pages explains the sounds that the symbols represent. Your dictionary, for instance, would include in its pronunciation key *to͞ol*, *āpe*, and *gō* or similar words) so you would know how to pronounce flo͞o, plā′tō, and ō dis′yo͞os. Also, accent marks will indicate which syllables should be stressed in speech.

Dictionaries also tell what part of speech a word is. This information usually appears right after the pronunciation in an abbreviation. In the following example, the *n* is the standard dictionary abbreviation for *noun*.

EXAMPLE: can·teen (kan tēn′) *n*.

Since many words can function as different parts of speech, often more than one part-of-speech abbreviation will appear in a main entry. In the following example, the abbreviations *interj.*, *n.*, and *adj.* tell you that *farewell* can be used as an interjection, a noun, or an adjective.

EXAMPLE fare·well (fer′wel′; *for adj.* -wel′) *interj.* [FARE (imperative) + WELL[2]] goodbye—*n*. 1. words spoken at parting, usually of good wishes 2. a leaving or going away—*adj.* parting; last; final [a *farewell* gesture]

The following chart presents commonly used abbreviations.

DICTIONARY ABBREVIATIONS FOR PARTS OF SPEECH			
n.	noun	prep.	preposition
vt.	transitive verb	conj.	conjunction
vi.	intransitive verb	pron.	pronoun
adj.	adjective	interj.	interjection
adv.	adverb		

Additional information may also be given along with the part-of-speech abbreviation. This information includes plural forms of nouns, parts of verbs, and different forms of adjectives and adverbs.

The etymology of a word—its origin and history—is given in brackets after the pronunciation or part-of-speech label. Abbreviations are used to indicate older words, many in foreign languages, that the entry word developed from.

EXAMPLE: **gup·py** (gup′ē) *n.*, *pl.* **-pies** [after R. J. L. *Guppy*, who first provided specimens for the British Museum]

Knowing a word's etymology can sometimes help you remember its meaning or use it correctly.

Definitions—the meanings of words—are what people most often seek when they use a dictionary. By just glancing through a dictionary you can see that most words have more than one meaning. Remember that when a word has a number of meanings they are grouped together by part of speech.

EXERCISE: Working with Main Entries. Look up each of the following words in your dictionary. Then use slashes to show how the word is divided into syllables, and put an accent mark right after the most heavily stressed syllable. Write out any alternative spelling given.

EXAMPLE: bandanna

ban/dan′/na bandana

1. aerial	6. epilogue	11. Xavier
2. altimeter	7. esophagus	12. heifer
3. amphitheater	8. formidable	13. docile
4. bougainvillea	9. hallucinatory	14. Beethoven
5. busing	10. oleomargarine	15. trough

DEVELOPING WRITING SKILLS: Pronouncing Words. Look up each of the following words and by using the phonetic alphabet and pronunciation key figure out how to pronounce the word.

1. long-lived	6. heifer
2. viola (musical instrument)	7. trough
3. Don Quixote	8. Xavier
4. docile	9. Okefenokee Swamp
5. Beethoven	10. jeopardy

Skills Review and Writing Workshop

Using the Dictionary

CHECKING YOUR SKILLS

For each of the statements below, write *True* or *False* on your paper.

EXAMPLE: A word's etymology refers to its origin and history.
True

1. A dictionary would alphabetize *port of entry* before *portable*.
2. A guide word on the left side of a page tells the last entry word on the page.
3. When two spellings for an entry word are given, the first is often the more commonly used or preferred spelling.
4. Dictionaries use a phonetic alphabet to give the origin and history of words.
5. If a word functions both as a verb and as a noun, it can have only one meaning as a noun and only one as a verb.

USING STUDY SKILLS IN WRITING

Explaining Dictionary Entries

Plan a paragraph that names and describes at least five kinds of information you would find in a dictionary entry. You may need to review the two sections of this chapter as part of your prewriting.

Write your paragraph. Be sure to begin the paragraph with an appropriate topic sentence and include enough supporting information. Use specific examples from a dictionary if you wish.

Now revise your paragraph carefully. Be sure that you have explained each term clearly and thoroughly. Then proofread your paragraph for errors in spelling, punctuation, and grammar.

UNIT VIII

Listening and Speaking

Chapter 57

Developing Your Listening Skills

There are people today who earn a living teaching others how to listen. Businesses, schools, and other organizations have learned from experience that success or failure often depends on how well people listen. It seems that many people do not listen well.

Maybe you too can recall times in your own life when not listening well led to your disappointing others or yourself. The problem was not that you could not *hear* what was said; it was that you did not pay attention to what was said. Hearing and listening are not the same thing. To hear is just to pick up sounds with your ears. To listen is to grasp the ideas that sounds such as words carry.

This chapter aims to make you a better listener. The first section presents ways of preparing yourself to listen well. The second section shows you how to spot the main ideas in the words you hear.

57.1 Preparing Yourself to Listen Well

The idea that you must prepare to listen may strike you as odd. Imagine, then, that you had gone without sleep or food for three days but still had to go to school. Would you be able to pay attention to what your teacher was saying? You would probably be struggling to stay awake or fighting against hunger pains. You would not be listening very attentively to the teacher! This imaginary situation makes the point that listening can be greatly affected by other things.

Get yourself physically and mentally ready to listen.

To be physically ready to listen means that you must get enough sleep, eat properly, exercise, and take care of your health. You can't listen well when you are tired or droopy.

MENTAL PREPARATION FOR LISTENING
1. *Do* tell yourself: "I will listen and pay attention."
2. *Do* focus your eyes and ears on the speaker.
3. *Do* put away things that can distract you.
4. *Do* take notes in class.
5. *Do* block out other concerns and thoughts.
6. *Don't* daydream.
7. *Don't* look around at your friends in class.
8. *Don't* doodle.
9. *Don't* stop listening to speakers just because their opinions are different from your own.
10. *Don't* ignore speakers just because they are saying things you already know.

EXERCISE A: Using Listening Skills. Follow the suggestions and advice on the preceding page during one of your classes. Afterwards, grade yourself on how well you listened by answering the following questions with a *Yes* or a *No*.

EXAMPLE: Did you get enough sleep the night before so that you were alert and felt good?

Yes

1. Did you remind yourself to listen and pay attention to everything said?
2. Did you keep your eyes and ears focused on the speaker?
3. Did you clear your desk of any and all distracting objects?
4. Did you take notes?
5. Did you keep your mind off all concerns unrelated to the class?
6. Did you avoid daydreaming?
7. Did you avoid looking around and talking with your friends in class?
8. Did you keep yourself from doodling?
9. If the speaker said something you disagreed with, did you continue to listen with attention?
10. Did you keep listening even when you felt sure that you knew what the speaker was going to say next?

EXERCISE B: More Work with Listening Skills. At home, listen to or watch fifteen minutes of a news show. Then rate your listening by answering Questions 1, 2, 5, 6, and 9 from the list in Exercise A.

DEVELOPING WRITING SKILLS: Listening Well to Write Well. Use your listening skills to carry out the following writing exercise. Write a summary report of a news show that you watched on television or listened to on the radio. Use a separate brief paragraph for each news item that you cover.

57.2 Listening for Main Ideas

Spotting main ideas is important when you read, when you write, when you outline, and when you take notes. They are also important when you listen. Not only do main ideas give you the most important points to remember, they also help you to organize and make sense out of the other things that are said.

Be alert for main ideas.

The following chart presents a number of methods for pinpointing main ideas when you are listening to a speaker. You will find them especially helpful in class.

HOW TO SPOT MAIN IDEAS

1. Listen for ideas mentioned at the beginning of a class, lecture, or other speaking occasion.
2. Listen for ideas mentioned at the end.
3. Notice which ideas are repeated.
4. Be alert for spoken clues; for example, "Remember. . .," "Most important. . .," "First of all. . .," "To summarize . . . ."
5. Notice what is written on the blackboard.
6. Notice when the speaker's voice becomes louder, slower, or more emphatic.
7. Ask yourself more than once, "What is the main point of what I am hearing? What ties everything together?"
8. If necessary, ask the speaker to make clear what the main point is.

You should also keep in mind that interesting facts or examples and entertaining stories are often just ways of clarifying or illustrating main ideas. They are not themselves main ideas. With experience and practice in listening, your ability to spot what are main ideas and what are not will increase greatly.

EXERCISE A: Spotting Main Ideas. Watch a television program on a real-life subject (a public-television broadcast on science, nature, modern life, and so on, would be excellent for this exercise). Using the suggestions in the chart on the preceding page, pick out and write down the main ideas of the program. Then answer the following questions in short sentences.

1. Were the main ideas of the program stated at the start?
2. Were they mentioned, or repeated, at the end?
3. Were they repeated during the middle portion of the program?
4. Were spoken clues ("Remember," "Most important," and so on) used to signal the importance of an idea?
5. Were other clues used to signal important ideas?
6. Did the speaker's voice suggest which ideas were especially important?
7. Which parts of the program were used to illustrate or support main ideas?

EXERCISE B: More Work with Main Ideas. Follow the directions of Exercise A for another television program or a radio broadcast that has ideas to present. (As an alternative, you may use a radio broadcast in which someone discusses a subject of interest to the public.)

DEVELOPING WRITING SKILLS: From Listening to Writing. Write a brief report on either of the programs that you watched or listened to. State what the main ideas were and how they were illustrated or supported. If you watched a television program, describe how the visual part of the program expressed or clarified the ideas conveyed by words. Which was more important: what was shown or what was spoken? If you listened to a radio broadcast, tell whether the program could have been presented more effectively on television. How would the program have to be changed to suit TV?

Skills Review and Writing Workshop

Developing Your Listening Skills

CHECKING YOUR SKILLS

Answer *True* or *False* for each of the following statements.

EXAMPLE: Listening does not require preparation.
False.

1. Listening is the same thing as hearing.
2. Listening requires attention so that ideas may be grasped.
3. To listen properly you need to be physically as well as mentally prepared.
4. To keep your ears focused on a speaker you should close your eyes or focus them elsewhere.
5. Listening properly to your teacher means that you must not be taking notes.
6. Grasping main ideas makes it easier to organize and make sense out of other things being said.
7. Main ideas are likely to be stressed at the beginning and the end of a speaking occasion.
8. If an idea is repeated it is probably a main idea.
9. An idea written on a blackboard is probably not a main idea.
10. A speaker's voice will usually not get louder or slower when a main idea is being stated.

USING STUDY SKILLS IN WRITING

Evaluating Your Listening

In this exercise you will write a paragraph that describes how good a listener you are. To plan the paragraph, review the two charts in this chapter and ask yourself how well you follow each instruction.

After you have identified your strengths and weaknesses as a listener, write your paragraph. Now revise your paragraph, and proofread it carefully for spelling, grammar and punctuation.

Chapter 58

Developing Your Speaking Skills

A famous writer named Ben Jonson once said, "Speak that I may see thee." He meant that speech is what allows people to make themselves known to others. To be able to communicate clearly to another person or to a group of people is extremely important to your personal development.

In fact, one of the main reasons why young people go to school instead of studying at home has to do with speech. School puts you into a situation where you must communicate both with your teachers and with your classmates. The better you can do this, the better you will be as a student. Also, communicating well will help you become a person who relates well to others.

In this chapter you will learn about two kinds of speaking—class participation and making a speech.

58.1 Participating in Class

Taking part in your classes enables you to learn more. It improves your understanding of a lesson. It gives you the satisfying feeling of contributing to a group effort. It also makes school more enjoyable.

To get the most out of your classes, be an active participant in them.

In most of your classes there are opportunities for you to participate.

EXAMPLE: When the teacher asks a question of the class
When you have a question about something
When a classmate offers an answer or an opinion that you wish to question or respond to

The following chart presents some suggestions for participating properly in class.

HOW TO PARTICIPATE IN CLASS
1. Do whatever studying and homework is required of you so that you come to class prepared to participate.
2. Listen attentively not only to your teacher but also to the questions or answers of your classmates.
3. To conquer self-consciousness and shyness, keep your mind on the class and off yourself.
4. Ask questions when you are unclear about something—it is likely that other students are unclear about it too.
5. Ask questions to follow up something said in a class discussion.
6. When your teacher asks a question that you can answer, raise your hand and, if called on, give your answer.
7. Do not interrupt other speakers or call out before your teacher has given you permission to say something.

EXERCISE: Evaluating Your Class Participation. Answer the following questions as honestly as you can. (Your answers will prepare you to do Exercise B.) The more questions you can answer *yes* to, the better your class participation is.

EXAMPLE: Do I enjoy contributing to class discussions?
Yes.

1. Do I study enough to be able to join in class discussions?
2. Do I do my homework carefully enough to profit from class discussions based on it?
3. Do I listen attentively to the teacher?
4. Do I pay attention to the questions, answers, and comments of my classmates?
5. Do I try not to think about whether a question or answer of mine will be poorly received by the teacher or my classmates?
6. Do I ask questions when something said or taught is unclear to me?
7. Do I follow up the questions or comments of others with my own questions or comments?
8. Do I volunteer answers to my teacher's questions when I am able to answer them?
9. Do I let others speak without interrupting them or being impolite in any way?
10. When I wish to ask a question or to say something, do I raise my hand and wait until the teacher calls on me?

DEVELOPING WRITING SKILLS: Writing About Class Participation. Write a paragraph on how you might improve your participation in class. First think about your answers for Exercise A. Then pick out a weakness in your participation. Next, decide what you can do to improve it. Your paragraph should describe the weakness and then tell what you can do about it. Mention other ways you can improve your participation.

58.2 Preparing a Short Speech

The ability to get up and give a brief speech is one of the most useful and admired abilities you can develop in school. And it is not hard to develop it, either. The chief difficulty you must overcome is nervousness about speaking before a group. Two things help to lessen nervousness: experience and preparation. You get experience by taking advantage of every opportunity to speak before a group. As for preparation, the following rule is fundamental for the kind of speech you are likely to make in school.

Prepare for a speech by collecting and organizing your thoughts on your topic and by practicing your delivery.

The following chart presents specific suggestions for preparation.

GETTING READY FOR A SPEECH

1. Build your speech on a single-sentence statement of one main idea.
2. Make sure any reasons or explanations you use are clear and easy to follow.
3. Think up simple, vivid examples and illustrations to clarify your reasons or explanations.
4. Plan to open your speech with an interesting, attention-getting statement.
5. Plan to conclude your speech with a vivid, memorable restatement of your main idea.
6. Jot your main idea and supporting statements on index cards you can glance at while speaking. Use very few words and write large.
7. Above all, avoid reading at your listeners: Look at them and speak slowly and clearly. Rely on your memory and, when necessary, quick glances at your cards.

EXERCISE: Making Notes for a Speech. Below are some general topics for a brief speech. Select one of them, and from it make up a specific subject. Then follow the numbered directions.

A Needed Improvement in My Neighborhood
A Memorable Experience
Advice to My Classmates
Up with ______ !
Down with ______ !
Saturday Morning Television
Why I Love the Dentist

EXAMPLE: A Needed Improvement in My Neighborhood
Let's Have a Recreation Center

1. Write a title on an index card.
2. Write a one-sentence statement of your main point on a card.
3. If you have a story to tell, think of the most important incidents or parts of the story; make up a brief phrase to remind you of each incident; and write each reminder on a card.
4. If you plan to use reasons to persuade your audience to accept an idea of yours, write each reason on a separate card.
5. If you have examples and illustrations to clarify your reasons, note them on the same cards that the reasons appear on.
6. On your last card, write a word or phrase that will remind you of your concluding statement, which should sum up your main point vividly and memorably.

DEVELOPING WRITING SKILLS: Practicing a Speech. Go over your cards, pausing at each one to think of what you would actually say if you were giving your speech. Then rehearse your speech with a partner. After hearing your partner's speech, write a paragraph naming at least one strength and one weakness of the speech.

Skills Review and Writing Workshop

Developing Your Speaking Skills

CHECKING YOUR SKILLS

Read the following statements. If a statement is true, write *True* on your paper; if it is false, or partly true and partly false, write *False*. Base your answers on the material in this chapter.

EXAMPLE: When your teacher asks the class a question, you should immediately call out the answer before someone else does.

False

1. Studying and doing homework are not necessary for good class participation.
2. When you want to ask or answer a question, you should not consider what your classmates will think or say about you.
3. You should not ask questions just because you do not understand something.
4. To give a good speech, write it out beforehand and read it to your audience.
5. You should restate your main idea when concluding a speech.

USING STUDY SKILLS IN WRITING

Writing About Speaking

Review the material in this chapter and plan a paragraph based on the following main idea: *The key to successful speaking is good preparation.* In your prewriting, consider such topics as how to prepare for a speech and why preparation reduced nervousness.

Now write the paragraph. If possible, support your main idea with specific examples or details from your own experience or from your study of this chapter.

When you have finished writing your paragraph, revise it. Then proofread it carefully for errors.

Preparing Papers

If you have written a good composition, story, or report, what you hand in to your teacher should look good, too. Neatness matters. It gives the reader a good impression of you and your work. So make sure that the final copy of anything you write at home or in school is neat and clean.

For handwritten papers you should also follow the suggestions in the following chart.

SETTING UP HANDWRITTEN PAPERS
1. Use white, lined, notebook-sized paper. But do not use pages torn out of a spiral notebook.
2. Use blue or black ink.
3. Leave a margin of space on the right and the left sides.
4. Indent every paragraph.

For papers you are typing follow the suggestions in this chart.

SETTING UP TYPED PAPERS
1. Use white, unlined notebook-sized paper.
2. Use a clear black ribbon.
3. Leave a margin of space on all sides.
4. Double-space all lines and indent every paragraph.

Your teacher may tell you what information to put on the front page. If not, use one of the forms shown on the next page. The one on the left is for a separate title page. The one on the right is for a first page with no separate title page.

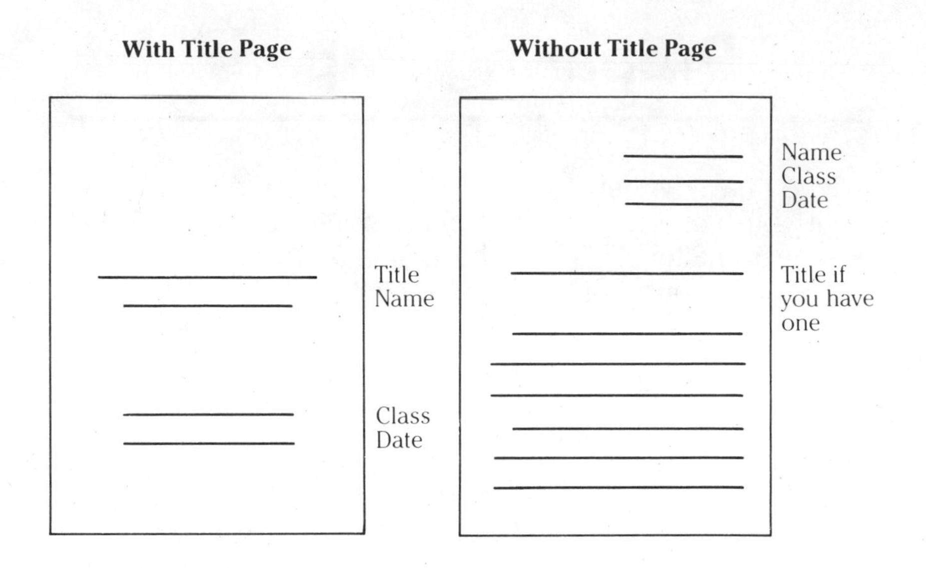

Correcting Errors

Even before you make sure that your paper is set up neatly and properly, go over it carefully for errors in writing. If you use the following chart, you can eliminate some of the most serious errors student writers make. The parentheses direct you to the sections of this book where you can find related information.

QUESTIONS FOR PROOFREADING AND CORRECTING PAPERS
1. Have I avoided writing sentence fragments? (16.2)
2. Have I avoided writing run-on sentences? (17.2)
3. Have I used appropriate language and avoided slang? (18.1, 18.2)
4. Do all the subjects of my sentences agree with their verbs in number? (23.1–23.3)

5. Do all pronouns agree with their antecedents in number and person? (23.4)
6. Have I used correctly such words as *did* and *done* (21.1), *lay* and *lie* (21.2), *set* and *sit* (21.3), *bad* and *badly (25.1),* and *good* and *well* (25.2)?
7. Have I used capitals correctly for the names of specific people, places, and things (27.2, 27.3) and for titles (27.4, 27.5)?
8. Have I used end marks—periods, question marks, and exclamation marks—correctly (29.1–29.3)?
9. Have I used commas correctly (29.4–29.9)?
10. Have I used apostrophes correctly and avoided using them with possessive personal pronouns (30.9–30.11)?
11. Have I used other punctuation marks correctly (30.1–30.8)?
12. Have I avoided double comparisons (26.1) and double negatives (26.2)?

One thing you should not need to be reminded of is this: Use a dictionary to check the spelling of any word you are unsure of. There may be some excuse for a spelling error if you do not have a dictionary available to you. There is no excuse when a dictionary can be consulted. Since many readers form a poor opinion of a paper with spelling errors, do your best to eliminate them.

Using Correction Symbols

Correction symbols are special marks that show where changes need to be made in a paper. Writers use them to note down changes and corrections that need to be made. But editors and proofreaders also use them to fix mistakes made by printers. There are many more correction symbols than are shown in this section. The following chart gives the most commonly used ones. If you learn them, it will be easier to proofread and make a revised copy of your work. Your teacher may also use them to point out needed changes.

SOME CORRECTION SYMBOLS

take out	ℓ	frag	fragment
add	^	RO	run-on
paragraph	¶	sp	spelling
add space	#		

The first sentence in each of the pairs on the following page has been marked with a correction symbol. The second shows the change that results.

MARKED: It slipped out out of my hand.
CHANGE: It slipped out of my hand.

MARKED: Molly was waring a summer dress.
CHANGE: Molly was wearing a summer dress.

MARKED: The last day of our trip was the best.
CHANGE: The last day of our trip was the best.

MARKED: Because the film was boring.
CHANGE: I walked out because the film was boring.

MARKED: I ordered soup, it was cold.
CHANGE: I ordered soup, but it was cold.

MARKED: We saw alot of horses.
CHANGE: We saw a lot of horses.

Index

Bold numbers show pages on which basic definitions and rules can be found.

Acknowledgments

The authors and editors have made every effort to trace the ownership of all copyrighted selections found in this book and to make full acknowledgment for their use.

The dictionary of record for this book is *Webster's New World Dictionary*, Second College Edition, Revised School Printing, copyright © 1983 by Simon & Schuster, Inc. The basis for the selection of vocabulary words appropriate for this grade level is *Living Word Vocabulary: A 43,000 Word Vocabulary Inventory* by Edgar Dale and Joseph O'Rourke, copyright © 1979.

Citations follow, arranged by unit and page for easy reference.

Vocabulary and Spelling. Page 466 From *Webster's New World Thesaurus* by Charlton Laird, Copyright © 1971 by Simon & Schuster, Inc.

Study and Research Skills. Page 564 From *Webster's New World Dictionary*, Second College Edition, Revised School Printing. Copyright © 1983 by Simon & Schuster, Inc.

Art Acknowledgments. Pages 340 The Granger Collection. **341** Robert Day, *The New Yorker*, © 1963. **342** United Feature Syndicate, Inc., © 1959. **350** OPC. **351** A.J. Wright, Taurus Photos. **367** General Motors Corporation. **368** Ken Karp. **382** Susan Kuklin, Photo Researchers. **383** John Blaunstein, Woodfin Camp. **384** Stanley Rowin, The Picture Cube. **400** Alon Reininger, Woodfin Camp; Eugene Gordon, Photo Researchers. **401** Photo Trends. **402** United Feature Syndicate, Inc., © 1985. **416** Leif Skoogfors, Woodfin Camp. **422** United Feature Syndicate, Inc., © 1959. **423** Phyllis Graber Jensen, Stock Boston; Howard Dratch, Leo de Wys, Inc.; Owen Franken, Stock Boston. **442** King Features Syndicate, Inc., © 1985. **444** Culver Pictures. **462** Ken Karp, Omni Photo Communications.

GRAMMAR US ME